"Someone once said that the best way to approach young children is as if they are distinguished visitors from another planet who have just arrived and don't know the ropes yet. The key is to see the world through their eyes so that you can help them learn how to make their way in the world. It takes a blend of knowledge and sensitivity that I call 'intelligent empathy.' Barbara Meltz has it. She has done her homework and she deserves an A+ for her book."

> —James Garbarino, Ph.D., co-director,
> Family Life Development Center,
> Cornell University

"Barbara Meltz is the keenest connoisseur of professional advice on raising children I know. . . . This book is a lively, sensible, solidly grounded compilation of do's and don'ts that speak to every parent's concerns."

> —Eli H. Newberger, M.D., director,
> Family Development Program,
> Children's Hospital (Boston, Mass.)

Put Yourself in Their
SHOES

Understanding How Your Children See the World

BARBARA F. MELTZ

A DELL TRADE PAPERBACK

A DELL TRADE PAPERBACK

Published by
Dell Publishing
a division of
Random House, Inc.
1540 Broadway
New York, New York 10036

*Portions of the material in this book were
reprinted with permission of* The Boston Globe.

Library of Congress Cataloging in Publication Data

Meltz, Barbara.
    Put yourself in their shoes : understanding how your children see
the world / Barbara Meltz.
        p. cm.
    Includes bibliographical references and index.
    ISBN 0-440-50823-1
    1. Parent and child. 2. Children—Psychology. 3. Parenting.
    I. Title.
    HQ755.85.M45   1999
    306.874—dc21   98-38609
                          CIP

Book design by Ellen Cipriano

Printed in the United States of America

Published simultaneously in Canada

February 1999

10 9 8 7 6 5 4 3 2 1

To Eli. Without you,
this wouldn't have happened.

Acknowledgments

· · · · · · · · · · · · · · · · · ·

Technically, this book began when my son did. At the time, I was the New England editor at *The Boston Globe*, typically working sixty hours a week. Even during my pregnancy I knew that once I became a mother, I wanted to work part-time but I couldn't think of what to do. Standing in the middle of the *Globe* newsroom one afternoon, I poured my heart out to my colleague and friend Evelynne Kramer. "You know what the *Globe* needs?" she asked. "A parenting column. And you could do that three days a week." Thus began the column that led to this book. The late Kirk Scharfenberg, my boss at the time, wholeheartedly endorsed the idea, as did Jack Driscoll, then editor of the *Globe*. In what is perhaps a touch of journalistic irony, Evelynne became the first editor of "Child Caring;" that the column got off to such a good start is due in no small part to the vision she had for what it could be. There are other people at the *Globe* I want to thank; Editor Matt Storin, for his support and friendship for more than twenty years; my current editor, Fiona Luis; Assistant Managing Editor for Features Mary Jane Wilkinson; Managing Editor Greg Moore; and my friend and colleague Ellen Goodman, who endured many tête-à-tête lunches where I picked her brain about how the heck you write a book. I thank also the many other *Globe* colleagues, too numerous to mention, who have shared their parenting woes and wonders so that I could turn them into fodder for my column. A very big thank you as well to all the readers whose support, enthusiasm, questions, ideas and fan mail have kept the column going for more than ten years.

I can never properly thank all the hundreds of sources I have interviewed who made this book possible: researchers, clinicians, teachers, psychologists, pediatricians, psychiatrists, professors and parents. But there are a few I'd like to single out. Pediatrician T. Berry Brazelton was one of the first professionals I interviewed for the column. Over lunch at the Harvest restaurant in Cambridge, he told me the column was going to fill a void for parents and that someday I'd write a book too. Barbara Willer of the National Association for the Education of Young Children has been a constant and invaluable resource. Professor Diane Levin of Wheelock College has helped me refine my thinking about child development and she's become a friend in the process. A special thanks to parent educator Linda Braun, director of Families First in Cambridge, who has never laughed at any of my questions and always made herself available to me, sometimes at great inconvenience. A giant thank you to parent educator Gloria Jurkowitz of Scranton, Pennsylvania, who was a frequent sounding board over the years and especially for the book. Her advice, insight, and wisdom have particular meaning to me because she is also my aunt.

When it comes to family and friends, I have been blessed. Thanks first and foremost to my husband, who, as the project neared completion, endured far more take-out meals and trips to the grocery store than he liked; to my son, the best kid on earth, who facilitated this turn in my career and taught me so much; to my mom, who has been an unfailing cheerleader all my life; and to my dad, who died years before I wrote this but whose influence is here, nonetheless. Thanks also to my niece Ariel, and nephews Adam and Michael, whose unseen influence is throughout the book, and to their mother and my sister, Ellen Thibault. This book absolutely wouldn't have happened without the prodding of my cousin Deborah Jurkowitz, who also happens to be a book editor par excellence. Although the idea for a book had been floating around in my head for years, it didn't crystallize until Debbie sat down with pencil and pad and helped me organize my thoughts. She was with me every step of the way, always dispensing sage advice. To my friends Betsy Hochberg, Donna Furlong Eidson, Patti Doten, Judith Robinson, Cheryl Di Paolo, Frank Grundstrom and Joan Koch—I couldn't have done this without you! Last but not least, thanks to a terrific and attentive agent, Nancy Yost, and to my book editors, Diane Bartoli, who defies publishing stereotypes by returning calls immediately, and Mary Ellen O'Neill, who helped me birth this book even as she gave birth to a baby!

Newton, Massachusetts
July 1998

Contents

Introduction

. . . .

On a wintry January morning, I stood transfixed in the lobby outside the gym of the Jewish Community Center while a twoish-year-old had a temper tantrum. It wasn't the toddler I was watching, though. It was his mother. She was a few steps behind him when he threw himself on the floor, crying and thrashing, and I was a few steps behind her. Without a word, she dropped her gym bag and baby pack to the floor and lowered herself down next to him. She didn't talk to him or touch him, she just got lower and lower, first squatting, then sitting, then lying on her stomach, until her head was at the same level as her son's and their noses were practically touching. Pedestrian traffic was unusually heavy that morning, but no one broke stride as they sidestepped the pair, and the mother seemed as nonplussed about them as they were about her.

The mother's single-mindedness struck me as remarkable. Wasn't she worried someone would step or trip on her or her son, hurting one or the other or all of them? How could she be so oblivious? How could she not be embarrassed? *How could she be so focused?* That was what really got me. I envied her selfless devotion to her child's needs, her unwavering sense of purpose and her patience. I couldn't take my eyes off her. Her face was almost expressionless. No matter how hard I searched for a sign of anger or frustration, I couldn't find it.

Her son's face, on the other hand, was registering a gamut of emotions, from shock and surprise to anger and, eventually, a kind of calm. His crying turned to a whimper and then stopped altogether. When he finally rested his flushed face on the dirty floor, his mother did too. (Ohmigod, I thought. I could never do that!) They stayed that way for perhaps two or three minutes. If he looked at the feet or legs or eyes of the people around him, she did too. If he stared into her eyes, she returned the look. Then, on some wordless cue, the boy sat up and so did the mom. He stood, she stood. She picked up her bags and offered him her hand. He took it, and they walked through the rest of the lobby, out the door. I followed them into the parking lot. The mother didn't stop to put on their coats and they broke into a run in the cold. At the car, she lifted him into his car seat, buckled him in, and settled herself in the car. As far as I could tell, she still hadn't spoken to him, but she had smiled as she snapped his seat belt and kissed him on the forehead.

As I got into my car, I wanted to applaud.

For weeks, the image of that mother stayed with me. Whenever I struggled with my son, I thought of her serenity. If I felt myself succumbing to frustration, I thought of her patience. I imagined she was a nurse or a preschool teacher. Who else could show that combination of restraint and insight? I wondered how much practice it had taken her to achieve it, if she had mastered this strategy on two or three older children.

Boy, did I get it wrong. Weeks later, I bumped into her in the locker room at the gym. I couldn't help myself; I plunged right in by asking if she worked outside the home. "I'm in marketing," she said. My mouth must have dropped. Marketing definitely did not fit. Now I was even more curious.

Did she remember that morning? I asked.

"Oh, God! Did I totally embarrass myself?" she said. "He'd had two temper tantrums already that morning and I had vowed to myself that the very next one, I wasn't going to try to reason with him or yell, I was going to try to see the world the way he does. That was why I did that," she said. "I had never done it before."

She also hadn't done it since. There hadn't been the need. Her son had not had a temper tantrum since that day. "I probably totally freaked him," she said.

"So what's it like, putting yourself in his shoes, looking at the world through his eyes?" I asked.

"It looks *really* different," she said. "It made me much more sympathetic to him."

When I told her how impressed I was by what she had done, she was surprised. "I have no idea how to be a mother," she said. "I'm brand-new at this. I was desperate."

So much for my theory. But was it any less admirable that this mother's success was due to luck, love, and intuition? She had broken a pattern of behavior by responding in a new and different way, and even though she didn't realize what she was doing, it was a stroke of genius nonetheless. As parent educator Linda Braun would say, there was a touch of humanity in what she had done. By wanting to gain her son's perspective, she let him know that she was friend, not foe. "When a kid senses you are with him, he has a feeling he has an ally," says Braun. "It makes all the difference in the world."

The idea of trying to look at the world as your child sees it is something I thought about even before I became a mother. Of all the women I know who are mothers, I've always been most impressed by my sister. She has three kids, 16, 13, and 11 at this writing, and, so far at least, she's always had a good relationship with each, no matter their stage of development. Whenever I've asked her, "How do you know what to do/say/think?" her answer is always the same: "I can remember what it feels like to be the kid. I can remember being there." Needless to say, her children have benefited from her exceptional memory.

For most of the rest of us, putting ourselves in our children's shoes does not come so easily. When we think of events that might be stressful for our children, we tend to mention divorce, unemployment, a move, illness or death in the family. These aren't wrong answers; those are stressful events for children. But ask children what *they* think of as stressful and the answers are not just life's megastresses.

I put that question to a fifth-grade class. Here's a sampling of what they consider stressful: lunch (who sits where); the bus ride (if there's a bully on the bus); being sick; staying alone after school; going to a boy-girl party; grandpa dying; the science test. In other words, Everyday Stuff.

In the ten years I've been writing a weekly parenting column, not to mention the ten years I've spent as a parent myself, I am continually struck by how the everyday stuff in a child's life is typically what causes the most difficulty for parents and children alike. I'm convinced part of the reason parents have difficulty is because not only do we lack a memory like my sister's, but we also aren't getting down and dirty on the lobby floor. We are looking at our children's lives from our perspective, not theirs.

It's no wonder, either. Taking our children's perspective is hard. It involves concentration and focus. It takes a certain amount of guts; often what your instinct tells you your child needs is not what your best friend and the mothers in your playgroup are doing for their children. It also takes an understanding of where a child is coming from and how she views the world. How she takes it in not just intellectually, but also emotionally and developmentally. It means understanding why the last day of school may be as stressful as the first, why sleeping at a friend's is not as simple as packing a few stuffed animals.

The issue for parents is twofold. We need to recognize the often small, concrete issues that cause our children to stumble, and then we need to know how to help them before they actually fall. There are four ways in which this book helps you accomplish this. The first is that, unlike many parenting books, this one does not use chronological markers to identify issues; age is arbitrary and not always a valid description of a where a child is. Every child's actions are grounded in a developmental context and so is this book. It gets you inside the head of your child so you are able to understand how he or she is thinking, which enables you to understand why she might have done what she did. Someone once told me that children move constantly between the stage they're coming from, the stage they're going to, and the stage they are at—and we're supposed to figure out where they are at any given moment!

Because it is developmental in approach, this is a book that talks about children of all ages. Parents of a 3-year-old will find it just as valuable as parents of a 7- or 11-year-old. Parents with questions about sleep problems at the beginning of the school year will get information that will help with a kindergartner as well as a third-grader. The parent who wants to know how to talk to his child about AIDS will get advice on what to say to a preteen and to a preschooler. This book gives you one-stop shopping!

The third distinguishing factor is a natural consequence of the first two. The events described in the book are, indeed, the Everyday Stuff of real people's lives. The anecdotes are not concocted, composite, or hypothetical. Although real names are not always used, the people behind them are real. While we're tangentially on the subject of names, also please note that throughout the book, *he* and *she* are used interchangeably.

That this book represents ten years of journalistic effort brings us to the fourth reason it's so valuable. In an ideal world, when there's a parenting problem, parents approach it like a term paper—research the topic, read the literature, interview sources—and then come to conclusions based on the research. Nobody has time for that today, unless they're getting paid to do it. Since 1987, I've been researching the issues parents bring to me, as well as those that crop up in my own life as a parent, and giving readers a consensus of opinion that enables them to take what information they need and come to conclusions that are appropriate for their family and their child.

Invariably, when parents describe situations they're experiencing with their children, what comes through time and time again is how they, the parents, have inadvertently dug deeper and deeper holes for themselves by highlighting the wrong problem. As parents, we tend to go for the mega issue. When our daughter is having a hard time concentrating in school, we think eye problem or learning disability, whereas she's simply worried because she hates blueberry pancakes and that's what her best friend's mother promised to make for them when she sleeps over for the first time Friday night.

For a number of very understandable reasons, we often don't realize how stressful day-to-day events can be for our children. It may be that we're desensitized to them or that we're too busy even to notice them. Perhaps we miss the source of the problem because what's causing the anxiety is something we view as pleasurable. "Children feel safest and most comfortable when there is routine and familiarity. Whatever changes that, whatever is out of the ordinary in any way, good or bad, is potentially stressful for them," says child and adolescent psychiatrist Mary Lynn Dell of Children's Hospital in Philadelphia.

I lost count of how many calls I had from parents after I wrote a column about sleep difficulties in school-age children at the beginning of the school year, but I can tell you what most of the parents said. It went something like this: "It never occurred to us that our child, who never had sleep issues before and has successfully begun school in other years, could be having difficulty sleeping at the start of school." Consider the child who ruins a family vacation because he won't leave the cabin to go down to the lake. Turns out, the problem is the mud: It feels so squishy. A twelve-dollar pair of water shoes or old sneakers could have salvaged a thousand-dollar vacation. But who knew?

This book has three goals. The first is to identify life events that children typically need help with. Some of them are the truly traumatic, such as the death of a parent or birth of a sibling. Others are milestones that are harder to spot, but milestones nonetheless: tattling, telling a secret, stealing. Some, such as the impact of media violence, the Internet or children's access to the news, are scary for us because we are breaking new ground in our parenting.

The second goal is to help us understand how and why a child may be reacting in a particular way. At each stage of a child's life, there is a threshold for what he or she can handle cognitively and emotionally. This is called developmental appropriateness. When life is presented within their developmental range, children thrive. When it isn't, there is discomfort that has the potential to get out of hand. *Put Yourself in Their Shoes* gives you a developmental map of real life. That, in turn, leads to the last goal: providing parents with strategies for coping. Having fingered events that are likely to cause difficulty for children, having offered a critical window into what a child may be thinking and the skills he or she brings to a particular situation, all that's left is for parents to respond in a way that feeds into a child's strengths rather than into his or her deficits.

Both the good and bad news about parenting is that there is no right or wrong way to do any of this. Just as there is no blueprint for us to follow that makes our job easier, there is also no such thing (short of abuse) that's a "mistake." Parenting is a cumulative effort. What it all adds up to counts more than any one isolated moment. So many of us think we are failing because we didn't say or do something according to a prescription. But any advice about parenting, including what's contained in this book, is only a guide. The ideas represented here are the result of years of interviews with hundreds of researchers and clinicians, teachers and parents, but they cannot and do not substitute for the intimate knowledge you have of your child. They are intended as a window, a way to get past the wall our children so often erect. But just as in architecture, the style of window that works in one house may be awful in another. As much as I hope there will be many ideas in this book that you can use in the life of your child, do so only after holding the idea in your hand. Does it fit with your child? Does it make sense for your family?

More often than not, my research makes me a wiser and, I hope, better parent. But whenever I wonder, which is often, how well I'm doing as a parent, my son is always my best guide. When he was 6 and I was applying (apparently rather transparently) a new strategy to our family's approach to chores, he told me I was taking my column too seriously. "I don't think you need to learn any more stuff, Mom," he said. "I think you're a good mother just like you are." It was a sweet message, even if his motives were a tad on the self-serving side.

CHAPTER ONE

Negotiating Independence

. . . .

When our children are very little and totally dependent upon us, we have this tendency to think they will always be that way. The intellectual side of us knows that isn't true but the emotional somehow doesn't believe it. The thought that there will come a day when they can do without us, well, like Scarlett O'Hara, we'd prefer not to think about it. So it happens that the first signs of independence take us by surprise. For me, there's a moment frozen in time when my son was 15 months old.

Every night at bedtime, we would sit in the rocker in his room and curl up with a book, his blankie, and his favorite stuffed animal, a penguin. It was a cozy time, something I looked forward to, an anchor to my day. On this particular night, though, after he cuddled in my lap, he climbed back down and headed for the window seat where more of his stuffed animals sat. I thought he was getting another one to join us but, no, he was getting a different book. That's fine, I thought. But then, instead of climbing back in my lap, he sat down on the floor and began to "read" by himself.

This had never happened before. Good for him, I thought. But moments later, I felt disappointed and sad. In bed that night, I thought about all the times ahead of me when I would need to let my son go: when he wants to walk outside without holding my hand, to dress himself, to cross the street by himself, my God, *to stay overnight at a friend's*! I remember feeling a sense of panic. There must be some way to prepare myself in advance for this, I thought. Otherwise, how will I know when to let go and when to hold on?

The next day at work, I couldn't stop thinking about it. I decided to do a column. Bruno Bettelheim, the late renowned child psychologist, scoffed at my question over the phone from his home in Santa Monica. "You never let go of your children," he said. "You just let them move toward independence."

It was a remark full of wisdom but also full of comfort, and it has stayed with me over the years. Unfortunately, though, attempts to be independent don't come with blinking neon lights: "I'm trying to be independent right now, Mom and Dad, bear with me." Not to mention that what often is a healthy sign of independence can also look a lot like brattiness to the nth degree. No neon lights for that, either. The trouble is, the move toward independence comes in fits and starts continually throughout childhood with great lurches forward and giant steps backward. To complicate matters even more, assertions of independence look different at each stage of development. Just when you think you have things figured out, you get hit with some new developmental twist.

Intertwined inexorably in all of this are our own feelings. No parent purposely sets out to overprotect a child, or to be neglectful. Yet sometimes our need to keep her close, physically and emotionally, compel us to be smothering while at other times we seemingly unfeelingly push her forward. Not surprisingly, the times when our buttons get pushed the most are when a child is feeling her oats. She experiences a burst of developmental self-confidence that enables her to do, or want to do, something for the first time and we feel threatened. She wants to soar and we clip her wings. In the life of a child, "firsts" are full of great excitement and high anxiety all at once, and that can fuel some pretty complicated behaviors. A child's world, after all, is full of rumor, myth, and misinformation, and whatever information she has, accurate or not, is bound to be embellished by her imagination. As parents, the better able we are to understand what's behind our children's behaviors, the better we will be able to negotiate them in a healthy, loving way that enables them to climb the next rung on the ladder toward competence and independent living.

Imaginary friends

There is a little man who lives in a corner of the basement of Courtney's house. He is small, under a foot high, and has a wife and children. Sometimes he goes on trips and brings back presents for them. His name is Mr. Neckit and he is Courtney's imaginary friend. "I believe he is real, but I know he's not," says Courtney, who is 6. "No one knows where he lives except me. He sleeps with me every night. I take him to school with me every day. And," she adds softly, "he has magical powers."

Having an imaginary friend is one of the early concrete ways in which a child exerts autonomy. For parents, it can be a rude awakening, especially if a child is as young as 3; there is no escaping the fact that she has a mind and a life distinct from you, totally beyond your control. You can enter this world if you want; in fact, it's preferable if you do. But many parents are uncomfortable with a child's imaginary friends. It feels weird to watch or encourage a relationship with something that isn't real, weirder still to become involved yourself. Other parents find a child's immersion into a fantasy character troubling. They worry that their child may be developing a personality disorder or suffering from an inability to distinguish fantasy from reality.

Research puts such fears to rest. Studies show that young children who have imaginary friends are perfectly normal and, if anything, tend to grow up to be more cooperative, less aggressive, more advanced in language skills, and better able to concentrate than peers who didn't have any. Psychologist Robert Brooks of Needham, Massachusetts, who lectures internationally on children's self-esteem, says bluntly, "It's a myth to think that kids with imaginary friends are disturbed." Indeed, he says, imaginary friends can serve important functions, providing companionship, helping a child fight off fears or express an emotion. It can even help develop a sense of conscience and self-control.

Spend a little time with Courtney and you can see what Brooks means. Angry one afternoon that her mother said it was time to stop playing, she stormed out of the room in a huff. Moments later she returned, considerably calmer. "It wasn't me who didn't want to stop playing," she said. "It was Mr. Neckit. I explained to him that it was just time to do carpool and we could play again later. That calmed him down."

Mr. Neckit first appeared in Courtney's life when she was 3, an age when imaginary friends typically materialize. "Suddenly he was just there," says Courtney's mother, Elizabeth. "She just started talking about him, volunteering information. Sometimes he would be a constant in her day, all day, for days on end. Other days, we wouldn't hear about him," she says. An absence can mean that the imaginary friend has disappeared, a sign your child has developmentally moved on, or it may be that she's still having internal dialogues but is better able to keep them private. Once, after not hearing about Mr. Neckit for several months, Elizabeth asked Courtney how he was doing.

"His children have gone away to college," Courtney said.

"Was he sad?" asked her mother.

"No, he was laughing with me on the stairs this morning. Besides, one of his sons just moved next door."

Elizabeth and her husband, Isaac, marvel at the ideas their daughter comes up with. Some of them reflect events going on in their lives—when the above conversation took place, their favorite baby-sitter had recently left for college—but many of the ideas are Courtney's alone.

Researchers say the only time parents need to be concerned about an imaginary friend is if it interferes with a child's ability to function in the real world—for instance, if she chooses to play with her imaginary friend rather than with real ones, or if she seems out of touch with reality in other ways, perhaps being consistently withdrawn, unable to solve problems, or choosing to sit on the sidelines rather than participate in age-appropriate activities. Otherwise, assume, as Courtney's parents have, that your child has a rich imagination and is using the imaginary friend to master social skills or find a way to work through an issue in his or her life, particularly a tough transition. A second-grade teacher relates the story of a child who was new in class and introduced his imaginary friend, a bat named Benny, to the class.

"Every day he had new stories about the bat and the children were drawn to him. Gradually, they joined in the fantasy," the teacher says. "After about a month, he told me the bat had moved away. By then, he had many friends."

Imaginary friends can be based on a real person or animal or on characters from TV or a book. Don't read a lot into the patterns or the scripts, but take your cues from them. If she's using the imaginary friend to work out an issue you can identify, acknowledge it. For instance, the parents of the boy with the bat might have said, "I'm glad to know that Benny goes to school with you. It's nice to have a friend when you start something new." When an imaginary friend first appears, parents are sometimes at a loss. Some good ways to respond: "George sounds neat. Did you make him up?" "Can I meet him?" "Does he hang around with you often?" "What do you do together?" "Why do you like him so much?"

Don't worry that you are encouraging too much fantasy. This stage will disappear when your child no longer needs the help the imaginary friend provides. In the meantime, every now and then get into a conversation with her about what is real and what's not on TV, in books, or on the news. If nothing else, it will reassure you that your child hasn't totally slipped into a fantasy world. You can also take advantage of an imaginary friend to help your child develop cognitive skills. If she's not particularly verbal, use the friend to draw her out: "What does George think about that?" If he likes to write or draw, ask him to write stories the friend tells him or to draw pictures about where the friend lives.

Psychologist Brooks encourages parents to join in a child's fantasy if they're invited to. "If you start with the premise this is normal, it's a great way for you to enter your child's world, have a good time together and see what's in her mind," he says. "It can encourage parent-child trust." Let your child take the lead. Ask a few questions—"What does George like to do? Is there anything he wants to talk about?"—but always respect the boundaries of the world your child has constructed. If you're not invited to join in, don't feel rejected. Some children, like some adults, need privacy more than others. Then, too, being invited in may be a function of age; older children may feel more self-conscious and therefore be more inclined to keep their friend to themselves.

> *Sometimes a child may pretend to*
> *Be the imaginary friend. It gives him*
> *a sense of control.*

If you are invited in but aren't interested, at least don't show any annoyance. A child will feel rejected if you tell him things like "George is not real. There's no one there and I'm not going to play with you." Instead, try a limited involvement that doesn't deflate your child: "George, I can't play with you, but I'm glad you're friends with my son because he's one of the neatest kids around." If an imaginary friend becomes too intrusive in your family life, it's okay to set limits around the friendship as long as you do it in a respectful way. If your child insists on setting real food out for George, for instance, instead of saying, "We can't waste food on someone that isn't even real," tell her, "It's fine to set a place for George at the table, but if he's hungry, how about if he eats pretend food?" To a child who says, "I didn't spill the milk, George did," a good response might be, "George may have been involved but I think you were, too, so you and George can help each other clean up."

While many imaginary friends disappear in the early grade-school years, it's just as likely that many others simply go underground. For the 8- or 9-year-old, the fun is in the secrecy, but even at this age there's still comfort to be had from an imaginary friend. Nine-year-old Amanda's imaginary friend is a boy with brown hair and eyes. They've been friends for five years. "When I was younger, I couldn't see him, but I knew he was there, he was just invisible," says Amanda. "Now I know he isn't real but I wish he were because he's a friend I've had for a long time and I enjoy being with him. I think younger kids have fun with imaginary friends. They are some-one to talk to if you are scared or unhappy or mad or lonely. Even when you're happy, it's fun to share a new toy with them."

Do her real friends know about her imaginary one?

"Only my best friend," says Amanda. "She has one, too."

Dressing for success

Clothing is another early arena in which children exert their inde-pendence. There's more to this than meets the eye, however. The 3-year-old girl who will wear only dresses or whose socks must have lace ruffles is working on gender identity, trying to learn what it means to be a girl; she'll wear pants again once she gets the identifi-cation part down. (Don't worry, by the way, if your preschooler girl wants to wear only pants; she's working on gender identification in other ways.) The toddler boy who throws a tantrum if he has to wear a pullover or something red may have a legitimate physical aversion to a fabric, style, texture, or color, sometimes diagnosed as Low Sensory Threshold; this is not about control but about comfort. The 7-year-old who insists on wearing his raggedy baseball cap wherever he goes is probably not developing a fashion sense. More likely, he's using that piece of clothing as a transitional object, a way to gain a sense of security as he moves toward more autonomy.

Whenever clothes begin to matter to your child, that's when you need to back off. My son was happy to have me pick out his clothes until sometime in the middle of third grade, long after many of his peers had begun to choose what they would wear. Nonetheless, all through kindergarten and first and second grade, every night as he got ready for bed, I would ask him, "Do you want me to pick your clothes for tomorrow or do you want to?" Once in a while he might have a shirt or pants that he wanted to wear, but for the most part he considered the decision a chore he was happy to relinquish. One day out of the blue halfway through third grade, I asked the same old question and the answer was "I'll choose." He had turned an invisible corner and developed a great sense of style, to boot.

> *Clothes consciousness knows no gender.*
> *Every sixth-grade teacher can point to*
> *some boys who are into clothes just as much*
> *as fashion-conscious girls, or to some girls*
> *who couldn't care less.*

Clothing is an important nonverbal communicator that can foster or impede relationships, not just among peers but also between parent and child. Atlanta psychologist Marshall Duke tells the story of a mother and her 10-year-old son who weren't getting along. In a session with the whole family, Duke gave everyone a handful of tokens with instructions to give a token to any family member over the next two days who did something they appreciated. At the next session, the mother had received tokens from everyone in the family except her son. She began to describe all the things she had done for him that week, including laying out his clothes.

"That's it!" the boy exclaimed, jumping up from his seat.

"That's what?" the mother asked.

"You put out that balloon shirt and all the kids made fun of me. They always make fun of how I dress."

The mother was chagrined but skeptical that this error in judgment about clothes, for heaven's sake, could be the cause of the problem in her relationship with her son. Duke was not. "Among other things," he says, "there was an issue of parental trust and credibility. He saw her as the reason he was getting teased. If her judgment could cause that to happen, how did he know he could trust her on other issues?"

Beginning in about first grade, clothing becomes a vehicle by which children accomplish one of childhood's most important developmental tasks: connecting with peers. At this age, wanting to wear what a best friend wears is not about label consciousness or status symbols (wait a few years!) but about making friends. The first-grader who wants sneakers just like Tommy's probably wants them because Tommy runs really fast and he wants to run as fast as Tommy so Tommy will like him. The second-grader is so admiring of the girl in her class who is reading chapter books that she wants to dress like her. Two third-grade girls who exchange one sock are using the mismatch to cement their status as best friends. A group of five fourth-grade boys who play together at recess every day wear neon shoelaces to show their friendship.

As parents, we need to think of these as survival instincts in our kids and, for the most part, trust and respect them. This doesn't mean, however, that from the moment your child announces she wants to pick out her own clothes, you are stuck watching her walk out the door in colors that clash or outfits that are inappropriate. There are plenty of ways you can grant her her autonomy and still have input. Begin by applauding her independence and offer yourself as a consultant: "Anytime you aren't sure about what clothes go together, I'm happy to consult with you." Suggest ways you can make it easier for her: "How about if we rearrange your closet so you can reach everything and so clothes are organized by category, clothes for school, clothes for play, clothes for special occasions"; "Would you like me to give you some ideas of what things go together?" Once you've done this, however, you mostly need to allow it to happen. If she goes to school in an orange skirt and red shirt, don't worry what the teacher will say. She's seen it all before and, if anything, she'll silently applaud your understanding of your child's need for independence.

By fourth and fifth grade, the touching, tentative ways in which clothing may have facilitated friendships now typically begin to become vehicles for exclusion. Marilise Flusser, a clothing researcher and author of an insightful book, *Party Shoes to School and Baseball Caps to Bed: The Parents' Guide to Kids, Clothes and Independence*, urges parents to keep a wary eye out for this. It's inappropriate, for instance, for friendship necklaces or twin dressing to be allowed in school because it's exclusionary, potentially hurtful, and distracting to other students. Reserve it for after school or weekends.

Clothing these days can take on frightening proportions for parents economically. Most parents would be willing to spend more than usual to buy a particular brand of jeans for a 10-year-old who is a social misfit if they thought it would mitigate against teasing. But what about the extravagant demands of a kid who is following the crowd? Cueing in to what your child needs and what your pocketbook can handle isn't always easy. Flusser says that whatever you do, don't use clothes to teach the lesson of individualism. If your 12-year-old is begging for certain jeans, don't insist she doesn't need them if all her friends wear them. Wearing the same clothes as her peers is a way for a child to say "I'm part of the group, I fit in." For the 9- to 13-year-old, belonging is of critical importance. One wise grandmother I know overheard a discussion between her 12-year-old grandson and his mother. The boy wanted a Bart Simpson T-shirt because all his friends loved the show. The mother wouldn't allow the shirt because she didn't allow him to watch the show. "If I think the show is inappropriate, why would I want you walking around in a shirt advertising it?" she asked him. The grandmother was able to figure out what the boy couldn't verbalize: He needed the shirt precisely because he couldn't watch the show. Having the shirt would help him fit in with his friends. The grandmother bought him the shirt (after alerting the mother she was going to do so). When Douglass opened the box, he was so happy and relieved, his eyes welled up. "This is the best present I've ever had!" he exclaimed. "The depth of his need surprised all of us, including his mother," says the grandmother. "It was a horrible shirt that only cost twelve dollars, but it was life and death to him."

Don't go overboard and buy items you can't afford or clothing that is offensive, but when something coveted is out of the question, don't minimize its importance or devalue it as an object. That only makes your child feel wrong, bad, or guilty for wanting it, or angry at you for not understanding her. Instead, acknowledge how important the item is to her and then discuss the cost. If you can, put it in a context: "This costs as much as going out to a nice restaurant three times, and you know how infrequently we do that." This is a good opportunity to suggest she earn some money to help defray the cost. Similarly, hand-me-downs may be a blessing for many of our pocketbooks, but they can sometimes make a child feel bad. Perhaps styles have changed. Perhaps the original owner projected an image this child doesn't like and she thinks she'll catch that image from wearing the clothes. Give her an opportunity to talk about why they offend her. If you frequently pass clothes down from one sibling to the next, make sure each child has something new now and then, something that's just for him.

For all the difficulties parents may have with children who are very clothes conscious, there is a whole other set of problems for parents of children who couldn't care less what they wear. These kids tend to be clueless; they become outcasts without knowing why. "It can be painful to watch as a parent," says Flusser. Even if there are other, more serious issues contributing to your child's social problems, at least make sure what your child wears isn't ammunition for ridicule. Start by paying attention to the rest of the kids in the class. Does your kid look like them? If not, suggest that you do some shopping together and steer him to clothes that will help him fit in. You don't need to knock him over the head with this; in fact, you don't really need to explain what you're doing unless he makes a comment such as "Oh, this is like a shirt that Adam has." The truth is, though, that kids who are oblivious to clothes are oblivious to clothes until one day when suddenly they aren't. That can happen at 6 or 9 or 16 or never. Even if your child isn't a social outcast but sticks out in some other way—he's very smart, very tall, not good at sports, overweight—it pays to run some interference for him and make sure his clothes aren't a reason for him to stick out even more.

Unfortunately, some parents can be as clueless about clothes as their kids. If you're an adult for whom clothes have never mattered and you find this whole subject offensive, or if clothes and dressing have never come easily, don't hesitate to ask the teacher or a parent you trust about this: "Is there anything about the way Johnny dresses that might be off-putting to his classmates?" or "Where do you buy Tim's clothes?" Be particularly sensitive to these issues any-time a child changes schools. Styles and fashions can vary even from one side of town to another. Make a point to check in with the principal before school starts: "Is there anything about the way kids do or don't dress here that could make my daughter feel like she doesn't fit in?" Any child who is an outsider by definition, whether he's new, an immigrant, overweight or handicapped, would be well served by a parent who runs interference in this way.

By 12, dressing alike gets ratcheted up yet another notch, for boys and girls alike. The issue of fitting in takes on even more importance for preteens because they feel awkward and uncomfort-able in their changing bodies, especially as they compare their bod-ies to body images they see in the media. It makes perfect sense that the "uniform" these days, at least, is baggy jeans and oversized shirts. What a great way for preteens to hide their bodies! At the other extreme are preteens who choose clothes that are sexually provocative. Stay away from arguments like "You're too young to dress like this," and talk instead about the values the clothes repre-sent. An 11- or 12-year-old may balk at your "strictness," but more often than not she'll be secretly thankful if you stand by your values.

Once your child reaches the point where clothes matter to her, there's little point in shopping for clothes without her. Mothers of girls always complain about how hard it is to shop for or with their daughters, but mothers of boys don't have it easy either. In any case, it is better to buy one outfit your child really likes than to buy three that she only kinda likes. They'll end up in the closet. Similarly, it's often a waste of money to buy a new school wardrobe before school starts. Wait and see what other kids are wearing. Even if your daughter loves what you buy her in August, she could hate it by September 15 if she feels like an outcast wearing it. While many kids like having something new for the first day of school, save any serious buying for October or November. Tell your child, "Let's wait and see what your friends are wearing." She'll appreciate your thoughtfulness (although she might not tell you), and you'll save yourself money and aggravation.

Clothes as a manifestation of independence take on particular poignancy for twins and other multiples. Dressing them in look-alike outfits is cute, but it can be stifling psychologically because it prompts people to lump them together: the Twins, not Jane and Mary. Eventually, the children come to think of themselves that way too. Better to dress your children as individuals from the start. As they get older, let them dress alike now and then because they choose to, not because you do.

No discussion about clothing as a statement of independence would be complete, of course, without also talking about hairstyles. For some reason, they can undo a parent-child relationship faster than you can plait a braid. Here's the question to ask yourself: Is this particular power struggle worth it? Before I was a parent, I was among those who would raise my eyes in disapproval at parents whose 5- or 6-year-old boys had a single long strand of hair hanging down their back or a shaved lower head with long hair overhanging it. Now it doesn't faze me; in the scheme of things, how a child wears his or her hair is not as important as nearly anything else you can think of and yet far more important to a child than we can imagine. Many kids feel as strongly about their hair as most adults; having a style they don't like or a bad hair day can affect their mood and sense of well-being just as it can for us. I'm also convinced that having control over your hair and therefore over how you look can be one of the biggest learning experiences a child can have. Visiting an elementary school one day, I stopped in the girls' room and came across a girl standing in front of the mirror looking very unhappy. Because I was wearing a visitor's name tag, she knew immediately that I was the reporter about to visit her fifth-grade classroom.

"I can't be in your picture," she told me, without preamble. "My hair has problems."

"I'm sorry to hear that," I said, thinking to myself that she was way too young to be having such thoughts. Besides, her hair looked fine to me. Thankfully, I had enough sense not to say so.

"I had it cut a few weeks ago. It was down to here," she said, gesturing halfway down her back. It was now in a short bob. I must have looked surprised, because she went on: "Well, my mom didn't want me to do it, and my dad *really* didn't want me to, but I wanted it short and my mom said it was my hair and I could do it if that was what I really wanted. But she told me a lot of reasons why I might be sorry. I really liked it at first but now I can see what she means. I have to get it cut like every four weeks to keep it looking good and that's a lot of time to spend at the hairdresser when you're only 10. People keep telling me that I look 12 or 13 instead of 10 and that was kinda cool at first, but now it's annoying. So I'm letting it grow back and I'm having a lot of bad hair days while I'm waiting for it to grow."

Clearly much wisdom and life experience had been gained from this haircut, and I bet this mother's advice will have more weight the next time a hair decision comes along.

That boys also struggle with their hair surprises many parents. But the reason many of them are so addicted to baseball caps is not always as simple as a liking for a hat. Tap the surface and you'll find the 8-year-old in your life loves his cap so much because it hides curls he hates, a haircut that's too babyish, or hair that's sticking out. And yes, even boys adopt hairdos for the statements they make. Timothy, 12, uses mousse to keep his two-inch Mohawk looking just right. Bo, a third-grader, got his hair cut to a half-inch crew cut when he had head lice, then decided to keep it that way because he was the only kid in his class with such short hair. "I like being different," he says.

Are the parents of these children neglectful or uncaring? I think not. My sister gives her three children free rein on how they wear their hair even though it's not always what she might choose. "First," she says, "kids don't have that many ways available to them to exert their independence. Second, I can remember how angry I was as a kid not being allowed to grow my hair long. If this is the worst thing my kids do, I can handle it."

The sleep-over

When Mary's son was 11, he hosted the slumber party from hell. That wasn't the theme she planned for the party, of course, but that's what she began to call it at about two a.m. after the boys put nail polish on the rec room doorjamb and before they put Tabasco sauce on the lips of the lone boy who had the misfortune to fall asleep. Laurel, on the other hand, has had only positive experiences with her daughters' sleep-overs. If the girls are still awake at one a.m., she parks herself in the darkened room to wait for them to fall asleep. They always do.

This is not about gender, it's about childhood. Slumber parties and sleep-overs are important for children, boys as well as girls. They are a way for them to test independence and cement friend-ships, to satisfy an innate curiosity about how other people live. But ensuring success involves a lot more than packing a sleeping bag and a toothbrush. Sleep, after all, is an intimate and ritualistic experi-ence. To be able to do it away from Mom and Dad is a milestone, a big step in the march toward autonomy.

The typical child isn't ready for a sleep-over until about 6 or 7, when he has the self-confidence to know he can cope if something goes wrong as well as the cognitive ability to carry an image of home in his mind. If he's sad, he can imagine being in his own bed in his own house. Although many 4- and 5-year-olds clamor to sleep at a best friend's, it's often because they are mimicking an older sibling's behavior, not because they are truly comfortable. It's rare for a first-born to be the one who wants to do sleep-overs at a young age. For a child who isn't ready and is pushed to do it, the psychiatric twist is that it feels like abandonment. No child should be pressured or coerced into sleeping over, not even by his best friend, not even for a birthday slumber party.

Don't worry if your child is the only one among her peers who doesn't want to sleep at friends'; children mature at different rates, and firstborns may be slower with this step than middle- or later-born children. Even though a child may spend lots of time at a particular friend's house, the first overnight should be at a house where *you* also spend lots of time, where your child knows you are very comfortable. That's an intangible that adds to her security and it's why a first sleep-over is usually at Grandma's or Cousin Michael's. Indeed, it's a bad idea for a child to sleep at a friend's house unless she's had a successful night alone at a relative's. One of the advantages (or disadvantages) of having your child sleep elsewhere is that she sees other parents for what they really are: in their bathrobes. With uncombed hair. At two in the morning. If she comes home happier to see you than you expected, it may be not only that she missed you, but also that she held you up to comparison and you fared well.

Because it is such an intimate thing to do, a sleep-over has the potential to seal a friendship and can be particularly strategic for a child who doesn't make friends easily. Not even that is a reason to push this on a child who isn't ready, though. Besides, for some children, the invitation alone can be an ego boost: "Wow! I must be her best friend!"

The first time she agrees to go is definitely a big deal and something you should support, even if she's only 5; if a child says she wants to sleep at a friend's and she's had a successful experience at a relative's, that's probably a good enough indicator that she is ready. But if she changes her mind at the last minute, find a way to let her off the hook with dignity. Don't say "But you promised" or "But your friend will be so sad." Tell her, "It's okay, you can try again another time." If backing out at the last minute becomes a pattern, then it is appropriate to talk about disappointing a friend: "You need to think about this very carefully because you've disappointed Jennifer three times before. How would you feel if a friend disappointed you four times? If you think you might change your mind again, it's better to say no to start with." If your child goes, certainly tell the host parents that you don't mind being called in the middle of the night. Most parents won't want to wake you without that explicit instruction.

For young children, sleep-overs tend to work best when they are spontaneous. Consider this scenario:

Two 7-year-old boys, Sam and Ian, are longtime friends. They've been getting along well all afternoon and they don't want to part. High on their good feelings, Sam says to Ian, "Let's have a sleep-over!"

"Yeah!" says Ian.

Sam's mother thinks it's a fine idea but it can't be tonight, it's a school night. Faced with their disappointment, she invites Ian to sleep over on Friday.

"Yes!" says Ian, arm victoriously shooting up into the air.

"Yes!" agrees Sam.

Ian's mother is consulted, a deal is struck. The boys part happily. Ah, but today is only Tuesday. Wednesday at school, Sam is full of plans for their sleep-over. They can play Monopoly for as long as they like, they'll go to the video store and choose a movie together, and his mom promised to make blueberry pancakes in the morning. What a treat!

Wednesday after school, Ian, normally an easygoing kid, is disagreeable and moody. By dinnertime, he's been sent to his room twice, once for hitting his sister, another time for being fresh. That night, he can't fall asleep. "Did something happen in class today to upset you?" asks his mother.

Ian thinks about that. "No," he says. After all, nothing happened in the classroom; his conversation with Sam took place on the playground.

"Do you feel sick?" she asks. No again. As she climbs into her bed that night, she comments to her husband, "Something isn't right with our boy."

Thursday morning, Ian doesn't want to go to school. This is so unusual that his mother decides to ask the teacher at pickup time if anything's going on at school.

"Now that you mention it," says the teacher at the end of the day, "he wasn't himself today." But it's nothing she can put her finger on.

That afternoon, Ian and Sam are scheduled to play, but Ian doesn't feel like it. He seems fine until dinner, when there's more of the same moodiness and fresh behavior. The next morning is the day of the sleep-over, although the subject does not come up. He doesn't want to go to school and starts to cry, sign enough for his mother that something serious is wrong. She decides to schedule a conference with the teacher. They'll have to brainstorm this together.

After school, Ian is quiet. She suggests he get his things ready for the sleep-over. "Do I have to go?" he asks.

"No," says his mother.

"Good," he says. "I'm not going. I hate blueberry pancakes!"

Now that's a non sequitur if ever there was one, but this mother knows her son well. "Was Sam's mom going to make them for breakfast? You don't like them, do you? I bet if you tell her you don't like pancakes she would make something else that you do like."

"Oh," says Ian.

"Is there anything else about sleeping over at Sam's that you were wondering about?"

A pause. "Well, he said we could go to the video store and get a video. . . ."

Ah, thinks his mother, the light dawning even brighter. "He likes to watch scary videos and you don't. Doesn't he like sports movies, too?"

"Probably," says Ian.

"Hmmm," says his mother. Long pause.

"I guess I could tell him I don't want to watch scary ones," offers Ian.

"That's a good idea," she says.

"But what if I have to go to the bathroom in the middle of the night? The bathroom is down that long hall. . . ." A few more sentences and Ian is reconsidering. His dark mood has lifted and shortly he decides he'll sleep over after all.

> *If an older child with plenty of sleep-over experience wants to back out of an invitation, trust her instincts.*

This mother handled the situation well, once she realized what the situation was. Even though she knew early in the week that something was amiss, she spent days jumping to conclusions. Even when she asked Ian some pointed questions, they weren't quite pointed enough, and if the pancake comment hadn't done the trick, it's easy to see how Ian's refusal to go to Sam's might have added fuel to the parents' fear that something more serious was going on. Perhaps Ian would have balked at sleeping over even if he hadn't had three days to think about it, but for this child, at least, mulling over the details was a source of worry, not pleasure.

Because of the level of intimacy involved with a sleep-over, parents need to do lots of communicating around it, not just for the very first one, but for the first time at any new house. As children get older and become veterans of sleep-overs, it may be your anxiety that increases because you are less likely to know the parents of the friends. This means going in and introducing yourself or asking other parents what they know about the family so you leave less to chance, including the worst-case scenario of an abusive parent who might harm your child. Even if you know the parents well, but especially if you don't, it is not unreasonable to ask about the plan for the evening. Will parents be home or will there be a sitter? Maybe that's okay and maybe it isn't. Will the kids watch a video? Choose it together in advance or at least let the parent know what your child can handle. What bedtime does the parent anticipate? Suggest one you are comfortable with. Once your child is 8 or 9 and a veteran sleep-over goer, subtly remind him of some family values before he goes off. Children often think that because they are in someone else's house, they should do what those people do, even if it's something they wouldn't do at home. Like watch an R-rated video, taste a beer, or play with matches. Always review the experience afterward, even if the kids sleep at each other's houses frequently: "Did Joey's parents treat you well?" "Did anything happen that made you feel uncomfortable?"

If a child has medical issues or food preferences or allergies, be sure to mention them if he's sleeping someplace for the first time. Something else that host parents ought to know about is bed-wetting. Most parents of children who wet the bed are too embarrassed to mention it. Don't be. It's easy for a host parent to take precautions and certainly it's better to ask someone to take precautions than for your child to be humiliated or teased. Bed-wetting can be a reason your child likes having friends sleep at his house but doesn't want to reciprocate. Let him know that you will quietly mention it to the friend's parent so that she can put a rubber sheet under the sleeping bag, or, if you and your child know the parent well enough, you can ask her to offer to wake your child before she goes to bed so he can go to the bathroom.

For children new at sleeping out, fear of homesickness can be a real factor. Don't be afraid to talk to her about it beforehand; it won't increase the likelihood she'll be homesick, in fact, it will do the opposite because you will have given her coping skills. Other suggestions for novices:

- Encourage her to take something from home to serve as a transitional object. Most kids, even middle-school-aged boys, like to take stuffed animals: "If you feel sad, you'll have Pooh with you to cuddle." A pillowcase from home or a picture of the family can also be helpful.

- Tell her, "Since I won't be there to kiss you good night, I'm going to give you two kisses when I drop you off. One to say goodbye, and one that you can save for bedtime."

- Talk about how every family has its own bedtime ritual so he'll be prepared for a ritual other than what you do at home.

- Tell her she can call you no matter what time it is. Don't, however, call her. A call could increase separation anxiety in a young child, not relieve it, and with an older child, a call can feel like you're checking up on him.

- For slumber parties, spell out ground rules and structure at the beginning of the party, particularly regarding lights-out. Try to anticipate in advance what the issues will be; for instance, for 10- to 13-year-olds, you may want a no-telephone rule.

The minefields of friendship

Observing school-age children's friendships, parents see a minefield. We never know when or where disaster will strike. Two friends who play happily for hours today could be bitter enemies tomorrow: hurtful, mean, downright cruel. When we hear children's tales of injustice—a snubbing by a first best friend, being chosen fourth for the soccer game at recess—we don't know whether to laugh or cry, whether to intervene or let them work things out themselves. Marsha Rogers Canick, a psychologist with the Wellesley, Massachusetts, school system is sympathetic. "It's hard to hear your child express hurts and worries around friendship issues and not feel like you have to whip into action and fix it," she says. Just as that isn't the answer, neither is brushing off an incident, as in "What's the big deal anyway?" That can hurt our credibility. What parent hasn't had a "You don't even care anyway" hurled at them by an enraged 7-year-old? To a child of any age, problems with friends are more important than practically anything else. Treating these problems with less than the attention he or she thinks they deserve, translates into not caring or not taking them seriously.

> *Always encourage and facilitate multiple friendships. Exclusivity, especially for girls, rarely goes smoothly.*

Part of what makes children gravitate toward each other is a sense of equity between them. Which is why, every now and then, children need to test things out to make sure they are not inferior. For girls, the testing is most likely to come up around the issue of exclusivity among best friends. Feelings of inferiority usually are expressed through rejection: "I can't play with Jenna anymore because she played with Lydia today." Boys tend to test their equality around competency issues—"Am I good enough? Do I fit into the group?"—and disagreements generally take the form of put-downs: "I'm a better soccer player than you!" "Yeah? Well, I'm a better skier." Whether you have a son or daughter, by the time the story gets home to you, it goes something like this: "I hate Joe! I never want to play with him again. He's mean and he doesn't play fair."

So what do you do with that? For starters, don't take it literally. It doesn't mean Joe, who was his best friend yesterday, has turned into a bully overnight. More likely, there's been a clash of egos. Child psychiatrist Stanley Greenspan tells parents to assume that your grade-school-age child thinks of him- or herself as king or queen of the universe. As long as he perceives he's better than or on a par with the other kings or queens who count, everything's fine. The problem is, with so many kings and queens walking around, there's bound to be rivalry sooner or later. The closer the friendship, the more it matters and the more intense the rivalry.

One-upmanship, which is so common among 6- to 12-year-olds and peaks at about 8, is each child's way of assessing the situation, according to Greenspan. He says, "These are years when kids see themselves as part of a larger group and define themselves by how the group sees them." They rank themselves on anything and everything, from height to hair length to math skills, on who has the best sense of humor, the most Beanie Babies, the biggest muscles, the most hair ribbons. Most of the time these assessments roll off their backs because they see them as fair. Overhearing a conversation among my son and his friends one summer day, I was beside myself at how much ranking was going on. I was imagining all the hurt being generated and the ego-soothing all the parents would have to do that night. But no, none of them seemed upset; if anything, there were nods and approvals all around and my son was fine with it afterward. When I asked him about it, he needed to be prompted to remember the conversation and all he had to say about it was "It was okay because it was all true." This was the order of things and it was comforting to them to have their perceptions validated.

Ah, but what if a child doesn't agree with the group's perceptions? What if the child who is ranked fourth in soccer thinks he should be first? "That's a challenge to their self-image," says Greenspan, who specializes in school-age children. How a child copes with this depends largely on her personality. A stubborn child typically makes things harder for herself because she responds by becoming more entrenched, therefore angry and bossy, alienating peers even more. A sensitive child may see even a potential rejection as a personal slight and turn peers off with her overreactions, while an easygoing child may be happy to be best friends again tomorrow. The more threatened a child feels, the more likely he is to assign blame: "Sam lies all the time. I can't play with him anymore." That gives him the rationalization he needs to leave the friendship and play with someone he perceives as more willing to see him as an equal. When any child is in the midst of a friendship crisis, even if the friendship is waning and you're cheering its demise, be careful about negative comments you make about the friend. In other words, never say anything you wouldn't want the friend to hear. Children of all ages tend to repeat and embellish comments we make to them about their friends, either to the friend himself after they've made up or to a third party who repeats it: "Ben's mom says you're a liar."

When any child is in the midst of a friendship crisis, you may see uncharacteristic behavior at home. Unable to control what's happening in the peer group, he may need to assert himself more at home, becoming impulsive and angry or finicky and stubborn, taking a stronger than usual stand on clothes or food choices, for instance. Even if you only have an inkling of what's going on, recognizing this for what it is makes it easier to deal with it. Pick your battles and don't take things personally. Before you make what you think is your son's favorite dinner, check with him to see if he wants it. Deciding as it's put in front of him that he doesn't like it anymore is a classic way to exercise control, even though it certainly isn't a conscious or malicious decision.

As parents, we shouldn't try to fix a friendship problem or take the other extreme of leaving it entirely in our child's hands. Instead, we need to help her thread her way through these complex relationships so she feels competent to solve her own social problems. The skills she acquires now affect how she'll fare in relationships later, too. For instance:

- Be supportive and empathetic without being judgmental. Instead of "Boy, isn't he a mean kid!" try "Tell me about it." Validate feelings, not behaviors: "That must have made you feel bad"; "I bet that made you angry!" Avoid offering opinions or criticisms.

- Help him focus. This detail is important for two reasons. First, it helps you; what upsets a child most is not necessarily what you assume was most upsetting. Second, it helps him. Kids often fuse and confuse details, losing sight of what really happened. There are several ways to get him to focus. One is to ask what bothers him most and to offer choices: "Are you upset because Kim teased you about your haircut or because you weren't first in line?" Another strategy is to make verbal or literal lists—"Okay, let's see what the problems are"—and then prioritize them: "So, what's the bigger deal here?" Recap what he says along the way: "So the problem is . . ."

- Offer a resolution in fantasy. Ask her, "What do you wish could have happened?" Sometimes the wish is simple: "That he apologized." Often, it's unrealistic: "That she'd promise never to play with anyone else again." Grant her the wish in fantasy—"It would be nice if it had worked out that way, wouldn't it?"—and then move her past it: "I wonder what *she* would wish could have happened?" Whatever you do, avoid judgmental comments such as "That's a selfish wish" or "Well, that could never happen."

- Talk about what she can do now. Children tend to get stuck here and the more you offer solutions, the less likely they are to accept them. Instead of trying to convince the typical 9- to

11-year-old who has been devastated by a rejection that there are other kids to play with, try to help her come to that conclusion herself. One way to do that is to help her create a list of options. Of course, she'll want to stop at the very first one ("Never play with her again") but don't let her. Tell her to come up with all the possibilities she can, even if she doesn't want to do any of them. Even if she insists none of them are viable and walks away from the conversation, don't feel like you've accomplished nothing. Often just the process of doing this will make her more open to ideas so that she'll think about it some more. Twenty minutes later or the next morning, she may tell you, "I know what I'm going to do," and have a solution that will incorporate some (or none) of what you talked about. What matters is that it will be *her* solution and therefore something she can buy into wholeheartedly.

Should you ever call the parent of the other child? Only if you already have a relationship with him or her, or if a child has been physically harmed. If it's a serious issue and you don't know the parents, mention it to the teacher. If you feel the need for a child to leave your house prematurely because problems have developed, serve as an escort so the information about what happened gets delivered accurately.

Getting your kids to pitch in

When our son was 4½, my husband asked, "Is he old enough to take out the garbage?" We had a good chuckle visualizing him lugging trash barrels twice his size, but we both knew that behind the fantasy were some serious thoughts. Doing chores is one rite of passage most parents eagerly await, not necessarily because we want to ease our own workload but because we recognize that it is through chores that children learn about responsibility and family life. Chores teach cooperation and instill a sense of belonging within the family; they help a child understand that things don't just "happen"—a house doesn't get clean unless someone cleans it—and that there are some things you do even though you don't like to. Since this is one move toward independence that parents, not children, initiate, the sooner we give them age-appropriate responsibility, the better. Our son may have been too young at 4½ for trash detail, but even at that age he was responsible for using the Dustbuster to clean up the floor after dinner. Of course, at that age he thought it was fun.

> *Children of all ages need to feel*
> *a sense of responsibility and success with chores.*
> *It helps them feel they're contributing to*
> *the good of the family.*

Very young children, 2- and 3-year-olds, love to help out. It's fun for them because it gives them a sense of mastery. For you, having them "help" often only makes more work, causing us to swoop in and do the job ourselves or to discourage a toddler or preschooler from "helping" in the first place. Stop yourself in midswoop. Somehow, you need to find the patience to tolerate the mess their help makes. One way is to ask a 3- or 4-year-old to help only when you know you have the time and patience to put up with it. Another is to be sure that the tasks you give them are age appropriate and can be accomplished without too much difficulty so they can see the fruits of their labor and feel good about them. A 3-year-old can't set the table, but he could carry to the table two or three objects that you set out for him— the salt and pepper shakers, napkins—and he could carry them back to the counter again after the meal.

One mother of a now 19-year-old tells how her daughter, when she was 4, happened to pick a dandelion, put it in a vase she had made in preschool, and put it on the dinner table. Everybody in the family commented on how pretty it was, including her two older siblings. The next day she did it again. The third day, she found a different flower, which prompted a discussion about how amazing nature is, that there are so many different kinds of flowers. The next day, she searched the backyard for yet another flower. Each time, it produced positive comments. By the end of the week, she named herself the "Table Decorator." It was her job, she declared, to make sure there was something pretty on the dinner table each night to "cheer everybody up." This self-defined responsibility may not be exactly what some parents have in mind, but it gave this preschooler a sense of importance within the family, a way to feel that she contributed something. This was not some here-today-gone-tomorrow fancy, either. This little girl stayed with her job all through the summer. When autumn ended and she couldn't find flowers, she put acorns and leaves on the table, which prompted a whole new round of positive feedback. The day of the first snow, she put a snowball in a dish, which led to another discussion entirely. This child is now a freshman in college, majoring in biology. Her mother is convinced her lifelong fascination with science and nature began with those dinner table discussions.

Just because we give children responsibilities, doesn't mean they'll want to do them, of course. What do you do when your child balks? With a young child, there's a tendency to say, "Okay, you don't have to do it this time." But what kind of message is that to send? That it's okay not to do something just because you don't feel like it? Researchers say how well we do or don't follow through when assigned jobs aren't completed may be more important than the chore itself. Don Fontenelle, a child psychiatrist in New Orleans, says, "Learning there are consequences is what builds responsibility. The worst thing a parent can do is set up a chore and not follow through."

What follows is a selection of my favorite strategies from various professionals designed to help us get our children to do the jobs we ask. Don't look for instantaneous results; like so many things in parenting, finding a strategy that works for your child is a matter of trial and error.

- Build the job into the child's sense of who she is. Psychologist Jacqueline Goodnow, known for her research on children and responsibility, calls this a Machiavellian strategy. It involves finding something positive to say about the kind of person your child is. Perhaps one day your 4-year-old organizes her stuffed animals by size. Tell her, "I can see you are the kind of person who likes to have things where you can find them." Does this mean this child will take pride in keeping her room neat? Not necessarily, but the theory is that if this idea gets planted, it can take root and become a positive self-fulfilling prophecy. You don't want to overdo it, however; perfectionists can be created too. Saying (and this is what Goodnow says most of us tend to do) "I can see you are the kind of person who likes to live in a pigsty," is a negative attribution that gets you nowhere and only makes a child feel lousy.

- Negotiate. All children, but especially school-age and older, are more willing to cooperate when they are part of the process. Discuss the responsibilities/jobs that need to be done and agree jointly on who does what and when and how. Post job lists on the refrigerator and rotate them from week to week. St. Louis family counselor Evonne Weinhaus offers a negotiating strategy she calls "I'm willing, I want." Parent: "I'm willing to do the grocery shopping, but I want help bringing the bags in from the car." Or: "I'm willing to pay you for mowing the grass, but I want to know it will be done by the end of the day Saturday." The trick to successful I'm-willing-I-want negotiating is not to give away the store. Always go into a negotiation knowing what your bottom line is, the compromise beyond which you aren't willing to go.

- Create a Job Jar. This is especially good for preschoolers, who will see it as a game. Write down the jobs on a piece of paper, put them in a jar, and take turns reaching in. Include jobs that are fun—decorating the refrigerator—as well as ones that are easy, bringing in the mail or newspaper. Do the picking once a week. A child might pick two chores that will be his for the week, or he might pick four pieces of paper and get to choose two of them. Don't change jobs in the jar too frequently; the longer a young child does the same chore repeatedly, the better he gets at it and the better he feels about himself. In Weinhaus's family, jobs in the Job Jar included setting the table, clearing the table, and wiping the table. Part of her deal with her children was that if they did it willingly all week long, she would do all three tasks on Sunday.

- Give your child room to make decisions. Telling her what to do, how to do it, and when to do it will feel too bossy. Educator Lucy Calkins says that when her sons have chores, she makes a point not to be too specific so they can think for themselves. "You're in charge of this," she'll tell them. "Apply your best creative thinking skills." Definitely don't redo the job yourself after she's done it. If you're unhappy with her performance, talk about why. Try to do it in a way that isn't critical, for example: "I bet you wiped the table with Ajax so you could do a really excellent cleaning job, didn't you? It's so clean, it sparkles! Did you feel the table top afterward, though? Feels gritty, doesn't it? Sometimes if you use too much, it leaves a film. Let me show you how much I use so that doesn't happen." In some families, giving room to move around in can include bartering among siblings, a strategy that can lead to improved sibling cooperation: "I overslept! I'll be late if I walk the dog. I'll trade you. I'll clear the table tonight." In some families, trading with parents can work, too. Indeed, offering to trade with your child may buy you untold goodwill: "I can see you have a lot of homework tonight. I'll set the table for you if you promise to give me ten minutes of your time tomorrow for something I need help with."

- Offer an appropriate amount of praise. Too much praise and your child may begin to think, "Hmm, maybe this is harder than I think it is." Too little and he'll feel taken for granted. A child knows when she's done a bad job and if you praise her too much too often, she may begin to do a bad job to test you to see if you say it's good even if it isn't. Carolyn Webster-Stratton, a child psychologist who spent twelve years studying why children don't comply, likes to complement verbal reinforcement with a point system. Most point systems work by giving a sticker or a point on a chart every time a child does the task successfully. At the end of an agreed-to period, the points can be traded for something he wants. This is a good strategy for young children or those who are difficult to manage.

- Agree to consequences at the time an assignment is made. All deals should be sealed with a contract that includes consequences for failure. That makes for fewer disagreements later. Talk together about what the consequences should be; often a child will be harsher on himself than you would be. Natural consequences are always the best ones—"I didn't know you wanted to wear those pants today. It's my job to wash them but it's your job to get them to the laundry basket." When you assign consequences in advance, be sure they relate to the offending action. Restricting TV viewing because she didn't pick up the clothes off the floor makes no sense to a child and feels unfair and arbitrary; not being able to wear something because it's still dirty has a logic she can follow.

So fine, you pick a strategy and sometimes it actually works. What about when it doesn't? Many parents, after reminding a child about a task for the seventeenth time—*"Did you pick the clothes up off your floor yet?"*—will drop the issue out of frustration, anger, or a sense of failure. That only reinforces noncompliance. When a child doesn't see follow-through, he'll also be more likely to test you. Which is why this last strategy of establishing consequences and following through with them is the single most important thing we can do. Too frequently we impose consequences as punishment, as an afterthought or out of anger. That's usually inappropriate and ineffective. When you ask children why they don't like to do their chores, the most frequent response is that they feel like they're being bossed. Webster-Stratton, after doing some parental observations, says it's not unusual for some parents to issue up to thirty-five commands in a typical half hour: "Put your dishes in the sink. Give the dog some water. Turn off the lights on your way upstairs." Is it any wonder children begin to feel put upon?

When your children don't comply, your first task as a parent is to ask yourself if you're being unrealistic in your expectations. What about consequences? Are you following through? If you aren't falling down on either count and you're still up against a wall, here are some other strategies:

- Renegotiate. "You haven't been helping bring the groceries in, like we agreed. What do you think we can do about it?" Avoid statements such as "I never can count on you"; "You're worthless"; "You don't belong in this family." If no ideas are forthcoming, try a variation on the I'm-willing-I-want strategy: "I'm willing to carry in the perishable groceries, but how about if you bring in the nonperishables"; "I'm willing to bring in the heaviest ones, if you can manage the others." Or even "I'm willing to do some, I just don't want to have to do it all myself. How about if every week we count how many there are and we each do half?" If no idea seems workable, you need to think about what choices you have that turn into consequences for your child. With the groceries, for instance, you could leave the stuff your child might want—snacks, cookies and drinks—in the trunk (yes, it would take an effort on your part to separate them out), or you could not buy them at all: "Well, there are so many bags to carry, and I wasn't getting any help with them, so I had to choose not to buy some nonessential foods." That will prompt a cry of "But I was gonna help you *this* time!" to which you can say, "That's great to know. Make me a list of what you want. Next week, I'll be sure to buy all that stuff, knowing I can count on you." Be willing to tolerate the unhappiness, knowing you'll likely get the compliance you need in the end.

- Remove privileges. This is your best strategy with kids school-age and older, but there are several pitfalls. The first is to remain neutral and matter-of-fact; otherwise you'll end up in a no-win power struggle. The second is to make sure the lost privilege matters to your child; if it doesn't, you haven't accomplished anything. Loss of TV for a day for an 8-year-old or of the telephone for an 11-year-old tends to be very powerful. As with consequences, it helps when the lost privilege has a connection to the failed action. When that isn't possible, spell out the connection for him: "I can't make you fold the laundry, but I can decide how much TV you get to watch." Be careful not to make loss of privileges too drastic, like taking away the telephone for a week. A child will feel he's in such a deep hole, there's no way out and it doesn't matter what he does.

- Problem solve. State your case clearly: "We have such a small family that if one person fails to do his or her family job, it puts a big burden on the other two people. But it seems like you have a hard time remembering that you need to set the table. . . ." Some children have a harder time than others getting themselves organized and need reminders: "Don't forget the table needs to be set before 5." In general, however, it's better if the power for the reminder remains in her control: "How can we help you remember to set the table? Do you want me to tell you when it's half an hour before dinner? Do you want to set the timer in the kitchen?"

- Time out. For children under 6, this can be an effective strategy because it eliminates negative attention a child might otherwise get for not doing the job: "Your job is to empty the wastebaskets. If you don't do them by dinnertime, you'll have a time-out." Have him sit in a designated time-out place for up to six minutes (a minute for each year of age). Then instruct him again on how to do the job and tell him failure to do it will result in another time-out. With some children, you may have to do this many times before they realize you are serious.

- Stop the world. In this scenario, also for younger children, you literally don't do anything until the job gets done, a strategy that comes from Judith Smith's book *Child Management: A Program for Parents and Teachers:* "Your job is to empty the wastebasket. I'm going to sit here and wait until that gets finished. I guess we'll be late for your playdate."

- Repeat back the rule. Asking your child to repeat back to you what it is he is supposed to do may sound ineffectual but many parents swear this works, especially if it is done in a matter-of-fact tone. Similarly, after the task is done, ask your child, "If you looked at the [completed] job through my eyes, what would you see? Will I be happy when I see how the job was done?"

Sooner or later, the question of payment will enter into the chore discussion. Usually this happens between ages 6 and 8, when a child begins to want some spending power. Many parents don't want to pay children for the chores they do. "It's not that I'm against them having their own money; there are important lessons for kids to learn about saving and spending," says Barbara, whose children are 9 and 6. "It's more that I want them to make these contributions because they are part of the family." So far, she isn't paying Pat and Carly for the work they do around the house. Any money either child accumulates comes from monetary gifts they get at holidays and birthdays and from a generous grandfather who hands out dollar bills whenever he visits.

In another family, Susan and James do pay their children for the chores they do. Matthew, 11, and Kristen, 8, each earn two dollars when they clean their room and two dollars if they help with the yard work on weekends. If Matthew baby-sits Kristen, he earns five dollars. "If they don't do the job, they don't get the money, pure and simple," says Susan.

Connecting chores to money is a personal decision that differs from family to family, and there is no consensus among professionals on whether it's a good or bad thing to do. Those who say that children should get an allowance no matter what, argue that allowance is an entitlement. Jerome Rabow, a sociologist and therapist in Los Angeles whose area of specialty is children, families, and money, says, "You explain to a child that the reason he gets an allowance is because learning about money is an important part of growing up. You also explain that another important part of growing up is having responsibilities around the house because that's what a family is all about. These are givens."

Those who argue that allowance and chores should be tied together say that otherwise, children never learn the value of money, where it comes from and why. But even sociologist Peter Adler, who researches the way children spend money and professionally advocates tying the two together, isn't locked into his position. When his children were 9 and 14, his son's allowance was tied to chores, but his 14-year-old daughter's was not. "Without the external reward, my son wouldn't do the job," he explains. As for his daughter, "I canceled her allowance because every fifty cents became a source of disagreement. Did you make your bed? Did you take out the garbage?" Instead, he gave her money as she needed it. In return, she agreed to do her chores without nagging. But this begs another issue: What about the experience children need handling their own money?

Earning and handling money

It's impossible to learn about money without firsthand experience. Unfortunately, research shows that many parents are loath to facilitate the learning. Like sex, money is a taboo subject in many homes; parents have difficulty talking about it with each other, let alone with their children. But the earlier children have experience with money, the better off they will be.

Start your child off in the preschool years with a piggy bank. At this age, the money she collects will come from coins parents and relatives give her for one reason or another, usually on holidays or birthdays. She'll assume that you collect money the same way you collect pine cones, so you need a conversation that goes something like this: "Money is something you save because it is a way to trade for other things you will want later on." Make the point that it's not just to buy things for yourself. Encouraging a child to use her own money to buy Dad's birthday present, even if it's only a pack of his favorite chewing gum, is a way for her to see that money brings pleasure and pride. It also helps preschoolers begin to learn relative value: Some things cost more than others.

It doesn't usually take a child long to see that money is a source of power because of what it can buy. Once that happens, generally early in grade school, a child is ready for an allowance. This can be a frustrating decision for a parent. Too much allowance and a child doesn't learn to value it; too little and it doesn't buy him the independence it ought to, not to mention that it will become a bone of contention between you. For starters, talk to parents of other children your child's age as well as to parents of older children to get an idea of the ballpark you ought to be in. You'll probably find quite a range. Aim for someplace in the middle; you don't want your child to be way out of sync with his peers in one direction or the other. A good starting allowance at age 6 is two dollars; if you're inclined to start higher, consider this: If a child gets four dollars when he's 6 or five dollars when he's 8, what will he expect when he's 12? And what would he possibly need or do with that much money at that age? On the other hand, if he is expected to pay for his lunch out of his allowance, five dollars may not be enough at age 8. Before you arbitrarily set an allowance at a certain amount, talk with your child about your expectations of what the money should be used for. Arrive together at what a good amount is. If part of the teaching experience is to be about saving, then the allowance needs to be enough so that a child can put some of it aside.

Economist Debra Sherwin, who works with parents to help children learn how to deal with money, recommends giving an allowance twice a month rather than weekly because it grants more responsibility and decision-making power. "The best thing that can happen is for your child to spend it all at once and have to go two weeks without any money or be forced to take some money out of her savings," she says. Kids hate to do that. By 8, they're very protective of what's in that piggy bank. In fact, by 8 they're protective of their money, period. Sherwin remembers her daughter was so tight with her money that she would make birthday cards rather than buy them, even though it might take her three hours. "She hadn't yet learned the value of her time," Sherwin says.

Whenever your child is begging and pleading for you to buy her something, the best way to gauge how important it is to her is to tell her she can have it, as long as she spends her own money on it. Most of the time, the item will immediately drop in importance. If it's a big-ticket item and it's something she still wants badly and she's willing to spend her last penny on it, then you can decide if you want to help her pay for it or not.

Once children have their own money, the biggest question is how much control to exercise over how they spend it. For most children under 12, giving them almost full control of their money is generally a nondangerous way to grant independence. Although you can have input into how your child spends his money, you shouldn't cut back or eliminate the allowance because of what you consider inappropriate spending. You may think blowing a two-dollar allowance on baseball cards is a waste, but in a 7-year-old's culture, those cards may be the most important thing in the world. Giving him the leeway to spend as he wants helps build trust, self-esteem, and experience. That doesn't mean you shouldn't know how the money is being spent or that you can't try to exert influence: "I can't stop you from spending this, it's your money, but I think this is a bad choice, it's not the kind of thing I expect you to spend money on," or "Christmas is two months away. Have you thought about a budget, or a gift list? I'm just wondering if you'll have money for all the people you like to buy gifts for if you spend so much on this CD." On the other hand, if a child is using his money to buy something you consider a poor choice or is overly generous in spending his money on gifts, you might want to talk about why this is not what you want him to spend money on and give him the chance to stop buying the offensive item, or agree to limits for how much is appropriate to spend on gifts. If that doesn't work, depending on your values, you may want to exert control by suspending the allowance or putting it in escrow until he agrees to spend more wisely. Since the idea underlying all of this is for your children to be making choices and decisions *and mistakes* about spending while you are still able to influence and teach them, the best limit-setting around money occurs when the limits are laid out from the start and when they continue to be part of an ongoing discussion about your values around good and bad spending.

Some children get into money in much bigger ways than others. When Christopher was 13, he earned the nickname Job Man. He had a paper route, which he began when he was 10. He had a regular dog-walking job, which led to three temporary dog-walking jobs, and in the winter he shoveled for neighbors. He also was paid for taking out the trash at home. By midwinter, much to his delight, Chris had earned—and better yet, saved—enough money to buy himself a hockey net ($100), hockey pants ($170), a basketball ($30), and assorted candy and pizza.

"Earning money has ups and downs," says Chris. "The ups are that it's fun to have your own money and not to have to ask your parents all the time. The downs are that your parents don't pay for as much as they used to." His conclusion? "More ups than downs."

There's probably more truth to this than Chris realizes.

> *Between 8 and 10, a child should be earning money at home, and by 12, earning something outside the home.*

Children who receive money by way of allowances and gifts but never actually earn it are at a disadvantage when they eventually are out on their own. There's a psychological empowerment that comes from earning money, a sense of confidence and mastery of the world that just isn't there when money is handed to you. That means that if an allowance has been an entitlement in your family and chores are done as part of the family work, select a few jobs for which payment will be issued: mowing the grass, shoveling, raking. Even if an allowance has been tied to jobs, it's time to throw some new jobs into the equation, making it clear these are not attached to the allowance but simply ways for earning extra money. My son has received an allowance since he was 6, but at 4 he earned money for the first time: for every two weeds he pulled, I paid him a penny. Lest you think earning experience isn't a big deal, consider this: Research shows that children who lack earning experience tend to be less successful as adults in their financial dealings, including being less able to negotiate employer-employee relationships, ask for a raise, or judge the value of work.

Young earners tend to be horrified at how much things cost because now they have a context in which to put that cost. If a child is struggling to save for something major and really being diligent about it, you may feel comfortable offering a matching-fund approach to a purchase: If he saves an agreed-to amount according to an agreed-to schedule, you'll match that amount.

Whether your child has a sporadic income or a regular one, he needs help to keep track of it. In other words, a budget. Sherwin likes to start a child off with a calendar that shows each week's income (allowance included) and expenditure: family birthdays, holidays, and so on. Then you begin to pose questions like these: "Okay, you earn twenty dollars a month. In April there are no birthdays, but May is Mother's Day. It might be too soon to think about what you want to buy specifically, but you might want to think about how much you want to spend so you'll know how much you can afford to spend on other things in April." Neale S. Godfrey, founder of the Children's Financial Network, which publishes a grade-school curriculum on how to handle money, suggests a more specific strategy for a child 10 or older who has a steady income: dividing earnings into thirds. One-third is for immediate spending, as the child wants; one-third is to save toward something he can't yet afford, like a bike or in-line skates; one-third is to save in an account for the future, like college or camp. Some parents might like a division into fourths, to include savings for a favorite charity. Location of the funds is important. The spending money can go in a wallet, the personal savings can go in a piggy bank, but the savings for the future ought to go in a bank account and your child ought to go with you to deposit it, just for the experience and exposure and to see how it adds up on an account record.

> *Having their own money to spend helps children learn the difference between need and want.*

With a savings plan in place, hopefully you'll be more comfortable letting her make her own spending mistakes. Bite your tongue to keep from saying "That's a waste of money," and stop your hand if it's heading for your wallet to bail her out when she's broke.

Tough as it may be, it's a mistake to loan money when your child runs out. If you don't resist the if-you-love-me-you'll-buy-it-for-me guilt trip, she'll never learn the consequences of overspending. This lesson is particularly important (and difficult to subscribe to) for parents of only one child. Since your money doesn't have to go as far, there's a tendency to be more generous. But bailouts create a rescue mentality, the idea that someone, Mom or Dad or Grandma, will always be there for you to turn to. When that happens, your child isn't learning how to delay gratification, which is one of the most important lessons that can come from managing your own money. Research shows that inexperience or inability to delay gratification is what leads later on to impulse buying, credit card abuse, and an inability to plan for the future.

Helping out is different from bailing out. If your 11-year-old wants sneakers that cost $115, it's reasonable to tell him, "I'm willing to pay seventy dollars for sneakers. If you want ones that cost a hundred and fifteen, you need to earn or save the balance. Or if you want to shop around at discount stores to see if you can find them for less, I'm willing to drive you around. If you find them for less than seventy dollars, I'll still give you seventy and you can use the extra toward the software you've been wanting."

Giving your child a wide range of experience handling money can pay off in unexpected ways. Chris and Erin's mom, Phyllis, is convinced that her children's need to budget their time for their various jobs helped both of them to be more organized with schoolwork. There was also a ripple effect for her 10-year-old son, David, who is not yet earning money but opened a bank account for his allowance so he could save for a basketball. But Phyllis has noticed a downside to Chris's earning. He has a tendency to treat friends to pizza and soda. Chris admits that's become a problem, especially after his mom suggested he keep track of how much he was spending on his friends each week and he saw it add up to more than twenty dollars. "I kinda feel rich sometimes, compared to my friends who don't have their own money. It makes me feel good to be able to treat them, but I'm trying really hard to make wise spending decisions and not to go crazy with it." On his own, he set a limit for himself of eight dollars a week on "treating."

The first crush

First love is one of the most poignant rites of passage, and although "love" in the teenage years looks very different today than it did even ten years ago, puppy love or crushes thankfully still look a lot like they did when we were kids.

Many children develop a crush sometime when they are in elementary school. Most parents tend to think it's harmless, even cute, and dismiss it without much thought. But a crush is no trifling thing to the child who's feeling it. Psychologist Elaine Hatfield, a researcher who is known for her work on children's emotions, says, "Kids fall in love as early as we're able to measure their feelings, and it has some of the same components as it does for an adult." A third-grader with a crush, for instance, thinks about the person a lot, idealizes him or her, wants to be with him, talks about him, thinks he's wonderful, feels good when he's paying attention to her and devastated when he's not. This is very different from the preschooler or kindergartner who has a same-sex or even opposite-sex attachment to a classmate. Although the 5-year-old's feelings of affection can be very intense and should always be respected, the 9- or 10-year-old has hormones that are beginning to kick in in a premature-budding kind of way that adds a tinge of chemistry to the feelings. First-graders often get caught up in writing love letters not for the message or any feelings behind them but because they enjoy the act of writing. Why love letters? Because somewhere they have seen or heard about them. One way to test this out is to encourage some other writing: "Grandma told me she's lonesome. I bet if you write to her, she'll write back." A third-grader with a crush won't be nearly so easily distracted.

My favorite illustration comes from Evan, a third-grader. There were certain mornings when Evan was so excited to get to school that his mother, Dana, asked him what he was looking forward to so much. He blushed. "He *blushed*! Can you believe it!" she exclaims, still incredulous herself. It dawned on her at that moment that he had a crush on someone. His answer at first was what you'd expect: "Nothing." But when she pushed him just a little bit, he said, "On Tuesdays, we have Open Circle and Molly and I always sit next to each other." A few minutes later, he offered, "We also sit next to each other in science." Also Tuesday.

A few days later, Evan asked if there were any of his school photos left. Told there were, he wanted to know how to mail pictures so they don't bend. Assuming he was mailing them to his granny, Dana got him some cardboard. "Are you going to write a letter, too?" she asked. "When he blushed again, I knew this wasn't going to Granny."

> *It's just as common for a boy to have a crush on a girl as the other way around.*

Dana couldn't decide how she felt about him mailing Molly his picture, but before she had much time to think about it, Molly's photo showed up in their mailbox. It had been hand delivered. "They obviously had agreed to exchange photos. The look on his face when he opened it was, well, magical," she says. Now Evan announced that he needed to go to the store to buy a frame. "I'll use my own money, don't worry, Mom," he told her. Things were moving much too fast for Dana: "I had no idea what to think of this. Was it good or bad?" She took him to the store and watched as he carefully chose a gold-colored frame. That night, as she tucked him into bed, Molly's picture was sitting on his nightstand, next to his clock radio, "so it's the first thing I'll see when I wake up," he told her. And then, after the lights were out, he confided even more: "When I feel sad, I just look at her picture and then I feel better."

Where was this coming from, wondered Evan's parents. Was it imitative behavior or was it real? And how were Molly's parents feeling about it? The answer to the last question came the next day when Molly's mother, a woman Dana had never met, telephoned. They agreed there was nothing wrong with what was happening since the crushes were mutual, but they also agreed not to let it get "out of hand," although they didn't define what that meant, something Dana came to regret.

If these feelings of affection are as real for children as they are for adults, they are not nearly as complicated or as intense. A crush is not only well within the range of normal childhood development, it is also a positive sign that a child is exploring his understanding of the way relationships work. It is not about sexual feelings. "If there seems to be a sexual component, it is curiosity-based, not sexually driven," says child and adolescent psychologist Dee Shepherd-Look. "It's a girl or boy wondering, how is he/she different?"

On the other hand, there's no question that some of what our kids do these days has a pretty adult-looking edge to it. That comes partly from what our children are exposed to in the world around them. Kids draw on the role models they see, not just from the adults in their life but also from the media. Evan, for instance, talked about wanting to have Molly sleep over. "Why do you want to do that?" asked Dana, her alarms going off. "It would be comforting to have her in the same house as me," he said. "And I could bring her breakfast in bed, like Daddy does for you sometimes." That made Dana feel better. "It was pretty clear to me that he had a warm feeling for this girl and that the way he was expressing it was simply a mimicking of what he's seen around him. Luckily," she adds, "what he sees at home is very positive." Dana granted Evan his wish in fantasy: "That probably isn't going to happen, but it's a nice thing to think about, isn't it?" Perhaps because she didn't belittle the thought or him for thinking it, Evan was satisfied with her answer. He didn't push her and he never brought it up again.

First love is not unlike a fixation. School-age children go through periods of time when they are trying to figure out how they fit into the world. Lots of things capture their imagination and they try them on for size. Very young children come to grips with new concepts through their play. But a 7- or 8- or 9-year-old boy like Evan knows it is no longer acceptable to play with a girl. That doesn't leave him many options when he has a feeling of connection to a person who happens to be a girl, so he draws on the role models he sees in the world around him.

As normal as all this may be, if the feeling isn't mutual, being the object of someone's fixation can be uncomfortable, even annoying. If your child is the object of unwanted expressions of affection, help her figure out some things to say: "I don't want to hurt your feelings and I'm glad you like me, but I like to play with lots of different friends, not just with you"; "It's okay if you like me, but it's embarrassing when you leave me notes or follow me around. I wish you'd stop." When Abby was in third grade, she was so embarrassed by the letters a classmate would leave at her desk and in her coat pocket that she didn't want to go to school. Unfortunately, her mother, Elaine, didn't know that was the problem until the boy mailed her a letter. Abby took one look at the envelope and ripped it to shreds, but not before her mom had seen the hearts on it and the return address.

"Did you know who that was from, without even opening it?" she asked.

"Yes. And I know what it said, too," her daughter said as she left the room in a huff. That night at bedtime, the mother probed. "I guess that wasn't the first letter you've gotten like that, huh?"

"He puts them in my desk at school. All the girls know he does it. They're calling me Mrs. H— and want to know what we'll name the baby. I hate him!"

Elaine called the teacher immediately. The teacher had noticed the boy busy writing at recess, but she hadn't paid attention. Now she would make sure he was engaged in other activities. Since Abby's mother didn't know his parents, the teacher promised to talk to them and to him, not in a judgmental or punitive way but to let him know that even though he wanted to make Abby feel good, he was actually making her feel uncomfortable. Once he realized that, he wanted to apologize to Abby, which he did at the beginning of school one morning with the teacher's help. She called Abby over and stood there while the conversation took place. It was short: "Abby, I'm sorry my letters upset you. I won't do it anymore." Abby: "Good. Thanks."

Evan's story does not end as happily. About two weeks after the initial contact, Molly's mother called again, demanding Evan stop "harassing" her daughter. Suddenly Evan felt like a criminal and was afraid to go to school. "Obviously something had happened to turn Molly off. I didn't know what, but my first priority was to repair his hurt," says Dana. "I told him that although it's nice to care about another person, sometimes it's possible to come on too strong." She also told him several times that even though Molly had stopped liking his attention, he wasn't a bad person. "I told him that not everyone likes you as much as you like them, that's just a fact of life."

> *Don't forbid your child to have a friendship with a child of the opposite sex unless you think she is in danger.*

Those were positive and appropriate messages to give her son, but in retrospect she wishes she had said things like that earlier. "Without realizing it, I had encouraged him to dote on this little girl. Frankly, it didn't occur to me that he might be overdoing it. I didn't even ask the teacher what was happening in class. Turns out, he was following her around. I don't blame the mother for calling me. I should have asked more questions. I wish I had been more tuned in, and I wish the teacher had called me when she saw these things happening." It's also possible that the object of a crush may be giving reinforcement without parents or teachers knowing it or, indeed, without the child herself realizing it. An 8-year-old boy might think a girl likes his attention simply because she says "thank you" when he hands her a note, even though she was just responding out of force of habit. It's our job to help identify that behavior for both of them.

Perhaps surprisingly, even a crush that is reciprocal can be damaging if it gets out of hand. "Exclusivity does not promote social development in the school-age years," says Shepherd-Look. If a boy and girl in fourth or fifth grade were engaged in couple-like behavior, either playing together at school or after school, or calling each other on the phone, she wouldn't make a big deal out of it, but she would encourage her child to play with others by saying something like "It's important to play with a lot of people because you have so much to offer them and they have a lot to offer you." Even in a two-way crush, parents need to examine the messages they are sending to be sure they are not somehow encouraging the behavior. A 7-year-old boy may enjoy a friendship with a girl in his class, but because his parents talk about how "cute" Tommy's crush is, he may start to write love letters. In other words, the "crush" may be in the minds of the adults, not the children. Parents who overreact to the other extreme create a different problem. If a parent is anxious, it can be her anxiety that makes this a difficult time for the child rather than the situation itself. Perhaps Molly's initial liking for Evan turned to annoyance because Evan did, indeed, "overdo it." It's equally possible, however, that Molly's parents came to be uncomfortable and their discomfort rubbed off on Molly.

An evenhanded approach is what works best. Rather than getting upset or being dismissive, get into a running dialogue about feelings with your children so you can gauge how they are coping. Give them coping skills along the way: "Last week you didn't seem to mind that Eric was paying a lot of attention to you. Now it seems like you do. What can you do to get him to stop without hurting his feelings?"

Crushes are not limited to peers, of course. What parent doesn't remember having a crush on a teacher? "*Very* normal," says Shepherd-Look. One reason it's so common for children to have a crush on an adult is because it is safe for them, almost like practice. Often that adult is the teacher. Mary Lou Dowd, a first-grade teacher in Hingham, Massachusetts, says mostly boys but girls, too, write "I love you" on worksheets or draw hearts with "MLD" and their initials. Her response is wonderful and 100 percent appropriate. She'll write back "I love being your teacher," or draw her own heart, no initials. What's inappropriate is if a teacher lavishes special attention on a child or humiliates him: "Oh, look, isn't this cute, Tommy brought me flowers *again*." If you get wind that anything like this is going on, talk to the teacher directly and to the principal as well.

On rare occasion, a crush turns into an obsession, where a child can't get through the day unless the object of his attention responds in certain ways. This leads him to resort to inappropriate behavior— pulling her hair, following her home from school, telephoning many times a day—just to make sure there is some kind of interaction. If you identify this kind of behavior in your child, early professional intervention is essential. If your child is the object of such behaviors, tell the teacher or school psychologist. Also rare but occasional is when sexual curiosity leads to sex play: "I'll show you my vagina if you show me your penis." Make sure your child knows it is inappropriate if someone ever says this to her, that vaginas and penises are private body parts that we don't share with other children. If you think your child is curious about opposite-sex body parts, tell her, "If you're curious about what boys look like, we'll find a book with some pictures." Certainly don't punish her. The interest is healthy, it's acting on it that isn't.

The dating game for 10-year-olds?

Not all children develop crushes, in fact, some never do. But sooner or later, most get caught up in boy-girl relationships. It happened to Zack when he was 10 and got an invitation to a co-ed Halloween dance party: "Wear a costume you can dance in! Bring your dancing CDs!"

Zack had never danced with a girl or even thought about going to a boy-girl dance party. He didn't like the idea, but he wanted to go because all his friends were going.

His parents were not happy. "It's one thing to go to a bowling or soccer party that includes the whole class but a dance party, well, that just has a different feel to it," says Susan, his mother. "This had a dating patina to it, the first step to a presexual stage," she says. "I felt like it was too early. It frightened me. He was only 10!" Her first instinct was to say no, but Susan and her husband, Ben, ended up giving Zack permission. "We felt it was important to allow him to be part of the crowd," explains Susan. "Peer pressure is so important at this age. And when I called the mother of the girl who was giving the party, she said I was the only parent who called to express any concern." Susan sighs. "It's very hard at this age to know what is right, to be able to say no."

This is a day in the life of a child that most parents would like to postpone as long as they can. Psychologist David Elkind of Tufts University says 10-year-olds are typically well-behaved, reasonable, logical children who enjoy being with their parents and whose sex hormones haven't kicked in yet. But today, even 10-year-olds are being pressured to grow up faster, leaving many parents as baffled as Zack's. "They're not 8-year-olds anymore, but they aren't 12-year-olds, either," says Susan.

Elkind and other professionals do not mince words: A dance party such as the one Zack was invited to is inappropriate for this age. "It's another example of rushing kids out of childhood," says Elkind, who is best known for his now classic book, *The Hurried Child*. In fact, it's unusual for 10-year-olds even to be comfortable with the opposite sex; those who are generally have older siblings. Developmentally, the typical 10-year-old is focused on a best-friend relationship, not on the opposite sex; certainly there is no developmental benefit from getting involved in stereotypical presexual behavior. It's not that boys and girls can't be attending parties together, or doing almost anything together, it's just that the activities shouldn't hint at a sexual orientation.

Zack admits he was pretty scared before he went to the party. Some boys didn't dance at all. "They were too embarrassed," he says. At first, he didn't either, but by the end of the evening, Zack had danced a number of slow dances. "I really had a very, very good time." He beams. "If my parents hadn't let me go, I would have been out of it."

> *If you decide to let your child attend a boy-girl party, make sure it will be supervised to your satisfaction. Don't hesitate to call the parents involved to ask for details.*

That may be true, agrees psychologist Gil Noam, of Harvard Medical School and McLean Hospital. He says, "A child very likely would feel left out, but probably only temporarily." He says that in the long run, the better decision might have been to say no. "There is more harm when the child knows the parent is ambivalent but doesn't say no," says Noam. "He perceives the parent has no backbone because he didn't stand up for what he believes in. That can damage your relationship, and you've got much harder stuff yet to go through." Besides, he argues, "What's wrong with a child feeling disappointed? With having things to look forward to when he's a little older? Isn't that how we all learn to deal with life?" A landmark study of twelve thousand teenagers conducted under the auspices of the National Institutes of Health supports Noam's thinking. The conclusion it comes to is that teens admire their parents more when they stand up for the values they believe in. When we don't, teens consider us wimps. A good message to take from that is that if you're uncertain about whether to say yes or no about anything, but certainly about boy-girl parties at the age of 10, there's nothing wrong with telling your child, "I need to think about this overnight. We'll talk in the morning."

Saying no to a 10-year-old means you'll have a disappointed, sullen, angry kid on your hands who will tell you you are unfair, stupid, old-fashioned, and have just ruined his life. This is not the moment to defend yourself, to rationalize with him or to punish him for talking to you rudely. The depth of his disappointment is real and needs to be respected. Let him have his sulk. Later, explain your thinking: "This activity is not appropriate for you until you are older. I know it's hard for you not to do something all your friends are doing, but I have to be true to the values I believe in." While it's important to be empathetic with your child's point of view, that doesn't mean basing decisions only on what he wants. Most children sense when they are in over their heads and may be pleased that you took them off the hook. But don't expect him to admit that to you. Look for evidence of his ambivalence in his behavior, not in his words: Does he seem nervous? Is he irritable and moody? Is he eating or sleeping poorly?

Zack wants to go to another boy-girl party but he says, "My parents would probably like me to wait a year."

Is that a problem?

"Well, yeah," he says. "I'd be very upset. It'd be hard 'cause I'd be out of the in crowd." He pauses, pushes back his glasses, and looks out the window. "If I think about it," he says, without facing his listener, "I'd probably say, 'Well, that's life.' I'd probably still respect my parents. I might even agree it's a little too early for me."

A *space of their own*

In the move toward independence, what often gets overlooked is that a child does not necessarily need a room of his own, but he does need a place of his own and a space of his own. The place is for the stuff, the space is for him. Privacy is an important part of growing up, and just as we expect children to observe our boundaries, we need to show them the same respect. It's not only a developmental need, but also a human one. Think about how you put out your belongings in a hotel room. It's not just a matter of convenience. Having your stuff in the space makes you feel at home. It tells you "I belong here."

Having spaces and places gives a child stability and self-confidence. Environmental psychologists say that personal privacy helps a child define who he is. External boundaries reinforce a sense of identity. Many young children are territorial about something as seemingly insignificant as their place at the kitchen table. I think about my son who, when we moved, immediately claimed a spot for himself at the new kitchen table and was unhappy if anyone else sat there. The familiarity of the spot and the view it afforded were undoubtedly a source of comfort and security.

> *If you're a recently divorced parent in a mostly empty apartment, find some way to provide personal space for your children, even if all you have are bins, boxes, or crates with handles.*

As parents, there are several ways we can support this process:

- Provide places for belongings: drawers, boxes, shelves. Beginning in preschool, children need a reliable place to work and store tools and equipment and to know these things are safe and secure; they shouldn't have to go rooting through the kitchen drawers to find their tools—markers, scissors, paper, or glue—or have to ask an adult every time they need them. Having these items stored in a consistent place and readily accessible, without having to bother an adult, fosters a sense of independence. If there are several young children close in age, each one doesn't need a separate bin for markers and such; they can share. But by third grade, children should have individual storage space. Personal belongings are another matter. Parents with many children should store each child's clothing separately from the beginning, even if it's only in boxes, to encourage feelings of individuality. This is especially important with multiples.

- Provide places to display handiwork. Every child in a family should have a place that honors his work—the refrigerator door, a bulletin board, a wall. The space should be divided so each child, regardless of age, has a defined area. Some parents need to be more creative with this than others. If your child doesn't draw and his interests are three-dimensional—Lego structures, for instance—find a way to display some of them. Most of us rush to pick up Legos or insist they be put away, a message that says we value neat-and-clean more than a child's handiwork.

- Provide space for every child, regardless of age. Even preschoolers need personal space, although it doesn't have to be elaborate; this is not about separate rooms but a corner of a room, a special chair and table. In homes where space is at a premium, creating mental space can substitute for physical space: "It's Tina's turn to use the table for homework. Let's pretend there's a glass wall around her." One reason private space is so important, especially when there are many children in a family, is because children, like adults, need a place to retreat where they can have peace and quiet. Pam created a reading nook for her three daughters by converting unused space under a stairwell. With oversized pillows and a comforter and a light, it's cozy and comfortable, a place where a girl can go when she needs time away from the hubbub of a busy, densely populated home.

The pitfall for parents is to create wonderful spaces and then impose our control over them. Once you give a child his or her own space, you can agree to some ground rules—no eating is a good one—but a child should be free to decorate the space the way she wants. Include even a 3-year-old in the decoration of his room by letting him decide between a Barney or Mickey Mouse quilt; having that input can help reinforce his sense of self. By third and fourth grade, decoration can become a bone of contention in many families. One family I know was redecorating and told their children they could choose the paint for their rooms. When the oldest daughter, 11, picked black, the mother didn't know what to do. "I guess I should have given her four or five colors to choose from, ones that I could live with," she says in hindsight. They reached a compromise: She could paint two walls black and have black accessories. In another family, the parents went to great expense when their son was born to create a sky on the ceiling and they carried the celestial theme through to draperies and accessories. By the time he was in second grade, he had outgrown the stars, moons, and rainbows, but his parents hadn't. Great unhappiness ensued over his efforts to hang sports posters. One night, when two friends were sleeping over, the room was transformed. The boys even put sports posters on the ceiling. The parents got the message: Children need at least some autonomy over personal spaces. It's a matter not just of individuality but also of self-esteem. On the other hand, while all children need some privacy, parents should be concerned about a child who consistently prefers to be shut up in his room rather than playing with friends or participating in other activities. This kind of withdrawal can be a red flag for unhappiness; professional help may be warranted.

When children share a bedroom, the space ought to be divided equitably. This can cause some pretty eclectic-looking rooms, especially when ages and/or interests are disparate. If the rooms are also used for play, time-sharing may be the best way to eliminate conflict: Tuesdays and Thursdays, John and his friends can play in the room, Mondays and Wednesdays, it's Tom's turn, and so on. While we're on the subject of privacy, let's not forget privacy in the bathroom. It can matter as much to boys as girls and it needs to be respected whenever it becomes important to your child, even if that's at the age of 5.

Home alone

Of all the steps our children take toward independence, perhaps none is as big as the decision to stay home alone. Eleven tends to be the youngest age at which professionals are comfortable saying it's okay to leave a child home alone; research shows that in emergencies, no matter how well coached they've been, children younger than that are too frightened to remember what they learned. Certainly there are plenty of children younger than that who are perfectly capable of staying home for short periods of time here and there, while mom drops off a sister at a birthday party or runs to the grocery store; in fact, little doses of staying alone is a good way to ease a child into more intense self-care. Unfortunately, nationwide, more than 7 million children a year aged 10 or younger care for themselves when they are not in school, according to the U.S. Department of Labor. Many of them are poorly prepared for the responsibility.

Whenever it is that your child announces, "I can take care of myself," it is maturity, not chronology, that should influence your response. Whether your child is eager to be more grown up, responding to peer pressure, or anxious to help the family out, her desire to stay alone should be your starting point for discussion, not the end. However, his saying he's ready is certainly not reason enough to do it; most children will tell you they are ready long before they are. And while you may be as eager as they are to be done with sitters or afterschool programs, self-care, like sleep-overs, is not something to be rushed. It might even be worth waiting until the second or third time a child brings it up before you take him seriously. Even then, there's nothing wrong with expecting your child to prove to you he's ready for this responsibility: "Before you can be alone in the house, you have to show me you're ready. I'll be keeping an eye out for the next three weeks to see how well you take responsibility for yourself." Keep in mind, too, that second- and third-born children often demand to stay home before they are really ready because they want to be as grown up as an older sibling. Try this response: "Your older brother proved he could handle this. When you are his age, it will be your turn."

To determine readiness, here are some questions to ask yourself:

- Does he have a history of responsible behavior? Of anticipating and avoiding danger? Children who tend to be irresponsible or erratic may not have the confidence to know, for instance, when it's appropriate to call the police. Psychologist Christine Todd, who researches the impact of self-care on children's emotions, has known children who called the police because they couldn't find their shoes. On the other hand, will your child be too timid to call if there's a real problem?

- Does she tend to be argumentative? Have a hard time following rules? If she needs supervision to follow directions or complete a chore, how well will she be able to follow a schedule on her own?

- Does he tend to be fearful? Panic when routines are disrupted? If so, what about the inevitable night when you're late because you're stuck in traffic? Corine, 12, was home alone after school during an electrical storm. Anticipating that the power might go out, she retrieved a flashlight. The batteries were dead. She called a neighbor, who was able to bring over batteries. Would your child have the presence of mind to do that? In an emergency, if she picked up the phone to call someone, would she be too flustered to be coherent? To remember her address?

- Is she an introvert or extrovert? A very social child who typically has difficulty entertaining himself may feel isolated, lonely, or bored. That makes him more likely to respond to temptation, including inviting friends in or leaving the house, or simply being miserable. A shy child who is home alone after school instead of attending an afterschool program may be losing out on the chance to develop better social skills or forge relationships with peers.

- What is she missing out on? Children of all ages need peer friendships and spontaneous play to maximize social development. If she's home alone after school, are there adequate opportunities at other times during the week when she is getting this?

- How physically strong and/or coordinated is she? Psychologist Todd was sure her 10-year-old daughter was physically able to take care of herself until she asked her to open a storm window. "She couldn't do it. It made me realize how much you need to think about what skills might get called upon in an emergency," says Todd.

- What type of community do you live in? Are there neighbors at home in the afternoon who can serve as resources, or will he be alone not only in an empty house but also in an empty neighborhood? Don't equate where you live—rural vs. urban—with safety. A child who is not developmentally ready faces the same issues no matter where he lives.

One of the first discussions to have with your child before you make a decision should be about the dangers of staying home, about the many things that could go wrong. This is a conversation most parents avoid for fear of frightening their child. But if your child is frightened in the abstract, don't you need to know that? Surely you don't want him alone with the possibility of the real thing and it will be reassuring to him for you to tell him so. If he's not frightened about potential dangers, that's a good sign of readiness and your discussion will be empowering for him.

A good way to have this conversation is to pose questions in the form of scenarios: "What would you do if you heard a strange noise? If you come home and the front door is ajar? If a stranger rings the bell and says your parents sent him? If you smell smoke? If you need to reach me and can't?" Role-play some situations, brainstorm together on how to solve them. If your child finds any of this daunting, frightening, or even boring, back off and wait a few months. These are signs he is either not ready or not fully appreciative of the scope of what he is proposing to do.

> *Don't dismiss a complaint of "I was bored."*
> *It can be code for "I was lonely."*

Most children experience some degree of fear when they are home alone, not necessarily traumatic but probably memorable. Not all will admit to it, especially if all their friends do without sitters. "Most kids want to tough it out," says researcher Michelle Seligson, director of the National Institute on Out-of-School Time at Wellesley College. If you sense the fear, take the initiative: "This doesn't seem to have been the right thing to do just now. How can we do this differently?" While your child may protest, he will secretly be relieved that you took responsibility for the decision.

In studies where latchkey children have been asked about problems they have, the most frequently reported difficulties revolve around siblings. Siblings who get along well and are respectful of each other probably will do fine alone together, but this is a slippery slope that needs careful examination and constant monitoring. Just because a 12-year-old is ready to be home alone doesn't mean he's ready to be home alone *and* responsible for one or two younger siblings. When siblings are close in age, leaving one in charge of the other often backfires. Jealousies flare, fights erupt. Better to put each child in charge of him- or herself but working as a team, so that each has an individual schedule to follow on his own. One child might be in charge of snacks and the other, of walking the dog. Success often depends on how well you are able to anticipate and talk in advance about areas that will get them into friction. A classic is time spent on the phone.

Safety is, of course, a critical issue. Look at the house through your child's eyes. Take nothing for granted: "This is the electrical box. Don't touch it." Agree on appliances that are usable and ones that aren't; the microwave is okay, not the stove or oven. As you do a walk-through with your child, you can get a sense of his comfort level with the house. If he won't go into the basement or the attic without you, if he tells you he won't go upstairs once it gets dark, he's not ready. Safety is not just knowing what to do when but how safe a child perceives she is. Seligson says that if a child stays alone even for just a few hours now and then and spends a lot of that time worrying about herself or worrying that someone will break in, it can have a profound effect on her personality.

Part of a child's sense of safety comes from knowing she can talk to you about her fears. If you pooh-pooh them with an of-course-you'll-be-fine attitude, she'll feel isolated. Don't overreact, either, though. Take concerns seriously and help her try to come to grips with them: "Now that it's getting dark early, it seems like you're feeling uncomfortable in the house. Would it help if you turn lights on before darkness falls?" That she's able to talk to you about these things increases the likelihood of a home-alone experience being successful, according to research. Other predictors of success include:

- Starting off in small doses and gradually leading up to bigger chunks of time. The first experience might be being home alone for fifteen minutes while you visit a neighbor or walk the dog, then an hour alone while you go to the grocery store.

Increase sporadically before you begin to leave him regularly or for many hours.

- Leaving him alone less than five hours a week; more than that and a child begins to feel lonely and sad.

- Checking in with him at agreed-to intervals. Children feel safer not only when they know how to reach you at all times but also when they feel you are monitoring them from a distance.

While you don't want to leave a child alone before he's ready, it's also a mistake to delay too long in granting this kind of independence. The 9-year-old who wants to stay home while you drive your 7-year-old to a birthday party probably should be allowed to do that unless there's something that has tipped you against it. By 12, most children should have had the opportunity to take care of themselves for limited periods of time. Otherwise, they will feel babied and babyish.

In addition to your child's readiness issues, there are also yours. If you feel anxious in any way, it will spill over to your child. Come to grips with your own fears before you go ahead with this. Beginning self-care gradually, thirty minutes first, then an hour, will bolster your confidence. So will a trial period. Tell your child you are willing to let him stay home on two different occasions, then you want to evaluate. If it goes successfully, continue week-to-week contracts for a month or so. When you anticipate what might go wrong, factor in that children don't take to new routines quickly. For instance, it's the first day your son is coming home after soccer practice instead of going to his friend's. He was supposed to call you at 4:15, now it's 4:20, 4:30, 4:35. You call the house. "Oh, hi, Mom. Yeah, I'm here. I was so hungry, I thought I'd eat before I called you. Well, I know I was supposed to call first, but I'm really hungry. What's the big deal?"

In fact, this is a big deal, not just because you were anxious and worried but also because you are laying a foundation for responsible behavior that you hope will carry over into the teenage years. Tell your child, "We agreed to a routine that includes calling me as soon as you get home, before you do anything else. If you're not responsible enough to do that, you aren't responsible enough to be home alone."

CHAPTER TWO

Milestones of a Different Kind

. . . .

For all the "firsts" we anticipate with pleasure, there are many we anticipate with dread. In fact, we hope they just won't happen. We all know that some toddlers bite and that some 10-year-olds steal, but we hope and pray our child won't be one of them. In truth, though, these behaviors signal change and growth as much as sleeping at a friend's or earning money. But if we're on the phone to Mom to talk about the first time our toddler bites or the first time we find a 9-year-old playing with matches, it certainly isn't with pride. We're worried. Are we doing something wrong? Is something wrong with our child? What does this mean? What should we do?

While these may not be milestones we celebrate, they are milestones nonetheless. Perhaps it is because we don't greet these moments with big smiles and words of congratulations that our children need so much help with them. Biting, tattling, stealing, running away—these are all behaviors we tend to blow out of proportion, imposing discipline and punishment. Yet a child who is biting or stealing has crossed a line not just in her behavior but also in her development. More likely than not, even she senses something is different; many children feel out of control, uncomfortable, or un-happy with these changes in themselves.

When toddlers bite

Even over the phone, day-care director Diane Lusk's sigh is loud. The topic—toddlers who push, bite, and are otherwise hurtful—is something that makes parents and providers crazy, she says. "Just the other day," she begins, "I had an 8-month-old who put her mouth on four different kids in four hours and left teeth marks on one."

Does this mean this is a difficult child, destined for tough times ahead?

"Absolutely not!" says Lusk. "She's a happy, sociable baby!" Then she adds with resignation in her voice, "These are exactly the kinds of conclusions parents mistakenly come to."

Does this mean the teachers aren't paying enough attention? That children aren't safe there?

Another audible sigh. "That's another conclusion a lot of parents come to. But no, that's not necessarily true either. Here's what is true," she says. "It is true that it makes parents hysterical. More parents leave centers over biting than for any other reason."

Lusk speaks with authority. Not only is she director of the Meeting House Child Care Center in Newton, Massachusetts, but she has been researching and working in day care for more than twenty years and is author of *Nothing But the Best, Making Day Care Work for You and Your Child.*

Biting and other aggressive behaviors are some of the earliest rites of passage in the life of a child; few children make it to 3 without having been both aggressor and victim. What parents need to know is that toddlers are being neither malicious nor evil when they bite. Rather, they are asserting a newfound sense of indepen-dence that leads them to solve a problem through aggression. Behind the biting (or pushing or hitting or hair pulling) is a reasoning that goes something like this: "This is mine! I want that! Now!" "Hey, you have what I want! You're preventing me from having it!" Biting isn't the sign of a social outcast or a maladjusted kid, either. If anything, the opposite is true. "These are very social kids," says Lusk. "They are kids who are in each other's faces all the time, kids who are in the social thick of things." Because they tend to have more social contact, they increase the likelihood of butting up against someone else's equally egocentric thinking.

The most commonly accepted theory on why toddlers become aggressive is that their repertoire for expressing themselves is limited. Without words and self-control, what else can they do? But there may be more to it than that. Lusk is convinced that what pushes a toddler beyond his tolerance for frustration is the degree of tension in his life. The tension can be from almost anything, including a mother who has gone back to work full-time or some struggle within the child: He's learning to walk, he's teething, perhaps he has an ear infection. In fact, whenever she has a toddler engaged in aggressive behavior, one of the first suggestions Lusk makes to parents is to have ears checked.

Given these possibilities, perhaps the best antidote for biting or any aggressive behavior is to help a toddler build up a repertoire and a sense of self-control by immediately offering acceptable alternative behaviors. Here's what Lusk did the day she was substituting in the infant room and realized she had a biter on her hands:

"Even though this was only an 8-month-old, I talked to her. I told her that biting other people is not okay. Then I showed her other things that are okay for her to bite: rattles and toys. I also held her a lot. When I couldn't be holding her, I made sure I knew exactly where she was at every moment, especially when she was in biting range of another child." With that strategy, Lusk was able to prevent anything more than lip contact three out of four times. The fourth time, when skin was broken, she says, "I was two feet away. I had turned my back for a second. Literally."

While the kids were napping, Lusk and her staff analyzed what had happened. Why was this kid so wired that she used such a primitive behavior? The answer was unanimous but not ominous: She was teething. Lusk felt miserable and guilty nonetheless, and she knew the parents would too. That afternoon, when she greeted the mother, she had a concrete plan for how the teachers were going to help her daughter at school and how her parents could help her at home. For instance, they could:

- Anticipate when she might be getting frustrated and redirect her behavior so that she won't have opportunity to get in biting range of another child.

- Offer language as an alternative for expressing frustration. With a child this young who is not yet verbal, keeping it simple is best: "Biting is no." For a toddler 12 to 18 months, a parent could say, "Instead of biting, use your big voice to shout, 'It's my turn!' " For 2- to 3-year-olds: "Use your words to tell someone what you want."

- Reinforce appropriate behavior by praising it: "What a terrific job you did of using your words!"

- Be physically involved with your child at her level so you can intervene directly.

- Don't punish her at home for behavior that occurred in day care. She won't be able to make the connection between what you are punishing her for and what she did, and will only be angry and confused. However, you should talk about what happened, even if you aren't sure how much she'll understand: "I heard you had trouble with Jane today, that you bit her. I'm sorry that happened. In our family, we don't bite people. It hurts when you bite people." If she's verbal, you could add, "What could you say next time so you won't bite her?"

- Examine what's going on in your home life to see if there is some out-of-the-ordinary source of tension that could be heightening her frustration level or if there is something going on with her medically.

An action plan like this is exactly what any day-care parent should expect from any provider, and as long as you are satisfied that the provider is on top of the situation, that she has a strategy to help the aggressor as well as one for keeping the victims safe, biting is not a reason to leave a center. If there is an outbreak of biting at your center where several children are involved over a short time, even if your child is not among them, you have every right to ask the director about the strategies she is using. A director who is defensive or dismissive probably is not on top of the situation the way she should be, and then it's time to talk to other parents. If you sense a pattern of unresponsiveness or haphazard responsiveness, you do have reason to look for new care.

> *If your child bites two to four times*
> *a week despite appropriate intervention,*
> *consult your pediatrician.*

Any toddler who is a social and active child and who interacts at home or in day care with other children will sooner or later end up on either the receiving or giving end of the biting equation. As embarrassed or humiliated as you may be as the parent of the perpetrator, as angry or outraged as you may be as the parent of the victim, the tables could turn tomorrow. That's a good thing to keep in mind whether you're the parents of the aggressor and you're apologizing to the victim's parents or whether you're the parents of the victim accepting an apology. A little respect for the unpredictability of toddlerhood, please! In fact, many parents whose child has been bitten assume a self-righteous attitude in the mistaken belief that their child has been frightened or traumatized. Many young children don't consider being bitten a big deal. It didn't hurt that much, they aren't upset by it, they still like the perpetrator, and they still want to play with him. It's only when we make a big deal out of it that they decide they should be upset. On the other hand, some *are* frightened and want to stay clear of the biter. Either way, you should talk to your child. Start off neutral: "I heard Tim bit you today. I'm sorry that happened. What can you tell me about it?" Whether he's matter-of-fact or not, you can offer strategies so it won't happen again: "If it looks like someone is going to bite you, what words can you use to stop him? Can you yell out really loud, 'No!' Or call the teacher: 'Help me!' " Also encourage your child to stand up for herself: "It's good when you tell people how you feel about things." If your child was the aggressor, don't force her to apologize but do try to help her understand the need to feel sorry for what she did: "What you did hurt Tommy so much it made him cry."

While parents of the aggressor tend to feel humiliated and embarrassed, parents of the victim tend to feel helpless and angry, sometimes even angry at their child for not defending herself. Both feelings are understandable. Nonetheless, it's helpful to remind yourself, "This does not reflect on me as a parent."

"Shut up! I hate you!"

As a toddler turns into a preschooler, the mouth continues to be a source of angst for parents. If few children manage to make it through toddlerhood without being biter or bitee, even fewer make it through the preschool years without shouting, with all the emotion they can muster, *"I hate you!"*

My first experience with this came from a child I had never seen before who turned to my son on a swimming pool ladder in a town pool and screamed, "I hate you!" I was dumbstruck; my son, who was 3½, was devastated. I tried to soothe him by saying, "She didn't mean it," but that sounded stupid. Clearly, she meant something. Even he knew that. But what?

Weeks later, the tables were turned. My son was the perpetrator and he was venting his rage at me. I had turned off a video after issuing three warnings that it was time to get dressed.

"I hate you!" he screamed at me.

I was stunned not only because it was my child uttering these meanest of words, but also because of his intensity. It made sense for him to be angry, but did he really *hate* me?

The use of the word *hate* is common and normal among preschoolers, a true rite of passage as they move from one stage of development into another. It does not have the same meaning for them as it does for adults. To us, *hate* means wanting the demise and destruction of another person. To a child, it isn't that loaded. Indeed, while it conveys a certain amount of intensity, it can mean almost anything from hate and anger to frustration, disappointment, or annoyance. It can even mean "I slightly prefer . . ." It's true children this age have very intense feelings, but they aren't able to discriminate among shades of a feeling. In addition, their vocabulary is limited, so they might use the same word to mean many things. Sometimes you can tell by the context what meaning your child is attaching to the word. Other times, you can't be sure. Which is why we should never respond with what comes almost instinctively to our lips: "Oh, you don't mean that!" Maybe at that moment, she really does hate the spaghetti or her brother or you. Even if she does, though, it's only temporary. She can say "I hate you!" one minute and "I love you!" the next and mean them both. Preschoolers, after all, live in the moment.

Whatever you do, don't back off from setting limits because you fear your child will say he hates you. Remind yourself that it's normal for young children to feel frustration and that the feeling will pass quickly. Indeed, when your child does respond to your limit setting or request with "You're mean! I hate you," avoid coming down on him for having those feelings. In fact, if anything, you should validate them: "I can understand you're angry with me right now. It's okay to be angry with me. You're entitled to your feelings. You still have to get dressed, though."

If a child finds satisfaction in the word *hate*, it's usually because of the reaction it gets. The first time he uses it, it may be because he heard an older sibling or a kid on the playground say it. He's trying it out, maybe for the sound, maybe to learn the meaning, always as a part of his effort to understand the world. The second time he says it, however, it will be for another reason entirely. Alice Sterling Honig of Syracuse University, well known for her work in how children acquire language, wonders if children today use more "I hate" statements than did previous generations because their lives are too scheduled. "They build up rage as a result of being too rushed, not having enough time to just be. Swear words, calling things stupid, or 'I hate' this or that—they all have appeal to them because there is so much emotion behind them," she says. When the parent or teacher reacts in horror, the word becomes even more attractive. "Children this age have this innate drive to have an impact on their environment, even a negative one," says Honig.

The more we make of an occasional "I hate" statement, the more we reinforce it. On the other hand, we don't want a child to get in the habit of hurtful verbal hostility. If frequent "I hate" statements go unnoticed, your child may not learn to recognize and correctly name his own feelings, to develop compassion or to consider the quality of a source who maligns him. The first time your child uses a word that offends you, ask him, "Do you ever try words to see what people do when you say a word like that? Some words hurt feelings and this is one of them. It's not a good word to use." On the other hand, sometimes saying "I hate you" becomes a game between two children and you don't need to intervene or interpret at all. You can tell by the tone of voice and intensity if this is playful or if it's escalating to hostility. Then you do need to step in.

One way to help a child is to tell her she can say words like that in her room with the door shut, so they don't hurt anyone's feelings. We can also get our young children away from "I hate" by encouraging other "I" statements that more accurately home in on the wide range of emotions they feel: I wish, I hurt, I'm frustrated, I want. Then, hopefully, he won't need to resort to "I hate" so often and instead of saying "I hate you!" to the child in the sandbox, he'll be able to say "I don't want to share right now."

Labeling feelings isn't enough, however. Children need to learn that words can hurt. Honig suggests telling a child, "You're using a word that makes other people feel sad and upset. That's not a nice thing to do." There is some disagreement among professionals over how big a deal you should make over hurt feelings. On the one hand, too much attention to them can give negative reinforcement, while on the other hand insisting on an apology can give the idea that saying "I'm sorry" magically undoes a wrong. Perhaps a good strategy is to first label and acknowledge the feeling the speaker is having—"I know you feel very angry at Sam"—before you continue with "It hurts his feelings badly when you use words like that." Equally important is to help him find an alternative way to express himself: "Can you find another way to tell Sam what you need?"

> *To avoid having a child think apologies magically undo a wrong, tell her, "It will make Rebecca feel a little better if you say you're sorry but her feelings will still be hurt."*

What's especially hurtful and confusing is when a friend turns on a friend. Often the outburst has nothing to do with the child. The aggressor could be angry about something else entirely (as must have been the case with the child on the swimming pool ladder) but doesn't know how to express herself. Projecting the feeling onto the friend is a safe way to express her rage, but obviously the victim doesn't feel very safe. Susan Ackerman, a former head teacher at the Lemberg Children's Center at Brandeis University, suggests taking children aside when something like this happens and asking them to explain why they are upset. Then she echoes their thoughts back to them: "Adam, you told Michael you hated him because you wanted to play by yourself, right? And Michael, you knocked over Adam's castle because he said he hated you. Is that right?" Although they might not understand this the first time, she says it helps them put their actions in a context. She believes, as do many professionals, that trying to make a child of this age feel empathy for the playmate whose feelings have been hurt is a wasted effort; their cognitive skills just aren't there yet. On the other hand, we don't want them to think that verbal hostility or physical aggression is acceptable. The key, then, is to try to extend their communication skills with the hope that this will eventually lead to a better understanding of another person's feelings. Honig is one who puts her endorsement on this approach. She's seen it lead one child to say to another, "It's not nice to tell me you hate me. If something is bothering you, tell me what it is."

As they get older, children ultimately need to learn how to figure out whether the speaker has any validity. In other words, how much attention does this person deserve? Is he credible enough for you to be crying over it, or is his credibility such that you shouldn't pay any attention? This is the kind of skill that helps build a child's resiliency and enables her to take a bully in stride, for example. We can help them with this by thinking out loud for them: "I wonder why she said a thing like that? Is it possible she was angry about something that happened before you sat next to her? Oh, she had wanted to play on the computer and it wasn't her turn yet. . . . Hmmm. I'm wondering if she was frustrated about that. I wonder if she would have been angry at the very next person who had the turn before her, no matter who it was. Maybe she doesn't hate you at all."

This strategy might have worked when my son's feelings were so badly hurt at the swimming pool. He might have learned what parents need to know too: that sometimes children say hurtful things for reasons that are dubious. Sometimes, what comes out of a child's mouth is random shrapnel.

When good children use bad words

The word *hate* is not the only word coming out of your young child's mouth that you could do without. What do you do when your 5-year-old calls you a "potty-head" or perhaps even worse? Child-rearing professionals offer a wide range of options, from ignoring what he said to setting a firm limit, but they generally agree on three points:

- This kind of talk is age appropriate for children 4 to 6 years old, girls as well as boys.

- It's funny to them.

- It makes them feel powerful.

What you might consider your child's preoccupation with what we euphemistically call bathroom humor stems from a growing self-awareness of her body and its bathroom functions: she's made aware of the connection between eating and having a bowel movement. Most likely, however, she is also confused. On the one hand, she has knowledge her parents have worked hard to help her gain. On the other hand, her parents are telling her this is not a nice thing to talk about. What's going on here? This doesn't make sense.

As a way to make this confusion manageable and to gain control over it, a child does the same thing adults do in similar situations: She tells jokes. "Humor is a way of defending yourself against those issues which are troublesome or threatening or psychologically challenging," says psychiatrist William F. Fry, emeritus associate clinical professor at Stanford University School of Medicine and one of the nation's eminent researchers on humor.

Riddle popular among 6-year-olds: What has four eyes and pees in its bed?

Answer: the Mississippi River.

Syracuse University child psychologist Rhoda Fisher says jokes like this are actually a way for a young child to discharge some aggression, a way of saying "All those crazy rules, I'm mad about them! You're restricting me! You don't even want me to acknowledge what my body does!"

So, okay, in a charitable moment you might agree the Mississippi River joke is cute, maybe even clever. But not funny. Not funny enough to make your child fall on the floor laughing. That's because you're applying adult standards to this humor. If you can't laugh at the joke, perhaps you can at least muster a smile watching your child laughing at it. Ah, but that brings up a critical question: If we laugh at it or even admit to its cleverness, aren't we encouraging more of the same?

Yes and no. Although the jokes and references may be crude, what a child is trying to do with them can be quite sophisticated, according to Fisher, who is co-author of a textbook on how children use humor. "A comic takes something taboo and detoxifies it for us, and that's what a child does for herself when she says, 'You're a potty-head!' She's trying to diminish tension, maybe not tension you feel, but tension she feels. That, at least, is one intent," Fisher says. She's also testing you, trying to see how much she can get away with. Where will you set the limit?

One school of thought is to set that limit the very first time you hear a word that offends you. Otherwise, the argument goes, a child will go on to the next level of language. If he doesn't have clear boundaries set for him, he'll also be more likely to use bathroom talk indiscriminately and to get into trouble for doing so, if not at home, then at day care or school. The other school of thought is to ignore scatological talk. That argument assumes that it will go away on its own for two reasons: first, because you don't give it any attention, and second, because children will grow out of it.

A middle road combines the common sense in both arguments. Let's face it, it's unnatural to be stern when something really tickles your funny bone. If your child tells a joke and you think it's funny, smile and enjoy it. Fisher says, "A child is pointing out the absurdity of the taboos. Besides, if he's trying to make you laugh and you don't, he's got to do something more to make you laugh. He'll keep working on it until he gets it." While you can appreciate a good riddle that uses bathroom humor, you can also set limits around words that are used just for the sake of their use. This isn't just a matter of applying a middle-of-the-road position; it's our job as parents to help a child learn social mores. Even with jokes, Fry says we can acknowledge the cleverness behind the humor but make it clear the language is not good manners: "I know you think this is silly and your friends think it's silly, but it's not good manners. These are not nice words. These are not the kinds of jokes people with good manners say and in our family, we value good manners." Don't mock her or imitate or exaggerate whatever it is she is saying. You'll make her ashamed, erasing the potential for growth.

> *For the inevitable "But Tommy says these words and his mom doesn't tell him not to," the best response is "Every family is different. In our family, we don't say them."*

It's okay to leave the impression that scatological jokes and language are acceptable among peers. Indeed, don't intercept or chastise children using these words in their play with each other unless they are imposing on each other in some way or a child is upset by them. It will be because of peers, in fact, that your child will gradually lose interest in this kind of talk. As kids move into the next phase of development, a playmate one day will say, "Ick, that's gross," instead of laughing, and that will be the beginning of the end of bathroom humor.

Researchers say the use of scatological language rarely becomes a problem that needs professional help. There also is no known correlation between the use of bathroom humor at 5 or 6 and swear words at 9 or 10. Tolerance of it, however, varies from family to family. If you find yourself annoyed because your child's sentences are sprinkled with *pees* and *poops*, it's gone too far. You're overreacting, however, if you wash his mouth out with soap or tell her angrily, "Don't ever let me hear you say that again!" You'll only make him feel awful over what is a normal developmental stage. Besides, the bigger deal you make of it, the more your child will be likely to use this language as a way to get to you. Instead, set a limit in a calm but firm way: "If you want to talk that way to your friends, that's your decision. It's not an acceptable way to talk to adults and Daddy and I don't want to hear those words."

This is the same approach that's appropriate with a school-age child who begins to use swear words; you can't control the way children talk to each other, but you can, and should, enforce the standards of your family. Indeed, for most families, bathroom talk is a minor annoyance compared to what lies ahead. By 7 or 8 (yes, that young!), *potty-head* shifts to something slightly more sophisticated, and by 10 or 11, it moves into something most parents consider obscene. Professionals may call this a developmental rite of passage, but most of us have a more colorful (and unprintable) label. When young children use an adult obscenity, they usually don't know what it means and are imitating older children or you. I have to admit that before I became a parent, I frequently used a swear word or two. (I am a journalist, after all!) But hearing swear words in the mouths of other people's toddlers quickly convinced me that I had to reform my language, lest my son imitate me. Now that he's older, he's always trying to catch me when I utter "Shoot!" in exasperation. He's quick to pounce, but honestly, that's the only *s*-word that comes out of my mouth, and it's gotten to the point where I don't even have to self-censor. If your young child does use an adult swear word, handle it informationally and calmly. Ask her what she thinks it means, then give her an age-appropriate definition and tell her, "Most people would be shocked to hear you say that. It's not a nice word."

"Timmy is a tattletale!"

"Tattling is a loathsome disease," declares Mrs. Hamilton, a character in Betty MacDonald's delightful children's classic *Mrs. Piggle-Wiggle's Magic*. It's obvious to Mrs. Hamilton that her daughter, Wendy, has the disease and now she fears her son, Timmy, is catching it too. If your children are in the midst of a tattling epidemic, you know Mrs. Hamilton is not overstating the problem. When you must endure yet another singsongy, "*Mom-mee!* Tommy says . . . ," it's little consolation to know that every 4- to 8-year-old tattles sooner or later or that tattling is a normal behavior with no serious moral implications. It can have serious social implications, however, and how we help children cope with tattling lays some of the groundwork for helping them to become independent thinkers with a sense of personal responsibility.

Children tattle for different reasons, depending on their age:

- **3- to 5-year-olds.** The preschooler who tattles has selfish motives but no malicious intent. She believes she is being hurt or treated unfairly by another child and she's looking to an adult for protection. By pointing out that someone else is doing something wrong, she is also proudly showing you that she knows right from wrong and *she* didn't do anything wrong. It's a not so subtle way of saying "See how great I am?"

- **6- to 8-year-olds.** Youngest school-age children tattle to get your attention, but before too long their tattling smacks of an ulterior motive: They're trying to get someone else in trouble.

This purposeful, revengeful tattling can continue off and on for several years until a child is able to see for himself that tattling has consequences he doesn't like—namely, getting a reputation for being a tattletale and losing friends. It's for that reason that tattling tends not to be an issue among children older than 8.

Even though children will stop tattling on their own, we shouldn't just let it run its course. For one thing, it can take years before a child will make the connection between her tattling and her loss of friends. Serious damage to her self-esteem, not to mention her social life, can occur. Second, there are some important lessons we can teach through tattling, although not to the youngest tattlers. A 3-year-old who tattles will be unnecessarily confused if you try to explain that it is wrong. At this age, a child tends to speak whatever it is she thinks, so it's better to simply acknowledge the information she is giving you and move on: "Yes, you're right. It is wrong not to share." With young siblings, it is especially important not to react strongly to either the tattler or the tattled upon. Each child needs to believe you are a safe person, someone who will protect both of them. So always listen to both sides of a dispute, not just to the tattler's. Certainly never label a child a tattler in front of siblings or peers. In fact, don't even apply the label to a child when you're alone with him; it can become a self-fulfilling prophecy.

By 4, you can introduce the concept of tattling: "You know, what you are doing is called tattling. Do you know what that is?" Explain in a nonjudgmental way: "Tattling is telling me or another adult something someone doesn't want us to know and it's something that we really don't need to know." The idea behind this is to get a child to the point where he asks himself, "Is this something that's important for an adult to know? Is telling a good idea or not?" Being able to think this through involves the ability to recognize and anticipate dangerous or destructive behavior, often shorthanded as "Double D," where someone is in danger or something may be harmed. This doesn't come easily to children; they need a lot of

coaching. You can start with a 4-year-old by pointing out the difference between behaviors that are annoying and ones that are
potentially unsafe and therefore important for an adult to know
about—hitting, punching, or biting another child, or breaking
something. Be as specific as you can: "It's a Double D if someone is
being hurt. It's a Double D if someone wants you to do something
you know is wrong, like stealing or breaking something that doesn't
belong to you. It's a Double D if someone wants you to keep a secret
about something you know is bad. It's not a Double D if something
is mildly annoying, like the baby scribbling on your paper over and
over again and it gets on your nerves, but it is a Double D if the
baby is crawling near the stairs and the gate isn't up." You can even
make it into a game: "Would it be a Double D if your brother won't
let you have a turn with the ball? What about if he climbed the
trellis to the roof? Would that be a Double D? How about pulling
the dog's tail?" Explain that when he thinks something is a Double
D, it isn't tattling, it's acting responsibly.

> *Stepping in and solving the problem*
> *a tattler is whining about only fosters more*
> *tattling and doesn't encourage a child to*
> *think for himself.*

Once Double D becomes a code between you, you can use it
proactively too. When you think your 5-year-old is on the verge of
tattling on his older brother, ask him: "Is what you want to tell me a
Double D or is it something you can work out yourselves?" Stating
this distinction as clearly as possible hopefully will pay off in the
years ahead, when your teenager will be able to see that a certain
kind of telling is an act of protecting a friend, not betraying him.

Perhaps the best strategy to help children evaluate and interpret
their own behaviors comes from educator Pamela Seigle, founder

and researcher of the Reach Out to School Project of the Stone Center at Wellesley College. She is program director of the Social Competency Program, which trains teachers on how to help school-age children problem-solve. She says that if your child is 4 or older when he starts to tattle, make a list with him of the kinds of things he thinks he can cope with by himself—his brother marking on his paper or taking an extra cookie, Tommy humming during story time so he can't hear. Do some role-playing and encourage him not only to describe the offensive behavior to the offender, but also to say what he would like to see happen next: "Tommy, you're humming and I can't hear. Please stop." Then take it a step further: "What if Tommy says it's a free country? What if he says he won't stop? Then what could you do?" Brainstorm alternatives: "Could you decide to ignore it? Could you ask him to move? Could you move?" This kind of proactive thinking has shown to be helpful in the school-age years when kids need to cope with bullies.

> *A child who is a chronic tattler may have difficulty getting along with others.*

Tattling among siblings can drive parents up a wall, especially at 4 and 5, when tattling tends to peak. Try telling the tattler, "You let Sally worry about Sally and you worry about you." If that doesn't work and if the tattler is tattling about something she, too, could be equally guilty of tomorrow, try throwing this in: "Hmm, that makes me wonder about everybody else in the family and whether they brushed their teeth." Believe it or not, this kind of message is reassuring. It lets her know you aren't going to come down hard on her transgressions, either, and that you are there to help them both live safe, comfortable lives. Another strategy with siblings is to help the tattler think about the consequences of his tattling.

Mom (whose 6-year-old has just told her that his 8-year-old brother drew lines on his drawing): "How do you think Josh will feel when he finds out you told me this?"

Child: "Mad."

M: "What do you think he will do?"

C: "Be more mean to me!"

M: "Is that what you want to happen?"

C: "No!"

M: "You know, since what you told me isn't a Double D, that means it's tattling and you're right, it will make your brother angry with you and maybe he won't want to play with you. How will that make you feel?"

C: "Sad."

M: "So what do you think you should do?"

C: "Not tattle!"

M: "Okay, so instead of tattling, what else could you do?"

C: "I could tell him this drawing was really special. I'll make a new one and ask him not to draw on it."

For a child who tattles only rarely, use a different tactic entirely. He needs to be taken very seriously, especially if he is 7 or older. He has probably internalized on his own the downside to tattling so that when he does tell on another child, in his mind it is for a very important reason. If he tells you something and you can't see the significance of it, before you dismiss it, be sure to ask him what he thinks is happening or why he told you. Chances are, his perspective of the situation is different from yours.

If you have an older child who is a chronic tattler—he resorts to tattling with regularity, many times a week—he needs to be taken seriously, too, but for a different reason. In families where there are many children, especially if they are clustered closely in age, chronic tattling may mean a child feels he isn't getting enough of your attention or that he wants to look good in your eyes. He may not care that tattling gets him in trouble with his siblings as long as it gets him attention from you, even if it's negative attention. Try giving him more one-on-one time and see if the tattling diminishes. If he also tattles on friends, it may be that he can't see that this will make them like him less, not more; this child may benefit from professional help.

Unfortunately, none of these strategies is as wonderful as Mrs. Hamilton's solution in Betty MacDonald's story. Mrs. Piggle-Wiggle supplied some magic pills to be given to the children at bedtime. The next day, when Wendy and Timmy opened their mouths to tattle, black smoke came out instead of words. "The puffs hung above their heads and grew small black tails," the story goes. But each time they started to tattle and stopped themselves, they discovered a puff would disappear. From then on, "Every time they started to tattle, they would gulp and look guiltily at the ceiling."

By all means, if your children are epidemic tattlers and even if they're not, find a copy of this old classic.

Taking stealing seriously

For most of us, stealing and tattling have nothing in common. We think the latter is endemic to childhood and only an annoyance; the former is a crime, something juvenile delinquents do. In fact, stealing is fairly common childhood behavior. Didn't you steal at least once when you were a kid?

The problem begins with us. Consider your first-grader who comes home from a friend's house and produces two plastic dinosaurs from his pockets. "Are those Tim's?" you ask. "Yes," he says.

"That was nice of him to let you borrow them."

Your son is silent. "He does know you have them, doesn't he, honey?"

He shakes his head no. "Does his mom know you have them?" No again.

What would you be most likely to say next:

- "Well, I'm sure Tim won't mind if you just borrow them for a while. You can give them back the next time you see him."

- "I'll call Tim's mom and tell her you took them by accident, in case Tim is looking for them."

- "Honey, taking something that doesn't belong to you and not telling the person is called stealing. We have to return them right away."

If you're like me, you'll opt for one of the two kinder, softer, gentler approaches. They're more sympathetic, and besides, you know your child didn't mean to *steal*, for heaven's sake. He's only 6!

As you probably have guessed, the last answer is the one professionals recommend. Age has nothing to do with this. Whether a child is 16 or 6, if we don't identify and condemn stealing for what it is when we see it, he has no reason not to do it again, no reason to think it's wrong. Professionals are unequivocal about this. Psychologist and pediatrician Gordon Harper of Children's Hospital in Boston, says, "Parents must know this: Every time you wink at stealing behavior, even with a 5-year-old, the likelihood for a path of juvenile delinquency gets increased." This is a strong statement and he knows it, but it is also a true one, he says, because ignoring it not only allows stealing to become easier but increases the likelihood that it can become part of a pattern of dishonest behavior. Once it is easy to steal, it is easy to be dishonest in other ways.

Let's keep things in perspective, however.

It doesn't mean you have a criminal-to-be on your hands because your preschooler takes a pack of gum from the grocery checkout. In fact, because children this young don't yet understand the concept of respecting personal property, it isn't really stealing at all when 3- or 4-year-olds take something. They're acting out of curiosity. They see it, they want it. It is still incumbent on us to say something, but our response can be simple: "That doesn't belong to you. Put it back." Or: "We didn't pay for that. We need to return it." If the gum has been opened, "Mama didn't pay for that, we have to go back and pay for it. Next time you see something you want, ask me about it before you take it." Even if it happens repeatedly, you do not have a stealing problem on your hands with a 4-year-old who has sticky fingers. Until about age 6, children may continue to take something simply because they are so egocentric. They think if it's there and they want it, they should be able to have it.

Sometime around 6, however, there is a dawning understanding of personal property. Now we cannot be ambivalent. Unfortunately, most of us are. We want to believe our second-grader when he says he "borrowed" the magnifying glass from the science room, so we rationalize: "I didn't see him do it, I'm sure he had the best of intentions. I don't know that he *stole*."

> *Professionals define a situation as serious if you suspect a child is stealing once every three or four months or more.*

As a parent, you don't need evidence that will hold up in court. If you wait until you are 100 percent sure your child has stolen, you could well have a child who has stolen successfully several times. Then it's not only a more difficult problem to deal with, but there's also the chance that your child may already have a reputation among peers or adults as a thief. Psychologist Ron Prinz, a researcher at the University of South Carolina whose area is how to prevent juvenile delinquency, says that all a parent needs in order to intervene is reasonable suspicion, reasonable judgment, and reasonable evidence. However, even if you are suspicious, don't go rummaging through your child's belongings looking for signs of theft; that only creates a trust issue in addition to whatever else is going on. On the other hand, if you discover a stolen object in the normal course of events, doing the laundry, for instance, don't pretend you didn't find it.

Before you accuse him of stealing, give him the opportunity to own up to it. Offer a nonjudgmental comment: "Gee, I'm wondering where this came from. . . ." If he just shrugs or says he doesn't know, give a second opportunity and be a little more pointed: "I know you didn't have that when we left the house." If he still doesn't own up, it's your responsibility to say "Well, we can't keep something that doesn't belong to us/we can't eat food if we don't know where it came from. I'll hold on to it until we can figure it out. Are you sure you don't have any ideas?" Give it overnight. If time passes with no response, label it for what it is. Don't pussyfoot around on this. As awful as it feels in your mouth, use that s-word: "I'm wondering if you took this from the grocery checkout. That's stealing. It's wrong."

Now comes an equally hard part. Tell your child, "Since this doesn't belong to us, we need to return it." It's an understatement to say that your child won't embrace the idea; he will likely protest mightily and insist you aren't being fair. This is a trap. If he gets you to the point where you are thinking that he's right, where you're asking yourself, "How can I be saying this about my child," remind yourself that if this was any other behavior—pushing, hitting, name-calling, swearing—you wouldn't hesitate to impose consequences. In this case, the logical consequences are returning to the scene and, probably with your help, apologizing for the crime. If she is too young, shy, or embarrassed to make restitution herself, speak the words for her: "My daughter took this gum and she knows now that was wrong." If the item was from school, go with her to return it to the appropriate teacher. If the item is damaged, offer to replace it and explain that your child will earn money to pay for it.

Your attitude throughout this is important. Try to remain matter-of-fact but unambivalent. Do not negotiate about what needs to happen: "You have something that isn't yours, you shouldn't have it, and there are consequences for that." On the other hand, avoid lecturing your child or humiliating him. Stay away from you-should-be-ashamed-of-yourself statements or statements that compare him to a sibling: "Your brother never did anything like this." Convey your family values in positive ways: "In our family, we take stealing very seriously. It's not something we do." With a school-age child, follow through with the consequences by assigning a chore so she can earn money to repay you for the item. The assigned chore should be boring and repetitive, raking leaves, folding laundry, and if there is a second offense, there should be a chore even if your child doesn't need to earn money to pay you back.

While most of us find it hard to admit to ourselves that our child has stolen, there are some parents who go off the deep end in the other direction, especially if there is a family history of antisocial behavior. Psychologist Harper cautions parents who develop a kind of anxious, self-confirming watchfulness not to jump to unfair, burdensome conclusions: "You're going to be just like your uncle, you'll end up in prison before you're 18!"

Identifying stealing by name, insisting on restitution, and assigning a boring task are appropriate responses to stealing at any age. But some circumstances call for more:

- **If a child steals from someone in the family.** With children 9 or younger, most parents tend to think of this as "borrowing." To the sibling whose favorite baseball cap is missing, however, this is a major crime, worthy of unspeakable punishment. The truth is in-between. Typically, when a school-age child takes something from someone else in the family, usually a sibling, it is more than borrowing. Your child is telling you something, most likely that family dynamics need adjusting. Perhaps a child feels deprived at some level or feels that a sibling gets more of your attention. First, get past the initial anger and the consequences. Tell her, "You need to give it back and you need to apologize." If candy or gum has been used up, reparations need to be made. Then have a private conversation with her: "We're concerned about the stealing but we're also concerned that you are hurting about something." Float some ideas: "We're wondering if maybe you'd like more time together/if you feel like your sister gets more attention," etc. With a child 10 or older, especially if it's money that's been stolen, you can't dismiss the possibility that he is stealing in order to buy drugs. Many parents will be bug-eyed at that idea; 10, indeed, seems young to us for this. Unfortunately, it is not unheard-of.

- **If she steals for the first time in the midst of a family crisis (separation, divorce, extended hospitalization of a family member) or when parents' attention is diverted for a time for any reason (new job, out of a job).** More likely than not, her stealing is a red flag she's waving in your face: "Hey there, remember me?" Once you realize this, a good response is: "I know I haven't been around as much as usual. I'm wondering if you stole because you're angry that I'm not available. Anyway, I'm going to pay more attention now." (Even though you understand what motivated the stealing in the first place does not mean you should absolve her of any wrongdoing. Apply the basic strategy as described.)

- **If he steals for the first time when he's 10, 11, or 12.** At these ages, what he steals is important. If it's petty items, like baseball cards or school supplies, it could be out of a newfound sense of materialism: He's equating possessions with self-worth. This can be a warning sign that a child isn't feeling good about himself, that his self-esteem is slipping. Perhaps she's entered middle school and has new friends. In that case, the stealing may be about accumulating for the sake of accumulating or about fitting in with peers. If the theft is of bigger items—money, especially ten- or twenty-dollar bills, CDs, cigarettes, liquor or beer from your cabinet—it could be in response to a different kind of peer pressure, probably from a new group of friends. They may simply think stealing is cool or okay or they may be interested in the items for their intrinsic value, in which case your child may be buying into a value system you want him to have no part of. Talking to your child is important, because you need to get a sense of motive. A possible response: "It worries me that your new friends equate how good a person is with the number of possessions they have/that your new friends have values very different from ours." At the same time, you also have to address the stealing: "Your friends may think stealing is okay, but we don't. You know our family values are against stealing. If your friends steal when they go to the mall, what can you do so you don't feel you have to steal too?" Brainstorm with her: "Can you say you have someplace else to go, so you just won't be there at the mall?" Talk about the chances of their getting caught next time, about the legal consequences. If you think they are stealing to smoke, drink, or buy drugs, let him know in no uncertain terms that these behaviors are not acceptable. Don't get sidetracked into tangential issues (important as they may be) such as who these friends are and whether he should even be friends with them. Stick to the stealing. Also, don't let the value of the stolen item influence how you react: Insist upon its return whether it's expensive or not, followed by an age-appropriate task to earn money. Restrictions of privileges should accompany a repeat episode for a preteen. If you have the conversations and get nowhere with them, or if the problem continues, seek professional help.

- **If your child has been stealing for a while and you've been in denial or didn't know.** The first thing to do is assess your own culpability. Has some system fallen apart in your family? Is there a lack of supervision or attention? Next, get a better handle on where your child goes and whom he goes with, then speak to him in a very direct way along these lines: "I've been seeing more and more things in your room, and I don't know where they come from. When I ask you about them, you give me vague responses, that you found them on the sidewalk or someone gave them to you. I'm hearing too many of these stories. I didn't want to believe that you are stealing, but I think that's what's happening. This is a terrible habit. It's wrong. It's my job to teach you to behave in an honest way. From now on, if I see things that don't belong to you, and you don't have a good explanation, I'm going to treat it as stealing, and here's what's going to happen." Then outline the consequences: The item will need to be returned to its rightful owner if possible, and/or he will have chores to cover its cost and/or privileges revoked. Expect your child to be furious, indignant, and stubborn. At the same time, however, he may also be feeling something he won't show: relief that you've figured it out and are rescuing him from something he knows is wrong. Bite the bullet and do what you need to do. With a child of this age, that includes calling the school (tell your child you are going to do this) to tell them you are concerned that your child has been stealing and wondering if they have similar suspicions. Unlike parents, school personnel, especially in upper grades, are slow to act on these suspicions, waiting until they have amassed airtight evidence. However, if you call them and ask for help, you can and should expect the school to be forthcoming, cooperative, and helpful.

In all of these scenarios, allowances need to be made for a child who comes clean. This should absolutely be the occasion for praise: "I'm proud of you for telling the truth, I know that must have been hard." Don't, however, go overboard in this direction and absolve him of any responsibility for the theft. A good response: "I'm glad you didn't lie, I hope you will always feel you can tell us the truth. We can't ignore that stealing is wrong, however, and there still needs to be some consequences for it. You need to return the item. Since you didn't lie, though, there won't be any further punishment." If you know your child has successfully fought temptation, lavish praise: "I'm so proud of you! I know you kept your hands in your pockets at the checkout today, just like we talked about. That was terrific!"

For many parents who come face-to-face with stealing, there is a sense of déjà vu. Long Island psychologist Leah Klungness recalls getting into a conversation with a fellow traveler as they waited at a Washington, D.C., airport to board a flight that had been delayed. She mentioned that she had been in Washington to deliver a speech on stealing to the American Psychological Association. Within minutes, a cluster of gray-haired businessmen had gathered around her to tell the stories of their childhood stealing. Each story had the same ending, with Mom marching the child back to the store to return the item and confess to the shopkeeper. Klungness even has her own story to tell.

When she was 8, she stole a roll of red Life Savers after her mother told her she wouldn't buy them for her. "We lived in the country, so the entire ride home, about twenty minutes, I clutched those Life Savers in my fist," she says. When they pulled up at the house, it was dark and cold and all they wanted to do was get inside. But out of the corner of her infallible mother's eye, Leah's mother spotted the red piece of wrapper.

"What's that?" she asked.

"Nothing," Leah replied.

"Open your hand," her mother said. When she saw what it was, she didn't hesitate a second. "We are going right back to that store," she said. Leah and her sister, Hattie, who was 5, piled back into the station wagon. Her mother drove the twenty minutes back into town in silence. "Not only did she make me tell the store manager, who looked nine feet tall, but I had to put it back on the candy rack. Luckily," says Klungness, "I hadn't opened it." They made the second trip home in silence, too, but when her father came home, Leah's mother announced, "We had a sad and terrible thing happen in this family today."

That Klungness remembers such details decades later is testimony to what a powerful life lesson the experience was. She never stole again because, as she says, "I was lucky enough to have a mother who didn't say, 'Oh, it's only a roll of Life Savers.'"

Secrets

Most young children delight in telling secrets. When my son was 3, he would put his mouth near your ear and "whisper" so loudly he could be heard across the room, meanwhile extracting a solemn promise that you would not tell anyone. Having this "secret" made him feel special because he had something to share, and it made him feel grown up. Children begin to have real secrets—about feelings, ideas, happenings—by age 6 or so. Instead of finding this cute, though, most parents feel left out, even threatened.

And why shouldn't we? A child with a secret, after all, is a child who is separating emotionally from her parents. This is not a bad thing developmentally, in fact, it's healthy and normal, but parents who overreact can inadvertently push their child away by becoming intrusive. When you say such things as "I want you to tell me everything!" or "You can't have secrets from your parents," what your child hears is "Your internal world is not sacred or inviolable." Because it is human nature to need some degree of privacy, a continually prodding, probing parent becomes an intrusive force, accomplishing exactly what she didn't want to happen: Her child becomes more secretive, maybe even lying, in order to gain the distance she needs. In early adolescence her reluctance to share information and your inability to get it can potentially put her in jeopardy. There's another way to look at this too. How well we do or don't respect a child's right to privacy can come back to haunt us years later. If you don't want your adult children prying into your affairs when you're 70, think about what you are modeling when they are 7. Don't tease her for keeping a secret, don't read her mail or her diary, don't pick up an extension to listen in on her phone conversations. If your child keeps a journal, don't peek inside, no matter how tempted you are; when you gain knowledge you aren't

ss, the combination of being secretive and disregard-
ment had the potential to be dangerous, and we talked
: "What if you had fallen off your bike and I didn't
ou were because you weren't where you were supposed
reed that if there's a time when he wants to do some-
't part of an agreement we've reached, that's a good
ime to renegotiate our agreement.

ild is very little, 2 or 3, there's little parents should say
secrets except to label them as fun—"Oh, I love
l respect them: "You shouldn't tell us your secret un-
to!" However, if your child is in day care or being
omeone else, and by age 4 even if he's not, it's impor-
a conversation about the difference between a good
bad one, and to make clear that telling about a bad
attling. To a very young child, keep it simple: "A
akes you feel good. A bad secret makes you feel bad. It
el nervous and unsafe." To an older child, you can
good secret doesn't hurt anybody not to tell it. You
night have a secret word and only the two of you know
and maybe it makes you giggle and feel silly. If some-
u promise not to tell something you know is wrong,
cret. Or when adults want to do something with you
ou feel nervous and unsafe and they want it to be a
crets you should tell to adults."

rents usually don't realize is that for school-age chil-
that make them uncomfortable come along pretty
pical child isn't forthcoming about them, but if we pay
n, we may discover she is constantly letting us in on the
rappling with. Think about all the times your 8- to 12-
your opinion about something without revealing why
ecause it strikes us as a non sequitur or because he asks
n the middle of something else, we answer almost ab-
and move on. The next time your fifth-grader goes on
t classmates you don't know or about an incident at
ikes you as boring, consider that she's sharing a secret,

supposed to have, you run th
information. If she ever finds
quite the same way.

In addition to the basic h
thoughts, children have secret
preschooler or early school-ag
a commodity, secrets are a wa
peers: "Janey really wants to kr
it secret, she'll play with me mo
tell her she's invited." If a chil
ally does not handle crises well,
gressions, he may keep secret:
won't get into trouble.

An 8- to 12-year-old may
maintain some freedom. At the
behaviors he knows are risky, t
you knew about them. After the
you can't prevent him from doi
my son was 9 and riding his bik
out the boundaries for an area m
knew he was champing at the b
did, but I didn't find out about
wanted to ride his bike to meet hi
the train station.

"What about that busy stree
that served as one of our bounda
that yourself?"

"Sure," he told me. "I've bee
By nature, he is not a risk-taki
thing that he knew we considered
we could get that he felt comfortal
was more of a surprise to me, hov
secret from me, an even clearer sig
ting. I realized that I was probably
stance and that he was capable of cr

so. Nonethe
ing our agre
about that t
know where
to be?" We
thing that i
sign that it':

If your
or do abou
secrets!"—a
less you wa
cared for b
tant to hav
secret and
secret isn'
good secre
makes you
elaborate:
and Tomm
what it me
one make:
that's a ba
that make
secret. Ba

Wha
dren, sec
often. Th
close atte
secrets sh
year-old
he wants
while we
sentmine
and on
recess th

that she may be talking about herself. There are many reasons why she'd do this. She may want time to sort her feelings out before she shares them; she may be embarrassed or humiliated or guilty; she may want your input but not until she can gauge your reaction: Are you going to be helpful or not, judgmental or not?

Perhaps she begins by saying, "The teacher is always making fun of Beth."

The quickest way to end the conversation is to ask, "Honey, are you talking about yourself?" To extend the conversation, you need to engage her in a dialogue. Play along.

"Gee, that must make your friend feel really bad. Has she told her mom or dad?"

"No. Besides, they wouldn't believe her."

"That's too bad. That's a hard thing to deal with. Most parents want to help a child figure out how to cope with something like that. I feel bad for Beth."

> *Being able to express themselves privately can help almost all children sort out feelings and deal with problems. Don't get locked into the idea that diaries are only for girls. Think computer journal or a small, unadorned notebook for your sons.*

Even such a sympathetic, nonjudgmental response doesn't mean your child will open up on the spot. She may need time to mull it over. While she does, we need to be able to walk away from the conversation without trying to pull information from her; otherwise she'll be even less likely to be forthcoming. Even when you know an older child is holding information you need to know, it's not a good idea to insist he tell you. Instead, find some way for him to volunteer it up. This kind of an opening may do the trick: "The way you're behaving makes me think something is troubling you. You don't have to tell me what it is, but sometimes kids get information that is hard for them to handle, and sharing helps. If you don't want to tell me, maybe there's some other adult you can tell."

Parents who push children to talk will be the parents who have the least amount of information, so when your child is young practice how to get information without pushing. You might tell an 8-year-old, for instance, "You don't have to tell me what is happening, but tell me why you can't tell me." If the answer is "Because you'll be angry," a good reply might be "I know in the past I've gotten angry sometimes. If you want to tell me something that you think will make me angry and that's why you don't want to tell me, just tell me that and I promise I won't get angry, I'll just try to be helpful." Then make sure you are. Again, don't expect your child to come around right away. It might take a day or two for your message to sink in. You can also use the Double D code here: "Is this a good or bad secret? Is it something that's a Double D? Because if it is, if someone is in serious trouble or something could happen to someone, you need to find some adult you can tell, even if it isn't me."

The secrets that are most difficult for children are the ones that come from parents, generally known as Family Secrets: Dad is an alcoholic, Uncle Jake is doing drugs. It puts a terrible strain on a child when parents either talk about these problems in hushed tones and pretend that children don't hear, or talk about them openly and then tell a child "not to tell anyone, this is just our family business." It is always better to be honest with a child than to try to put a false face on something. If Daddy can't get up to go to work because he's been on a drinking binge, instead of saying "Daddy must have a touch of the flu," tell the truth: "Daddy drank too much last night. It made him sick." Anything less insults a child's intelligence and, in time, leads to a sense of shame. Acknowledge facts and explain why you don't want your child to tell anyone: "Daddy's been drinking too much. You probably know that this happens a lot. We're not ready to tell people until he agrees to get help, so we're just going to tell them he's sick, and keep why he's sick between you and your brothers and me." Or "We're not going to tell Grandma that I lost my job until I get a new one because it would worry her so much." These kinds of explanations are easier for a child to understand and process.

A more benign example comes from a family I know where the dog ran out the front door one morning when the mom answered the doorbell and was hit by a car and killed. The kids were at school, so she and her husband made the decision to take the body immediately to the vet for disposal and to tell the children that Salty had run away. When they came home from school that afternoon, the mom pretended she had been searching all day and attributed her red eyes to allergies. For the next two days, the children, a first- and third-grader, were preoccupied with finding Salty, first making posters they tacked on trees in the neighborhood, then spending hours scouring the neighborhood and asking people, "Have you seen my dog? Here's her picture." Their sleep was fitful, their schoolwork ignored. On the third day, the older child's interest in the search cooled. "She probably got hit by a car," she announced. "Salty is dead."

Instead of grabbing on to this lifeboat, the parents insisted she was just missing. The more convinced the older daughter was that the dog was dead, the more upset the younger one became and the more determined the parents were to shield them from the grief of the truth. Two and three weeks later, however, the first-grader was still going out on her bike after school in search of Salty.

By this point, the parents realized their error. "We wanted to protect them from the pain of dealing with her death but it was really our own pain we were hiding from," says Mark, the father. "At first, we couldn't bear the thought of having to see their sadness, but after three weeks we realized there would never be any closure for them unless we came clean." They told their daughters the truth, including that they had made a bad mistake trying to keep it secret to begin with.

It was a bitter pill for them to swallow in ways they couldn't have expected. Salty's disappearance had been a big topic of discussion in both girls' classes. Now there was a discussion about what had really happened. "As parents, we knew we didn't look very good," says Mark. Luckily for them, the teachers bailed them out. They invited Mark and Arlene to talk to the classes about the mistake they made by keeping Salty's death a secret, and what they learned from it. So although Arlene and Mark had deprived their children of a good model of how to confront emotional pain in a healthy way, they did model for them how keeping some secrets can be bad and how to confront a mistake with integrity.

One of the biggest secrets that has traditionally been kept from children is that they have been adopted or, in recent years, that their birth was the result of collaborative reproduction. There's been a sea-change in the thinking on both subjects, largely due to longitudinal research on adoptees. Specialists now almost unanimously agree that children should be told the truth. (See Chapter 6 for how to talk to your children if you had help conceiving them.)

Truthfulness doesn't come easily

A few years ago, when Diana Peters was 2½, her father, Douglas, a professor of psychology at the University of North Dakota, took her to his office with him. It was a weekend and no one was around, so while he worked he allowed her to wander the hallway. At the very moment he came out of his office to see where she was, Diana pulled down on the lever that activates the fire alarm. At the sound of the alarm, Diana was frozen with fear and her father was stricken with astonishment. "Diana, what have you done!" he gasped. Her response was instinctive: "Nothing, Daddy! I didn't do it! Brian did it!"

Brian, her 4-year-old brother, wasn't even there, but a frightened Diana stuck to her story as police and six Grand Forks fire trucks arrived.

For Peters, the moment was a curious blending of personal and professional lives. For eight years, he had been researching children's lies; here was his daughter publicly providing him with a whopper.

There's a lot of speculation and research about whether children as young as 2 or 3 lie. Until the late 1980s, the prevailing thinking was that children under 7 could state something falsely but weren't capable of actually lying, which researchers define as the purposeful attempt to deceive another person. According to psychologist Stephen Ceci, who researches why children lie, the thinking was that young children are too egocentric and not cognitively sophisticated enough to lie. Newer research disputes that line of reasoning. Peters thinks his daughter did lie. "It was scary, all those people running into the hall, the loud noise, the firefighters," he says. "She was afraid of being punished. It was a human reflex to say, 'I didn't do it!' "

Nonetheless, he didn't argue with her or insist that she "tell the truth." She was, after all, only 2½. Hours afterward, however, Diana voluntarily owned up. "Daddy, I pulled the switch," she told him.

Peters remembers remaining casual, saying only "I thought so. It's good you told Daddy that you remembered you pulled the switch."

To know how to handle your child's lies, it helps to understand why she lied. Not surprisingly, this is often developmental. A preschooler usually lies to avoid punishment, get a material reward, or to keep a promise. Peters thinks Diana lied to avoid punishment. School-age children lie for these reasons as well as some others: to impress a peer or to challenge authority, to get out of an awkward social situation, and, by 9 or 10, to get privacy from an overly intrusive parent. Children of all ages lie simply to see if they can get away with it: " 'Did you wet the bed last night?' 'No, the dog did it.' 'Did you have a cookie?' 'No, the baby did.' " Parents of 6- to 10-year-olds will also recognize a form of lying that psychologist and researcher Paul Ekman refers to as "tricking." "It's a kind of game they play," he says. "They're trying to get you." For instance:

"Mom, the cafeteria had yak burgers today! It's a nutritional experiment the school signed up for." Just as your skepticism is beginning to fade he pounces: "Ha, ha, I tricked you!" At some point, though, they stop announcing the I-tricked-you part. When they let you dangle and leave you believing them, they've moved into a power trip, according to Ekman. "They're bragging to their friends, 'Can you believe it! She fell for it!' "

Because of the ultimate damage lying can inflict—the erosion of trust between two people, including between parent and child—we need to let even young children know that lying is not nice, even when it's not much of a lie. This message can be lost on preschoolers if we overreact. If Peters had screamed at his daughter, "I know you're lying, I saw you do it!" he might have frightened her so much that she'd be afraid ever to tell him anything, let alone the truth. Getting a preschooler to see the truth of the moment is not nearly as important as establishing a fundamental value of honesty and truth-fulness. Peters accomplished that by waiting for an opening (Diana's confession) and then praising her for telling him.

By 5, children are able to see that lying is unfair and to label it cheating. They also can understand the consequences of a lie. Peters says that if Diana had been older, he would have explained that she should tell the truth because firefighters need to know why the alarm was pulled, whether there was a real fire or not. At about age 8, you can begin to get to the heart of the matter by introducing the idea of the boy who cried wolf by lying so often, no one trusted him when he finally did tell the truth. Even if your child has heard this idea before, reintroduce it at this age. He's more likely to get the concept.

School-age children engage in all sorts of little lies as they grap-ple with various social situations. Because lying is so common, there will be times when you may begin to worry that you have a serious problem on your hands.

Unfortunately, we often contribute to the problem by in-advertantly pushing a child to lie. Here are pitfalls to avoid:

- Don't accuse him of lying. That will only make a school-age child more entrenched and indignant. Instead, tell him, "I'm not sure if you are telling the truth. Before you say anything else, I want you to think some more about this."

- Don't try to trap him or tempt him to lie; that's modeling deceit. Instead, be straightforward and present him with the evidence you found. If he still lies, Ekman's advice is to say, "I don't think you are telling the truth. I'm not happy to have a rule broken, but I'm even less happy if someone lies about it."

> *A preschooler's face is an open book and gives his lie away instantly, but school-age children are a little harder to read. Telltale signs that he's lying: He avoids eye contact, puts his head down, turns his back on you, or engages in a nervous gesture such as rubbing his arms or hands.*

Because your goal is to help him not to lie, a child needs to see you as understanding and approachable so that he can conclude, "Even if I do something really stupid, my parents might understand. I can tell them." One way for that to happen is if you create an environment that supports and rewards telling the truth rather than punishes lying. Researchers say that punishing a child for lying rarely acts as a deterrent because the typical child simply resolves to learn to lie better next time. A child who starts off lying and then tells the truth shows courage that should be rewarded, even if he was trying to cover up for something he shouldn't have done. If it's a first-time transgression, tell him, "I'm so proud of you for telling the truth, I'm not going to punish you this time." If it happens again, be clear that you still admire the truth but can't overlook the transgression; keep the punishment reasonable, not so severe that he'll think telling the truth was a wasted effort: "I'm glad you told the truth. Unfortunately, the lamp is still broken. Since you were honest, I'll go easy on you. You need to earn some money to help replace it, but not as much as if you hadn't been truthful. What do you think would be fair?" Keep in mind that some children are punished enough by your strong disappointment.

By far, what influences whether your children do or don't lie is whether you do. Parents who say it's wrong to lie and then lie themselves send a powerful message that is hard to undo. If you need to lie to spare someone's feelings, label it as such to your children: "I don't like the scarf Grandpa gave me for my birthday, but I don't want to hurt his feelings, so I'm going to think of something good I can say about the scarf, like that it goes with my jacket. That will spare his feelings and it won't be lying." A sensitive child may try to do the same thing, telling a friend, for instance, that she can't play tomorrow because she has a doctor's appointment when, in fact, she's going to a party that the friend wasn't invited to. While her intent is admirable, she needs you to help her project to the potential negative outcome from such a kindness lie: The friend could find out about the party from someone else and then be angry at her for lying to her. Perhaps the best way to help a child with a dilemma like this is to explain that the truth is always the better choice if there's any chance for a bigger hurt as a result of the lie.

Young runaways

When the 7-year-old daughter of a friend ran away, she stuffed her backpack with essentials—pajamas, underwear, toothbrush, and favorite doll—and left via the backdoor. At first, my friend could see her out the window, hiding in some bushes. But then, when she turned her back to tend to her crying younger daughter, the 7-year-old disappeared.

She didn't go far. The next door neighbor spied her looking

teary and forlorn and invited her in. She didn't need coaxing to call her mom. "I'm next door," she said. "Don't come get me right away." Twenty minutes later, there was a happy reunion.

Initially, my friend looked at the episode as insignificant. Cute, not worrisome. But there were lingering, unsettling questions. No one thinks of 7-year-olds running away.

Ah, but they do. It's true that teenagers are more likely candidates; of the nation's 1.3 million runaways each year, most are teens, according to the National Network for Youth. But an estimated 260,000 kids under 14 also run away, about 20 percent of the total number of kids who run away each year. Many of them are under 10 and most of them run away during the summer, usually for a few hours or less. Any absence of any length of time should be taken seriously, although an overnight absence by a young child signals something more serious.

Although only a small number of young children make a plan and execute it, it's a rare child who sometime or other doesn't at least make a plan to run away and *fantasize* about executing it. Nonetheless, it's shocking when it's your child. Even though I had done this research, I was surprised when my son admitted to me there have been times when he's been so angry at us that he's thought about running away. He even identified a specific incident where he made a plan but didn't execute it because it got dark.

Thinking about it is different from doing it, however. A child who runs away, even for a short time, is waving a red flag. It's a communication not to be ignored. For a child to resort to something as scary as leaving home means her hurt or frustration is at least temporarily very high. There are many reasons why she might leave home: She feels angry, sad, unwanted, unloved, isolated, or betrayed. She thinks she is a disappointment, a failure, or a burden. She has been abused sexually, verbally, physically, or all three. Home life is so chaotic or rigid that the lure of freedom from rules and parents' rigidity is overwhelming.

The runaway's age is an important clue in understanding motive:

- **3 to 6 years.** Living in the moment, the young child leaves on impulse. Something is really bugging him and he wants to get away from it. Not having verbal skills to express how he feels, he acts out his feelings by escaping the scene. Usually he can be found someplace very nearby, in a tree or under a bush. When Eve, a first-grader, was found an hour after she was missed, she was sitting under a tree as far from the house as she could possibly get and still be on their property. Her mother knew immediately why she had run away. The family was living in France at the time and the house was overflowing with guests from the States. There was too much noise and too many people, and Eve couldn't get her mother's attention.

- **7 to 9 years.** This child is more a hideaway than a runaway. Like the younger child, you'll probably find her behind the boiler or under the porch, someplace very close to home. If you could get into her mind, you'd likely find out she's run away because something "wasn't fair": Mom was unduly harsh, Dad made a promise he didn't keep, her siblings get all the attention. Because she still needs you to interpret feelings for her, if she perceives something getting in the way of that— a new baby, a sibling, a demanding job—she's ripe to feel misunderstood: "Nobody loves me, nobody cares." A third reason a child of this age might run away is because he's done something wrong and fears being punished.

- **9 to 12.** For a child of this age, the hiding place will not be close by but in the extended neighborhood, at a nearby relative's, even the nearest bus station. Like Tom Sawyer, this child is not feeling rejected or fearing punishment but is rejecting and punishing you: "I'll show her! Boy, will she be sad!" His reasons for leaving are varied: He has too much responsibility in a single-parent home, thinks he's disappointed you in school or sports, feels lost or left out in a newly blended family, or (and this is the most typical) feels a need to assert his independence. It's a hostile gesture but not necessarily an unhealthy one. This child's fantasies about leaving home revolve around freedom: "No rules, no nagging! I'm old enough to make my own decisions. I'll show them I can." It's not that he can't name or express his feelings but that he chooses not to. He packs his bag and storms out of the house thinking, "I'm not going to live in *that* house anymore!" Child psychiatrist Daniel Rosenn has a vivid memory of thinking exactly those thoughts when he was about 12 and packed his clothes and carried them to the woods behind his house, where he neatly laid them out in the field. He remembers feeling exhilarated, indignant, and free. Hours later, as it began to get dark, a sobering sense of reality set in. "I'm not ready for this," he decided, and went back home.

Perhaps what we need to know most of all about these runaways is that the behaviors are all within the range of normal behavior, according to the Reverend Mark-David Janus, a Paulist priest and child psychologist who is an authority on runaways and author of a textbook on the subject. Normal or not, as parents we end up upset, worried, and hurt, and that's how we come to make a big mistake: When we are reunited with our child, instead of expressing our love, we express our anger. "You may think it's obvious how much you love your child," Janus says, "but if it was obvious to him, he probably wouldn't have run away."

No matter what you are feeling, no matter how old your child is or how unusual the circumstances under which he ran away, the first thing you need to say is how much you love him and how glad you are that he's home. Otherwise you can exacerbate the problem that caused him to run away in the first place. If all you do is clamp down—"You're grounded for two weeks!"—you reinforce feelings of being misunderstood. Save your anger and expressions of worry for some later time. Don't punish, devalue, joke about, or otherwise make light of what she did, but don't glamorize it either. Focus on her immediate needs—"Are you hungry, cold, wet?" Get the mending process under way: "Tell me why you felt you needed to run away"; "Let's think about what could have happened differently so you wouldn't feel like you needed to leave." Reaffirm your bond by making some individual time together, not necessarily for a heart-to-heart but just to reestablish your connections. If your child is 10 or older, there is a promise you need to extract from her, not that she won't run away again but that she'll talk to you if she's ever feeling bad enough to want to run away. If she won't make that promise, seek professional help.

The dangers that could befall a child who runs away cannot be ignored, of course. With a child 10 or older, you can be specific about what they are and ask him, "What can we do to remind you how dangerous this is, so you won't do it again?" Make it clear this isn't a punishment but an act of love. With younger children, make sure they know their phone number, including area code, and how to use 911. Impress upon them how important it is for you always to know where they are.

> *When your runaway returns, tell him,*
> *"I'm glad you chose to come home." It will*
> *make your child feel more in control, and*
> *control is often a big issue.*

Here are a few *if*s to be aware of:

- If a child has run away once, it could happen again, especially if issues don't get talked about. It also increases the likelihood that a younger sibling will try it: Running away is now a viable option to him when things aren't going his way.

- If a child of any age runs away three or more times, that's a pattern that shouldn't be ignored, even if all he did was hide in the backyard; the cry for help isn't diminished by the scope of the geography. Seek professional help.

- If you think your child is thinking about running away, tell her: "I've noticed you seem upset lately. Some kids, when they are very upset, think about running away. If that's on your mind, I want you to know we don't want you to run away. We love you and if there's a problem, we want to work on it together."

- If your child threatens to run away, don't tell him "You can't do that." Instead, sit down and talk with him, right then. Family psychologist James H. Bray of Houston tells parents to turn running away on its head by telling a child, "You stay here, I'll run away." That will either strike them as so silly or so scary that it will get issues out in the open right away.

In my friend's family, it took a few days before she and her husband got to the heart of the matter. Reading in bed with her father three nights later, the daughter confided why she had run away: "Mom loves me less. She always pays less attention to me." Knowing that enabled my friend to be more sensitive to her daughter and eventually to approach the subject head-on. Happily, there has never been another runaway attempt.

Playing with fire

Sometime before your son hits 14, possibly as young as 4 but almost certainly at 9 or 10, odds are that he'll play with fire, literally. Odds are also that you won't know about it. That's good, sort of. If you don't know about it, it means nothing tragic happened. But what if there's a next time?

Unfortunately, beyond keeping matches and lighters out of the reach of very young children, most of us dismiss the thought that our child might start a fire. We tend to think of children who play with fire as "troubled" kids from "disadvantaged" families. This kind of thinking is dangerous. Research shows that only one-third of fires set by children are on purpose with intent to harm. The typical child who starts a fire is neither sick nor angry. He's playing. In other words, it could be your kid or mine. More than likely, it will also be your son, not your daughter.

Child psychiatrist Stuart Goldman, director of the Fire Sense Program at Children's Hospital in Boston, says every parent of a son should have a conversation about fire play with him sometime before he's 9. "I have little doubt that by 9, most boys will have done some match play. It's almost a rite of passage," says Goldman. "If your 9-year-old son hasn't, then his friends have." Social psychologist Robert Cole, who has collected nationwide data on children and fires since 1983, says 40 percent of children under 14 admit to playing with matches at least once. In addition:

- Children under 14 are known to be responsible for setting 100,000 fires nationwide each year. Not all fires get reported, however, because parents are able to put many out themselves.

- Fires started by children cause 2,800 injuries and 400 deaths nationwide annually. In one month in Boston in 1997, three people died in three fires set by children under 7 who were playing with matches out of curiosity.

That young children, boys more than girls, are drawn to fire is not in itself cause for concern. Fascination with fire is not exactly developmental, but it is virtually universal among toddlers and preschoolers. After all, fire is colorful, beautiful, and mesmerizing. Not only that, but from a young age, children are socialized to associate fire with pleasurable events. Amid much hoopla, we put candles on a birthday cake, turn out the lights, and urge a child to make a wish and blow them out. Nothing scary about that! That fire takes place in a warm and wonderful context continues to be true in most succeeding exposures: The family congregates around the fireplace or woodstove for a cozy winter evening of board games or gathers around a campfire at the beach and sings songs.

It is not surprising, then, that the very young child who plays with matches (or, more likely, a lighter because matches are too difficult to manipulate) is motivated by sheer curiosity: "Can I make that beautiful thing happen too?" Because children under 6 are developmentally unable to make the connection between lighting the match and starting a fire, they are responsible for a disproportionate number of fatal fires. Not being able to make this cognitive connection, they are more likely to experiment indoors. In addition, they don't respond appropriately if a fire does start. Because they don't understand the potential consequences of not telling, and because they are afraid of the flames and perhaps afraid of getting into trouble, they are more likely than an older child to ignore it, walk away, and not tell anyone.

By second grade, the child who wants to play with fire is more cognitively advanced. He now knows enough to think about safety and to play with fire in such a way that he won't get caught. If he's going to light matches, he'll do it in the sink or tub, or clear away a place in the basement, the backyard, or, most typically, at the foot of his bed. He'll light a leaf, a tissue, or a piece of newspaper. When he becomes frightened, he'll drop it, stomp it out, and push the residue under his bed or wipe it up with a cloth. He may or may not tell someone, an older sibling or a friend, but if he does, he'll probably be bragging about it. At this age and older, children typically are attracted to fire precisely because it is dangerous; it gives them a sense of mastery and control and makes them feel grown up. The play is impulsive, not planned, and often the result of opportunity: He has access to matches and time on his hands. "That's why you see so much more of this in the summer," says Goldman. It is only after about age 11 that fire play is sometimes fueled by more ominous motives: an angry child lashing out at something or crying out for attention.

There are a number of red flags that indicate your child may be engaged or thinking about engaging in fire play. Watch for:

- A school-age child who spends a lot of time alone in his room or the bathroom with the door shut or who stockpiles wood, newspapers or other flammables.

- Burn marks or residue under the bed or elsewhere in the house.

- A pattern: He was caught with matches a year ago, three months ago, and two times last month.

Because fire play has the potential to be fatal, it is one of the few behaviors psychiatrists treat as emergencies. Parents should too. Contact your pediatrician immediately if you think your child has experimented even once with fire, or if he seems preoccupied by it; that is, not just staring into a fire and finding it beautiful, but frequently urging you to make a fire, insisting on being involved in its construction, and being disproportionately disappointed when you won't make one.

> *Take seriously reports by teachers or other adults that your child was talking or bragging about fire play.*

All it takes to keep our children safe from fire play is instilling in them a healthy respect for fire. And all it takes for that is a series of conversations:

- **With a preschooler,** acknowledge the beauty of fire but also the dangers. When you light the barbecue, the woodstove, or the fire in the fireplace, say, "This is really hot. The flames are pretty, but they're dangerous. Fire hurts people. See how careful Mom and Dad are with it?"

- **To the 5- to 8-year-old,** reiterate fire's danger frequently: "I know it looks easy to strike a match. It's a very tempting thing to do but it's very dangerous and not something you are allowed to do."

- **To the 9- to 11-year-old,** acknowledge peer pressure: "Probably some boys you know are interested in fire and may even light matches, but fire is unpredictable and dangerous. No one ever thinks they'll get hurt or start a real fire. You should never play with matches. If you know someone who does, you should tell an adult." If your 10-year-old is anything like mine, he'll interrupt you halfway through to say, "Mom, I *know* that." Tell him you know that he does, but it's your job to remind him about it anyway, because it's so important and because it's the kind of thing that even adults sometimes forget. Even children of this age should never be allowed to handle firecrackers or fireworks.

According to Cole, children under 15 should not have responsibility for lighting a match, not even under adult supervision, not even for something like the Hanukkah candles. When Cole first told me that, I suggested that he was taking a particularly conservative view. I had a selfish motive: At about age 8, my son had begged to strike matches to light the Hanukkah candles, and we had reasoned that it was a good thing for him to learn how to do it correctly, while we watched. Alas, interviews with other researchers indicate that Cole is not alone in his position; in fact, although some will vary the age by a year or two, there is pretty solid agreement among them about this, although they are careful to make the distinction between striking the match and holding a lit candle. Cole patiently explained that my reasoning wasn't sound, at least not when you think about it developmentally. "Teaching a child of 9 or 10 how to light a match correctly gives them a false sense of security," he said. "Children who have been given responsibility for fire are more likely to play with it because they feel empowered. They think they can do it safely."

When the time does come that you feel your child is ready for the responsibility, Cole says you can't overemphasize the safety factor. "Tell him, 'I'm letting you do this because I trust you, not because it's not dangerous.'"

CHAPTER THREE

School Days

. . . .

The day my son started first grade, I was very excited. When it came time to pick him up, I was bubbling over, dying for every last detail of his day. Here's how our conversation went:

Me: "So how was your first day?"
Him: "Okay."
Me: "Well, what happened? What was it like? How were your teachers? How were your friends? What was lunch like? Gosh, tell me everything!"
Him: "Mom, it was *okay*. Can we get home to have a snack now?"

Sound familiar? The unfortunate truth is that most children clam up when it comes to talking about school. Coping with this recalcitrant conversant is impossibly difficult for us as parents. What goes on in our children's lives while they are in that building is important to us not just because we love them so much, not just because we need to know what and how they are learning, but also because what happens there impacts heavily on what they say and do at home, indeed, on who they are becoming as individuals. Everything that happens while our child is in school contributes to shaping him into the person he is becoming. Everything contributes to his overall sense of well-being and self-esteem.

While we may think the academics are what count, in the eyes of a child, everything else counts far more. When things aren't going well interpersonally for a school kid, things aren't going well, period. No way the child who's been picked on at recess, or who thinks the teacher doesn't like him, can "settle down" and learn. He can't concentrate. He can't focus. He can't compartmentalize. With young children, when something goes wrong, you know about it quickly. But the older they get, the harder it is to know and the more complicated it is to be helpful.

Getting—and keeping—your child talking

Children themselves ought to be our first source of information about school, but to hear them tell it, nothing happens that's worth remembering and if it is worth remembering, then it was either absolutely awful, terrible, and stupid or it was *okay*. Fortunately, a child's stingy answer is rarely a purposeful attempt to thwart us. Beginning at about age 6, girls tend to be more readily talkative than boys; even boys who were talkative as preschoolers tend to become more reticent now. How our children respond to our interest and inquiries depends largely on their stage of development and personality:

- **Preschoolers.** Three- and 4-year-olds are so egocentric, they think the world revolves around them. They assume we know everything they know, so when we ask about their day, they think it's a rhetorical question: "Why is Mom bothering to ask? I don't need to tell her, she already knows." The preschooler may be a little confused about what happened anyway. Cognitively, she is not yet able to sort out events and people and may actually expect *us* to tell *her* what happened.

Because things get mushed together in her mind, she may also need time to work through the doubts and uncertainties she has about the day before she can talk about them. For some children that can be fifteen minutes. For others, it can take a day, even longer, to process. If a preschooler refers back to something that happened several days ago, it's because she is just now processing, or reprocessing, some aspect of it.

- **Five- and 6-year-olds.** Now that they are in "real" school, children want to feel grown up. The lack of an answer is not malevolent in intent, just a normal and healthy way for them to separate from you and establish autonomy. Beginning in first grade, your child may tell you "I forgot" so many times that you begin to worry something is wrong. Consider instead that it's just a kinder way for her to say, "I don't feel like telling you." Help her identify the feeling, though. Ask her, "Honey, is it that you really forgot or that you just don't want to talk about it now? That's okay, if it is."

- **Second-graders and older.** Having to stop, think things through, and give you an answer takes time and effort, an anathema to most school-age children, and their reluctance to talk may be as simple as that. Then, too, there's the issue of privacy: The older a child gets, the more valuable it is to him. While the younger child isn't consciously withholding to maintain a sense of autonomy, a child of this age may be: "School is my world and I'll let you in when I want to."

As normal as it may be, for some parents this withholding is emotionally wrenching. For years, we have known every little detail about a child and now we know next to nothing. There are two sides to this, of course. As parents, our job is to be emotionally connected to our children, so we feel shut out. Our children's job is to be more and more autonomous. They feel intruded upon. Can't you remember squirming under your own parents' questioning? Now for the paradox: Just because children have a need and a right to separate doesn't mean they don't want to be still connected. As much as they want autonomy, all of them, even teens, also want to know we care. Psychologists say parents who see a child's demand for privacy as a signal to butt out run the risk of being neglectful and of sending a message that says "Hey, kiddo, you're on your own."

Walking this parental tightrope is quite a balancing act. The trick is to learn how to get information without seeming to be nosy, without making a child feel like she's just been put through the third degree. When you ask a barrage of questions, the way I did of my son the first day of first grade, it begins to sound like you are checking up on him, that you don't trust him to take care of his own business. If your child consistently doesn't want to talk to you about his world, ask yourself these questions: Is there something about our relationship that makes him hesitate? Is it possible something is happening at school that he doesn't want me to know about? Is there something about my questions that is making him feel intruded upon? Although your inability to engage him at this moment is most likely a function of how and what you are asking, it is also tied up with the whole of your relationship. If you are never respectful of his privacy (see "Secrets" in the preceding chapter), then he may feel a more urgent need to hold his school world apart from you.

Engaging our children in conversations is every parent's best strategy, starting when they are very young, but timing, tone, and topic are critical.

Timing. You need to be available to talk when he wants to talk to you. His timetable, not yours, is what counts. If this feels annoyingly like a one-way street, well, it is. But then, we're the adult, he's the child, and we're supposed to be able to handle these inequities. Invariably, of course, he wants to talk when you can't (the baby is crying, you're rushing off for work) or when you're unprepared. If he consistently approaches you when he can see it's not a good time, rather than lose your patience, consider why he does this. There's a good chance he's feeling neglected or left out, but can't find any way to tell you other than to seek negative attention. Make a point to talk about his strategy: "You know, I've noticed you often want to talk to me at a time when I'm busy doing something else, and you end up being frustrated and so do I. Maybe we need to make a point to find some quiet time each day for the two of us." If she only infrequently seeks you out when you're busy, tell her, "I can't be late today. Let's make a plan to talk later." Then make sure you follow through. On some occasions, and you'll be able to see this happening, the message you send by putting your own needs aside to talk to him at the moment he wants you will be worth whatever inconvenience it causes. Cindy, mother of four, says, "My kids know that I'll stop what I'm doing if it's really important, but they also know that if it turns out to be something that could have waited, I'll be angry." If someone grabs her as she's running out the door to get a sibling to hockey, or when she's rocking the baby to sleep, she'll ask, "Is this a Now, Not Later?" which is short for "Are you absolutely sure this can't wait?"

Timing is also affected by location. Where are you and your child physically in relation to each other? One mother I know says one of the most important conversations she ever had with her 12-year-old son about sex began when she was standing at the sink. She doesn't think it was coincidental that he chose to ask her about French-kissing when her back was turned. Another mother recalls that the first time her daughter asked a question about menstruation was from behind a closed door. And what about the fact that so many of us have our best conversations with our children when it's just the two of us, alone in the car, or at bedtime, after the lights are out? You may think these are terrible times for an important conversation, but to a child they may be perfect. Lack of eye contact has a lot to do with it. When a child is embarrassed or scared or even just a little bit unsure, eye contact increases anxiety; it makes things more real. From her perspective, the car is ideal because there are distractions—she can look out the window, you have to drive—and because she knows the conversation can't go on indefinitely, which is especially important if she thinks you're going to lecture or yell.

Knowing when to initiate a conversation means knowing when

your child is likely to want to talk. There's no science to this. What works one day may not work a week later. Many kids are most talkative right after school, when everything is fresh in their minds. This need not be a hardship for working parents. Establish a routine phone conversation. If that's not possible, get an inexpensive tape recorder that he can talk into or a journal for him to write in; even at an afterschool program, he can steal a few private minutes. Other kids are happier to have quiet time when they first come home, almost as a buffer zone between one piece of their life and another; some are too hungry to talk when they first come home, or too close to events to be able to make sense of them. These children may be more willing to talk at dinner or bedtime, after they've decompressed. In that case, allow for the bedtime routine to be leisurely enough for you to have time for a conversation. Sometimes older children look forward to having private time with a parent after the younger kids have been put to bed and as a way to break up their homework. Boys tend to be less talkative about school than girls, in part because fathers tend to talk less than mothers and young boys imitate that. A father can counter by telling his nontalkative son, "You know, I'm not so good about talking about things that happen to me. I wish I was better at it, and I'm going to work on it. Can you help me?" It's not a bad idea for both parents to think about the model they present to their child when it comes to sharing information. Make a point at the dinner table to give everyone in the family a chance to talk about their day.

Tone. Timing isn't everything. Tone of voice can make or break your opportunity; many parents don't realize how off-putting their tone can be. For instance, "Is it that you really forgot or that you just don't want to talk right now?" can sound accusatory or sympathetic. If you frequently start off friendly and conversational but turn into an interrogator halfway through—"Well, what *did* you get on the test?"—a child learns you have a hidden agenda and will avoid conversations. And one of the quickest ways to squelch conversation is to quiz a child hungrily, the way I did with my son.

Topic. Getting information depends on what we do—or

don't—ask. For instance, you're better off talking about feelings than accomplishments, and you're more likely to learn something from specific questions than from general ones. Asking "How was your day?" will almost always yield a nothing response. For children who haven't learned that that's a social idiom meant to start a conversation, it's too broad a question; they have no idea how to answer it. Instead of asking "How was reading today," try "What book is your group reading?" Instead of "How was math?" ask "Did you find out how to solve that complicated problem?" Every once in a while I'll ask my son to tell me FSGB: something funny, something sad, something good, something bad. Most days he's not in the mood, but every once in a while I get lucky.

> *When something bad has happened and your child doesn't want to talk about it, give him a choice: "We can talk about it now or save it for after dinner. You decide."*

If you're a parent who's blessed with a child who doesn't clam up when you inquire about school or, even better, who offers information before you ask (it always astonishes me to come across a child like this!), being an appreciative audience and praising the communication process—"You're such a good reporter!"—increases the likelihood she'll keep on talking. Even with the talkative child, though, there are times when we need to figure out how to get more information than she's offering. If your second-grader tells you out of the blue one day, "My teacher yells a lot," you need to know if this means the classroom is unsafe, the teacher out of control. Are there serious discipline problems in the class? Did the teacher yell at *her*? The questions shout inside your head. For the time being, at least, keep them there.

What your child needs, even though she doesn't know it, is to get to her feelings. If you help her get her needs met first, there's a good chance your needs will get met along the way, that the information you want—"I pushed Jennifer in line and I got yelled at"—will come out naturally, without your ever having to utter those intrusive, judgmental, interrogatory words: "Did you do something to make your teacher angry?"

> **Questions to never ask your child: "Who got the highest grade?" "What did Michael get?" "How come you only got a B+?"**

You can never go wrong with an answer that parrots back, in a sympathetic tone, what your child just told you: "Hmmm, your teacher yells a lot, huh? . . ." If you're met with silence, you could follow it up with something equally benign, "I wonder what that feels like to the kids to have a teacher who yells a lot. . . ." She may just shrug and walk away, or she might open up more: "I can tell you! It feels awful. Today she yelled at me in line for no reason and she was *really* mean." Even if she walks away, it's registered that you aren't jumping down her throat and that you are approachable. If you do get some information but not enough, avoid asking "What happened? Why did you push Jennifer?" Instead, go with another reflective response: "She yelled at you while you were in line." Work hard to keep your tone from registering surprise or passing judgment. Imagine yourself in the situation and go with that emotion: "Gee, that must not have felt very good to you." That's called being an "active listener" and gives a child room to move around in because it is so nonjudgmental and sympathetic. There's something else about that kind of response, too: it's relaxed. Asking "What happened?" almost always has a worried tone to it, as in "I can't bear to think anything awful might have happened to my darling!" Even "Tell me about it" is better; it signals to your child that you aren't going to rush in offering solutions. Parents who are quick to offer here's-what-you-can-do-next-time responses unwittingly cause a child to clam up. Kids can't project to next time because they are stuck on now, and they don't want to know what to do because they are immersed in feeling. What kids need to enable them not only to talk but also to feel better is often nothing more than a sympathetic ear.

Teacher trouble

In the eyes of the typical young child, a teacher is a kind of god, all-knowing and all-seeing, with powers that are endless and far-reaching. Even as they get older, their awe may diminish but rarely does it disappear. It's not surprising, then, that one of the most unsettling feelings a young child can have is to think the teacher doesn't like him. Whether it's true or not doesn't matter; it's his perception that counts. Even if the issue is only in a child's mind, it needs to get fixed quickly. Most children withdraw when they are upset with a teacher. They become quiet, sullen, and unresponsive in class. They stop listening, stop paying attention, and tend to get into trouble. In its extreme, this can spiral out of control, negatively affecting classroom behavior and academic success not just this year but in the future as well.

Thinking the teacher doesn't like you is very common in lower grades. It's most likely to occur in the first six weeks of school when teachers haven't had a chance to know how each child reacts to various situations, and when children haven't had the time to learn to read a teacher's signals and moods. Six- to 9-year-olds are particularly prone to misinterpreting a teacher's behavior. There are two reasons why. One is that about 80 percent of interpersonal communication between teacher and child is nonverbal, making it easy for kids to misread. Another is what child psychiatrist Stanley Greenspan, well known for his research and clinical work with school-age children, calls "all-or-nothing thinking."

> *Try to learn something about the teacher that he and your child have in common, a shared hobby or sport, perhaps: "I heard Mr. Lee loves to fish, just like you!"*

Your second-grader approaches his teacher, who is sitting at a table working on a math problem with another child. He interrupts her. She turns to him and says, quite civilly, "I'm helping Timmy now. Can you wait your turn?" Knowing only that he wants his teacher *now*, he doesn't hear her in the matter-of-fact way she intended. Instead, his feeling translates to an all-or-nothing thought— "She hates me!"—rather than the thought of a slightly older, less egocentric child with more reasoning capacity: "She likes me, she's just too busy right now."

There are other reasons misunderstandings occur. A young child may:

- React to a comment directed at someone else;

- Personalize a comment meant for the whole class;

- Become jealous of attention given to another child;

- Blame the teacher for not protecting her from a child she doesn't like or who doesn't like her;

- Dismiss his own culpability in the situation.

Figuring any of this out, of course, is not easy. It's always possible your child will announce, "My teacher hates me!" and with a few sympathetic "That must not feel very good" responses, you're at the nub. More likely, however, you need to pick up on nonverbal cues. Look for a child who was excited at the start of school and isn't now;

was motivated at first but isn't now; liked doing homework and doesn't now, or doesn't want to go to school. Especially if any of this occurs in the first few weeks of school, there's a good chance it has something to do with the teacher. Use your best information-getting techniques (timing, tone, topic) to play detective. Perhaps you might start by identifying the behavior you've observed: "I've noticed that you don't seem as enthusiastic about school as you were in the beginning. . . ." Although most of us are tempted to tack a question on to the end of that ("Has something changed/Is something bothering you?"), it isn't really necessary and will probably feel intrusive.

Sometimes, specific questions will get you more information: "Do you ever have a chance to do anything with your teacher, just the two of you?" "What kinds of things does she help you with?" "When you couldn't zipper your jacket, was your teacher helpful?" "Does she call on you much?" Don't ask all these questions at once, that's what feels like a grilling to a child. But if you ask them over a day or two, even if you get only yes or no answers, you may begin to be able to fill in a picture of a teacher who is or isn't responsive to your child. Get him to elaborate as much as possible and, most important, encourage him to tell you how he feels about what he describes. For instance, if he says, "She calls on Thomas all the time, hardly ever on me," ask him to close his eyes and picture the teacher in his mind calling on Thomas. Ask him, "How does that make you feel, when that happens?" If you assume your child is to blame in a negative teacher-child interaction, you not only force him to be defensive, but you also isolate him: "It's me against all of them."

With this, as with many of our children's problems, the tendency for most of us is to try to solve the problem. While you can intervene without much difficulty on the behalf of a first-grader, it's much harder as well as less appropriate to do that with a seventh-grader. Which is why it's so important to begin when they are very young to provide them with coping and human relationship skills so they can solve their own problems. Our job is to listen, gather information, and then ask, "What do you think you can do about this?"

Even first-graders will have solid, valid ideas. In the above situation, for instance, you might ask, "What can you do to get her to call on you more?" If she has no ideas or gets defensive, depersonalize the situation: "Let's list all the reasons a teacher might not call on a child." Offer a possibility: "Maybe the child waits too long to raise her hand." It won't take long before the two of you generate a list: Maybe she doesn't raise it high enough; maybe she calls out while she raises her hand; she waves it too wildly; she raises it just a tiny bit and the teacher doesn't see it. The typical child probably won't admit that any of this describes her, but one of these possibilities might cause her to pause and then you've probably hit on it even if she doesn't admit it. Don't knock her over the head with it. Instead, respond with a thoughtful "Hmmmm" and let the subject sit for a while. She may come back to it. If not, in a day or so, you may see a change in behavior or moods. Even if you can't, bring up the original issue: "How are you feeling about your teacher these days?" Don't be surprised if she doesn't answer that question but goes directly to, "She called on me today!"

Some children are especially sensitive to criticism from a teacher. Jeremy, a kindergartner, came home from school sad because his teacher "yelled" at him. To Jeremy, whose parents were low-key and never raised their voices, even a slightly raised voice qualified as yelling. When asked about it, the teacher remembered the incident well. She hadn't yelled at him, but her voice had taken on an edge. She had reminded him it was time to clean up and when he didn't respond, she had said, somewhat impatiently, "Jeremy, we're waiting."

To Jeremy, the incident meant Mrs. Little didn't like him and that's what he told his mother that afternoon. She did some role-playing with him: "You be the teacher and I'll be the child. How would you tell me to finish cleaning up? What would you say if I was being really slow?" But taking the teacher's point of view didn't help. What did help was a straightforward comment his father made: "Sometimes I'm angry at the way you tease your sister, but I still love you. You can be unhappy with something a person does, but still like the person." "You mean," asked Jeremy, "how I yelled at Sparky [the dog] when he chewed my pencil? But I still wanted him to sleep on my bed?" Because this all unfolded in one afternoon and evening, Jeremy was feeling fine by the next day and there were no lingering aftereffects, but in hindsight, his mother wished she had told the teacher at the beginning of the year that Jeremy is particularly sensitive. It might also have been helpful for these parents to tell Jeremy that because their style of talking is very quiet even when they are angry, he might mistake someone else's loud voice for anger when it was really just a regular way of talking.

If a child's complaints about a teacher last for two weeks, it's time to talk to the teacher. (If a child is upset every day, you might not want to wait that long.) As is true for all classroom problems, always talk to the teacher directly first, even if you suspect a problem is going to end up needing the help of the principal or other school personnel. This conversation will be easier if you've already met and established a rapport with the teacher, something parents should make a point to do within the first two weeks of school, no matter what grade their child is in. As our children get older, or as there are more siblings in school, there's a tendency to slack off on this. You assume that because your older child had the same teacher, you don't need to reestablish a relationship, or that because your child is in fifth grade, it's no longer appropriate for you to initiate a conversation with a teacher. It's always uncomfortable, however, to have your first conversation with a teacher in the midst of a crisis.

When you're talking to a teacher about a problem, be direct but diplomatic, concerned but not condemning. Make it clear you want to approach this as a team. For instance: "Mary doesn't think you like her. I knew you'd be as concerned as I am, so I wanted to bring it to your attention. Do you have any idea what might be going on? What can we do to help her?"

Few teachers won't respond positively to a parent who wants to collaborate and most will go out of their way to make a child feel better. When a child thinks the teacher doesn't like her, a conversation between the two of them is a good idea: "I'm sorry you thought

I don't like you. Can you tell me what I did that gave you that idea, because I do like you and I don't want to do the same thing again." If your child is noticeably happier after the teacher makes an effort, send in a note: "Susan had such a good day yesterday! She was so happy when she came home. Thanks for being responsive."

There are those few teachers who won't respond, and there is always the possibility that the teacher really *doesn't* like your child. In either case, stay in the diplomatic mode for a week or two, touching base with the teacher every few days. Go in to the class to observe and gather evidence; even if a teacher knows you are coming, she can't be on such good behavior that her style and attitude toward your child won't come through. If nothing changes, now is the time to go to the principal, keeping in mind that not all teacher-child relationships can be resolved positively. If you conclude that's the case, try to turn the situation into a learning experience for your child. Talk about how you can't always like every teacher in your life, share an experience from your childhood where you didn't get along with a teacher, explain that learning to work with people you don't get along with is part of life. If you're faced with an extreme example, where the teacher is humiliating, ridiculing, or otherwise harming your child, it's not inappropriate to request that your child be moved to another classroom.

Penny wishes she had been more of an advocate on her oldest son's behalf when he was in second grade and the teacher picked on him. "He began complaining in November," she says, "but I didn't really believe him until March. By then, it was clear that my son was simply shutting down in class." The fact that he didn't learn much that year turned out to be a secondary issue compared to the damage to her relationship with him. When Penny, a single mother, didn't respond to his complaints in November, he felt abandoned and began acting out. Unfortunately, Penny attributed all of this to the absence of a father figure. By the time she paid more attention in March, her son was so far behind academically, he needed tutoring. That helped him regain some self-confidence, but the year never really got salvaged. Only later, when Penny transferred Jake to a private school, did she learn that that second-grade teacher had a reputation for picking on one or two boys in his class each year. It was also only many years later that she learned how deeply he had been hurt by her unresponsiveness. He often refers to second grade as "the year Mom didn't pay attention to me."

"Don't make me go to school!"

One reason it's so important to deal with teacher trouble ASAP is because it is the kind of thing that can make a child not want to go to school. There are various degrees of not wanting to go to school, from the normal, developmental separation issues of a preschooler, through school-age reluctance (often called school refusal), to anxiety that's so intense, it's accompanied by physical illness and is commonly called school phobia. This is something to take seriously at any level. Psychiatrists do. Like fire play, this is one of the few situations they consider an emergency, not because it is so dramatic but because it can escalate so quickly. What is perhaps most unfortunate is that parents frequently end up as unwitting abettors, which is why professionals who study children who refuse to go to school are unanimous in their advice: If your child isn't sick, send him to school anyway. Even if he's miserable, even if he's crying.

This can seem pretty harsh. Their reasoning is that by keeping him home, the message you send says: "Yep, everything you fear is true, and then some. I'll keep you home because that's where you are safe. What's going on in school is more than you can handle." Allowing him to stay home just one day makes it that much harder for him to return to school the day after. Just that one day can make the problem worse and begin to move you along the continuum from reluctance to phobia.

There are generally two possible sources of the problem. The first is a separation issue of some kind that makes it difficult for him to leave home, perhaps a change in development or an issue at home, a dying grandparent or an out-of-work parent. The second is that something is happening at school that makes him not want to be there, either some specific one-time situation, such as a math test, or something more chronic, such as a bully picking on him. Luckily, there's lots of perfectly normal, age-appropriate I-don't-wanna-go behavior that need not be cause for worry, as long as it gets handled appropriately:

Preschoolers' separation anxiety. Preschoolers who don't want to go to school are almost always experiencing a developmental anxiety over separation that has nothing to do with the quality of the program or how much your child likes it. You need to be sure about this, though, just in case. So ask yourself: Is my child sick? Is there some stress at home causing her to be upset? At the top of the list is a new sibling, but also consider whether there's been a change of routine at home or parental stress of some kind. Also look into a change of routine at day care or preschool—a new teacher, a teacher out sick, a favorite friend whose schedule has changed. Next, rule out philosophical issues: program too long or too structured, teacher turn-over too high, a problem in safety or supervision. Now it's safe to conclude you've got a separation problem on your hands.

The typical 3- to 5-year-old goes in and out of periods where she looks at the big, grown-up world ahead of her and feels competent, confident, and conquering: "I'm terrific! I can do anything!" At other times, though, she looks at the same world and sees it as too much to handle. Literally overnight, she can go from feeling she's the boss of the world to feeling she's a baby who is overwhelmed by everything. It's in this mode that she'll give you a dozen reasons why she doesn't want to go to preschool: "My tummy hurts!" "I forgot my blankie!"

Sympathy is appropriate—"I'm sorry your tummy hurts," "I know how upsetting it is not to have your blankie"—capitulation is not. Don't keep her home *in case* she's getting sick, don't go back home for the blankie. Tell her instead, "I'll call when I get to work, to see how you feel," or "How about if I leave you my scarf today, since you don't have your blankie, and tomorrow we'll make sure not to forget it." Separations can be harder on Mondays and on days after vacations, and winter makes for tougher transitions for preschoolers; just having to put on all those extra layers of clothing makes some kids not want to leave the house. A new sibling at home can make a preschooler anxious enough not to want to go to school. "I can't go to school!" she thinks. "That baby will have Mom all to himself and she'll forget about me!" A parent's best recourse is to remain calm, comforting, and confident: "I love you but my job is to go to work today/to stay home and take care of this crying baby and your job is to go to preschool. I know you can do this."

School-age reluctance. Starting in first grade but most typically in years of change and transition (second grade and fifth through seventh, where noticeably increased demands are made on kids, as well as the first year of middle or high school), parents are likely to get at least one dose of school reluctance. The protest can range from mild to intense, but what makes it manageable from a parent's point of view is that a child is almost always able to give you a specific reason why she doesn't want to go and, in the end, she does go without too much difficulty.

> *Refusal to go to school can appear for the first time at age 7 or 11, even in a child who has never had separation issues.*

The reason she doesn't want to go usually is because something has caused her to be anxious, afraid, or embarrassed. He was teased because he forgot to pull up his zipper. She stood up abruptly, knocked over some books, and the class laughed at her. A teacher reprimanded him, a bully pushed him. If she clams up and can't or won't give you a specific reason, it's reasonably safe to assume it's something along these lines. The other possibility is that something is happening at home that makes him not feel safe at school. Have you started a new job? Perhaps he's worried about you or about how the school could reach you. When something like this is on a child's mind, it can distract and derail him. Our job is to be supportive and understanding, never belittling. At the same time, however, we need to be firm, positive, and unwavering in our conviction that school is where he belongs. He needs to know there is no doubt: He will go to school.

Offer empathy but also let him know there's no wiggle room here: "I'm sorry something happened to embarrass/upset/concern you. I know some days things happen at school that make you wish you didn't have to go. But you do have to go. Tonight we can talk about how the day was for you." Obviously if there is a specific problem that needs fixing, you need to cope with it, but that still doesn't mean he shouldn't go to school. Offer support and reassurance and try to help him to figure out how he can solve the problem. If it's appropriate, offer to talk to the teacher, perhaps both of you together.

What to do is much less clear if a child can't give you a specific reason why he doesn't want to go to school, if her reluctance becomes a daily or an every-Monday or an after-every-vacation event, or if her upset is so intense she becomes physically sick with a headache, stomachache, fever, or vomiting. With a sick child, look first at the context: Was he sick last night? Did he sleep through the night? Is anyone else in the family sick? Is there something going around the school? If you're on the fence, send him and tell him to go to the nurse if he doesn't start to feel better. If you keep him home, the surefire way to know if his sickness is related to a school problem is if there's a quick, although not instant, recovery. It's not that he was faking it, just that with the anxiety removed, he feels better. One way to prevent this from happening again is by not making the sick day a fun day. Insist he stay in bed, just in case he starts to feel bad again. If the recovery occurs early enough in the day, send him to school late, not in a punitive way but matter-of-factly: "Gee, it's only eleven o'clock, you might as well go to school so you don't miss math." The behavior you see around this may be as close as school-age children get to a temper tantrum: "Please, please don't make me go!" "I'm scared to go to school!" "I'll hate you if you make me go!" "I'll stay in the bathroom!" Unless you think your child is physically unsafe, a bully's beating him up on the school bus, for instance, failure to respond with appropriate firmness can lead a child to think, "If I don't want to deal with a problem, it's okay to avoid it." It's not an exaggeration to say that a continued dose of that kind of thinking can lead to a lifelong inability to face problems.

Just because you get her to school that first day doesn't mean you won't see a repeat performance of not wanting to go to school. I can remember going through this myself in seventh grade, the first year of junior high school. Several elementary schools had merged and I had the misfortune of being the only one in my home economics class from Jefferson School. I didn't know anyone in the class. To make matters worse, we sat at tables instead of desks and worked in teams. No one wanted to work with me, so the teacher assigned me to her team. Naturally, everyone hated the teacher. That I was the one stuck with her made me even more of an outcast. On the days that I had home ec, it made perfect sense to me not to go to school. I would refuse to get out of bed or, once out, I would develop an awful stomachache. I can remember days when my father pulled the covers off me, once when he even put my sweater on over my pajamas, insisting he would send me to school dressed like that. One day I left the house, walked about a third of the way to school, and plopped down on a curb, fully intending to spend the day there. My father happened to come along—a sixth sense, perhaps, had taken him on a different route to the train—and he drove me to school. I cried and cried, refusing to leave the car. Finally I was able to verbalize what was happening. He went into school with me, talked to a guidance counselor, and within a day my schedule had been changed.

Not every child has such a clear-cut event that makes her want to stay home. For many, it's a series of stresses that create a cumulative anxiety. Each one may be small and manageable—there's a new bus driver who doesn't control the wild kids, the teacher is out for the week, her best friend has been ignoring her—but as one problem piles on top of another and she realizes they are beyond her control, a child takes control of the one thing within her power: "I won't go to school and you can't make me!" That gives her instant relief, even if it gives you a migraine.

On the other hand, maybe it doesn't give you a migraine. Maybe you like the company of having her home for the day, just the two of you. Maybe you're happy to have an excuse not to go to work. That may be pleasant for you both, but the ultimate message your child gets is that it's good she didn't want to go to school: "Mom needs me at home." In other words, she convinces herself that she's staying home because you need her to. This does not mean you and your child shouldn't have a cozy day at home together if you think you need it. Even children deserve mental health days once in a while. I know one mother who does this routinely for her three children once or twice a year if she thinks one is on the verge of exhaustion or extreme stress. But here's what makes this okay: She initiates it. She's not giving in to an I-don't-wanna-go refrain, and she only does it once or twice a year. Another mother I know tells her children at the beginning of every school year that they can each have one mental health day a year as long as it's not the day of a test. In four years, none has ever requested it. Her theory is that just the knowledge that it's available is a source of comfort for them.

Starting a new year

Just as it often surprises parents when a child who has always liked school suddenly doesn't like it, many parents are similarly stumped when a child who has always had no difficulty with transitions suddenly has trouble starting a new school year. We expect kindergartners and maybe even first-graders to be anxious, but not fourth-graders. Yet why not? No matter how many times a child has done it before, there are still issues to face: Will the teacher be nice? Will my friends still like me? Will I be able to do the work? While parents shouldn't assume that the entry into any grade is necessarily going to be difficult, they also shouldn't assume it will be flawless. There are four transitions in particular that stand out as troublesome for children:

Kindergarten. The summer before kindergarten can be a mini hell for parents as a child vacillates between wanting and not wanting to be more grown up. But let's not forget that some of what can make this the summer from hell has more to do with you than with your child. Marjorie Kostelnik, an early-childhood educator at Michigan State University, is only half kidding when she says, "It's parents, not children, who need to sit around in a circle and talk about beginnings and endings." Even parents whose kindergartner is a second- or third-born child are not immune to emotional blips over this transition. If you're having them, let your child know. Otherwise, he'll pick up on your sadness and think you think he can't cope with kindergarten. Keep the conversation age appropriate: "I'm proud you're grown up enough to go to kindergarten, and I know you'll do a good job. I really enjoy you as a big kid, but sometimes when I see how grown up you are it makes me want to remember what you were like when you were a baby. That's called being sentimental, and being sentimental sometimes even makes me want to cry." If your sadness is more than you can manage, find someone to talk to about it. A friend who's lived through it herself can be very helpful.

For most children, the subject of kindergarten will come up now and then over the summer. Rarely is it a constant worry; if it is, call the school system and find out who is available over the summer for you to share your concern with. Anxiety that seems to come out of nowhere can often be attributed to a passing comment made by an older child in the neighborhood. To a temperamentally anxious 5-year-old, a 7-year-old speaks with the voice of experience. Comments like "Mrs. Mahoney is really tough," or "If you don't behave, you get sent to the principal," can be scary. Whenever possible, put your spin on this: "I've never heard of kindergartners being sent to the principal. I wonder if Jaimie is talking about older kids. Let's ask him." Although you don't want kindergarten to be the focus of the summer, you also don't want to leave the topic untouched until just before school starts. That's asking for trouble. If the subject hasn't come up at all by August, find some way to drop it into conversation.

Perhaps the parent who has the hardest time with all this is not the parent going through it for the first or last time, but the one who has been through it before and figures it won't be a big deal. Because he hasn't prepared himself to be sad, this parent doesn't face up to whatever mixed feelings he might have. By the way, the use of *he* is not random here. Fathers are more prone to this than mothers; they don't expect any emotion around it and therefore don't prepare themselves for it.

Some parents are more worried than sad: Will her special needs be attended to? Will she make friends? Will the school be welcoming? Logistics often are what stresses parents most about this transition: Will the carpooling work? Will the childcare work? The best solution is to get arrangements in place as early as you can and to do the best you can to make sure they are suitable to your schedule and your child's temperament. Ultimately, the more you can show your child that you are confident and settled, that you feel good about the school and the choices you've made about kindergarten as well as about your child's ability to be there, the happier your child will be.

Even though all children entering kindergarten had an orientation last spring, that was a long time ago in the life of a 5-year-old. Visit the playground in the week before school starts, even if you visited a few times during the summer. If your child seems particularly anxious, visit the teacher as she's setting up the classroom; call ahead to see if you need an appointment. Rather than just remind him about his visit last spring, make a story out of the visit so he can place himself in the classroom again: "Remember the day we went? It was raining really hard and because we forgot the umbrella, we got so wet we needed to go to the bathroom and wipe our faces with paper towels? But the class was so cheerful, it felt like the sun was shining inside. . . ."

For most children, the single biggest worry is about having to go to the bathroom. What if I have to go really badly? What if I have an accident? What if I forget where the bathroom is? Another big worry may be about you: How will we say goodbye? Where will you pick me up? What will you be doing while I'm in school? Since few children will verbalize these concerns, walk through the day for them, providing as much detail as you can about the bathroom, goodbye and pickup procedures: "We'll walk to the bus with Tim and his mom, I'll kiss you goodbye. . . ." If she says she'll miss you, tell her you'll be thinking about her and all the fun she's having. If she says she's scared, validate her fear: "Lots of people are nervous the first time they do something, even me. I remember when I went to kindergarten . . ." Or: "This is the first time I'm taking my child to kindergarten, so I'm a little nervous too." Draw a simple map to help remind her where the bathroom is.

Help your prospective kindergartner to be more independent over the summer by making sure he picks up after himself and can do simple dressing tasks such as zipping and snapping. Having him routinely perform a household chore will make him feel more capable and confident.

At the end of the day, help her process her experience through play, perhaps reenacting the parting with stuffed animals or puppets, by playing school, or having her dictate a story to you. If an issue surfaces, one puppet pushes another, for instance, don't stop the play to find out what that was about, and don't feel you need to personalize it to your child. Just keep going, perhaps having the teacher puppet say, "What can we do next time so there's no pushing in line?"

First grade. While parents tend to be more anxious at the start of kindergarten, kids are more nervous at the start of first grade. The child entering first grade is cognitively aware enough to begin to compare herself to classmates: "I can't read yet and Sasha can." "What if I can't do what the teacher asks?" Remind your child offhandedly of the many things she can do, from writing the names of family members to cutting on the line. Acknowledge concerns, don't dismiss them: "I can tell you're worried about how nice the teacher will be. I would wonder about that too, if I were starting first grade. I remember meeting her at the assembly last year and she told me she was looking forward to being your teacher. She seemed friendly to me." Help him feel a sense of control by doing something concrete, perhaps playing in the "big" playground, or writing on lined paper.

Changing schools. A child of any age who is switching schools for any reason needs a lot of parental support. The child who will have the hardest time is the one whose parent is traumatized or preoccupied by the move and unavailable to the child; for instance, a parent who is recently separated and not coping well. Many parents arrange a family move over the summer so a child has time to get used to the new location. It's not unusual for a child to seem to adjust to the new house and new neighborhood and then to be a wreck in the days before school starts. Most likely, he's pushed away the thought of school all summer long. Now that it's getting closer, he's angry: "I hate you! You made us move! I don't have any friends at school!" Not all children will actually say things like that, but it's what they are feeling and the anger is more likely to come out in behavior, often by picking fights with you about things that have nothing to do with school. Educators increasingly say that summer moves are not the best way to go, that moving during the school year provides instant structure for a child and reduces anxiety because she is immediately able to be in the school and to make friends.

Get the issue on the table by asking open-ended questions that don't necessarily need an answer but will get your child thinking: "Most kids who move are nervous about starting a new school." "I remember when my family moved, I was really angry at my father for changing jobs." If he responds, stay away from comforting platitudes, such as "Oh, honey, I know you'll be fine," and validate his feelings instead: "I'd feel the same way. It's tough to start at a new school." At the very least, this should help a child to move his thinking a little bit forward instead of staying stuck on the why-did-we-have-to-move part. You can also try to help him by reminding him about a previous successful transition; by brainstorming things he can do to ease the transition; by role-playing; and by finding out what the school does to help new students. Ask the principal to assign a buddy to your child if she doesn't offer to do so.

Definitely go with your child the first day of school, even if he's going into fifth grade and protests, even if he's successfully handled transitions of this magnitude on his own before. Don't be fooled by nonchalance or insistence that he'll be fine. Just because a child is older doesn't mean he isn't scared or doesn't want your support. However, do grant him his dignity. Tell him you're going in because it's your job to meet the new teacher. If he has friends to go to school with and he insists he can go without you, you don't have to go in along with him but rather at about the same time, so you arrive slightly before or after. The flip side of the coin is a child who wants you to accompany him to school every day for the first week, or even for the first two weeks, and you feel that's inappropriate. Try to back off a little bit more each day, first walking him to the entrance of the building, then to the sidewalk, and so on. You aren't babying him by doing that, and just because he needs that support doesn't mean he's becoming too dependent.

Middle school. In Boston, the transition to middle school is considered so significant that the school system offers a voluntary five-week summer course to help students make the jump. Whether middle school begins in fifth, sixth, or seventh grade, this can be a traumatic transition for parent and child. No one knows it better than the kids themselves. "Going into middle school is the hardest of all the schools, even high school and college," one 11-year-old told me.

While academics may be what's on your mind, that's the last thing on your child's. As he stares at the start of school, he's worrying: What if I can't remember my locker combination? How safe are the bathrooms? What headings do I put on my papers? Do I need a different heading for each subject? Do eighth-graders really shut sixth-graders in their lockers? Middle school administrators and teachers caution that if we don't deal with these concrete fears, the academics are irrelevant; kids become so stressed out by the social and emotional issues that they can't even pay attention to the learning. Here, then, are some of the issues most likely to be on your child's mind, with some suggestions about how to be helpful:

- **The locker.** Informal surveys of students around the country conducted by the National Council of Middle Schools identified locked lockers as kids' single biggest issue. The fantasy they tend to have is of standing in front of the locker and being unable to open it while dozens of kids they barely know stand by laughing at them. Students typically report being so nervous, they forget their combination, or being too flustered to remember they have to go by the middle number once before stopping on it. Practice at home with a combination lock, write the combination on the inside of his hand or on a note he puts in his pocket.

- **The Bathroom.** Notice the capital *B*. There are some kids who don't go to the bathroom at school the entire sixth-grade year because they've heard so many horror stories about what goes on there. Unfortunately, many of them are true, so don't pooh-pooh whatever your child tells you. Instead, call the school to find out what the bathroom policy is. Can children go in pairs, if only the first week? Then you can calm the fear: "Did you know there's a buddy system?" In some schools, there are separate bathrooms for the sixth-graders.

- **Housekeeping.** How papers need to be headed, what equipment they need, who they turn papers in to—these are issues that consume enormous mental energy. Help your child pick out a new binder for the first day, complete with paper, pencils, eraser, and a calculator. There's nothing worse than having to raise your hand that first day to ask for a pencil and to see all those kids watching you.

- **"Teenagers."** To many middle school kids, all the older kids look big, mean, and threatening. Even though your child may already know that sixth-graders are separated from the older grades, a reminder can't hurt. Tell your child that stories about new kids in junior or senior high school getting locked in the lockers were circulating even when you were in school. Listen sympathetically if he tells you stories he's heard about drugs, smoking, sex, and violence. While the stories may (or may not—check it out) be just stories, the fears are real. Just being able to talk to you about them can be helpful. But also engage in brainstorming to come up with some concrete suggestions that will make him feel safer: prearranging with a friend to ride the bus or to walk from one class to the next.

- **Body changes.** It comes as a shock to many beginning middle-schoolers to see such a range of body shapes at school. Early developers may feel self-conscious, late developers feel inadequate or think something is wrong. Reassure your child that bodies change at different times. Whenever it happens, it's normal.

So much for your child's anxieties. What about yours? Because our kids are bigger and older and demanding increased independence, and because the middle school is typically less warm and fuzzy than the elementary school, there's a tendency for parents to see this as a time to back off. It's true middle schools may not seek our involvement as much as elementary schools do, but this is not the time to back off, literally or figuratively. Indeed, what may ease the transition for both of you is to learn more about the school. Specifically: Is this a true middle school, with a middle school philosophy, or is it a junior high in disguise? With the trend these days toward middle school and away from junior high, the distinction is important. Junior highs typically don't cater to the developmental needs of 10- to 12-year-olds and middle schools do, at least theoretically. The more you know about middle school philosophy and about how the school functions, the better you'll be able to help your child make the transition. Here's what you want to know:

- **Is there a "house" program?** A true middle school moves kids from class to class as a group and keeps that group together from year to year. This is often called clustering or teams or a "house." Researchers say children feel more secure and thus perform better in this kind of configuration.

- **Are there advisories?** A term unique to the middle school philosophy, advisories are glorified homerooms. Ideally, this teacher has the group for a minimum of three hours a week to discuss personal-growth issues, current events, and nonacademic subjects. This is a good teacher for a parent to touch base with at the beginning of the year. Sixth-graders in middle schools without advisories are twice as likely to be expelled as sixth-graders who remain in an elementary school structure, and researchers are convinced it's because kids lack a supportive personal relationship with any one teacher. This pseudo-homeroom teacher can make a difference, at least in the beginning.

- **Is there team teaching?** If so, these teachers generally meet as a group several times a week to discuss each child. Plugging into this structure early is a good idea.

Kindergarten and first grade

Okay, so you and your child have made it through the start of school. Don't get too comfortable. Every school year brings its own set of stresses, but researchers agree that kindergarten and first grade are by far the most stressful years in the first ten years of childhood. This tends to surprise parents. I once mentioned this to a friend whose son was entering kindergarten, and she listened politely but clearly didn't believe me. Several months later, she called. Her son, who had been acting up for days, had just announced that he no longer wanted to go to kindergarten. "It's too hard," he told her. "I have to write my first and last name on every paper."

The stress that a child feels comes from many places, including his own internal pressure. Some of it also comes from such unlikely sources as the checkout clerk at the grocery store who says, "Aren't you in kindergarten now? You're too big to whine about gum!" Comments like these are innocent enough and certainly there's not much we can or should do about them. But they are not lost on our children, who see that the world expects different things from them now that they are in kindergarten. These comments affect us, too, whether we want them to or not. We tend to think that because our 5- and 6-year-olds are more grown up and more capable, they don't need as much support from us. Research shows the opposite is true; kindergartners are more emotionally needy than at any time so far in their lives and more needy than they will be until they hit preteen. So if she suddenly wants to know your whereabouts at all times, take it in stride. She's just expressing her neediness in a time of stress. Go through your schedule with her. In fact, anticipate and try to alleviate her anxiety: If you're going to be late picking her up at a playmate's, call ahead.

Children vacillate between being grown up and regressing because they don't know for sure what being grown up is all about. They wonder, "If I'm big, do the same rules apply? Will you still take care of me?" Both regressive and precocious behaviors are their way of testing things out. On the day she acts feisty, she's subconsciously trying to see if that's what being big is all about. In trying on her new role, you may be astounded at how bossy she is to younger siblings or how sassy she is to you. It's her way of telling the world "I'm one of the big kids now," and of testing: "Will you still take care of me? Will you still be the same mom/dad?" The very next day, however, she can't dress herself. Her regression is an expression of her ambivalence: "If I act like a baby, maybe I won't have to go to kindergarten." Literally tell your child, "You know, Mommy and Daddy will still take care of you, even though you are grown up enough to go to kindergarten." That will reassure her and help keep regressive behavior to a minimum.

> *Tell a worried child, "No kindergarten teacher will ask you to do something you can't do. If she does, just know that that was a mistake."*

Whether your child exhibits newfound big-kidness or regression, the message you want to convey is that, yes, the same rules still apply. As tedious as it can be, you may need to go back over this again and again, reiterating limits and following through with consequences. On occasion, you might also use these behaviors as an entree into a conversation about kindergarten: "I've been thinking about kindergarten, what about you?" Few children will answer yes, simply because they can't identify their feelings. Don't push the point. You have helped him just by making the topic talkable.

This obviously is not just the result of the grocery clerks making passing comments. Our kids are getting even more powerful messages from within themselves, the result of internal developmental change. A 5-year-old may organize herself in a new way, taking on new tasks at her own initiative, or doing an old task with more sophistication. She will think of herself differently or have her own high-minded expectations that surprise you. How many times have you heard about kindergartners who come home from the first day of school disappointed they didn't learn how to read?

The expectation of learning how to read, whether self-imposed or introduced by parents or teachers, is a good example of bad stress. In his books *The Hurried Child* and *Miseducation: Preschoolers at Risk*, Tufts University professor and psychologist David Elkind made famous the theory that expecting too much too soon has negative effects on our children. It's a point worth repeating here so that parents of kindergartners and first-graders can make the distinction between the kind of stress that may spur a child on and the kind that can put him at risk. What helps a child is the stress of a challenge that is within his reach; what hurts is the challenge that overwhelms. The best kindergarten classroom, that is, the one with positive stress, is developmentally appropriate. It allows each child to practice skills that are within his range of ability without feeling compared to peers or judged and pressured by adults. Some 5- and 6-year-olds, especially boys, have difficulty with small motor skills and struggle to hold a pencil and/or form letters. If they come to feel inadequate, either because they look around the room and see (to their mind) no one else struggling, or because of comments from a teacher—"Oh, for heaven's sake, you can do this"—they can be on their way to not wanting to go to school or to academic risk, even at this young age. At a time when they should be excited about learning, they become frustrated, possibly blaming themselves: "I must be dumb because I can't write my letters and everybody else can. I can't learn." This is so common that professionals have a name for it, "pencil anxiety." Luckily, there's a simple antidote, something all parents of first-graders should do routinely, whether you see signs of pencil anxiety or not. Assign a family task that gives them pencil practice—copying over items for the grocery list, making name cards for a family dinner, writing a list of Saturday errands. All kids this age, but especially those with older siblings, love feeling they are grown up. Meanwhile, it won't take them long to become more competent in their pencil skills. Children who have this fear but don't get this competency typically tune out, becoming inattentive or bored. They get labeled as troublemakers because they aren't paying attention, or as unmotivated and slow learners. What started as pencil anxiety in first grade may be labeled as underachievement in fifth.

While one child struggles with small motor skills, others in the same classroom are forming letters and may be ready for words or even sentences. In a developmental setting, there is room for each child to proceed at his or her own pace without others feeling inadequate. This is the kind of classroom you want for your beginning learner, and you shouldn't hesitate to ask a principal or prospective teacher, "Is this a developmental kindergarten?" If not, why isn't it? If it's not and you can afford to, investigate private kindergartens. It's that important.

Extracurricular activities are generally not a good idea for kindergartners, especially if it's a new activity. Five-year-olds have enough to deal with just going to school each day. If you're a working parent and your child can't literally go home after school, what's the closest equivalent? If she was in day care, that probably feels like home to her. Does your center have a half-day program? Can your family day-care provider pick her up? Afterschool programs with classrooms specifically for kindergartners are also an option.

That your kindergartner or first-grader is feeling undue stress is generally easy to spot. Your child may be alternately more feisty, whiny, or resistant than normal; he may be temporarily unable or unwilling to do tasks that came easily to him a few months ago; he may revert to bed-wetting or have troubled sleep, or complain about head- or tummyaches. Here are three ways to help him through this:

- **Promote competence whenever you can.** Let her choose a task she can do well, putting plates on the table for dinner, for instance, and encourage her to do it routinely. Praise her when she does something well, especially something new.

- **Lavish undivided attention.** Children blossom from our time alone with them and from feeling that they are important enough for us to give them that time. We should be doing this with our children no matter what their age, but when they are 5 and 6, it's particularly important to set aside time each week for an activity they can look forward to. It doesn't matter whether it's something you do outside the home, like bowling on Saturday mornings or breakfast at the local diner, or something you set aside time for at home like playing a board game or reading, as long as it is just the two of you. If it is an activity at home, make that time inviolate. Nothing makes a child feel better than when you let the machine get the phone or when you tell a caller, "I can't talk now, this is my time alone with Matthew."

- **Show an interest in school activities.** When you're a classroom volunteer or doing some school-related activity with your child, you are sending a powerful message: This place is important, this learning is important. That will make him value school more and make him feel more capable.

At the same time all this is happening, the typical kindergartner is struggling to figure out where she fits into this new world that's unfolding before her. She's likely engaging in countless comparisons: "I'm smarter, I'm stronger. Am I bigger?" "Who's older?" "Who's taller?" After a while, of course, all a parent wants to say is "Who cares?" But our kids are trying to get at something important: Who am I in this world? Am I a little one who gets protected? Am I a big one? What is my relationship to bigger kids, to smaller ones? Answer these questions truthfully and matter-of-factly. Provide opportunities to create; that gives them something to control, a source of pride.

Psychologist Howard Gardner, a professor of education at Harvard University and author of *The Unschooled Mind*, offers an insight into the typical 5-year-old that is not necessarily comforting. He says the mind of the 5-year-old is making so many strides at such a rapid pace that it's as if there are two minds in one body. One is creative and imaginative, often bubbly and innocently bumbling, and it sees the world in delightful ways that we, as adults, can't. The other is rigid, simplistic, and stubborn. Played out against the school backdrop, the dichotomy can leave parents alternately awestruck, puzzled, bemused, and confused. When it comes to living with this creature on a daily basis, Gardner says, "This can be the best and worst of times." Consider the 5-year-old who is fascinated by the piano and says over and over that he wants to play. So you sign him up for lessons. Very quickly, though, he's uninterested and you end up in battles that always begin "But you said you wanted to play. . . ." As parents, we are putting our adult construct onto that child's statement. He said he wanted to *play*. To us, that meant taking lessons. To him, it meant sitting down at the piano and producing the sounds of an accomplished pianist.

In these first two years of school, if we are to succeed as parents, we must first be willing to accept these discrepancies as a normal part of development. Then we need to set a goal for ourselves not only to minimize the stress the classroom and society place on our kids, but also to maximize our availability to our kids. The one thing that can make the biggest difference between whether these two years are stressful in a good way or stressful in a bad way is a child's knowledge that he can depend on you. In the years ahead, the trust that comes from that will form the foundation for future success.

School-age children and sleep

Whether your child is 6 or 12 when he has a school-related problem, here's a good first question to ask: Is he getting enough sleep? As parents, we tend to overlook sleep as a source of trouble, but researchers link it to poor school performance, low self-esteem, moodiness, and a decreased ability to handle stress. Two scenarios typically surface:

- The sleep-deprived child begins to have problems. Never thinking to look at sleep as the irritant, parents look everywhere else instead, creating more problems in the process by making issues out of non-issues.

- Parents realize their child needs more sleep but feel helpless to change poor sleeping habits. Instead, the bedtime ritual becomes such a struggle that the struggle takes on a life of its own and, P.S., the sleep problem never gets fixed.

Ironically, it is not all that difficult to help a school-age child get more sleep, certainly not as difficult as it was to help him when he was an infant! The starting point is to figure out about how much sleep a child his age normally needs. Pediatrician Richard Ferber, the nation's preeminent sleep researcher and director of the Center for Pediatric Sleep Disorders at Children's Hospital in Boston, says 8- to 11-year-olds need nine and a half to ten hours a night, while children 11 and older need about nine hours. There are three reasons why kids tend not to get the sleep they need:

Nightmares, night terrors, and sleepwalking. Nightmares are the most common source of sleep deprivation for school-age children, affecting almost every child for a period of time almost every year. About 10 to 20 percent of 6- to 10-year-olds also experience night terrors and/or sleepwalking. (Some younger children do too.)

Nightmares sometimes come in clumps, sometimes for reasons you can identify—a scary movie, a sad or traumatic event in his life—but just as often not for any particular reason. Your child is usually wide-awake and often demanding: Don't leave me! Pediatrician Ferber is well known for his answer to this: "Do whatever you have to do to take the fear away," whether it means searching closets and drawers for a monster or not leaving her alone. Avoid being dismissive or angry: "You've had a bad dream, go back to sleep"; "You're too old for this!" It will only make matters worse; on top of being afraid to fall asleep because she's afraid she'll wake up with a bad dream, now she's also afraid of your angry reaction. Be willing to stay in her room until she falls back to sleep (my husband and I have been known to lie down in our son's bed thinking we'll only stay a few minutes, only to awaken hours later with a limb that's fallen asleep from being in a cramped position) or have her come sleep in your room, preferably on a mat or sleeping bag on the floor. Keeping her in her own room is the better solution, however; otherwise she may make a habit of not wanting to sleep in her own room anymore, and then you've got another problem on your hands. Whichever way you handle it, the goal is for her to see that you are available to her, that she doesn't have to deal with the fears alone. That usually takes a few nights, but then you can begin to negotiate to get to the point where the nightmare isn't so disruptive: "Is it enough to know I'll come to you? I'll stay a few minutes, and then I'll just be in the next room and I'll check up on you?" Try negotiating case by case. On a night when he's really frightened, you may need to sleep in his room, but on a night where his fear is minimal, you may be able just to tuck him back into bed.

Night terrors are very different and very distinctive. They tend to happen in the first third of the night. A child wakes up screaming, crying, or otherwise agitated, but when you go to him, he doesn't seem to wake up; pediatricians caution not to try to: no wet cloths on the face. Instead, hold him close. If he's thrashing too much for that, talk calmly and softly. Stay with him until he settles down, usually ten to thirty minutes. If it's any comfort, this is scarier to you than it is to your child; there's no known lasting or harmful effect. In fact, he probably won't remember anything in the morning and there's no reason to remind him about it, although there's also no reason not to unless you think it will worry him.

Children who sleepwalk generally have something in mind that gets them out of bed, but their execution is lacking: they end up in the closet instead of the bathroom. The behavior is not purposeful or mischievous, so don't punish your child. It's generally better not to wake her but, rather, to redirect her back to bed. Once you've discovered a child sleepwalking, though, take some safety precautions, such as putting a gate at the stairs.

The creeping sleeping time. If your family is anything like mine, it's hard to be consistent about bedtime. Between parents' work schedules, evening meetings, kids' extracurricular activities, homework, instrument practice, and household chores, not to mention a little family fun time, it's easy for a nine o'clock bedtime to slip to nine-thirty. The problem is, as the bedtime creeps later and later, a child's body clock gets reset to the point where he can't fall asleep at the earlier time. Researchers call this "sleep phase delay" and it means that the child who whines he can't fall asleep isn't being manipulative.

Sooner or later, when parents decide they want their evening back, not only do they have a battle on their hands because their child really can't fall asleep, but they also have a whole new set of problems. Have you ever lain in bed at night in the dark, sometimes for an hour or two? Exactly. Your imagination runs amok. Whatever it is you start to think about gets blown out of proportion. Kids, however, don't realize it's out of proportion, so real anxieties and fears can develop. The way to dig you and your child out of this is to match bedtime to the time when your child is able to fall asleep. That eliminates both the lying in the dark and worrying and the struggle. The trick is to make sure he's still getting up in the morning at the same time every day—don't let him sleep in, not even on weekends!—and expose him to as much sunlight as possible during the day. The goal is to get the body clock reset so that he can eventually go back to sleep at a more normal hour. Insisting that he wake up early on Saturday and Sunday won't win you any popularity contests and could cause a secondary battle over wake-up time, but if you explain what it is you're trying to accomplish, hopefully he'll buy in. The good news is that this process usually only takes a few weeks before he'll be tired enough to get to sleep earlier and thus get his body back to the normal schedule, which includes sleeping in on weekend mornings. In the meantime, maybe you can plan some early Saturday and Sunday morning activities, like going out for pancakes, just the two of you, or going for a brisk early morning walk together.

> *A child who has nightmares as well as irrational fears during the day may benefit from a professional evaluation.*

Many children have a terrible time with sleep at the beginning of middle school because they have to get up so much earlier than they are used to; in some towns, it's not unusual to have a school bus pick up at seven-fifteen, which seems downright cruel for 10- or 11-year-olds. No wonder kids fall asleep in class! The solution often requires a superhuman family-wide effort that involves rescheduling everyone so that dinner is earlier and homework is finished in the afternoon so a child can get to bed early, sometimes by seven-thirty or eight p.m. This can be hard if younger siblings have a later bedtime, but at some point your child will be so tired that he won't mind. It's also easier if he knows it's happening in his best friend's family too. This truly is the kind of issue that takes advance preparation and coordination, but it can make a big difference in how a child feels physically as well as emotionally. Kids who are sleep deprived don't function well, can't concentrate on their work, and definitely are mood-challenged. I know of one family where everyone was so supportive of their sixth-grader's plight, they all went to bed at eight for a few nights in a show of sympathy.

Battling the bully

When Marilyn first learned her 9-year-old son was being taunted on the way home from school by a boy two years older, she wanted to thrash the brat. "I hated him," she says. In the next millisecond she wondered, "What is my kid doing to provoke him?" At the same time, she wanted to hug her son tightly and promise no one would ever hurt him again. Wisely, she didn't act as impulsively as she felt.

As much as we would like to, we can't always protect our children from the meanness of others. Children get picked on by other children for reasons as complicated and wide-ranging as the children themselves, and even if you can pinpoint the cause—he wears glasses, she's overweight—it doesn't mean you'll be able to do something about it. The good news is that whether your child is the bully or the bullied, there's been a sea change in professionals' approach to helping these children. Instead of dealing with them individually, surreptitiously, or under a cloak of shame, researchers and teachers now realize that if even one child is being bullied in a classroom, it's not just that child who is affected; bullying interferes with everyone's ability to learn. "A kid who's being taunted at recess—'Hey, fatso, you can't play!'—can't exactly walk into the classroom and put that behind him. His concentration is shot," says Carmen Wilson, health coordinator for three schools on Martha's Vineyard. "And what about the kids who watched it happen? They aren't exactly feeling safe, either. Either they're feeling badly because they didn't intervene, or they're worried: 'Am I next?' "

Jeffrey was not different in any obvious way. He had friends, did well in school, was liked by teachers and peers, and was on two sports teams. It shocked his parents to learn he was being picked on. "One kid was following him home, calling him names, grabbing his books, pushing him down," says Marilyn, his mother. "It was agonizing for us."

Because it wasn't happening on school property, Marilyn and

her husband, like many parents, operated on their own at first, and they made the mistake many of us make. Instead of beginning in a neutral, nonjudgmental, and supportive way ("Let's think about this together. Do you remember what was happening right before this happened?"), Marilyn's first question put Jeffrey on the defensive. She asked, "What are you doing to make him do these things to you?" While the typical school-age child doesn't have the maturity or objectivity to acknowledge that he might have a role in this, he usually does have enough sense of self to be embarrassed or ashamed that it's happening. Marilyn's question showed no sensitivity to his sense of self-esteem, an error she realized instantly when Jeffrey responded angrily: "I didn't do anything and even if I did, I would never tell you! You always take the other person's side against me!"

> *Don't assume your child is blameless,*
> *whether he's accused of being a bully or*
> *he tells you he's been bullied.*

Before you respond to your school-age child, it's helpful to remember that by the time she's willing to admit to you that she's being teased, it's likely that it's been going on for some time. If a preschooler's playmate grabs her toys or won't share or teases her, she's so egocentric that she can't help but tell you about it as soon as it happens: "Jody is mean to me!" School-age children will be more likely to stew on their own, absorbing the blows, literal or figurative, and suffering some amount of damage to self-esteem. While a preschooler typically feels angry if she's been victimized, a school-age child is more likely to feel helpless. A response like Marilyn's only adds to his distress, says developmental psychologist Myrna Shure, a professor at Allegheny University of the Health Sciences in Philadelphia and author of *Raising a Thinking Child*. In other words, "Let's wait and see what happens" is not a good response. Usually by the time you hear about a problem, it's happened more than once and may well be spiraling out of control: What starts with one child picking on another can quickly become sanctioned by an entire social group. As soon as you hear about something, even if it doesn't involve your child, let the teacher know.

Marilyn felt awful about her tactical error, but no matter what she said to Jeffrey, he couldn't be placated. Two days later, when she happened to bump into one of his former teachers, she told the story. The teacher urged her to go to Jeffrey's current teacher and to the principal, because the problem involved a child in another grade. Fearing that her son would be mortified, Marilyn procrastinated. Meanwhile, because she worked out of her home, she was able to rearrange her schedule so she could pick Jeffrey up at school on days he normally walked home, thinking that would show that she did care and was willing to help him. Her rescue of Jeffrey eliminated the problem temporarily but didn't get to the heart of the matter and certainly didn't give him any coping skills. A week later, when the older boy picked on him again at recess, Jeffrey started to cry. At home that night, he told his parents he couldn't go to school anymore, and Marilyn told him what his former second-grade teacher had said.

"Do you want me to go to the school and talk to the principal and your teacher?" she asked.

To her surprise, he said, "Mom, I'll take any help I can get. Otherwise, I might get killed." She went in the next morning. The principal called Jeffrey in to their meeting and assured him that the school would help to keep him safe and would also do whatever it could so that this kind of thing wasn't happening to anyone else, either.

This incident took place in 1990, and the principal was slightly ahead of her time in recognizing the need for a community response to bullying. Today many schools across the nation have a more formal and proactive system for dealing with bullying. At the Chilmark School on Martha's Vineyard, health coordinator Wilson is one of many educators nationwide using "Bully Proof," a six-week curriculum for fourth- and fifth-graders developed by the Wellesley College Center for Research on Women Project on Teasing, Bullying and Sexual Harassment. (There's also a curriculum for younger grades, "Quit It! A Teacher's Guide on Teasing and Bullying for Use with Students," in grades K–3.) It's the kind of thing most parents wouldn't think to ask about until they have a problem on their hands, but it's definitely worth lobbying to have something like it in their child's school. In addition to helping children, a curriculum like "Bully Proof" sends an important and hopefully comforting message to parents: While it's critical, for you to be working with your child at home to bolster self-esteem and unravel whatever it is that has led bully or victim to this precipice, you cannot, should not, and need not be working alone. What attack plans like this are proving is that the school and the teachers need to be involved in an active, constructive way. If a child is being picked on, the classroom is failing as a community, and no matter how much work you do with your child at home, if he is walking into an unchanged, uncaring, and unfair environment at school every day, your efforts will be for naught.

When Wilson asks her students, "Why do people bully?" the answers are surprisingly sophisticated: "Maybe he's being bullied at home." "Maybe he doesn't know how awful it feels to be on the other side." "Maybe no one ever taught him other things to do." "It makes him feel powerful." It's developmentally difficult for school-age children to take another person's point of view, but sooner or later, children in Wilson's classes begin to say, "Wait a second, I did that once! I bullied my little sister."

Researcher Nan Stein, co-author of *Bullyproof*, says one of the goals of the curriculum is for the children to construct a new norm for behavior that revolves around courage. "I put it to kids this way," she says: " 'What would be the courageous thing to do when someone is being teased? What can you do to make a difference to reduce bullying in your school?' " One of the perhaps surprising results is that not only does everyone begin to see the bully in a new light, but the bully sees himself differently too. By the time the group gets around to strategies, Stein says children are ready to intervene on behalf of a victim or to help a bully redirect his anger. In one school where name-calling had been a problem, third-graders agreed to divulge to each other the name they most hated to be called. "That was pretty risky behavior because you're providing material that could be used against you," says Stein. But the class had established a sense of trust, and even the child who was most responsible for name-calling stopped doing it. The victim of one such incident wrote "Now that people know how I felt when they called me 'shrimp' or 'shorty,' and other mean things, they stopped."

Researchers say the only child who is immunized against being bullied is the boy who is an excellent athlete. Most other children are teased or victimized sometime during their elementary years. Indeed, studies show that at any given time in any grade school, 5 percent of the children are being victimized. Those who don't get the support they need are not only at risk for being unhappy now but also at risk later in life for depression, juvenile delinquency, substance abuse, and/or a lifelong attitude of helplessness.

The best way to help a child who is being teased is to help him figure out what, if anything, he's doing that provokes this response.

Psychologist Robert Cairns, who has studied children's social groups for more than thirty years, says it's easy to profile the child who is vulnerable to being victimized: "He's physically clumsy, or he's a poor loser. He's a know-it-all, bossy and obnoxious. Be alert for ways in which your child might not be fun to play with—she doesn't know how to jump rope and all her friends do, she can throw a ball but not catch it. Can you teach her? Can someone else? The characteristic that makes his peers dislike him could even be something you, as parents, admire: he's smart."

It's a rare parent who can look objectively at her own child and figure this out. What you need are specifics of the situation, details that you want to be careful to obtain not by grilling your child but by putting together disparate pieces of information. Here are the kinds of questions you need to be able to answer: Is he being victimized by only one other child, a recognized bully, for instance, or is it coming from a friend who has targeted a soft spot? Where did it happen? When did it happen? Was it a one-time incident, or has it happened more than once? (One-time incidents are less serious. It's the ongoing stuff that is so problematic.) Perhaps your child is an easy target, someone who won't stand up for himself and is intimidated, has a quirky trait, like sticking his tongue out when he concentrates. Luckily, there is something likable enough about most children that enables their playmates to overlook the negative: The withdrawn child is great on the basketball court, the child who dresses differently from his peers has a greatly admired sense of humor. It's the child who can't compensate at all or who is oblivious to what's going on around him who is most likely to be taunted or teased. He may not realize he talks too loudly, for instance. Sometimes a victim admires the bully and wants to be his friend but does something strategically wrong, like being too bossy. This child typically doesn't even realize he's been rejected and blames everyone else for his problem.

Since the last thing you want to do is add to your child's pain as Marilyn inadvertently did, approach and tone are critical. While specifics are nice, the older your child is, the less likely you are to get them, so don't make yourself crazy trying to. Instead, go directly to the next step: solutions. Whether your child is in preschool or fifth grade, the goal is to help her take control through brainstorming and problem-solving. Start by asking, "What do you think you can do or say if this happens again?" Often in the course of answering this question, your child will unknowingly give you the details you need. Psychologist Shure's favorite example is of a boy who said he had no idea why he was being picked on and couldn't remember what was happening just before he got teased, but when his mother asked what he could do so it wouldn't happen again, he said, "I could stop staring at him during math."

The pitfall to avoid is feeding your child answers. That creates a dependency and a rescue mentality. Instead, get your child to frame time. "They have the language to talk about it, they have the sense we are all in this together. We're turning the problem on its head," Wilson says with a touch of pride in her voice.

Jeffrey's problem got worse before it got better. Although he felt safer in school, teachers reported that at recess or lunch, he would unwittingly provoke his teaser into taunting him, usually just by positioning himself literally in the kid's path. He surely didn't intend it to come across as a what-are-you-gonna-do? taunt, but that was the way it was perceived. The school eventually suggested his parents seek professional help for him, which enabled him to take stock and ownership of how his behavior affected others. Jeffrey, who is now in college, remembers clearly that year of his life, but what he remembers most is that the turning point came after his father told him, "It doesn't have to be this way, but only you have the power to change it."

Should your child ever fight back? Except where size or age differences make it dangerous or where family values make it abhorrent, many researchers say fighting back in self-defense can be a good idea, even if it means your child will get beaten up. (Don't worry, they say, young kids can't do all that much damage to each other!) Personally, however, I subscribe to the theory that there are ways for a child to stand up for himself without exchanging physical blows. Just saying, "Hey, why did you do that?" or walking with his head held high may be enough to challenge a bully, and it can work wonders to change a child's perception not only among peers but also for himself.

Overcoming test anxiety

As destructive as bullying can be on the social side of the ledger, that's how destructive test anxiety can be on the academic side. Unfortunately, test anxiety often doesn't get identified until after damage has been done because parents don't expect to find it in young children.

the problem. This may take some coaxing: "The problem is, h[ow]
you get this kid to stop picking on you. Any ideas?" Talking i[n]
third person is easier for some kids: "If this were happenin[g]
someone else, what advice would you give them?" In the begin[ning]
your child may have nothing to say. It's okay to let her think abo[ut]
for a few hours or a day before you come back to it: "Any ide[as?]
Shure says this process is critical because a child is more likely to [buy]
into a solution when it's her idea. "It has to come from her innar[ds,]
Shure says. If it comes from yours, she'll find half a dozen reasons [to]
shoot it down.

In the process of doing this, hopefully your child will be thin[k]
ing not only about his actions and their cause and effect but al[so]
about his feelings. Ask him: "How did it feel, when this happened?[]
"How did you feel afterward?" Also hopefully, a child will come u[p]
with more than one idea for what to do next time. If he doesn't
reinforce the process he went through for coming up with the one
idea, rather than the idea itself: "I'm proud of you for thinking this
through. You're good at analyzing problems when you set your mind
to it." A child who doesn't place any value on the thinking process is
less likely to try again and more likely to give up if the first idea
doesn't work.

Having a repertoire of responses means he'll be likely to do or
say something unexpected the next time an incident occurs. That
alone can improve his stature in the eyes of his peers and might even
make a bully an ally. Shure tells parents and children not to be
discouraged if the first attempt doesn't work; indeed, there may be
many failures before a success.

Ownership of one's behavior is at the crux of what's going on in
Wilson's Vineyard classrooms. "We see the behavior of bullies
changing," she says. "We see bullies finding other strategies [for
expressing themselves] and we see victims feeling less isolated, less
victimized." She says it's not unusual for a whole group of kids to
come in after recess and talk about something that happened, how it
made them feel, what was bad about it, and what they could do next

For Julie, a first-grader, every Thursday night was a nightmare because Friday was spelling test day. Even though the words were ones Julie could spell correctly for her parents at night—mat, cat, sat, moon, soon—no amount of drilling could convince her that she'd be able to spell the words correctly Friday morning at nine-fifteen. She would insist on being drilled on the words over and over, even though she got them right each time, until her parents' frustration would put an end to it. "You'll be fine," they would tell her, only to be proven wrong the next day. Every week, she would get four or five of the ten words wrong. Sometimes she would leave lines blank. Her teacher knew she knew how to spell the words, and her parents did too. At the second conference they had on the subject, the teacher suggested that she was just nervous because it was a "test." Her parents agreed. After all, she had two older sisters who moaned and groaned about tests, and she was probably just mimicking them. She would grow out of it. Not to worry.

They were only partly right.

For 10 to 20 percent of children in fourth through twelfth grades (researchers haven't measured this for younger children), test anxiety is not about preparation or even intelligence. Instead, say researchers, it is about how a child is wired as an individual and about a physiological function that crowds out the ability to retrieve the information the brain has stored. In a test-taking society such as ours, where tests open doors to everything from schools and colleges to jobs, children who routinely panic on tests can be in trouble, not to mention how debilitated they can be from the panic itself. Even as a first-grader, Julie knew that something was wrong. All she had to do was look around the classroom and see that while everyone else was calmly writing the words the teacher dictated, she alone sat frozen, unable to answer.

Educator Patricia Lawrence of Wheelock College, a consultant to Boston public elementary schools on children's emotional response to testing, explains that it is emotions that often get in a child's way, literally and figuratively. The problem, she says, is physiological. The short-term working memory, which contains the material studied last night, is stored in the prefrontal lobe of the brain, the same place that controls emotions. "A child who is prone to a high level of anxiety sits down at a test, sees two questions he can't answer, and panics. That emotional response is so powerful that it overrides and intrudes on the ability to use the working memory," she says.

This can happen to children as young as 7 or 8, although it's more common beginning in fourth grade. It can happen because a child studies the wrong material or the right material the wrong way. Julie, for instance, knew how to spell the words as long as she was doing it aloud. With a blank piece of lined paper in front of her, she couldn't function. Many children are fine until they come to a question that causes them to hesitate. They decide they are ill-prepared—"I don't know this! I can't do it! I'm doomed!"—and work themselves into such a tizzy that they can't function. Other children may know the material and feel prepared, but with the test in front of them, they can think only about consequences of failure: "What will my dad say if . . . ?" "If I do badly, I won't stay in my spelling group!" For this child, the what-if worry steals her concentration so she can't focus on the test.

> *Standardized assessment tests are scary because they are timed. Provide practice through timed games—"How many math problems can you do in a minute?"—and timed writing.*

This is an awful feeling for a child; she feels temporarily out of control. An obvious problem is that the panic can be a self-fulfilling prophecy. If she associates this bad feeling with taking a test, she begins to think, "I'm a poor test taker," and then gets so anxious that she is. As young as she was, that's exactly what was happening to

Julie. As the paper was being handed out each Friday morning, she would say to herself, "What if I can't do it again, just like last week?" In effect, she talked herself into not being able to do it.

For many children, especially those who don't become anxious about tests until middle school or later, the anxiety may be because they are placing too much value on a test. Studies show that this can happen to fifth- and sixth-graders who know the standardized tests they are taking will help determine their acceptance at independent schools. Although it feels comforting to tell a child, "It's not a big deal, don't worry," it's more helpful to validate a test's significance rather than dismiss it: "You're right, this test is one of the things admissions looks at. But what's the worst thing that will happen if you don't do well? They also have your portfolio to look at, and your recommendations, and your personal interview."

More commonly, third- through seventh-graders don't take tests as seriously as parents or teachers think they should. This may be developmental: Third-graders can't see the significance of tests because they don't yet cognitively understand the relationship between the present and the future. Tests will have more meaning and be less threatening to them if you can give them a context: "Tests help teachers see if they are doing a good job of teaching what you need to learn. It's a tool for teachers." Sixth- or seventh-graders who seem cavalier about tests are probably more tuned in to their social life than to anything else, so that when they finally do focus, it's not until the night before and then they panic. What helps a child of this age most is some organizational tools: for instance, a personal calendar that has such entries as "Two days till Spanish test." Of course, getting him to look at the calendar may be another story.

Not surprisingly, children are better able to keep tests in perspective when we do. Statements to avoid: "Is that the best you can do?" "Your sister got 100's when she was in fourth grade." Instead, set reasonable goals: "You did better this week! Good for you. Your studying really paid off."

In many ways, standardized assessment tests are in a category of their own. Not only are students judged by them, but so are teachers, schools, and entire districts. Unfortunately, that pressure often gets passed on to students. Public school principal Mary Nash of the Mary Lyons School in Brighton, Massachusetts, says she works hard to minimize the impact of standardized tests, even though they are a fact of life. At her school, where one-third of students have special needs, Nash urges teachers to keep anxiety down through games in which pupils learn to look for "trick" questions, and by presenting material in multiple formats, so they can add horizontally as well as vertically, in words as well as numbers. Knowing there are many ways to approach a problem is one of the best antidotes for test anxiety. A child who can say to himself, "Maybe this question is upside down," may be able to keep himself from panicking.

> *When a child does badly because he didn't study, use supportive rather than punitive consequences. Not "You're grounded," but "Next test, we'll figure out how to schedule your weekend around study time."*

Most children do talk to themselves during a test, according to educational psychologist Harry O'Neil, a professor at the University of Southern California, whose area of research is test anxiety. What they're saying, however, is usually negative and self-defeating: "'I wish I'd studied harder. I don't know this.'" O'Neil tells parents to have a litany of positive things a child can say to himself; for instance, "Okay, you studied for this, there must be something on here you know, keep looking." Lawrence likes self-talk, too, because the child who stays calm enables her brain to get into gear to retrieve information. In other words, she pushes the emotion aside.

One problem parents and teachers are up against is that a child may not realize what happens to her during a test. Not all children are as self-aware as Julie. In fact, it was Julie who diagnosed her own problem. One day she told her mother, "When I take a spelling test, my brain is like that old typewriter Grandpa has."

"How's that?" asked her mother.

"If you hit too many letters at once, they get stuck together and you can't type any letters until you pull them apart. I think my brain must be like that. The letters in my brain get stuck together and I can't spell the words because there's no way to pull them apart."

Her parents and teacher had already realized that there was a discrepancy between her classwork or homework and her test scores. But it took Julie's 7-year-old insight to get them to figure out that she actually froze during a test. One little-used technique that can help you figure out what's happening for your child is to ask him to draw a picture of himself taking a test. When Stephanie Sartain was a doctoral student at Boston College, she asked 322 first- through seventh-graders at schools in Los Angeles, Chicago and Atlanta to do just that. For the students who don't take tests in stride, the self-portraits were very helpful. One seventh-grade girl's thought bubble says, "What am I going to do? Start guessing," while a boy shows himself preoccupied with thoughts of lunch while he's trying to solve an equation. One fourth-grader's drawing shows how threatening the situation was for him. He drew himself at a desk with a grim expression on his face, huge sweat beads on his cheeks, and giant, menacing pencils floating in the air next to him.

Once Julie's mother knew what was happening to her, there were several concrete things she could do to help her. The simplest was to test her on her spelling words by having her write them down, just like in the real test, on the same kind of lined paper. She and her husband also talked to their older daughters who then talked to Julie and explained that some of their complaining and worry about tests wasn't because they were *really* worried but because when kids get older, "You aren't cool unless you think tests are a pain in the butt. Actually," said her oldest sister, a freshman in high school, "I really like tests because I like a challenge. But I would never tell my friends that!"

Extracurricular activities: too many too soon, too bad

Considering that it's not unusual to find that some 10-year-olds carry Week-at-a-Glance calendars in their backpacks and that children these days can sign up for everything from computer skills to Mandarin Chinese, it's no wonder that parents (and children) get overwhelmed. The when, what, and at what cost, financial and otherwise, of extracurricular activities is no simple matter. Here's a good rule of thumb: not too young, not too many, your child's choice, not yours.

Walk into almost any preschool and you'll find parents who are enrolling their kids in all kinds of weekly lessons: gymnastics, ballet, karate, violin. They do it out of the best intentions, of course, but it's misguided nonetheless. Tufts University's David Elkind tells parents not to start extracurricular activities until kids are at least 5 or 6, preferably 7, and even then no more than three activities a week. By 10, some children can handle more than that, but kids who can juggle that much, *and* do their homework, *and* have time for play, time for chores, time to take a shower, time just to *be*, and get to bed on time, well, we all know something has to give. At Elkind's advice, you can almost hear the collective moan from parents across the country: "How can I possibly limit my 9-year-old to three activities when he's involved in three sports alone?" "If my preschooler isn't doing preschool soccer and violin, won't he be at a disadvantage in kindergarten?"

Not long ago, as I visited an elementary school, I waited in the hall while a third-grade teacher finished a conversation with one of her students, who had lingered at dismissal.

"School is the best thing ever invented," the girl told her.

Clearly pleased, the teacher asked what it was she liked so much.

"If it wasn't for school," she said, "I'd never see my friends."

Then she ticked off her activities: gymnastics, soccer, ballet, violin, cello, Hebrew school and Sunday school.

The teacher tried not to show her astonishment. "Do you like doing so many things?" she asked.

"Not really," she said. "But that's the way my family is."

After she left, the teacher said the girl was a good student who lately was getting into trouble because she was so busy socializing. "Now I understand why," she said.

Unfortunately, this child is not an anomaly, and while parents may hope their extracurricular dollars are giving their child an edge, the opposite may be true. Research shows that children who start an activity, especially a sport, at an early age are more likely to drop out in middle or high school than if they had started it at a later age. They burn out. In addition, there are decided disadvantages to a child's having too many activities. They become overprogrammed. Without time to just be a kid and play, they don't know how to relax and veg out. (For more on this, see Chapter 4.) Studies show that imagination and creativity suffer. The one notable exception for young children is music lessons, specifically, lessons where parent and child are involved together. In families where parents play an instrument daily, music is a way of life for the child too. There's no guarantee a child will love the instrument as you do, but research shows there may be long-term benefits to a child who plays an instrument, including heightened intellectual development. There also are emotional benefits: Young children love the togetherness of sharing the activity with you or the family.

Third grade is widely considered the best entry point for activities. Developmentally, a child is interested in other people now, especially in peers and in group involvement, and she's able to understand rules and regulations and even the need to practice. She is also less apt to get worn out physically and better able to relate to the adults who serve as coaches and teachers. At this age, too, a child can see her own progress and take pride in her accomplishments. There also can be other, more subtle, benefits. An 8-year-old who isn't having much success in school but is physically well coordinated might get a boost to his self-esteem from being valued on a soccer team, and that could carry over to his schoolwork. A 7-year-old with no age-mates in her neighborhood may become more socially competent from joining a Brownie troop.

Children benefit most from extracurricular activities when there is variety. All sports or all music doesn't make for a very well-rounded individual. If Elkind were orchestrating a third-grader's activities and money were no object, he'd have one sport or physical activity, a musical or artistic activity, and a third activity that is more general and social, such as scouting. Whatever the choices, it's important a child buys into them because he wants to, not because you want him to. The one exception, again, is something that is an established piece of a family's identity, such as going to Hebrew school.

As you examine options for your child, also examine your motives. Are you giving your child skating lessons because he wants them or because you never learned how to skate and always wished you had? I'm guilty of that. I used my son's skating lessons as an opportunity to take skating lessons myself. He got the basics down, he can hold his own on the ice, but as soon as I stopped my lessons, he had no interest in continuing. He's been on the ice maybe once or twice a year since then. That turned out to be an eye-opener; most of us underestimate how powerful an influence we are when it comes to activities. Many children will stay with something they dislike because they know we want them to. They may even insist they like it because they know it pleases Mom or Dad. Eventually, however, their unhappiness or frustration will come out. Alex started soccer when he was 3. By 9, he was a star player and in several leagues. Most years, his father was the coach; they had lots of together time traveling to away games throughout New England. In his freshman year of high school, Alex was recruited for the varsity team, a rare occurrence. But Alex had discovered drama. Rehearsals and practice were at the same time. He couldn't do both and he wanted out of soccer.

"All those years, all that money, it was tough to hear," admits his dad who, to his credit, didn't pressure his son or show disapproval of his choice. "At least we had all that time together," he says.

But something bothered him, nonetheless. "Did you hate soccer all that time?" he finally asked Alex. "Did you really do it only to make me happy?"

"I liked it when I was little," Alex said. "I never hated it, but there were times when I wished I was doing something else, like baseball. The last two years, it got kinda old."

The father learned his lesson. With his youngest son, he's much more laid back, exposing him to a variety of sports. Indeed, shopping around for a few years may be the strategy in any child's best interests. There's nothing wrong with trying hockey one year, basketball the next, piano one year, clarinet another, so that a child can find the one or two things that really excite him. Unfortunately, the organizations that sponsor many of the sports teams behave as if only their sport counts, and they don't allow kids to have the flexibility that appropriate childhood development demands, often penalizing kids who don't give their sport priority. A child shouldn't be made to feel he's giving up if he wants out or wants to try something else, and as parents and coaches, we shouldn't be so invested in an activity, emotionally or financially, not to allow for that. A child who feels pressured by parents or coaches often feels guilty or just plain unhappy because he doesn't like what he's doing. That can not only turn him off to the activity but also make him resent you.

CHAPTER FOUR

Summertime

. . . .

One summer, my niece and I invented a water game. While we held hands, I took minileaps, propelling us from one side of the pool to the other. She, meanwhile, bounced up and down in the water, up and down, up and down. Eyes squinched tightly shut, she would take a deep breath each time she popped out, but would never pause and never open those eyes, not even when she couldn't resist grinning broadly at my off-key musical accompaniment. I called her the Battery Girl.

She didn't tire of the game and neither did I. We made our way back and forth across the pool so many times that parents sitting on the edge were grinning just from watching us. It was mostly her enjoyment of such a simple pleasure that kept me going, but there was something else too: Every few bounces, the sun would catch the drops of water gathered on her long lashes, creating the world's most beautiful natural glitter.

Pure summer.

Lying in bed that night I called up the scene and others appeared, uninvited. The week before, on a family biking outing, we had been gliding down a hill. On our left was an open field sprinkled with wildflowers, on our right a thick glen of trees shading the bike path. It was quintessential New England, something tourists pay to come see. But it wasn't only the scenery that exhilarated me.

"Doesn't the air feel wonderful on your skin?" I shouted to my son, just ahead of me.

"Yeah," he shouted back. "It does."

Such simple moments, such simple pleasures, and yet, how they stand out! Even now, I can call them up and relive the pleasure they brought. If you're like me, you, too, covet the gifts this season gives your family to be in touch with nature's wonders, to be flexible with time, to decide at the spur of the minute to go for a swim or walk to town for ice cream, to have time together as a family.

But a curious thing often happens.

When you take an hour on a summer afternoon to sit on the porch with a book, a glass of iced tea, and a contented smile, your daughter wants to know what's wrong. "Why aren't you *doing* something?" she asks.

When you finally arrive at your vacation destination, before you've even unpacked, your 7-year-old is already whining. "What can I *do*?"

Our children are, after all, creatures of habit, and the environment we give them nine months of the year is frantic and frenetic. They have activity piled upon activity. They are pushed and pulled every which way, taught to squeeze meaning into every minute. As soon as they are old enough to tell time, children are taught to live by it. All the more reason why adults herald summer's arrival, of course. We're thrilled to give them—and ourselves—the opportunity to slow down.

Well, maybe you and I can switch gears literally overnight, but our kids can't. They may not like all the specifics of the school year routine, but they thrive on the predictability it gives their lives. In the life of a child, the loss of that routine is typically more stressful than we realize. Our kids aren't used to big chunks of time on their hands and they don't like change. What we remember as the ideal summer day from our childhood—no plans! A whole day to create what we want of it—is the ultimate in frustration to them: "I'm *bored*!" As healthy as unstructured time may be for them, our children aren't used to it. Surely they need some time just to be, surely they need the gifts summer can bring, but just as surely they need our help in the transition to them. As surprising as it sounds, our children need our help to enjoy summer.

When school ends

When our kids reach the end of a marker year—the end of pre-school or elementary school—we tend to greet it with great fanfare and celebration. But what about the years in-between? Most of us do very little, perhaps nothing at all, to mark the end of them. We're too busy and excited looking ahead to summer and they are too; they're not interested in looking back.

Well, yes and no. Young children, especially those with older siblings, can exhibit behavior that looks like they're excited, but it may not be genuine, which is to say, it's not internally driven. More likely, they are mimicking what the older kids are saying without any real understanding of what it means. Ask a 4-year-old why it's so good school is ending, and her reason is likely to be "Because my sister said so." Her third-grade sister, meanwhile, may be genuinely happy to have certain aspects of the school year ending, homework, for instance, and she may be able to conceptualize what summer will be like. But even she is likely to have some trepidation.

Children of all ages need to get through the present before they can consider the future. Focused on the here and now, they tend to see that something is ending, not that anything else is beginning. That can be downright scary. For many of them, regardless of age, the end of school is one of the worst and most stressful times of the year, a far more difficult transition than going from the end of summer into the beginning of school. The end of school means they are leaving important things behind: friendships, teachers, a classroom that fits like an old shoe. For a typical child this can generate a range of emotions: excitement, fear, anxiety, loss. The stress can surface in a variety of ways, from mild depression, changes in sleep patterns and regressive behavior, to physical symptoms such as colds, diarrhea, constipation, headaches, or stomachaches. Often, these symptoms are temporary and pass before you connect them to their cause; sometimes, they linger.

Just because children have these feelings does not mean they are able to verbalize them or identify where they come from or what they are all about. It falls to us to do that for them, something we're frequently too preoccupied to do: We're dealing with our own set of feelings. Perhaps we're so excited to get on with what is coming next that we gloss over what's happening now. Perhaps we're too frazzled by the effort to replace school as a source of childcare that we can't focus on anything else. Or perhaps we're too sad. For many of us, the end of the school year is a blinking neon sign: Childhood is slipping away! Not wanting to make our child sad, we keep the feelings to ourselves or we pump up the next step as a way to avoid dealing with them.

> *Ask your young child to draw a picture of what he is leaving behind and what he is looking forward to.*

This is not healthy for us or our children. Letting the year wind down without acknowledging anybody's feelings denies children what they need most: closure. Looking at the year past to see her own growth is what helps a child go forward.

Preschoolers. Three- and 4-year-olds may not cognitively grasp the significance of a change in classroom or school, but they do understand that they are leaving their classroom, the teacher they love, the familiar faces of their classmates, and a routine that is very comfortable. Teachers expect regression among some children either at the tail end of school or after the last day, and so should we. Signs that a child is feeling stress typically include reversion to behaviors they have outgrown like thumb-sucking, bed-wetting, daytime accidents, clinginess, and difficulty falling asleep at night. Just as teachers anticipate that more transitional objects will come out of the cubby and into the classroom, we should expect our 3- and 4-year-olds to want to take stuffed animals or favorite toys to school. Most teachers don't discourage the proliferation of teddy bears and neither should we, although it never hurts to let the teacher know what's happening. If your child confides in you or a teacher, "I'm not going to the 4-year-old room, I'm going to stay here," don't even bother dealing with the facts. Get right to the feeling: "I know you feel that way. It must make you very sad to leave a place where you've had so much fun." Don't feel like you need to add the "but you are going to go," either.

Preschoolers are more likely to get anxious when they've had too much notice that the end of the year is near. Two weeks is just right, even for those who are excited about going to kindergarten or changing classrooms; anything more fuels anxiety, anything less and it's not enough time for processing. Many preschool teachers wisely incorporate end-of-the-year rituals into the last two weeks. Some of the best ones: making yearbooks of favorite activities from the year; trying on the extra set of pants Mom brought in at the beginning of the year and marveling at how small they are now; a picnic with families and teachers; discussions at circle time on growth and change. While the focus should be on the knowledge and skills each child has gained—"Remember how you didn't like to share at the beginning of school, and now you're a person who likes to share?"— there should also be an acknowledgment of the losses: "It would be nice if all of you could go to the same kindergarten, wouldn't it? But you can't, and that makes me sad, too." Once these feelings are out in the open, a child will instantly feel safer. If he keeps talking about it, it doesn't mean that he's unduly upset or upset in an unhealthy or troubling way but, rather, that he feels safe enough to verbalize the thoughts when they come to him.

School-age children. Just because your child is now a veteran of end-of-the-year goodbyes doesn't mean she's any better at coping with them. Indeed, the older a child gets, the tougher the departure can be, especially in upper elementary grades and junior high. Perhaps it's *because* they have been through it before that they are sadder: They know things will change. Next year will be different—she and her best friend may not be in the same class, the teacher may be stricter, the work harder—and next week will be different too: she and her best friend are going to camp, but not the same one. They won't see each other for four weeks! No matter what the summer holds, there are plenty of reasons to feel sad right now.

By far, it's the loss of friendships that affects children most. Even first- and second-graders will miss the friends they don't see every day. Two days before the last day of school, one soon-to-be ex-first-grader sat silently through an entire circle-time discussion about saying goodbye, refusing to talk when it was her turn. The teacher had so many obviously sad children on her hands that she didn't pay attention. An hour later, as they were cleaning up to go home, the child sat at her desk crying. "I'll miss my best friends," she told the teacher, and then rattled off twelve names, all the girls in the class.

Such poignant and sophisticated thoughts don't surprise Marilyn Niehoff, a retired first-grade teacher formerly of Marblehead, Massachusetts. In her years of teaching, she perfected closure to an art. Every year, she would have a day at the beach, an authors' breakfast where children read parents a story they had written, and a picnic at her house where students presented awards of appreciation to people who had helped them during the year. It was only after there had been considerable discussion of the year's accomplishments that Niehoff would turn students' attention to next year. They would visit the second-grade classrooms, locate the bathrooms, and hear from her what second grade would be like. On the last day of school, she always stood at the door to dispense hugs. "Even the boys want them," she commented one year, noting that in the upper grades, teachers are much more matter-of-fact on the last day. "Isn't that a little bit sad?" she asked.

By sixth grade, some of these relationships can be as important and intimate to them as our marriages are to us. Their friends are a source of support and comfort; to know you aren't going to see that friend every day for a bunch of weeks or that you won't be in the same class next year can be very upsetting. If your fifth-, sixth-, or seventh-grader is temperamentally moody and oppositional anyway, it may be hard to distinguish end-of-the-year blues from everyday behavior. Better to assume he's experiencing it than not because if he hasn't thought about the transition, he needs to. Initiate a conversation: "Gee, you've been so busy this year, I bet it will be a little weird at first to slow things down." Parents of 10- to 13-year-olds often report that their kids walk around the house in the first few days of no school looking like they are lost, shadowing them the way a toddler does. Even though a child this age is somewhat able to create opportunities to get together with friends, you may need to plant some ideas and help facilitate plans: "Tuesday would be a good day for me to take you and Todd to the beach, if you want"; "I'm going to the mall Friday, would you like me to give you and some friends a ride?"

There is the potential for other losses for the school-age child, too. Some are obvious—a special support group the school provides for a disabled youngster—but many might not occur to us. For instance:

- **Lunch.** For most school-age children lunch is a pleasurable, social time and the lunch box itself a source of conversation: "Hey, wanna trade your sandwich for my dessert?" "Wow, look what Lydia has today!" Creating a ritual for lunchtime at home can help—eating picnic-style under a tree, perhaps even continuing to pack a lunch (and a surprise or two). On the first day of no school, simply acknowledging the loss can help: "Well, how does it feel to eat in our quiet house instead of that rambunctious lunchroom?"

- **Routine.** Many children are lost without the structure of school. For them, knowing the day's schedule in advance can help ease the transition to summer.

- **The joy of learning.** Some kids are lost without the stimulation of the classroom, even though they couldn't (or wouldn't) admit it. Before school ends, ask teachers and librarians for ideas for projects you can do together and books you can read as you ease into summer.

Special needs children may require the most help making the transition from the school year into summer. Even if they are attending a summer program in the same building or only switching to a summer program they've attended before, there will likely be a change in staff and routine. Photographs of the new teachers can be a great help because that's something concrete to focus on. Also look through snapshots of the year that's ending, as a reminder of the skills he's taking with him, and snapshots of the previous summer, as a reminder of the fun he had.

Closure is just as important for older kids as it is for younger ones, and while teachers may provide it in the lower grades and the school will provide it in the marker years, it's often up to the parent to fill a void for those in-between years. About the week before school ends, begin to talk about what will be different once vacation starts. Don't dwell on it, but be concrete: "The first day of no school, you can sleep as late as you want and we'll have time for French toast for breakfast." As the end gets closer, help a third-grader think of something to give the teacher, not so much a gift but a way to mark his learning: a letter, a story, a picture. Ask a fourth- or fifth-grader which friends she wants to play with in the first week after school and then help her put the plan in motion. Create a ritual in your home, an end-of-school dinner where each child talks about what he learned that year. I know one family where the children present a "show" at the end of the year. Relatives are invited, cupcakes are served, and each child chooses four items for a show-and-tell presentation of what he or she learned. Ask first- and second-graders to draw pictures or write a story about what they are leaving behind and what they are looking forward to. In our family, at the end of each school year we give our son a card of congratulations on the last day of school: "We're proud of you for doing such a good job in third grade!"

It's nice if you can build in some breathing room between the last day of school and the beginning of structured summer activities. Some mothers I know who work outside the home purposefully take a few days of vacation just to hang around the house and help their children make this transition; others who are at home full-time often treat these days as something special. Even if your child only has a weekend between the end of school and the start of a new program, the key to success is to give the days some structure. Otherwise, he will be discombobulated. It's an admirable goal to want to knock back the level of activity, but it helps to think of it as going from high to medium rather than into low all at once. On the other hand, you don't want to keep it at high. Some younger children may like the idea of posting the day's schedule on the fridge: 7:30 to 8:30, TV; 8:30 to 9, breakfast; 9 to noon, play in the yard. . . .

> *Most school-age children love to collect things. Get them started on a summertime collection: seashells, insects, wildflowers.*

As you make this transition, it's helpful for most kids to have something to look forward to each day, but try to keep activities open-ended and noncommercial so there's room for the creativity and spontaneity that summer should hold. A walk in the woods may open their eyes to wildflowers, which may lead to a collection, which could lead to the library, which may lead to a scrapbook. Suddenly, there's a summer-long project.

"I'm bored!"

Sitting with a friend on our porch one summer afternoon, her preschool daughter kept coming to her saying she was bored. "Use some other words to tell me what you mean," my friend said the first time.

"I'm hot," her daughter said.

"Do you want to run through the sprinkler?" the mom asked. The 4-year-old brightened up and ran off. Moments later she was back, dripping water on her mom's lap. "I'm bored," she whined.

"You're bored?" asked my friend, in her best reflective-listening mode. "Do you want to water Barbara's flowers?"

With permission, she was happy again, only to return very quickly doing a telltale little dance. "I'm bored," she said.

"Hmmm," said the mom. "I'm wondering if you need to go to the bathroom."

"Shhh," she whispered loudly. "I didn't want to ask you in front of Barbara." As they walked away hand in hand, I could hear her say to her mom, "Adults are really silly to think that children could be bored that many times."

She was right, of course. There are times when we can take "I'm bored" at face value, when a child really is tired of the activity at hand, and times when it is code for something else entirely. Real boredom—being uninterested in or weary of an activity—typically only occurs in children 12 and older and typically is a sign they need more structure and purpose in their summer. For children younger than that, "I'm bored" can mean many things: I'm sad; I'm not doing anything exciting; I'm lonely. It can even be a cry of panic: I'm lost without my friends/routine! Some children can even feel guilty or worried about the time they suddenly have on their hands. When in doubt, interpret "I'm bored" as a cry of help.

There can be times in the life of a child when a little boredom is a good thing. Jeri Robinson, early childhood program director at the Children's Museum in Boston, urges parents to see boredom not as a problem but as an opportunity. This gets back to all that structure we're constantly putting into their lives the rest of the year. There can be so much that we rob them of the chance to be creative and spontaneous in their play, to daydream and stare at the sky. I don't know about your child, but when mine has time on his hands, he's most likely to plop in front of the TV or computer for a shot of instant gratification. Robinson worries that our children are growing up learning that only a programmed, goal-oriented activity is worth doing. "The joy of childhood is getting lost in our busy world," she says.

> *If your normally good-humored child is cranky and bored, especially at the end of the day, it may be he's more tired than usual. Have you stretched his summertime bedtime too late?*

This does not mean leaving an unhappy child entirely to her own devices; that tends to lead to dangerous activities like playing with matches or picking fights with siblings. Instead, acknowledge a child's feelings and help her try to figure out what's behind them: "All your friends are away, I wonder if you're feeling lonely"; "It's been raining for three days, I'm feeling really antsy. How about you?" Sometimes what a child needs is permission to chill out, literally. Have a conversation with an 8-year-old about the value of unstructured time. Let her know it's okay to sit under a tree just because you're in the mood to be lazy. And then when she does it, don't assume something is wrong.

Getting her to understand what's behind her feelings is one

thing, getting her to do something about it is something else. It can be pretty frustrating trying to get a child to take ownership of her entertainment when all she wants is for you to entertain her. We tend to think of this as an issue only with young children, but an 8- or 10-year-old who feels lost and rudderless can be harder to engage than a preschooler. One mother of four reports that on family vacations it is always the older two children, 13 and 10, who need the most attention, not the 5- and 7-year-olds. "The older ones want something *real* to do, like playing tennis or water skiing," she says. "The little ones can gather a bunch of acorns and sticks and get lost in pretend play."

When a normally self-sufficient school-age child gets bored, you probably need only to remind him of his options—"Remember how you talked all winter long about wanting to organize your baseball cards?"—or set him up in a useful task: "How about if you go through your bookshelves and decide which books you want to give away?" Offering him a way to earn some spending money is almost always guaranteed to get his juices going. With a preschooler, you may need to be more involved, perhaps starting off playing with them and gradually extracting yourself and increasing the time he can play without you. The more experience a young child has playing by herself, the more likely she'll be able to amuse herself when she is older.

The most trying child for any parent is the one who is bored not once or twice a week but once or twice a day. If you think this is a habitual response, especially in an older child, ban the words *I'm bored* from his vocabulary, explaining that he needs to find a better, more exact way to express his feelings. If you think this is an indication of another kind of problem, short attention span, for instance, consult your pediatrician. Otherwise, assume she's either too dependent on you or chaffing under the lack of routine. "Let's make some plans," you might tell her, and sit down together and block out the day. Be willing to spend time planning options for her, but not necessarily implementing or orchestrating them. Robinson suggests having an idea jar stuffed full of activities he can do. Have a separate list or jar of ideas that need your supervision or involvement. When he's bored, let him keep pulling out ideas until something strikes his fancy. When no idea pleases him, and assuming he's not suffering from lack of time spent with you, there's no reason to feel responsible for his having a good time every minute of the day. Remind him that the ideas in the jar are all things he once thought were terrific. Tell him, "You really need to sit quietly and think about what you want to do." (When you load the jar up, make sure they are things you'll want him to do at any given time. If you think you're both miserable now, just wait until he pulls an activity out of the jar and you say, "Ooops, sorry, that's too messy for today.")

Perhaps the single most important aspect of summer for children of all ages is the opportunity to be outdoors creating and directing play that they dream up, without adults breathing down their necks. While children are engaged in play all year long, there's a qualitative difference between what happens in the classroom, playground, afterschool program, or on a team and what happens outdoors, on their own, in the summer. Outside on their own they are engaged in play that is not planned, directed, or supervised by adults: no teachers to organize which children are in which groups, no coach to tell them what position they have to play, no parent to tell them it's time to do homework. It's up to the playmates to negotiate the activity, the rules and the roles, and it is the combination of being outdoors, away from adult scrutiny and free of time constraints, that helps make summer play so powerful and so important developmentally.

Researcher and environmental psychologist Roger Hart goes so far as to say that it is only through this self-directed outdoor play that children learn what true cooperation is. Indeed, if he had his way, every child would have access to something he calls an "Anarchy Zone," either in the backyard or in a public community space. This is a place set aside for children only. The space has some basic raw materials suitable for building some kind of structure that can function as a clubhouse or playhouse: logs, large branches, lumber, or a tarp. (A purist, Hart says a tent isn't good; it's like buying a minibike instead of building a soapbox car, although a tent certainly is something children of all ages enjoy for play.) It's no coincidence that children's literature is chock-full of treehouses and clubhouses; they provide fun and privacy and also long-term benefits. "Children who have this opportunity will be better at cooperation later in life," Hart says. "Independence and creativity in adulthood are related to having had autonomy and free time in childhood, to having been allowed to manipulate their environment." So when your child and his friends are complaining that there's nothing to do and why can't they play computer games all day, think about encouraging them to build a fort. Hart says it can turn a summer around.

Family vacation as oxymoron

If a vacation is supposed to be a respite, a time when you do something new and exciting and relaxing so you can return to your daily life refreshed and energized, a family vacation might well be an oxymoron. If anything, a family vacation has the potential to be awful: You plan and look forward to it for months, but it can disintegrate within hours. Your sleep-deprived toddler won't stop whining, the older siblings won't stop bickering. Your 3-year-old asks ten times in two hours when he can go home to his real house, and your 10-year-old is pouting because she misses her friends. And then it rains.

The best insurance for keeping your vacation from falling apart is to set reasonable expectations. Most important among them: Don't idealize what the vacation will be like or what your kids will be like. Your kids will still be your kids. They will not be different people just because you are on vacation, just because you have anticipated this for months and spent a fortune on it. If they fight at home, they'll fight in line at Disney World. If they don't do well in restaurants at home, eating out three times a day will be worse, not better. No matter what you do, you can't change their personalities or how they deal with change. What you can do is minimize and diffuse the stress.

> *It's no coincidence that vacation frequently is a time when children make developmental leaps. Not only are you more available, you're also more relaxed, more fun, and more focused on them. That makes them feel safer and more secure, which breeds a level of comfort that encourages trying new things.*

Maryann and Gary learned the hard way. When their children were 10 and 7, they decided to re-create a trip that they had taken before they had kids. "We wanted to share it with them," says Maryann. Their children were veteran travelers and, they thought, at just the right ages to appreciate the beauty of a place like the Grand Canyon. They retraced the steps of their earlier vacation, seven destinations in two weeks, which included two flights and up to seven hours at a stretch in a rented car. One night, a flight was delayed, they didn't get to the hotel until one A.M. and they had to get up the next morning at seven because they were on such a tight schedule. They were in some places only overnight and often all four of them were in one cramped room. One night their daughter fell asleep over dinner in a restaurant. One day their son refused to climb back into the car.

So what happened to these veteran vacationers?

Until this trip, Maryann and Gary had always taken their kids on single-destination vacations. So, yes, they'd been away from home, they'd been in airplanes, and they'd been to different countries. But they had never been on a schedule that demanded travel every day and a different location almost every night. "We overplanned and overpacked," says Maryann. "We didn't factor in exhaustion. We didn't factor in hang-out time. You don't plan your dream trip and expect to bring kids along."

Of all the lessons Maryann and Gary learned, perhaps this observation from Maryann is the most important: "If you want your kids to rise to the occasion, you have to give them occasions that are realistic."

But how do you know whether what you are expecting is realistic or not, especially if you've never done it before? All you need to do is answer this question honestly: Will my kids think this is fun? I don't know any 4- or 6-year-olds who are happy spending two days traipsing through an art museum, even if it is the Louvre, and if your 12-year-old is at the mall-and-movie stage, she may find nothing appealing about camping. In some ways, babies are the most mobile of any age because they don't care where they are.

Linda says she and her husband, Scott, camped with their son when he was 8 months old and thought it was a breeze. By 18 months, it was a different story. "We were at the Sagamore Lodge National Historic Site in the Adirondack Mountains, on a guided tour of the Vanderbilt family home, and my son was fascinated by the bugs on the ceiling. Every time the guide spoke, Billy would say, 'Bug, bug.' We had to walk out. But as long as you're prepared to leave, it's not a big deal."

The thing is, kids have expectations for vacation just like we do, and when their needs and expectations aren't met, they feel as frustrated and disappointed as we do. The problem is that their frustration comes out in cranky, whiny, difficult-to-deal-with behavior that only adds to our disappointment and frustration, setting off a vicious circle that can ruin any vacation. When your kids get to the point that they are acting out, stop and wonder if you're pushing them too hard. Are you doing enough things they enjoy doing?

When a preschooler gets excited about the prospect of a vacation, it's not because she has any concept of what it will be like, it's because she sees you getting ready and being excited and that rubs off on her. She may think, "This will be a good time," but what, after all, does that mean to a 4-year-old? The truth is, young children have no idea what to expect. Even if you have been on a vacation before, even if you've been to the same place before, that doesn't necessarily compute for a preschooler, whose memory is exceedingly limited. If you are going to someplace you've been before, about a week before you're going, pull out the photo album and go through it together. Turn the pictures into little stories: "Oh, I remember that afternoon! We decided to go canoeing and the dog followed us all along the edge of the lake and jumped in the water and swam out to us. . . ." She may or may not remember, but the pictures may prompt pleasant associations.

With toddlers and even 3-year-olds, don't start to talk about the vacation with them until about a week beforehand; with children 4 to 6, about two weeks. Show them on a calendar when you'll be going. Most young children are full of anxieties. If they could verbalize them, their questions would revolve around the basics: Where will I sleep? What will I eat? Where will I eat? Who will I play with? Answer these unvoiced questions as specifically as possible. As the time for departure nears, some parents find themselves in a struggle over such things as stuffed animals. Keep in mind that it's hard for preschoolers to leave behind things they love. Give them choices when you can: "We can fit two stuffed animals in the suitcase. You can choose which ones we take." Make a ritual of saying goodbye to what stays home.

School-age children, on the other hand, have lots of ideas about what to expect, especially if they are vacation veterans. While they may not have accurate or clear memories of past trips, their associations will be strong. My son, for instance, especially looks forward to any vacation that includes staying in a hotel because it means the three of us share one room. He loves the coziness.

The best way to deal with these expectations is to talk about them beforehand. Ask questions: What do you think it will be like? What would you like it to be like? What are some of the things you hope we'll do? Make your discussions comparative: "Here's what will be like the trip to Washington, and here's what won't be like it." Involve a school-age child in some aspect of decision making, both beforehand and once you're there, but only if you're willing to abide by his choice: "We could either go whale-watching or deep-sea fishing, but it's too expensive to do both. Which would you prefer?" Look at the route you'll be traveling, talk about where you want to stop along the way, or how you'll occupy your time during an airport layover. If you're going to another country, go to the library for some travel books and peruse them together. Whatever you do, talk about the food. Young children don't expect variations in food and most parents don't think to include this in their advance discussions. If you have a picky eater, and even if you don't, you can be in for some tough times. Some families arrange for hotel rooms with kitchenettes or travel with easily portable food. In all our travels with our son, one of the biggest disappointments he experienced was going to Mexico and finding the food different from the Mexican food he loved in restaurants back home. We had prepared him in advance for this possibility and he was 10 at the time and old enough to take it in stride. Nonetheless, on the first night home, we ate at our favorite Mexican restaurant.

Sometimes the biggest hassle is the traveling. Three suggestions:

- **With infants, toddlers and preschoolers,** if you're traveling by car, think carefully about the time of day you do your driving; a young child who sleeps all day in the car probably won't sleep at night. Plan frequent stops, not just for essentials but for them to play in a grassy area and do something physical to get rid of pent-up energy.

- **With 3- to 7-year-olds,** answer the inevitable "Are we there yet?" by linking your arrival to something they understand: "We'll be there in time for dinner." "The time it will take us to get there is as long as watching two *Barney* videos."

- **For 3- to 10-year-olds and even older,** for plane as well as long car travel, help them pack a backpack with snacks as well as activities. This is especially important for plane travel: Kids are always hungry long before the attendants break out the food. Also pack surprises for your children. They don't have to be expensive, just something they've never seen before.

To the school-age child, vacation is a time when all rules are off and, to some extent at least, that should be true: Bedtimes may be later, junk food may be allowed, privileges will be granted. But life isn't—or at least shouldn't be—a free-for-all. As parents, it's important for us to see how the world is changing from our children's point of view but it's equally important to establish what rules there will still be. Call them Vacation Rules, make it clear they are for vacation only—"When we get back home, the regular rules will apply again"—and set them out as specifically as you can. Since you don't want to make rules you're constantly breaking, you might not want to set a bedtime, for instance, but, rather, to outline parameters around bedtime: "There will be some nights when you'll be staying up later than usual, but once we say it's bedtime, no arguing." "You don't need to make your bed in a hotel but you still need to pick up your clothes and put them away." Because vacation presents situations that don't arise in our daily lives, anticipating the challenges and setting limits around them can be helpful too. You might want to have a family meeting when you first arrive at the hotel/vacation house to set down three or four important rules (not too many, they'll tune you right out): "No one can go to the pool without an adult; the elevator is not a toy, you can't ride up and down, up and down," and so on. To eliminate whining about what your school-age children want you to buy, give them a vacation allowance. Make it enough for them to be able to buy trinkets they'll want, discuss what happens if they spend it all in one place, make it clear whether you will or won't buy anything in addition to this, and then let them spend as they choose. Have them keep a tally of the spending, though, and if the money runs out before the trip ends, talk about how they spent it, but stick to the rules you established. Keep in mind that limits are not only how we keep children safe, but also a way children have of knowing that we care about them. That's as important on vacation as at any other time of the year.

One of the most common reasons why family vacations fall apart is because parents and children are working at cross-purposes. As adults, we're looking for breaks in the routine; for children, the farther they get from their routines, the more they fall apart. The younger the child, the truer this is. If you have children of varying ages, plan activities around the schedule of the youngest. If you're sightseeing, go back to the room in the middle of the day for the 2-year-old to take his nap while the older kids have a quiet activity or swim at the pool. As frustrating as it may be to cut activities short, the more you are able to accommodate your youngest child's needs, the happier everyone will be in the long run. Psychologist Hy Day of York University in Ontario, who has done considerable research on vacation and prevacation anxiety, says parents who end up with crises on their hands on vacation—kids who melt down, act up, and can't be brought back under control—typically have pushed kids to their limit day after day, much as Maryann and Gary did. His advice is that if you want to push your children on Day 2, give them a treat on Day 3: "We know yesterday wasn't so much fun for you, and we really appreciate your patience, so since you put up with what we wanted to do yesterday, you two get to choose today's activity." In general, the more you can allow your children to dictate the agenda for vacation, and the more you plan activities around them, the happier you all will be. When my son was 9 and we were visiting friends in France, my husband and I took him to the Louvre. We spent less than two hours there. Before we went in, we promised that he would be in charge of what we stopped to look at. We headed straight for the *Mona Lisa*, because he had learned about da Vinci in third grade, and then we looked only at the artwork that caught his eye. Was that a sacrifice for two adults who don't exactly get to Paris very often? Well, yes. Was it a fun afternoon free of whining? Also yes.

For all the attention most of us tend to put on the transition to vacation, the transition back home again typically gets ignored. It's not unusual to hear parents say, "My kids were so great the two

weeks we were away and now that we're back home, they're awful!"
Usually, it's for good reason.

> *Children of different ages like to do different
> things. Instead of dragging them to things
> they don't think are fun, split the family
> into two groups, one with each parent, and
> swap groups the next time.*

In my family, the last night of a vacation, my husband and I take
out our calendars and start to process what we are returning to.
Who has which meetings when, what we need from the supermarket, when we can pick up the mail. Before we even get home, we
have begun to shuck our vacation skin. Walking in the door, we're in
high gear, unpacking, throwing clothes in the washer, taking messages off the machine, watering plants and grass. What's a child to
make of all this? You are not the same person you were two days ago.
Period. End of discussion. How this affects your child will vary:

Babies and toddlers. For the youngest of our kids, the biggest
issue upon reentry often is sleep. Kim and Janet recall having a
terrible time with Eric after their first vacation with him, when he
was 12 months. "We let him sleep with us in the king-size bed in the
hotel, something we never do at home because our bed is only a
double. It was fun and it wasn't a problem because the bed was so
big. Even though it was only for two nights, once we got back home,
he didn't want to sleep in his own bed." A word to the wise from
Janet: "Don't change sleeping habits like that, at least not with a
very young child, without realizing the potential consequences."

Toddlers and preschoolers. Your distracted demeanor once
back home and your unavailability is disconcerting: Why *can't* you
play with me? Who *is* this person? What happened to Mommy?
Verbalize their feelings for them: "Boy, it's hard to get back to

normal after vacation, isn't it? It was so nice to have all that time together and now it seems like we're all so busy with our lives."

School-age child. He may not even notice your shift in gears when you first get home. After all, he has friends to reconnect with, TV, toys and computer games to welcome him. But after a period of so much emotional and physical closeness, he may find it hard to be separated when you go back to work or he goes back to school. Once again, advance work can mitigate against this back-to-normal transition difficulty: "You know, it might be hard for us when we get home, because we won't be together as much. But isn't it nice that we have vacations when we can be together all the time?" Not only are you identifying and validating the feelings she may have, but you're also letting her know there will be more vacations like this one. Often when my son is having a wonderful time on vacation, he'll ask repeatedly, "How many more days?" When he was young and would ask that early in the vacation, we thought he was unhappy. It didn't take us long to realize that that wasn't it at all; he was asking because he didn't want it to end.

If the thought of going on vacation with your children sometimes seems more trouble than it's worth, don't beat up on yourself for thinking the thought; it is a lot of work to take children away. Parents who enjoy family vacations also tend to be parents who have worked out ways to make sure some of their own needs get met, too. If you have young children, plan with your spouse to carve out some time when you alternate kid duty so that each of you has some private time for exercise, reading, walking on the beach. Or plan a vacation with another family. As our son has gotten older, my husband and I have come to see the benefits of having built-in friends, especially since there is only one child in our family. We've also done a fair share of travel vacations where it's just the three of us, and when we do, we make sure to choose activities he will like.

One family I know literally stumbled upon a way to get all the benefits of a great vacation without ever leaving home. The year their three young children were 5 and 3 (the 3-year-olds are twins), the kids got the idea that they wanted to go camping; they had seen snapshots of their parents, pre-children, on a camping trip and they wanted to sleep in a tent too. Mom and Dad weren't interested in attempting camping with such young kids, but they carted out the tent and set it up in the backyard for them to play inside, thinking that would be the end of it. But, no, they wanted to sleep in the tent. All of them.

"We said what the heck and, on a whim, we decided to pretend we really were camping. We got out all our equipment and ate outside and spent the day and the evening in the yard," says Monica, the mom. The kids made a rule that they could only go inside to use the bathroom. "We broke that after they fell asleep," says David, grinning. "To get some wine."

Sunday night, as they were packing up, Monica remembers David looking at her and saying, "You know, I feel terrific. I feel like I've been on vacation. Let's do this again."

That was seven years ago. What began as a way to make the kids happy has turned into a family tradition. Now that the children are older, this family also goes away from home for vacations, but it is this backyard trip that they talk about all year long and it is this vacation that consumes hours of planning, even in the deepest winter. "It's been a real interesting process to watch as it's unfolded," says David. "And definitely cost-effective."

Summer's pitfall: parenting in public

You have been in line to get onto the USS *Constitution* for just five minutes when your 4-year-old tugs at your shorts. "When will it be our turn, Mommy?" he asks.

"Soon," you say. "Soon. You have to be patient."

Uh-huh.

Less than a minute passes. "I want it to be our turn now!" he whines.

It is at this moment, of course, that your baby decides to register her complaints, going from a whimper to a full-throated wail in less than 4.3 seconds. In the time it takes to lift her from the stroller, your son has stepped on the toes of the senior citizen in front of him, crawled through her husband's legs, and is perched on the rickety railing that defines the line. You can feel the sweat coursing down your cleavage. You can feel the looks of your fellow line-dwellers boring holes in your back. You know what they are thinking: *What kind of a mother is she?*

Is this parental paranoia? Not this time. Sometimes it is just our imagination that people are watching. But in the summer, when you are parenting in public more often, there really are people watching. And judging.

The question is, is this a reason to change your standards? When your toddler asks for a second Popsicle at home, you say, "The rule in our family is only one Popsicle. You just finished one. You can't have another." You know that as soon as you set the limit and hold to it, one of two things will happen: She'll either be only mildly upset and accept the limit or she'll throw a tantrum. Now let's take the same situation and put it in a public place, say, in line at the aquarium. You don't have a time-out chair and you're worried about what *they* will think. It's human nature, after all, to want people to think well of us, even when they are people we don't know and will never see again. So, fearful of what might happen if you set the limit you would normally enforce, you either become uncharacteristically angry—"Stop whining!"—or you become uncharacteristically compliant: "Okay, here, have another one."

Understandable as they are, these reactions are problematic. You are giving in to *your* feelings, *your* needs, *your* agenda to shift the attention away from your family and onto someone else's. But what about your child? At the very least, you have thoroughly confused him: "Why is Mommy acting so different?" You may even be reinforcing the behavior you're trying to squelch, because she's apt to think: "Mama's not very upset with me. I guess this is a good way to get her attention."

Here's another parenting-in-public situation: At home, if your 4-year-old hides behind you to avoid greeting a visitor, you indulge him, perhaps shrugging your shoulders in bemusement. At a wedding reception, the same behavior embarrasses you. Perhaps you speak sternly, almost threateningly: "I want you to say hello, Timothy." Perhaps you squeeze his shoulder and literally remove him from behind your legs. Patricia Henderson Shimm, director of the Barnard College Center for Toddler Development, says, "This is scary to him. He knows he's done something wrong but he can't figure out what it is; the same behavior at home doesn't get you upset, so that can't be it."

Inconsistency of any kind confuses a child. Even though she's begged and begged for it, when you give in and buy the second Popsicle, her thoughts can be downright scary: "Mommy doesn't love me anymore." In other words, because you aren't setting the limit your child is used to, she thinks you don't care. That thought is even more upsetting than wanting the Popsicle and not being able to have it, so she may be more upset now that she's got what you thought she wanted than she was to begin with, making you more aggravated, causing her to act out even more. Suddenly you're into negative attention so quickly, you don't even know what happened.

Being a successful parent in public means having the courage to do what you know is best for your child, regardless of what *they*, your unadoring public, might think. This requires some advance preparation:

- **Anticipate your child's reactions.** By taking her temperament into consideration, you can sometimes head off a disaster. Does she normally do well in crowds or get overstimulated and whiny? How does she react when her nap is cut short? Is it fun for her to wear unfamiliar "special" clothes or is that a source of annoyance and discomfort? Family therapist Linda Budd of Minneapolis offers an example from personal experience. Her father was getting remarried and the wedding coordinator wanted her to bring the kids to church two hours before the ceremony for photos. "My kids were 3 and 7," says Budd. "I looked at the coordinator and said, 'That won't be an option. We'll be there in plenty of time, but two hours is not going to happen.' My sister-in-law complied. Her kids fell apart before the reception. It was too much and too long for them."

- **Tell your child what to expect.** Children of all ages benefit from knowing there will be long lines, big crowds, or loud noises. The younger the child, the newer the experience, the more specific you need to be. When possible, refer back to a previous experience as a point of comparison: "Remember how unhappy you were at Great-grandma's birthday party because it was all grown-up food and there was nothing for you to eat? Well, this party might be like that, too, so I'm going to pack a special lunch for you so you'll have some favorite things to eat."

- **Establish limits.** With toddlers and preschoolers: "You'll see lots of things you want to buy and eat. You can choose one souvenir and one treat." "The rule in restaurants is to keep bottoms on the chair and to use an inside voice." With a school-age child, set the limits jointly: "Let's make a deal: One souvenir under three dollars, one refreshment, no complaining. What do you say?"

- **Equip yourself.** Take along snacks and drinks, small toys, markers, dolls, books, whatever it takes to engage your child. When my cousin's three children were very young, she would take them to some of the fanciest restaurants in Manhattan, places I wouldn't consider taking a child. After dining out with her and her children a few times, I realized the secret to her success. She would take along enough paraphernalia to last a week; her kids never had the opportunity to get unhappy (well, hardly ever). In the process, they became familiar and comfortable in restaurants.

- **Help your child feel part of the process.** "Can you be the navigator? Here are the directions." "At the museum, it's your job to decide where we go first."

Once you are in public:

- **Anticipate antsiness.** If the line is longer than you expected, ask the person behind you to save your place while you and your child step away to do some jumping jacks or toss a soft ball. In a restaurant, step outside for a break. In other words, put yourself in your child's shoes and don't let things get to the point of no return. In museums or at performances, be prepared to leave at the first sign of antsiness. If you wait until your child is beyond squirmy and miserable, not only will you be miserable, too, but all he'll remember of the experience is how awful he felt at the end; he won't want to do it again. Whenever we travel, I always carry a soft Koosh ball in my purse. It's come in very handy over the years waiting in lines at boarding gates and on layovers.

- **Respond quickly.** At the first sign of inappropriate behavior, remind your child of the rules or your deal. Kneel at her eye level and speak quietly to her. Be sympathetic, label what she's feeling; sometimes validation is enough to help her be able to conform: "You must be so frustrated that this is taking so long. I am too." "I know this is hard for you. Can you try again?" If that doesn't work, then:

- **Be prepared to leave.** When all else fails and misbehavior is escalating, you need to go. This is not easy to do, but if you do it just once—"Waiter, can you take his food and pack it up for us, right now?"—you'll be more likely to get compliance next time. One word of caution: Once you have said you are going to leave, don't give in to pleas of "Daddy, I promise to be good." Young kids may mean to keep a promise, but they often can't help themselves, so if they don't behave, you'll be even angrier. Meanwhile, you'll have issued an empty threat that could undermine your future effectiveness.

- **Compliment good behavior.** Words of praise always go a long way with children, especially when they are trying hard. Let them know you notice: "I'm so proud of how patient you are being."

After any outing, it never hurts to have a casual conversation of assessment, including of your own behavior: "This was a terrific afternoon. Nobody got impatient, not even me! And nobody lost their temper. What did you think?" If there were problems, address them: "What do you think happened that you got so upset?" With an older child, do some problem-solving: "If we want to do something like this again, we need to think about ways to make it work out better. Any ideas?"

Perhaps one of the most upsetting things about being in public is witnessing another parent verbally abusing their child or hitting or spanking them. They could be feeling the same pressure you are, or this could be the way they operate all the time. Either way, you feel helpless and awful. Is there anything you can do? Parent educator Fran Litman, retired director of the Center for Parenting Studies at Wheelock College, has personally struggled with this question for years. In the past, she didn't say anything for fear of infringing on a parent's right to privacy. In recent years, she's become more proactive. "Many parents just don't know what to do and they welcome support," she says. She calls what she does "cautious intervention." She might offer an empathetic look and say, "That looks familiar. Could you use an extra hand?" or "I've been in that situation, my kids used to do that all the time." If the parent throws her a hostile, outa-my-face look, Litman is quick to back off, hoping that by letting a parent know he is not alone, she will have raised his consciousness, even if only for a moment.

Conquering water fears

It's 91 degrees lakeside at Camp Q., a day camp west of Boston, but Brian, 9, and Dante, 12, aren't swimming today. They didn't even bring their trunks. It's seven days into the session and Brian has been swimming once, to take the deep-water test, which he passed. Meanwhile, a third camper, Mike, 8, decides not to swim either, even though he brought his trunks. If these kids aren't sick, what's going on here?

"I only like pools," Brian explains. "The ocean makes me feel sticky and weird and in a lake, you never know what your feet will touch. Rocks and stuff. Once, seaweed in the lake scratched my back. That really scared me. And there's all these little fish. They're tiny but, still, that's pretty weird, you have to admit. And if your eyes are closed, a fish could come really close to you and you wouldn't even know it." As if that isn't enough, Brian has another reason: He misses the best friend he made last week at swimming, a camper who attended for only one week.

Dante went swimming last year for the first time, right here in this lake, at the same camp, with the same swimming instructor. This year, he stayed out of the water the first two days of camp and has gone in only a few times since. "I used to think I would drown," he says, "or that I would choke on the water. I kinda like it again, but I kinda don't, too."

Cold water is what bothers Mike. Cold air, too. Swimming is okay, he says, sometimes even fun, but both temperatures need to be just right, something he admits isn't easy to come by. Besides, he says, "I like to play in the water, not to swim."

If this sounds familiar, you probably know only too well that this stuff can ruin camp, family vacations, and summer in general. All three of these boys, however, are sending a message that often gets overlooked by parents: Not wanting to go in the water may have more to do with some aspect of the water *scene* than with the water itself. What's turning your child off can range from Brian and Mike's discomforts to a dislike of the noise at the pool, the undertow at the ocean, or the lack of privacy in a locker room. The summer after first grade, my son hated his day camp. Every day was a struggle to get him there. Luckily he was able to tell us why: He disliked the chaos of the locker room scene and the noise level at the pool. At his next camp, swimming was optional.

Finding out what the problem is isn't always easy, and sometimes identifying it doesn't necessarily mean you can do anything about it. For instance, despite repeated conversations with Brian about why he didn't want to go in the water, the camp director didn't get to the bottom of the problem. It was only when Brian spoke to me, a reporter he'd never seen before, that it surfaced that swimming had lost its appeal because Brian had lost his best buddy. "That's something I can try to fix," the director said, hoping he could help Brian make another friend. But Mike's problem with the water temperature, well, that's another story.

It would be nice if all of us with water-wary children could find a camp director who is as respectful of a camper's qualms as Bob is. "When I know a child is timid, we work to support him, step by step," he told me. Always tell the counselor and swimming instructor about your child's concerns and ask for their suggestions and help. A step-by-step approach is the best way to help a child overcome trepidation, and it is not unreasonable to expect some accommodations to help a child get over the hump—for instance, for a 7-year-old who doesn't like the locker room to be able to change someplace else. The swimming instructor (or parent) who insists a child go in, who pushes him or dunks him, even playfully, or who puts a you're-a-wimp trip on him, will only make a child more fearful and make himself an adult who can't be trusted.

On the other hand, the water and its trappings shouldn't be avoided altogether. If you're away on vacation and one of your children doesn't want to go in the pool but your other two do, insist he come to the pool *area* with the family. Psychologist Richard Gallagher, a cognitive behavioral therapist, says you only make it worse when you totally give in to the fear, for example, pulling a child out of day camp in the middle of the session. Better to make accommodations, like finding an alternative place to change. If you are in the water with a child who becomes frightened or panicky, that's the worst time to get out. "He'll think that leaving is what made him comfortable, that this is just something to be avoided," Gallagher says. Instead, he advises, "Pick him up and settle him down again while you are in the water. Leave when he is calm" so his lingering memory is not of panic and fear. It's helpful to verbalize for him what happened. For instance: "I bet you thought you were choking and going to drown. You gulped a little bit of water. You were able to cough it out. I'm holding you and, look, you can stand here."

Don't be surprised if your young child loved being in the water last year but won't go near it this year or vice versa. A child's concerns vary with developmental stages; changing cognitive abilities can change her perspective. Parents who do water baby swim programs with infants are often very surprised when the baby who loved the water is a toddler who hates it. The reason is that fear mechanisms don't kick in until about 12 to 14 months of age. Do an infant water program because it's a fun way for you and your baby to do an activity together, not because you expect your child to learn to swim (although some do) or never to be afraid of the water (although some certainly never are).

Two- and 3-year-olds often don't like having their face in the water even to be washed, so why would they like having it in a lake or a pool? One trick with a child this age is to recognize that we inadvertently feed into a fear by catering to it, for instance, letting a child wear goggles in the tub because she hates the water in her eyes. This can translate to a fear of the water at the pool. A good strategy is to start out with the goggles but then to gradually remove them: "How about if you try not having the goggles on for two minutes? I'll set a timer." Or: "Let's take turns sprinkling a tiny bit of water on our face before we put on your goggles. You sprinkle me first."

Getting a fearful toddler beyond the water's edge takes a lot of patience and a gradual approach. The first step is sitting on or by the edge and watching. This can take days, depending on how often you go. One day he may be willing to dip his toes. Don't push beyond that; in fact, if he wants to do more, express surprise: "Gee, I wasn't expecting to do more until another day. But if that's what you want . . ." That way, it's his decision and he'll feel totally in control. Gradually, you may be able to immerse more and more body parts: ankles, knees, and so on, slowly moving up the body and gradually adding parts of the face: chin, mouth, nose, eyes. The whole process could take weeks, maybe even a season, because some children get stuck on a particular part of the body. The key to this is supportive perseverance. Beth, the mother of a 3-year-old and a psychologist whose specialty, ironically, is fears, started in April taking her daughter to an indoor pool once a week. She would stand at the top step with water on her ankles, nothing more. By July, they had made no progress. She decided to make a commitment to be in the pool with her daughter every day for as long as it took for the child to overcome her fears. It took five days of going after work to make the difference. "All of a sudden, on the third day, she stopped crying. On the fourth day, she went in up to her waist and sort of liked it. By the fifth day, I couldn't get her out. It's actually harder for me now," she says, "because she thinks she is more competent than she is."

> *Most camps don't allow flotation devices because they give a child and a parent a false sense of security.*

The step-by-step process that helps a younger child will also help an older one, but it gets complicated by peer pressure and the fear of embarrassment. Dan, a third-grader, was best friends all year long with Nick. They were practically inseparable. When the warm weather hit, though, Dan no longer wanted to play with Nick. Nick would call and Dan wouldn't even want to talk on the phone.

"Did you guys fight about something?" Dan's mom asked.

"Nope."

"Did he do something you didn't like? Did he ignore you? Play with someone else?"

"No, Mom, I don't want to talk about it."

Out of desperation, the mothers decided to have a family pool party at Nick's house. Hearing the news, Dan refused to go. That night, Dan's mother gently initiated a conversation: "I think I figured out why you don't want to play with Nick. It's because he has a pool, isn't it?"

Silence.

"Would you like to try private swimming lessons this year, at the Y? We could go and meet the teachers and see if there was one you liked." Dan refused.

His mother bowed out of the get-together at Nick's family's house, figuring that this wasn't something she could force and remembering, as well, her own fear of the water as a child. (No, this isn't hereditary and, besides, Dan's mother mastered her fear as an adult. But parents can pass on a fear through a hesitant, fearful, or overly protective attitude.)

Two weeks later, Nick invited all the boys in the class to an end-of-school party. The day the invitation arrived, Dan asked his mother, "Do you think we could go to the Y today?" After two lessons, Dan agreed to go to Nick's pool with just his mom. Once he was comfortable with the setting, he agreed to go another time before the party when just Nick and Nick's mother would be there. When Dan got in the water and was clearly tentative, Nick said to him, "I'm a lot better swimmer than you but you're a lot better soccer player than me, so I guess we're even," a comment that Dan's mother says "endeared him to me forever." By the time of the party, you could barely notice that Dan was less comfortable in the pool than the other boys.

Dan was lucky to have a mother with a lot of patience who was able and willing to orchestrate events in his favor. She also didn't get into a power struggle with him. Many children Dan's age dig themselves in deeper simply because we so badly want them to swim. (You can substitute almost any other behavior in this kind of scenario.) Dan's mother was pleased with the way things went, but there was a poignant P.S. to the story. Weeks into the summer, when Dan and Nick were spending hot afternoons at the pool and were once again inseparable, Dan told her he had known all winter long that he would have to stop being best friends with Nick when summer came. "It made me so sad to think he had spent the winter steeling himself to end the friendship," his mother said.

Another problem with older children is that they are cognitively able to imagine all kinds of catastrophes: "The water is dangerous, I could drown." "No one will be there to make sure I'm safe, the instructors don't pay any attention." "There are sharks in the ocean!" "I could step on a sea urchin or get stung by a jellyfish!" There's some truth in these fears, but there also is irrationality and untruth. In fact, it doesn't matter if the fear is totally irrational. To her, it is real and telling her she's being silly doesn't help. What does help this child is to see that some fears come from reality and some from imaginings, that the imagination can create real feelings but not realistic ones. The trick for parents is to let your child know you take him seriously, to validate his fear and to be respectful of it—strategies, by the way, that can be applied to almost any childhood fear. Start by saying, "It's true that if someone goes in deep water alone and doesn't know how to swim, that person could drown." At the same time, offer a solution: "But if you stay in shallow water and you're not alone, and you know to call for help if you need it, and you learn to swim, those are things that will keep you safe." When he counters that he read about someone who drowned, don't dismiss it: "Yes, that happened. We all could drown, but for people who learn how to deal with the water, it becomes less of a possibility. We don't know anything about why or how that person drowned or if he knew how to swim or what. Being safe in the water is a learning experience."

With a 5- to 8-year-old, help her to quantify the fear as a way to see progress: "Last week, you were frightened to your knees. Today, you're only frightened to your bellybutton. So let's stay in bellybutton-deep water today." When she seems comfortable at that depth, suggest that you try it a tiny bit deeper. The same strategy can apply to children like Mike or Brian who don't like some aspect of the water scene. Psychologist Gallagher suggests taking this child to the locker room or the pool when no one else is there and hanging out for a while. The idea is to demystify the situation. "Kids who are afraid need to be gradually introduced to the scene in a way that gives them a sense of control," he says. Like anything else, parental attitudes rub off on our children. If you're afraid of the water and you don't want your child to be, honesty is the best policy: "I've been afraid of the water ever since I was a little child. I wish I wasn't and I'm still trying not to be, but I definitely don't want you to be afraid too." Try to show that you are making some effort, even if it's only putting your toes in. If you get anxious when the kids are in the water, then don't go there with them. On the other hand, it's very important for you to feel comfortable with the safety regulations at camp. Several years ago, the drowning of a 13-year-old girl on a school outing in a Boston-area lake prompted parents to become more safety-conscious than ever. Camp directors wisely invited parents to visit camp during swimming to see safety precautions in action. If you request to do that and the camp doesn't want you to, you don't want your child at that camp.

Brian, Dante, and Mike have some suggestions for parents too. "Tell your child to at least try," says Dante. "I don't like to try, but some days I do anyway," says Mike. Adds Brian, "Some days your child just might not want to get wet. That's okay."

Is your child ready for overnight camp? Are you?

The best insurance for a happy camper is advance preparation. For starters, it should be your child who fuels the discussion to go to overnight camp, not you. Children most easily move away from parents when they do it at their own pace. That's also when they will most benefit from the experiences camp offers. The general consensus is that most children are ready for overnight camp at 8 or 9, but age is less a sign of readiness than maturity and experience. Is she successful when she sleeps away from home, not just at relatives' but also at a friend's? Is she able to take care of herself—brush her teeth without being reminded, willingly take a bath or shower, take responsibility for her clothes?

Having a good fit between child and camp goes a long way toward determining the outcome of an experience, and there is a cottage industry of camp consultants who help match camper and family to camps. When you find the right situation, it can be enough to make a child forget his trepidations: A child who really wants to play basketball all day long may put aside hesitations about leaving home. On the other hand, a 9-year-old who enjoys batting the tennis ball around on the street may be miserable at a tennis camp where five hours of tennis daily is de rigueur and where tennis is what campers and staff talk about at breakfast, lunch, and dinner. Timing is critical, too. A week of basketball may be terrific; two weeks might be overkill. Making an educated and potentially expensive guess about what your child will be able to handle in July is a difficult thing to do in November or December, when many private camps begin to fill up. The best decisions tend to be those based on camp visits the previous season, but the next best thing is to watch videos, talk to directors and other campers, and attend open houses. Don't just do one of these things, though; it's the combination of several of them that will give you and your child a real sense of the camp. Your camper-to-be needs to be able to see herself in the setting and to see what, exactly, she's getting herself into.

If you are considering a special-interest camp, make sure it is the child's interest, not your interest for him, that is pulling you there. Although not all camps have special interests per se, many have specialties. Some may have a fabulous array of activities but pay little attention to social relationships, while others pride themselves on group problem-solving and group dynamics or on competitive athletics. Some base all activities on competition—one cabin versus another, blue team versus red—while others stress cooperation or individual achievement and downplay competitiveness. These are important details to know. If you have an antisocial child, or one who is shy and inhibited, and you put him in a competitively based camp where he's expected to deal alone with his problems around social interactions, teasing, or being left out, you can be setting him up for failure.

> *Discuss with counselors any fears your child raised before camp: "He sleeps with a stuffed animal and he's worried about being teased." "He often goes to the bathroom at night and he's frightened of walking through the woods." Make sure your child has mail the first day he's there; send it before he even leaves home.*

The more nitty-gritty questions your child asks about camp, the more you know she is putting herself in the situation. That should guide you in your decision not only about whether to send but also about where to send. Ruby says it was from her 11-year-old daughter's questions that she was able to choose an appropriate overnight camp.

"When we talked about it, she kept asking questions about sailing and canoeing," she says. "She had had it with crafts from day camp. She wanted a camp with a lot of boating."

Ruby's concerns focused on accident prevention and access to medical facilities and about how child-oriented the staff is. "It was important they be attuned to the kids, really care about them," she says. "I looked for flexibility, too. My daughter was used to making decisions about what she does. Most kids her age, after being regimented all year long in school, need summer as a time to have alternatives and to take responsibility for their choices. She wouldn't do well at a place that's highly regimented."

There are some kids who would never choose to go to camp on their own but might benefit from camp and love it nonetheless. For them, parents need to be the initiators of the discussion. The trick is not to push too hard. Plant the seed casually—"Have you ever thought about going to overnight camp?"—and make the subject part of your child's consciousness. Talk about your own experiences: "I never went, my parents couldn't afford it, and I always wish I had been able to try it, just once." Before you get too deeply entrenched in thinking he should go, examine why you think it's a good idea. Keep in mind that camp is not a way to solve problems that have plagued your child for years: A third-grader who's been a loner since kindergarten isn't going to turn into a social butterfly from two weeks at overnight camp. Ditto for the child who has trouble making friends and relating to peers. On the other hand, a child who doesn't do well in new situations but otherwise is socially adaptable may get over the hump of initially not wanting to go by being very involved in the choice of a camp; feeling in control may predispose him to respond more positively. Some other do's and don'ts:

- Don't send your child as a way to avoid having him at home during a difficult time: a parent's hospitalization, a family move, parental separation. Even though you're trying to spare him, it translates to him that you are getting rid of him or punishing him. Some children will feel guilty at not being around to help you.

- One- and two-week stays are the best introductions for first-time campers. They give a child a feeling of not being locked into something forever. But:

- Don't send her to a two-week session at a camp where the majority of kids stay longer. If she's arriving in the middle of their longer session, friendships will already have been formed; if she's leaving sooner, kids may cool off toward her, considering her a short-timer.

Crunch time often occurs as you begin the preparations to go or just before it's time to leave. Almost every first-time camper, including the child who is good in new situations, experiences some last-minute hesitation. Many often get stuck on very specific issues: What will the bathroom be like? What if I don't like the food? The question for parents is how much attention you should give these concerns. That depends in part on your child's normal reaction to new things. Look to her for clues: If she doesn't want to be involved in the buying of camp gear or doesn't want to help pack the trunk, if she's preoccupied with the idea of sleeping in a strange bed or is uncharacteristically worried about some minute aspect of camp, say, insects, she's more than just mildly anxious. This doesn't mean she shouldn't go; most children really want to go deep down inside. It does mean she needs extra help to feel able to cope. Pepper your conversations about camp with simple and specific reassurances: "Remember, there are peanut butter and jelly sandwiches available at every meal"; "I bought you plenty of insect repellent."

Camp directors report that once in a while, parents may decide at the last minute not to send a child who has been anxious all along. To come to this conclusion, you'd want to see serious signs of anxiety: sleeplessness, listlessness, change in eating, withdrawal or acting out. This is a tough call to make, and if you are facing it, look hard for any glimmers of pleasurable anticipation. If you find even one, it's probably better to proceed.

> *Be especially alert to a normally adaptive child who is homesick or to a veteran camper at a new camp who is homesick. There may be inappropriate activities or behaviors, an inattentive staff, even an unsafe environment.*

Part of the preparation for camp should include a conversation about homesickness. This is a topic most parents avoid, figuring that talking about it gives a child the idea to get homesick. In fact, the opposite is true. If you talk about it openly and matter-of-factly, you normalize his emotions for him and give him a framework in which to put them. You don't honestly think your child is going away from home for the longest amount of time in his life and it hasn't occurred to him that he might get homesick, do you? So get it out on the table: "Some kids get homesick. I did when I went to camp. I just want you to know that if you do, it's very normal. Getting involved in something usually makes it go away within a few days."

A *homesick camper*

As a child, I was one of those ambivalent campers-to-be. Two of my best friends were going to Girl Scout camp for two weeks and I got caught up in the excitement and decided to go. But I vacillated in the time leading up to camp and then, wouldn't you know, the morning I was supposed to leave, I woke up with a fever. From my bedroom window, I watched as Nancy's and Lynn's families drove slowly past my house with their loaded cars. I made it to Camp Hoover on

Tuesday, only two days late but it might as well have been a decade. Group dynamics of 11-year-old girls will never be described as inclusive; to the girls in my tent, I was "the girl who came late." Combine that with my own ambivalence and homesickness set in quickly.

Despite a camp policy not to allow calls home, three days of my crying convinced the director to make an exception. I can remember the relief that washed over me when I heard my parents' voices. I even wanted to talk to my sister. For the remainder of my two weeks, I was allowed to call home every evening before campfire. It was the only thing about the day that I looked forward to. Looking back, I don't know if the calls gave me the boost I needed to stick it out or if they gave me an emotional out from participating more fully. All I know for sure is that camp is not a fond memory and I never tried it again.

A no-phone policy may seem harsh and cruel, but many directors and camp professionals adhere to it, arguing that children need time to work things out themselves. Krystal, now 19, remembers being terribly homesick during her first session at camp. When she wrote home, she would print in big letters, I MISS YOU. During the day, she rarely thought about home but at night she would often cry herself to sleep. According to camp policy, she couldn't talk to her parents until the second week of her month-long stay. She and her mother both remember that first phone call.

> Krystal: "I was crying, but I was trying to be quiet."
> Betty: "She was real quiet on the phone. Her voice sounded funny. I asked her if she had a cold."
> Krystal: "Then I really cried."
> Betty: "I went crazy. I wanted to run up there and be with her. Instead, I told her we'd see her soon, that I was excited about the activities she was involved in, and I reinforced how much I loved her. Then I got off the phone as fast as I could because I didn't want her to hear *me* cry."

As often happens with most children who battle homesickness, Krystal got reinvolved in activities and quickly recovered. Back home, meanwhile, Betty and husband John didn't. They agonized for days, going back and forth. Had they been right to send her to camp? Should they call the director? Should they just go up there? "I didn't sleep well for three nights," remembers Betty. Luckily, the director called them to say everything seemed much better. Krystal, now a counselor at the same camp, says that if she has a homesick camper in her bunk she is very sympathetic because she remembers one particular counselor who came to her bunk every night when she cried and sat with her until she fell asleep. Interestingly, she discourages homesick campers from calling home. She was lucky, she says, because her mother knew the right things to say.

"But what about parents who don't?" she asks. "If parents say, 'Oh, honey, I miss you so much too,' they could make the homesickness worse."

> *Discuss proper camp behavior, not just his own, but also what he should and shouldn't expect from counselors. Appropriate and inappropriate touching should be a matter-of-fact part of the discussion.*

As painful as her homesickness was, Krystal says she learned an important life lesson from it. "I learned that I could manage it myself. It wasn't exactly that I could talk myself out of it but that I could tolerate it and then it would pass." It was a skill that took time for her to acquire, though. Krystal says she liked camp well enough after that first year to want to go back, but she says she gets a little bit homesick at the beginning of every year, even now, and also did at the beginning of her freshman year at college. "I always miss home, but I always have a good time and want to go back," she says.

Hopefully if a director does allow your child to call, he will have called you first so you aren't hearing from your child out of the blue. That's incredibly upsetting. Flustered parents literally don't know what to say. A good director will call you first, explain what's happening, tell you how serious he thinks the problem is, and coach you in how to handle it. If you do get a call out of the blue from your child, be sympathetic, supportive, and firm: "You're really feeling lonely, huh? Got any ideas about how to get yourself through this?" "I really think you can handle this, I have lots of faith in you." As soon as you hang up, call the director. Don't be satisfied with a "Don't worry, ignore it, he'll be fine" answer. What you want to hear is a strategy for how they are trying to engage your child. It's important for the staff, as well as you, to acknowledge the homesickness, not to slough it off. It's not a bad idea, by the way, to have a conversation about homesickness with a director when you are choosing camps. It's one thing to find out in the middle of a crisis that the director's approach to homesickness is tough-it-out, something else entirely to find out that he's also unfeeling and unsympathetic.

Unfortunately, parents can unwittingly trigger homesickness. When you say goodbye to your child, don't let her walk you to the car for one last hug. Say goodbye in her cabin, where she will immediately be engaged by the counselor or cabinmates. When writing to her, tell her how much you love her but don't use the words *miss you*. Many children feel guilty about going to camp. They think they have somehow abandoned the family, particularly if there's a problem at home, or if they are only children and left you home alone. When you say "I miss you," you run the risk of fueling that guilt. Your tears can do the same thing when you say goodbye. In letters, it's not a good idea to give glowing details about what you are doing at home—if she's already feeling lonely, the idea that she's missing out on something special can put her over the edge—although it's also not a good idea to flat-out lie.

Homesickness generally happens in the first three days of camp. The trigger is usually interpersonal: She feels alienated or estranged, singled out or excluded because she doesn't have cool sneakers or doesn't like a particular rap group. But just as often there may not seem to be a specific reason, at least not one she can name. The question we all want to know in the midst of a homesickness crisis is whether to bring her home or not.

The camp director is your guru on this, which is one reason it's so important to meet and feel a rapport with the director beforehand. In a crisis, there can be a lot of phone calls back and forth, perhaps several a day. Be prepared to be emotionally exhausted. What you want to be hearing from the director is how your child is doing during the day. Is she moping all day long, not involved in activities and not engaged with friends? Or is she involved and looking pretty normal most of the time? A child who is tearful at a specific time of day, generally bedtime, but functioning pretty normally otherwise will probably overcome the homesickness in a matter of days. You are not damaging your relationship with her or inflicting unnecessary pain to tell her to stick it out for two or three days. Three days, however, is usually telling. By then, if she still isn't involved in anything, isn't eating, and/or talks about running away, and especially if she isn't responding to the counselors (who should be making great efforts to facilitate her acceptance in the group; expect to talk to them and ask for specifics), you probably should bring her home, even if the director wants her to stick it out. If the director says you should come get her, even if you disagree, go get her; having her stick it out in an environment where she isn't wanted and isn't supported is not healthy.

Once you decide to bring her home, how you handle it is important. She's undoubtedly having all sorts of contradictory emotions. "I hated them! They were mean, I'm glad to get out of here" can be quickly followed in her mind by "There must be something wrong with me, all the other girls were having a good time." She may be feeling guilty—"I wasted all your money!"—and probably is determined never to go to camp again. For starters, make sure she knows you aren't angry with her. Tell her, "Listen, it didn't work out for you. Camp isn't for everybody. I understand how you feel. If you want to try it again sometime, you can and if not, that's okay too." Whatever you do, don't talk about wasted money or how she doesn't appreciate all you do for her. You'll only make her feel awful about herself and that could carry over into other aspects of her life. If you have to adjust the rest of the summer to accommodate her presence, do that without making her feel guilty too: "Let's find a fun family vacation" rather than "Daddy and I were really looking forward to . . ." Involve her in the decision about how she will fill the time she now has for the summer and make sure it's something that she will be able to feel successful at.

For most children, of course, camp is a positive experience that they remember always. Here's how 11-year-old Alex described camp: "Camp is a great place to make new friends. The best thing about camp is that you meet people from different parts of the country. My best friend last year was from Florida. Some of my counselors were from different countries. One was from Scotland. Last summer I went for four weeks but I had such a good time, this summer I'm going for eight. I never got homesick."

Not being able to attend parents' day practically guarantees sadness and homesickness. If you can't go, can some relative go in your stead?

While we're on the subject of homesickness, have you given any thought to being "childsick"? Even for parents who were campers as children and know what a great experience it can be for their child, even for parents who look forward to some time alone together, sending their child off for two, four, or eight weeks of camp can be bittersweet. What adds to the bitter side of the ledger is when parents aren't prepared for the onslaught of their own ambivalent feelings. Liz was one of those mothers:

"Two days after I sent my 10-year-old daughter off to camp, I broke out in hives. One week later I was nauseous to the point of being sick. My doctor said it was too coincidental that Leah left and I got sick." Sure enough, her symptoms resolved themselves on visiting day. But her happy ending has an ironic twist: "I couldn't stop hugging and kissing her. I regretted it two weeks later, though. Leah had an advanced case of head lice and passed it on to me!"

Another mother remembers missing her three children so much that she organized a group of five mothers with similar "childsickness" into a semisupport group. "We met once a week at each other's houses for the weeks the girls were at camp. In the beginning, we talked only about the girls and their letters, and how much we missed them," she says. "After that, it became more of a social group. But we knew we could call each other on the phone and cry if we needed to. Each of us did that at least once."

Meanwhile, back at home: siblings left behind

With any luck, your camper is having a great time. What about your kids at home?

When older children are gone, there's a hole in the family that may wear more on your other children than you think. The night her older sister left for camp, Erica, who is 6, brought all of her sister's Beanie Babies into her bed "so they wouldn't be lonely." This symbolic expression was as close as Erica was able to come to acknowledging her own loneliness. In subsequent days, she became her mother's shadow, almost literally. "She'd want to come with me to do an errand rather than stay home with Daddy," says Jane. "When I was busy doing something, like getting dinner, she'd want to know, 'Why aren't you playing with me, Mommy?' Whenever I sat down, she'd want to be in my lap. It was unbelievable. Very out of character."

To this mother, behavior that was at first sweet and poignant began to seem "almost desperate and definitely annoying. It was as if she couldn't be by herself, even for a minute, and it started to drive me nuts."

To Erica, of course, it was something else. The house was empty, even spooky, without her sister around. Indeed, what their parents didn't know is that Elana, who is five years older than Erica, served as a surrogate parent for her younger sister. It wasn't just a playmate Erica was missing, but also a protector. Erica was at a stage where she didn't like going upstairs by herself; Elana would almost always indulge her and go with her. And it was more than sisterly love that would prompt Erica to quietly color in Elana's room early on summer mornings while Elana slept; Erica simply didn't like to be up and about in the house by herself.

Faced with these behaviors and not understanding the depth of Erica's loss, there were several paths Erica's parents could have taken. One was where they seemed to be headed: annoyance, frustration, eventual anger: "Why are you hanging around me so much? What's wrong with you, you're acting like a baby." Erica, already feeling defenseless and vulnerable, would likely have responded by becoming withdrawn or by acting out; either way, her stress would have increased. Her parents might also have expressed confusion— "You never used to be like this. Is something wrong? Are you sick?" That could have ended up in them carting her off to the pediatrician, which could have brought stress of another kind: Maybe there really is something wrong with me. A third possibility was to assume that the change in behavior was connected to her sister's absence, to gently point this out to her, to indulge some of her behavior, and to give her time to settle into the new routine. This was the appropriate choice and, happily, the one Erica's parents made.

The absence of a sibling is a loss, even though it is a loss by choice, even though it is temporary, even though the sibling may normally be a source of annoyance and tension. With patience and help to adjust to it, most siblings fill the vacuum in ways that bring pleasure and growth. In most homes, it doesn't take long before the siblings left at home discover that they have more access to you, which means more attention from you. When there is only one child left at home, the newly created threesome is often able to do things they wouldn't otherwise do and to interact in new ways. In one family, dinnertime became a longer, infinitely more enjoyable time. Sandra says that when her daughter, Amy, was home, she dominated conversations at dinner and her younger brother would sit quietly by. If he did talk, Amy was quick to put him down, tease him, or dismiss his ideas. Dinner, says this mom, was always an ordeal: "Amy can't stand to sit still for very long, she couldn't wait to get up and get to the telephone or her homework or something, which would make dinner a battleground and make Danny rush through it too, because the rule is she can't leave the table until he's finished too." With Amy gone, Danny suddenly had lots to say and no one to interrupt him, sneer at him, or steal his thunder. His parents discovered that he was a charming conversationalist and very witty. "We found ourselves saying to each other with great joy, 'He's so funny!'" says Sandra. But in the same breath they felt guilty: Why had they not realized this before? What kind of parents were they to have allowed one child to so dominate the environment?

> *Avoid statements that place blame on any child: "This wouldn't happen if your brother were here!" "Why can't you two get along this nicely when your sister's home?"*

The simple truth is that it is impossible for parents to know any child in the same way that you know your first; everything they do is a first for you, too, and that in itself forces you to focus on it in a way you don't need to the next time around. Only if you are truly neglectful are you actually shortchanging later-born siblings. However, the absence of your firstborn provides an excellent opportunity.

Rather than buy into any guilt you may feel, seize instead on the delight. That's what Sandra and Richard did. "We felt lucky to have time alone with Danny and to get to know him in a new way. I'm sure he sensed this because he came out with all kinds of great observations. It was pretty clear that he enjoyed the time with us," says Sandra. Enjoy it yourself, too. Miss your camper but don't feel sad at her absence. Consider it a gift that you don't have to split yourself into pieces. This not only makes you more available; hopefully, it makes you more relaxed, too.

> *If your child finds you crying or sad, acknowledge simply: "I miss Sara. I bet you do, too, sometimes." Then move on. Talk about her as often as it comes up naturally in conversation but avoid constant chatter about her, especially talk that's full of longing: "Oh, your sister would love this. . . ."*

For children like Danny who live in the shadow of an older sibling, especially if they are close in age or feel competitive with each other, this may be a chance to be more independent. They may revel in being able to strut their stuff. They feel more powerful, become more verbal, more self-sufficient, more opinionated, more assertive, and, yes, sometimes more difficult. Some children, on the other hand, become more dependent, especially younger children who are separated by many years from the absent sibling. This is the child who, like Erica, wants to run errands with you, sit in your lap, cuddle and hug whenever possible. Consider these signs that he's happy to have you to himself, not that he's regressing. All year long, most younger siblings put lots of energy into keeping up with the older one just in order to exist. Now he doesn't need to do that. He can be who he is, exactly at the stage of development where he belongs. He doesn't have to act more grown up to get the sibling's attention and he shouldn't have to to get yours.

In a family with more than one child left at home, the change in pecking order can be problematic although also healthy for the kids. "It gives them a different perspective on life. I think that's been good," says Elissa, the mother of five daughters, three of whom were left behind when the oldest two, who are twins, went to camp. What she liked best was watching the evolution of the new relationship these three daughters forged with each other. Interestingly, they did some of it in the twins' bedrooms. At first, the three of them would go into their rooms individually, almost reverentially, just to look around. After a while, they would go in there together to paint their nails, dry their hair, and play. What a wonderful way to get a sister fix!

Your children left at home may also be:

- **Ecstatic.** Cries of "Yippee, she's gone!" tend to aggravate parents. When you think about it, though, why shouldn't she be thrilled to have more attention, more power, and potentially less grief in her life? Instead of responding with hurt and anger, be accepting of your child's thoughts, including the meanest one of all: "I wish she'd never come back." Don't make him feel like a bad person because of them. Instead, hold yourself to descriptive comments made in a nonjudgmental tone: "I can see you're enjoying your time without your sister."

- **Sad and lonely.** Is your toddler or preschooler roaming aimlessly through the house, even going to the front door and announcing, "Here comes Brian"? As frustrating as this might be, it's not behavior to be upset about, even if it happens every day. It's a sign of a strong and healthy attachment, a very young child's way of showing he misses his brother and is hoping for his return. A good response communicates a sympathetic and realistic message: "You're hoping Brian will come home soon, aren't you? You must be missing him a lot. He will come home, but not today." Since young children have little concept of time, engaging them in a discussion about when Brian will return is often not worth doing; however, you could tell him: "Brian isn't coming home today, it will be another day and I promise to tell you which one it will be." Divert your toddler's or preschooler's energy into something constructive by encouraging him to draw a picture to send to his brother.

- **Anxious.** True clingy behavior goes beyond what Erica's mother described and includes not wanting to sleep in her own room, literally hanging on to you, and regressing—sucking her thumb, bed-wetting, or having accidents. This is most common in children under 7 and can be due to fear. The thinking might go something like this: "They must have sent Brian away because he was bad and maybe they'll send me away too." It's worth asking a simple question of this child—"I'm wondering if something is bothering you or worrying you"— but few children will be able to respond to that. Try matter-of-factly making the point that this was something Brian wanted to do: "Did you know that Brian wanted to go to camp? It was his idea. He asked to go and we said yes, and we helped him find the right camp for him. Going to camp is a fun thing older kids like to do. When you're older, it will be your decision to go to camp or to stay home." Clinginess can also be because a child thinks you are sad and need cheering up. If you think that might be what's going on, tell him, "If you think I need cheering up because I miss your brother, that's very thoughtful of you. Sometimes I do miss him but I know he's having a good time and that makes me happy." If your child's clinginess doesn't respond to your probing, and if it seems to be getting more and more regressive, mention it to your pediatrician.

▪ **In denial.** A child who says, "I don't miss her at all," makes us think we have a mean, unfeeling kid on our hands. In fact, the opposite could be true: Some kids' insistence that they don't miss a sibling is a cover-up for sad feelings or for a kind of sour grapes/angry reaction: "She left me, I'll show her!" It can also be a sign that something happened between them before she left. Either way, it's a good idea to ask (although not in direct response to an I-don't-miss-her announcement), "What kinds of thoughts are you having about your sister?" No matter what she says, including "I hate her," accept the information without judgment. Ask, "Are you angry at her? Did something happen between you?" and talk about how it is possible to have good and bad feelings toward a person, to miss them and also be glad they are away.

Whatever changes you observe in your child, comment on them in a descriptive way. When you see the need for some self-esteem repair work the way Danny's parents did, make some gentle comments. They began a conversation by saying, "We've noticed that you're much funnier when your sister is gone." Danny smiled. They continued: "What do you think it will be like when she comes back?" The smile disappeared. "Well, let's talk about it," they said. "How would you like things to be after she comes home?"

When Danny had nothing to say, they tabled the topic. But at dinner the next night, he asked, "When Amy comes home, can we tell her that my sense of humor is much better than it used to be, and she might enjoy some of my jokes?"

Danny's parents did three things right: They brought up the topic in the first place, validated Danny's feelings, and didn't rush to a conclusion. Another strategy is to offer some observations: "You seem happier with your sister gone. I'm wondering if there are some changes we should make after she's home?" If he has no ideas, offer some choices, although not all at once. For instance, "Do you think I spend too much time doing things with her and not enough with

possibilities. Use it before you lose it: "You've been wanting to see this movie. Would you like to invite one of the kids from school to go see it?"

Not all changes, of course, may be ones you like. Your child may have picked up bad language, she may be too cocky, too independent, too full of herself. Give her a day or two of breathing room before you bring her back to reality. Be prepared to hear a lot of "The way we did it at camp . . ." The reply that wants to come out of your mouth—"Well, this isn't camp"—is dismissive and will put your child on the defensive and make him unlikely to want to share with you. You might as well be saying "I don't care about camp!" So bite your tongue and say instead, "Tell me more about that," even "Is there some way we could adapt that idea to work at home?" That not only will nip his anger in the bud but increase the chance that he'll feel more favorable toward home.

As hard as it is for us to accept it, fitting back in can be a real challenge for some children. It's not that it's bad to be back home, just that it's different, not from what it was before he left but different *from camp*. For the moment, at least, that can be a devastating loss, especially for a child not used to coping with loss. It's not just the obvious things that he's missing, like friends, routines, and activities; sometimes, it's more subtle. The smells are different. It's quiet at home. You can't see as much of the sky.

These things may be worth pointing out because he may not be able to identify them for himself: "Did you ever notice how different the air smells here, compared to Maine? I noticed that when I came back from visiting day. The smell of pine trees makes the air so fresh at camp. We don't have that here." It's food, however, that parents say gets talked about the most, especially with boys: How much food there was, how fabulous the desserts were, how they could have seconds or thirds, how there were several choices at each meal. There are lots of creative ways to respond to this without getting defensive. I know one mother who asked her 12-year-old daughter to plan the menus for her first week at home so she'd be sure to have meals she liked. Another mother got so tired of hearing about the salad and dessert bars at camp that she adapted the idea at home, putting out salad stuff each night for a make-your-own and once a week putting out the makings for make-your-own sundaes. Interest in the salad bar quickly waned but the dessert bar was still going strong six months later.

As the parent of a returning camper, perhaps the most helpful thing you can do for yourself is to compare your child to a spouse returning from a six-week business trip in Europe. You'd expect an adult to be happy to be home, but also both frazzled and exhilarated and maybe just a tiny bit preoccupied, still slightly in a European mind-set. You'd give her a few days to recover from jet lag and from the travel routine, and you certainly wouldn't expect her to cook dinner the first night home.

> *If your returning camper is moody and unhappy for more than four or five days, call the director. Perhaps something happened at the very end of camp.*

Your returning camper needs some emotional space, too. She has a powerful need to hold on to good feelings about camp, although the way she goes about it may mystify or worry you. A normally communicative child may be unusually silent, neither talking about camp nor reengaging with friends but moping around the house, watching lots of TV, ignoring or being mean to siblings, and being unusually oppositional. This can be hard on parents. Don't assume something is wrong, don't take it personally, and don't push. What's going on is that many children under 13 think that they can't hold on to two feelings at the same time. A camper who loved camp wants to hold on to it for as long as possible and she's afraid that if she reenters fully into home life, she'll lose camp. She doesn't want to talk about it because that gives her complete and personal ownership and keeps the experience from being diluted. So her body may be living in your house but inside her head, it's still camp. Allow your child the freedom to decompress without pressure; in the long run, the transition will probably be smoother, even if there are a few unexpected bumps along the way.

Sammy, who is 10, came home from camp, plunked down in front of the TV and stayed there for two days. At first his parents were indulgent; after all, he hadn't had TV for a month. By the end of the second day, his mother was building up a head of steam. "I'm going to unpack your trunk, come help me," she said. Sammy didn't budge. Mom unpacked the trunk. As she was dumping everything into the laundry, she discovered two T-shirts and a pair of shorts that didn't belong to Sam. Gingerly holding them with two fingers, she waved them in front of his face as he stared at the TV.

"Whose mother is missing these clothes today?" she asked.

Suddenly Sammy came alive. "What are you doing?" he screamed.

He snatched the clothes from her, ran to his room, and slammed the door. She waited a few minutes, then knocked. No answer. Ten or fifteen minutes later, as she was literally pacing the hallway outside his room, Sam came out wearing one of the T-shirts and holding the rest. "These are Todd's," he said. "We traded. These are too dirty for me to wear. Can we wash them? And Mom," he said, "I want to unpack my trunk myself from now on."

Needless to say, she didn't object.

For many children, the trunk is sacred. They hold off on unpacking because they know that once they do, the last tangible piece of camp is gone. Some kids will even object to having you wash the clothes. Cleaning won't wash away just the dirt, but the smell, too, and maybe the memories. Psychologist Muchnick says of trunks, "What's inside is the last vestige of camp. Don't unpack without permission. It's an intrusion. Unless you hear things inside it or it smells funny, hands off."

Hands off your child, too. Literally. As parents, we're dying to get our arms around our kids and some kids are as hungry for that as we are. For others, it's smothering. If your child sends you threatening looks or puts you off, respect the distance he's requesting. It's one more sign of his newfound independence. He'll come around in a few days, if you're patient. Patience, in fact, is what you need most during this period of transition. Gently help your child to acknowledge feelings and put meaning to them. For instance: "You look sad. Are you missing camp?" "It must feel weird not to be living in a bunk anymore." Let her know, too, that it's possible to hold two feelings at once, to be sad to be gone and glad to be home, and that memories are forever. After about two days of this, begin negotiations to get her back to normal routines: "I don't think you have any clothes to wear. They're all inside your trunk. When were you thinking about unpacking?" If your child is wallowing in sadness after two days, tell him kindly but firmly: "It's time to get back into regular routines now," and offer him choices, much as he would have at camp. Some families identify the first week home as "family camp," posting chores and activities on the refrigerator, as well as the day's schedule, and having "honor room" instead of "honor bunk," where the occupant of the neatest room at the end of the week gets a treat.

If your child is oppositional or changed in ways that are negative, remind her about your family's values and get back to center in your limit setting: "Since you've been back, you haven't wanted to help clean up after dinner. I guess you need a reminder that this is one of the things everyone does in this family." "We didn't allow that language in our family before you went to camp and we don't allow it now." "You've been really tough since you came home. Do you realize it? Can you help us understand what it's all about?"

In addition to patience, there's one other thing that will help you get through this transition: the ability to distinguish between your hopes and your expectations. You may hope your son or daughter will come running into your arms, but if you expect it, you'll be disappointed; you may hope that she'll be so glad to be home, she'll be cooperative and cheerful, but if that's what you expect, her moodiness will be that much harder to take. Instead, expect that things will be different in some way, that your child will have grown emotionally, interpersonally, cognitively, and/or physically. But keep yourself from doing anything more than hoping about what those specific changes might be.

CHAPTER FIVE

Our Children and the Media
. . . .

Some things your children say stick with you forever. One of those moments for me was a conversation my son initiated when he was 7. "Mom, I have a grown-up question," he said at breakfast. "Is all the violence we see on TV what the world is really like?"

That question really got to me. For starters, TV does not play a prominent role in our family. My husband and I are not big viewers. Except for sports, any viewing we do tends to be after our son's bedtime, including the news; the TV is never on in our home as background, and the house rule has always been no TV on school days. Even when he was little, TV was on only for specific programming. He never watched things like *Teenage Mutant Ninja Turtles* or *Power Rangers* (his choice as much as ours), and as he's gotten older he mostly watches Saturday morning cartoons, sports events, and an occasional sitcom on Nickelodeon. As for videos, we have always handpicked them, and movies were never an issue because he didn't much like them until he was about 9. His real life doesn't have violence in it either. There is no personal violence in our home, our neighborhood is not tough or unsafe and neither is our suburban town.

His question also begged another: If my child, with monitored, minimal exposure to screen violence, is worried about his safety, what is the impact on kids who watch lots of TV, including real-life violence on the news and dramatized true-life police stories? What about kids who have a steady diet of violence in their videos and movies, or worse, whose screen violence is augmented by violence at home?

A developmental psychologist once related this anecdote to me, told to him by a 13-year-old client. The youngster would regularly gather with three of his friends to watch one of the four *Faces of Death* videos, which depict markedly gruesome, allegedly real-life, violent death scenes. Their game is to see who can watch the longest. The one who turns away first, or who cries or vomits, is not the winner. So the kids watch it again and again and again, sometimes alone at home. To practice. The psychologist didn't doubt his client's story, and as I interviewed boys of similar ages, I didn't doubt that something like it might be true for many others.

Anecdotes like these are why researchers are so concerned and why all of us as parents ought to be too. There's a growing mound of evidence that the more violence children watch, the more they come to accept it as normal. Researchers call this desensitization. (My son recently told me it was my fault he doesn't like violent movies. "If you had let me watch them when I was young, then I would be desensitized, like all my friends," he told me.) For years, studies have shown that exposure to television affects children in ways that reach far into their psyches, affecting deep-seated attitudes and behaviors. Unfortunately, in today's world it's not enough to worry about how many hours our children spend in front of the television screen. What about the other screens in their lives? What about all the other media exposure?

In her insightful book, *The Shelter of Each Other*, psychologist Mary Pipher says there's nothing necessarily wrong with each of the individual technologies available to our children today. "It's the whole pile of them put together," she writes. I couldn't agree more. The cumulative effect of the various screens is what's so troubling because the messages they get from all the screens together add up to a worldview of violence and destruction, of racism and sexism. That's bad enough, but unfortunately it's not all. All this screen time takes time away from other, more developmentally important, kinds of play. There's also the fact that the media are so extensive and that parents have so few defenses against them. There was a time when parents hoped their child wouldn't be exposed to older kids on the school bus uttering the *f*-word. Today, by third grade, there's not only the *f*-word to worry about, but the *a*-word, the *b*-word, and even the *c*-word. Forget the *s*-word. They all know that by second grade. Where do kids get all this? Song lyrics. PG 13–rated movies. Chat rooms on the Internet. Radio DJs. What's a parent to do? Campaign for censorship? Raise our kids in bubbles?

In the life of a child today, the good and the bad news is that there's more access to information than at any other time in the history of our planet. It puts the world at our children's fingertips, but it also places a tremendous burden on us to teach our children to be good communicators and good communicat*ees*. My son's question was poignant proof that even with careful, controlled exposure, a child can perceive the world as a violent place. It happens just from being alive in these times.

The violent screen

The morning my son asked me his question about violence on TV, I dropped him at school, went to the office, put aside the topic I was working on, and embarked on a column on the influence of the media on children. The first person I called was child psychologist James Garbarino, an international expert on the impact of real-life and media violence on kids. He was more than sympathetic. "This is something all parents living in America need to come to grips with," he said. "It doesn't only take firsthand experience for a child to be affected."

By the age of 18, the typical American child will have seen 30,000 violent deaths on TV.

Many children, he said, become desensitized to violence: Because they see so much of it, the only way they can make sense of it is to accept it as commonplace, okay, normal. Otherwise the world is too scary to cope with. Indeed, those who see lots of violence and don't get desensitized typically become fearful or even traumatized. Either way, Garbarino has no doubt that exposure affects a child's worldview and influences how likely she is to use violence in her own life. In its extreme, exposure can cause a child to lose confidence in the future. Ask a 12-year-old growing up in a crime-ridden inner-city neighborhood, "What do you expect to be when you're 30?" and you may be saddened but not surprised when he says, "Dead." Unfortunately, Garbarino's research shows this same bleak view of the world is widely held by children in suburbs all over this country.

Desensitization begins as a defense mechanism. Children use it to work through common childhood fears: You take the extraordinary and turn it into the ordinary so it doesn't scare you. All children do this to some extent. It's healthy adaptive behavior. But with violence, this works like a double-edged sword: The more violence a child is exposed to, the more desensitized he becomes to it, so that he begins to accept it as normal. The more he accepts violence as normal, the more likely he is to use violence himself and to accept violence he sees others using. This doesn't happen overnight, it takes years of exposure, and the more intense the exposure, the more dramatic the results. It explains how an 8-year-old comes to view hitting not only as okay but even as good, or why an 11-year-old who walks down the hall at school and gets accidentally bumped by a schoolmate turns around and hits the kid and then truly doesn't understand why the adults make such a fuss. It's true that the child with extensive personal experience with violence is the most likely to formulate such a worldview, but it can also happen to any child with constant exposure to media violence. Children, after all, construct meaning out of their experience, whatever it is. Author David Elkind says, "Children form images of themselves from what they see on TV and if the images are too mature, too sophisticated, too savvy, they don't handle them well. It produces a set of inappropriate expectations. It's very stressful."

> *Involving an older child in the process of controlling a younger sibling's viewing— "You know, I'm thinking this is too violent for Ariel to watch. What do you think?" —will help teach him to become a more discriminating viewer himself.*

The critical question is, What is any given child's threshold? There is no magic answer but age and stage of development certainly play a role:

- **Toddlers.** Even children as young as 1 and 2 are affected by daily exposure to violent programming, according to researchers at the Zero to Three National Center for Clinical Infant Programs. At this young age, they don't internalize or even understand much of what they see, but because imitation is the fundamental way young children learn, they mimic whatever behaviors they see most frequently on the screen. If what they primarily see is aggressive behavior, and especially if they see that at home as well, over time that affects the way they react to people, and they become either overly aggressive or overly self-protective. A 2-year-old, for instance, might strike out at a playmate for no reason you can figure, but if you could get inside his head, his reasoning might go something like this: "If

I don't hit him first, he'll hit me." Or he might become totally passive, not engaging at all with age-mates for fear he will be hurt. He might be thinking: "If I just sit here behind the blocks, I'll be invisible. He won't notice me and he won't hurt me." It's precisely because of this imitative tendency that appropriate programming is so crucial at these young ages. Shows like *Mister Rogers' Neighborhood*, *Barney*, and *Blue's Clues* may be boring to you and maybe even to your 2-year-old's 4-year-old sibling, but when multiple-aged children are viewing together, programming should cater to the youngest child, not the oldest. This is an important point, one you'll see made frequently in this chapter. If your 4-year-old protests, carve out a separate "grown-up" viewing time for him, when the 2-year-old naps. Notice, by the way, that *Sesame Street* is not mentioned here. Its fast pace makes it more appropriate for preschoolers' viewing than for toddlers'.

- **Preschoolers.** Cognitively, the 3- , 4- , and 5-year-old typically can focus only on one thing at a time. That explains why children like to watch the same video over and over: It takes repetition for them to absorb more than just a few salient features. Initially, however, they focus on what stands out the most to them. So if they're watching something with violence, that's what they take in because it's most noticeable. The violent message is also what's most likely to stay with them, even after repeated viewing, not only because it stands out the most but also because the violent themes tend to be repeated from show to show almost in a formulaic way. The logic or sequence that led up to the violence, as well as any pro-social moralities that may follow, are lost on them. The susceptibility of a child this age to what he views was made most obvious by the *Power Rangers*. At the height of its popularity, many preschool teachers in the Boston area banned "Power Ranger" play in their schoolyards and issued advisories to parents of the dangers of 3- and 4-year-olds watching the show. "In all the

years of various superhero TV show popularity, even including *Teenage Mutant Ninja Turtles*, I've never seen anything like
the imitative aggression this show encourages," one teacher
told me, referring to the kicking and fighting she was seeing in
her playground. In addition, because children this age are developmentally still very egocentric, they automatically relate
what they see to themselves. So even if his only exposure is a
playmate's telling him about a scary or violent scene, his
thought is: "Am I safe? What can happen to me?" It's this line
of thinking, by the way, that probably was responsible for my
son's concerns.

> *If professionals offer one cardinal rule*
> *about children's TV viewing, it is to never*
> *put a television set in a child's bedroom.*

▪ **School-age.** As children become more cognitively sophisticated, they are able to take in more and more, so that starting at
about 6, they begin to see the fuller context and story line. The
older they get, the more shades of gray begin to emerge and the
more they begin to see connections between cause and effect.
The typical child might wonder: Can a good guy do something
bad and still be a good guy? Unfortunately, research shows that
the more exposure they've already had to violence, the less
likely they are to ask these questions. Instead, they want to up
the ante. In other words, the level of violence that entertained
them five months ago is old-hat now, sissy stuff. Riding on the
subway one day, I overheard two third-graders on a class field
trip to a downtown museum. A boy and girl were arguing the
merits of *Terminator 2*. The movie was rated R. The boy had
seen it with his father, the girl with her teenage stepsister. "I
thought it was a little scary," said the girl. "Are you kidding?"

the boy replied. "There's nothing scary in it. I was bored." The teacher assured me this was not just bravado. "He sees R movies all the time with his dad," she said. A child who sees this much screen violence becomes inured to it. It's not just violent messages he's absorbing, either. Because so many of the bad guys in these movies are represented by people of color who don't speak English, researchers say a child is more likely to buy into the stereotypical thinking the movies propagate. Curiously, not all school-age children exposed to media violence become more and more aggressive; some become more and more fearful. Like the toddler who wants to hide, they develop a perception that the world is basically a dangerous place and their anxiety leads to a heightened need for self-protection. According to researchers, as teens these kids are likely to be among those who will carry guns and weapons, not to be aggressors but because that's the only way they feel safe. Ironically, they often are among those who commit violence, albeit in what they perceive to be self-defense.

Of course, we can all make the argument that we were exposed to violence on TV when we grew up and we turned out okay. There are significant differences, however, between the violence we saw and the violence our children see. What we watched wasn't violence with cars or violence involving children. It wasn't violence in homes that looked like ours with families that looked like ours. The violence didn't mimic what we heard about on the radio and on TV news or in headlines at the breakfast table. When we were growing up, the violence we saw on the screen generally didn't have anything to do with our lives, it wasn't as intense, it wasn't as realistic, and it wasn't as, well, violent. We also couldn't watch it every day of the week, whenever we turned the tube on. *Charlie's Angels* and *Mission: Impossible* weren't in reruns seven times a week. The violence wasn't available as video or computer games or on little palm-sized screens we could carry with us in the car and into the doctor's waiting room. Two of the nation's most respected researchers in the field, psychologist Leonard Eron of the University of Michigan and early childhood educator Diane Levin of Wheelock College, believe the impact of video and computer-game violence is far more harmful than TV violence. "It's because the child is actively involved. He's not just watching and listening, he's doing something," says Eron. "He's connecting kinesthetically. *He's making the violence happen.* Not only that, but if he doesn't make the right choice, which is usually the most violent one, *he loses the game.* What kind of message does that send?"

This physical connection creates what Levin calls post–video game trauma. She says that players are so completely absorbed in the video world they enter that when they turn it off, it's hard for them to switch gears to come back to the real world at hand. There are other problems with video games too. To be a skilled player often means you are trying to second-guess the programmer, not engage in creative thinking of your own. With one particularly popular computer game among school-age boys, *Doom*, the kids spend as much time in one-upmanship as they do in playing—"I killed more than you did today!" They also spend a fair amount of time trying to "break the codes," which is a polite way of saying "cheating."

> *Counter "But Joey's parents let him watch/play this!" with "Every family is different. In our family, we don't think this is good for you to watch/play."*

Also troubling to researchers like Levin and Eron is the addictive quality of video/computer games. Even if a child is spending hours immersed in relatively harmless, nonviolent games like *NFL Hockey, Golf* or *Treasure Mountain*, it means he is spending less time engaged in one of the most important and fundamental tasks of childhood: play. A preschool teacher once commented to me that many of the 4-year-olds in her class were more computer literate than the teachers. "Put them in the Pretend Corner, though, and they're at a loss," she said. Fantasy play is a preschooler's most important vehicle for making sense of the world. Is it possible children might lose their ability to play in this way? This teacher, at least, fears it is.

Luckily, parents still count for something. When we set limits, intervene, and interpret what's on the screens, we can, in fact, count for a lot. Because a child can feel threatened whether the violence he is exposed to is real or pretend, we are most helpful when we provide a secure, predictable environment where a child feels not only that we are doing everything we can to keep her safe, but also that she has tools to protect herself. If your 2- to 7-year-old has been frightened by something he's seen on TV or in a video or computer game, it's likely to show up in a bad dream that very same night. The younger the child, the more obvious the connection will be. Astonishingly, some children will insist on watching the same show or video the next day. Don't assume it means they're ready to handle it. More likely, they're trying to conquer it, much the way the middle school boys were doing with *Faces of Death*. Remind them: "Remember the bad dream you had last night? That was because this show was too scary. It's my job to protect and take care of you. You can't watch this anymore." It's that middle thought—"It's my job to protect and take care of you"—that they need to hear most. Older children may be better able to make the connection themselves. When my son was 9, he awoke one night with a nightmare. He didn't tell me what the bad dream was about, but after I helped him settle back down, he told me sleepily, "I probably shouldn't play *Doom* very much anymore." He didn't either, at least not for a while.

About the best way to protect our children from all the malevolence of TV and videos is to ban them altogether or tape everything the kids might watch and then prescreen. Peggy Charren offers a less drastic measure. A tireless national advocate for quality children's programming, she's spent decades hammering home the message that we need to put our values between our children and the screen. "Even a rotten show three hours a week isn't going to ruin your child's life," she says. In other words, once or twice a week is okay. It's the repetition of the same show with the same theme—hurting people is an okay way to solve conflict—that's detrimental. This includes commercials, by the way. When there's a commercial that you think is demeaning to women, say so: Comment on it, interpret for your child what she is seeing, help her to question it, to not just accept it simply because it's there. Charren says the goal in limiting TV viewing is to make discriminating viewers of our children so that they learn to watch programs, not TV, and so that they turn the set off when the program ends. This is more likely to happen if you begin when your child is young: "You can watch up to two hours a day. Here are the programs you can choose from."

> *Too much TV viewing has been
> linked to poor reading skills, low SAT scores,
> and an inability to initiate ideas,
> be creative, or organize oneself.*

With school-age children, have an agreement about how much and what they can watch. At the beginning of the week, look together at the upcoming programming and circle the shows you agree to. (This strategy also helps them learn time management skills because they have to organize their homework around the programming.) If they violate your agreement, pull the plug, literally. If you have a school-age child and you want to impose viewing limits for the first time, it will be harder than if you're starting with a preschooler, but it's not impossible. Go for an honest approach: "I made a mistake by letting you watch so much TV. Now I want us to have a joint agreement about how much you watch and what you watch." Ask him to list all the shows he likes and to put them in order of priority, then go through the list together. Don't make decreased viewing a punishment and don't link it to poor grades. Let the merits of less watching stand on their own.

> *When your school-age child watches prime-time shows, watch them together as often as possible and talk about them afterward. Many shows raise topics that children can relate to, but sometimes the irony and sarcasm are lost on them.*

Whenever you can, watch TV with your child no matter what her age but especially if she's under 5. Not only will you know what's influencing her, not only will you be able to interpret on the spot, but your credibility will also be higher when you tell her she can't watch something: "I looked at this program with you and I don't like what it says." Or: "You're not old enough to watch this and make good use of it." Perhaps the best reason: "These values are not values our family approves of." Don't just watch one program once, either; check it out every few weeks to see the continued messages your child is absorbing. Don't just watch the terrific stuff, watch the shows you can't stand, too, like cartoons (they're often incredibly inappropriate), and don't disappear during the commercials; children don't tune them out the way we do and in fact are very much influenced by them.

Even Disney can be the enemy

Unfortunately, one of the worst perpetrators of scary images for our youngest children comes from a source we have come to trust the most: Disney.

Jacqui Sears is a mother with a story that illustrates the point. When her daughter, Jenny, was 6, she was afraid of dogs. Given her age, this was not particularly unusual, in fact, rather normal. But Jacqui was convinced her fear was more than developmental. When Jenny was 3, they had watched the Disney video *Beauty and the Beast*. In the scene where the wolves chase Belle to the forest, there's a close-up of the wolf's teeth biting her cape. It's mean- and vicious-looking.

"Jenny started to whimper," remembers her mom. "I said, 'Oh, Jenny, it's only a cartoon, it's not real. Snuggle up to Mommy.' "

A child's fear is real even if it is irrational.

That night, Jenny had a nightmare about a dog chasing her. She's continued to have the same bad dream off and on ever since, up to the time of this writing four years later. If that was the beginning of Jenny's fear of dogs, it was also the end of her mother's naiveté about Disney films. To this day, Jacqui Sears regrets how she reacted when Jenny objected to the movie. "I was trying to toughen her up when I should have shut it off," she says. "Because it was Disney, I figured it was okay." Like Sears, I have a similar story. I mentioned earlier that my son doesn't like movies much. Until about age 9, he was rarely interested in going to a movie in a theater and only slightly more interested watching a movie on video. I'm convinced it's because he was overwhelmingly frightened by the very first movie he saw in a theater, Disney's *Fantasia*. He was 4. I had consciously waited until he was that age to introduce him to movies, and I had purposely chosen this one. It was Disney. It had to be good. It wasn't.

Over the years, Disney has become a symbol of wholesome Americana, right up there with motherhood and apple pie. But its reputation as child-friendly is as much the result of image making as it is of deed. Disney films are laden with issues that make them inappropriate for toddlers and preschoolers. They're too scary. Joanne Cantor, one of the nation's premier researchers on the impact of scary films on children, says the biggest problem with Disney movies is that children tend to see them before they are developmentally ready to deal with the issues they raise. Of course, kids aren't going on their own. We're taking them! Because we've bought into the image. If nothing else, Disney is king of aiming movies and movie products at young children, fooling parents and kids into consuming them long before our kids are ready. Here's what happens: If, like Jenny Sears, a child is presented with scary material before she's developmentally able to handle it and it's scarier than her own worst fantasy, she defends against it either by becoming desensitized or by becoming more frightened, not less. In Jenny's case, she developed anxieties and unnecessary stress. Other kids may develop fears around it or misinterpret altogether, which leads to a different set of anxieties and stress.

> *Children categorize things as real and pretend before they understand that what's pretend can't get them in the night.*

The scariness factor is amplified for preschoolers because of their developmental inability to distinguish fantasy from reality. *Bambi*, re-released as a video in 1997, is a good example. The shooting death of Bambi's mother introduces a concept most preschoolers have not yet thought about: Will my mother die? This is a very heavy issue, one many children do eventually explore, but not at 3, probably not even at 4. Knowing this could be a problem, Jacqui Sears purposefully waited until Jenny was 4 1/2 before letting her see it.

Jenny watched without any apparent difficulty but days later, when classical music was playing on the car radio, she said, "This is the music they use when they shoot Bambi's mother." Then she let loose a torrent of tearful questions: What happened to the mother? What happened to Bambi? Are you going to die? Is Daddy? Jacqui vowed not to make such a mistake again. She outlawed Disney films for her second child, screens them religiously for Jenny, and founded MOM (Mothers Offended by the Media).

> *While some children will tell you they don't like a video, many will not, especially those with older siblings. Look for nonverbal signals that a video is causing discomfort, especially restlessness or an inability to focus.*

Like many of us, Jacqui found out the hard way how impressionable 3- and 4-year-olds can be. Her impression meshes with Joanne Cantor's research. In one of her studies, Cantor asked college students to identify some of their worst childhood fears. Unprompted, what many of them remembered were Disney movies they'd seen as preschoolers. One had been frightened when naughty children in *Pinocchio* were turned into donkeys; she worried for years that might happen to her. Another blamed her lifelong fear of cats on the Cheshire cat in *Alice in Wonderland*, also a Disney release, while another was frightened by a scene in the same movie, where the queen yells, "Off with her head! Off with her head!" That college students had such vivid memories so many years later prompted Cantor to comment, "It's as though the movie's visual image burns in the brain. Once there, it stays."

Researcher Diane Levin has a theory about why this happens: "Disney takes hold of the issues that are deeply important to kids and makes them scary. Instead of helping kids work them through, Disney exploits the scariness. For young kids, when they get the wrong message at a young age, it's so salient that it stays with them. When they see the world as scarier than it really is at an age when they can't handle it, it has potentially long-lasting effects."

It's not just the action and plot that are the problem, either. Even though Disney is wonderful at creating cute, adorable, and endearing characters, it's even better at doing ugly and grotesque ones, and 3- and 4-year-olds are supersensitive to looks. They get stuck on appearances because they don't have the cognitive capacity yet to reason that a visual image can hold two qualities, that something that looks ugly and scary (the hunchback, the beast) could also have good qualities. They also aren't yet sure that mean and scary villains (Cruella de Vil, the wicked witch in *Snow White*) are just make-believe. What scares one child may not faze another, of course, but here are a few examples of Disney fare that typically are too scary for a 3- or 4-year-old: The chase scene with the rat in *Lady and the Tramp*; the hunt scene for the puppies in *101 Dalmatians*; the scene where Jafar turns himself into a cobra in *Aladdin*; the concept in *The Lion King* that Simba is responsible for his father's death; the good-toy-versus-bad-toy scenes in *Toy Story*; the hunchback in *The Hunchback of Notre Dame*; Hercules in *Hercules*; Ursula the sea witch in *The Little Mermaid*.

So how can you protect your child from unnecessary nightmares and fears? Joanne Cantor's guideline to parents is that until your child is 7 or 8, "don't assume that anything is automatically okay in a Disney movie." If your child does see something that prompts her to be afraid, never belittle the fear or sweet-talk her out of it the way Jacqui Sears did. Help a child connect a bad dream to the movie (although not in the middle of the night): "I wonder if that bad dream last night was because of the wolves in the movie?" Once again, when siblings are watching together, they should watch what's appropriate for the youngest, not the oldest.

It's also important to read your child's cues. Many young children, boys particularly, are not verbal or emotive and find other ways to tell you they aren't comfortable, if only, alas, you pick up their signals. I have to admit I wasn't always alert to my son's. When he was 3 and 4, *101 Dalmatians* was one of the videos I always felt comfortable popping in the VCR. Neither my husband nor I ever stopped to wonder why it was that whenever Cruella de Vil appeared on screen, he would click off the video or get involved in some other activity. A few years later, when Glenn Close starred in a live-action *101 Dalmatians*, I couldn't wait to see it. My son wasn't interested. "Seeing that movie will remind me how much I hated Cruella de Vil when I was little," he told us.

"I didn't know you hated her," I said.

"I thought she was really scary. She gave me bad dreams."

Oh.

Off the screen, Disney performs another disservice to young children. When a 3-year-old sees promotions for *The Hunchback of Notre Dame* in every store, he thinks it's *important.* When he sees the logos on everything in his life, from pajamas to baby bottles to books and tapes and even with his hamburgers at McDonald's, he assumes this is part of life, the same way brushing teeth at night is. Disney is a master at convincing kids to convince us to purchase on their behalf. That's called purchasing influence, and it makes it incumbent on us as parents to be good consumers on behalf of our children and to teach even our 3-year-olds to be smart consumers. Disney's goal is to get children to establish brand loyalty by the age of 3. Is there any question of its success? When a 3-year-old throws a tantrum because you don't want to buy her a Jasmine backpack, she's not just being difficult; she truly believes that she *needs* that backpack for her well-being and happiness. Psychologist David Walsh, president of the National Institute on Media and the Family, tells of a woman who realized the power of Disney's marketing when her 5-year-old daughter announced, "*The Lion King* is the best movie I've ever seen." "She hadn't even seen the movie," the woman told Walsh.

The problem is that kids are so developmentally vulnerable. Says Walsh, "When little kids start to get the message they won't be happy unless they have X, they buy into it wholeheartedly. They can't separate all this out." At the age of 3 and 4, it doesn't take much before children can't help themselves from incorporating this into their worldview.

The antidote is balance. There's nothing wrong with a 3-year-old having a Jasmine backpack. But when she also has Jasmine pajamas, sheets, and pillowcases, T-shirts, headbands, and pencils, we are feeding into the message that Jasmine, and by extension, Disney, is the key to happiness. To combat Disney's intense cross-marketing, we need to introduce the concept of media literacy to 3- and 4-year-olds: "See how that toy fills up the TV screen so it looks giant size? In real life, is it that big?" "Remember how badly you wanted the *Lion King* toy and then it broke the first day you had it? I wonder if this toy will be disappointing too?"

As for Disney movies themselves, we need to evaluate each one on its merits, thinking about the susceptibilities of our individual children. It's not that Disney doesn't make good movies; it's that it's not safe to assume they are good enough for our children under 5. When Jacqui Sears first outlawed Disney movies for her preschool son, her friends told her she was overreacting. Now they thank her for enlightening them. Researcher Cantor certainly is on her side. "I can't think of a Disney film that doesn't carry a concern for parents of young children," she says.

When television remakes romance

Several years ago, when Mira Dobrow was 5, she asked her mother why her 2-year-old brother liked to watch the *Cinderella* video so much.

"Maybe he likes the music," suggested her mother, Julia.

Mira thought about that. "Maybe," she said finally. "I don't think he understands the romance part."

If Julia Dobrow was taken aback—what, after all, does 5-year-old Mira know of romance?—it wasn't for long. A researcher at Tufts University, she studies the effects of media on children and knows that even preschoolers experience incidental learning from whatever they watch. She had been saying for years that they pick up information we don't even realize they are getting and often wish they didn't have, and her daughter proved the point. Like many parents, Dobrow screens and protects her children from media violence. But romance? Who thinks about that? The fact is, though, that television also sends powerful, often sexist and unhealthy messages about relationships. This time the problem is that we're so desensitized, *we* don't notice. Among the skewed messages children get: Girls "cast spells" over boys and compete with each other for affection; girls are bossy and boys are strong; you have to "make" a man love you and the best way to do that is to be dumb, have a tiny waist, and long hair, preferably blond; the best way to "make" a girl love you is to be lean, mean, and rich; there are certain ways to behave when you fall in love and certain things that happen when you fall in love. In some sitcoms popular among the under-12 set, women are constantly putting down their husbands and men in general; and in others, men are constantly putting down their wives and women in general. Renee Hobbs, an associate professor of communication at Babson College and a national leader in media literacy research, says, "These shows normalize one person deriving pleasure at someone else's expense. In fact, they idealize it."

> *Some of the most sexually violent or graphic scenes on TV are on promos and movie previews. When one comes on, seize the opportunity and put your spin on it: "That's horrible, to see a man treat a woman like that. Some people think this is entertaining, but I think it's awful."*

As adults, we can laugh at a TV husband's teasing of his wife and put it into a context. Children aren't able to do that. And although we grew up watching sitcoms, once again the difference between our viewing and our children's is dramatic: We only had three channels, our children have sixty; we could see our favorite programs once a week, our children can see a sitcom in reruns every day. As with violence in programming, there's a cumulative effect from viewing sitcoms, too. The more children see men and women put each other down or treat one another as objects, the more they accept it as normal, as behaviors to model. Hobbs wonders if girls and boys are being bred to expect to be unhappy in love.

If cynical = cool were the only misconception our children were getting about romance from TV, it might not be so bad. But there are so many mixed messages out there that it puts kids in a position of having to make choices of which messages to pay attention to. Whether we realize it or not, even preschoolers begin to wonder about such things as "Do you have to be a beautiful princess for the prince to love you?" "Do you have to be a strong, brave prince for the princess to love you?" "Who will love me if I don't look/act like that?" Disney was rife with these stereotypes when we were children and continues to be today, too, only in greater quantity. And what about the dysfunctional, problematic love relationships that children see on dramatic shows, police shows, and the news? What sense can they make out of a husband beating a wife, the person he is supposed to love more than anyone else in the world, or of a wife who falls in love with her best friend's husband, two themes popular in made-for-TV movies? Even if our kids don't watch the movies themselves, they see the promos or movie previews, which typically highlight the most graphic scenes. Researchers say the long-term impact of these messages can affect how children view their own relationships.

In most adults' lives, successful love relationships usually come at the end of many years of trying love on in different forms, including idealizing romance. But children today aren't exposed to many, if any, examples of old-fashioned, idealized love. They come to see true love or romance not only as unobtainable but also as undesirable. Does this account for why so many teenagers end up in relationships of a nontender, nonromantic kind?

Once again, the good news is that children are learning about romance not only from the media but also from us. How we manage our own love relationships gives them a context for evaluating what they view. The more loving and respectful we are as husbands, wives, and significant others, the more we mitigate against the cynicism they are exposed to. Hopefully they will conclude that TV images are unfortunate exceptions. But what about the child whose real-life models for romance are not happy or are even similar to or worse than what's on TV? In such cases, the two images probably reinforce each other, although research shows that there is sometimes an ironic kind of backlash. Some children will seek out images on TV to compensate for the negative relationships they see in real life. This doesn't mean that in the normal course of life, you and your spouse can't express honest differences of opinion and even be angry at each other. But if you are going through a tough time in your marriage or through a divorce, it helps to have conversations with your children about those differences rather than leave them to their imaginations.

The bottom line is that just as we need to monitor children's exposure to violence, we need to monitor their exposure to romance by watching what they see, looking at it through their lens and putting our interpretations on it. Recently my son and I watched a rerun of *Home Improvement*. As usual, Tim, the husband, badmouthed his wife, this time to the guys in the hardware store. My son knows themes like this aggravate me, so he tried to hide his laughter and was surprised when I laughed along with him. "Well, it *is* funny," I said. "It's very funny and very clever. I really admire writers who can think up things like that, but that's what this is, writers and actors who get paid to make people laugh. In real life, I don't know people who behave that way, do you?"

While visiting at the home of an 8- and 6-year-old, I sat in the family room with them while I waited to interview their mom. They were watching a rerun of the sitcom *Married with Children*. The episode was full of sexual innuendoes that I hoped were beyond them, and the plot, no surprise, revolved around the husband's being in the doghouse for not being attentive enough to his wife.

"What do you think of this show?" I asked.

"Good," said the older one. "It's just like our house," said the younger one. "Mom is always complaining that Daddy isn't nice enough to her."

"She is not," said the older one.

"Is too," the younger insisted. "She said yesterday that Daddy didn't thank her for getting his cleaning. That's a way he wasn't nice to her."

"Maybe she should complain *more*," the older one concluded. "If a man really loves a woman, he tells her nice things all the time about how beautiful she is and he smiles at her a lot and kisses her and brings her flowers. Otherwise she might divorce him."

"How do you know that?" asked her sister.

The older one pointed to the TV, the younger sister fell silent.

> *The next time your school-age child is home sick or out of school for a snow day, rent an old-fashioned love story and watch it together.*

When the mother and I were alone, I mentioned the conversation to her. Two days later, she called me. When her husband had come home from work that day, the 6-year-old was waiting in the driveway for him with a bouquet of flowers picked from the garden. "These are for you to give Mommy," she said. "Daddies are supposed to give mommies flowers. I'm going to help you so you don't have to get a divorce."

This couple was lucky: Their daughter was able to verbalize her fears. Many children might have worked themselves into a real tailspin, thinking their parents were headed for divorce because Daddy didn't bring Mommy flowers. These parents used this opportunity to talk about the many ways husbands and wives show they love each other, and about how TV shows aren't the same as what happens in real life.

In addition to modeling and interpreting, there's something else we can do that's very concrete. Just as adults love hearing a good, old-fashioned love story, so, too, do children. Telling your kids your own personal love story in age-appropriate ways is one of the best tools we have to counteract the cynicism they are exposed to when it comes to romance. If you're a single parent, find a love story you can tell about people they know, grandparents or an aunt or uncle. If your marriage is intact, let them know they come from a relationship that is loving and beautiful. Even if they giggle or cringe at the we-were-so-in-love part, that's what your children are dying to hear. And don't forget Valentine's Day. Even if you think it's corny, commercial, and artificial, it's a visible part of our culture that kids take note of at a young age. You don't have to be mushy, you can even talk about how you show your love for each other all year long, but celebrate it in at least a modest way and certainly don't put down the sentiments. Otherwise, your children may wonder—and worry—why you don't observe the day. After all, everyone else does. And isn't that what people in love do? And aren't parents supposed to be in love?

Megabyte babies? Maybe not

Of all the screens in our children's lives, the one that tends to confound us most is the computer screen. Pam remembers being 21 and panicky the first time she sat down at a computer. "I was scared to death I'd blow up the world if I pushed the wrong button," she says. Her daughter, Dana, was 18 months old when she first sat at a computer. Finding her father at the keyboard, she climbed up on his lap and said, "Me too."

The contrast speaks megabytes about the difference in generations. For our children, computers are just another fact of life. For us, there is still ambivalence about these machines, especially when it comes to our youngest children. We all want to know: Is there an ideal age at which to make the introduction? Do computers hinder learning or help it?

Putting ourselves in our children's shoes would have us view computers as they do: like a telephone, a washer, or any other appliance. We use a vacuum cleaner because it's the best, most efficient way to clean our carpets. When it comes to computers, we should apply the same principle: Children should use them when they have an efficient purpose to serve.

In 1994 when I first wrote a column about children and computers, educators encouraged early exposure, saying that computers stimulate creativity, cognitive learning, and social skills. Although they went so far as to say that children who didn't have exposure to computers by kindergarten were at a disadvantage, they warned parents to take certain precautions; namely, to make sure programming was age appropriate and that computer time didn't come at the expense of traditional play activities like blocks, board games, and bike riding.

Unfortunately, parents tended to hear the first part of that message and not the second, even though educators and researchers were careful to point out that this was a technological disadvantage, not an academic one. Parents should not think of computers as electronic tutors that would give their children an academic edge, they said. There were no educational benefits to be accrued from putting young children at the keyboard.

Now educators and researchers are more strident, taking back what they said about any benefits and asserting there may even be harmful effects for young children from the computer. Perhaps the loudest and most respected voice calling for a reevaluation of computer use for young children is educational psychologist Jane M. Healy of Vail, Colorado, who spent several years in classrooms around the country amassing data for her book *Failure to Connect: How Computers Affect Our Children's Minds—for Better and Worse.*

> *Pay as much attention to your child's posture on the computer as you do to software. Even kids can get carpal tunnel syndrome. Fluorescent lights can create a glare that is hard on their eyes.*

"There is no reason to give a computer to a child under 7," Healy says. Indeed, if she had her way, she'd throw computers out of kindergarten and preschool classrooms and keep computer time at home very limited and highly monitored.

That's because researchers are turning up evidence that early exposure in all but the smallest dose can potentially undercut brain development, interfere with the way a child learns, intrude on social and emotional development, and put health at risk. And what about children being technologically backward? Educators say experience has shown that that was an unfounded fear. Kids take to computers quickly; they'll make up for lost time without any problem. Besides, being temporarily technologically backward is nothing compared to the possibility of being cognitively confused, perhaps for a long time.

Much of the evidence for this comes from a small but growing chorus of kindergarten, first-, and second-grade teachers around the country who say they are seeing more and more children who lack self-motivation, have short attention spans, and can't focus. The response from researchers, also small but growing, is mostly one of chagrin. Technology researcher Douglas Sloan, a professor at Teachers College at Columbia University, says, "It's something of a scandal that it's taken us so long to figure this out."

What we know from years of motivational research is that from an early age, children instinctively want to do better and develop their skills because it satisfies an inner human need. The reward for doing better is sometimes a parent's or teacher's praise, but it is often also simply their own personal pleasure at successfully meeting a challenge. "If the reward for doing a tough math problem is the child saying to herself, 'I worked hard and I got that right,' there's a good chance she's next going to say to herself, 'Now I'm ready for something even harder!' " says Healy.

Computer games mess this up.

Parents tend to love "skill and drill" electronic flash card computer programs because they seem so educational. In truth, they're worse than the flash card you hold up for your child; at least when you do that, you can help him figure out why he didn't get the correct answer. Computer games give a child two or three chances to come up with the correct answer and then move him along anyway. If he gets the wrong answer, it doesn't tell him why, and when he gets the right answer, it gives rewards regardless of how hard he did or didn't work at the problem. The typical 4- or 5-year-old doesn't play the game to solve the math problem and feel that intrinsic sense of satisfaction from knowing the correct answer; he plays to "get to the next level" where the special effects are even better.

When you give them rewards for something they already know or even for something they don't know but can second-guess, they work for the reward and pick the easiest possible way to get it. Playing enough games that operate like this (and most of them do), children become less creative and less willing to take risks. The only strategies they're learning is how to get to the next level, how to beat the game, not strategies that lead to independent thinking or translate to solving real problems in the real world. What it does translate to in the real world is the parent-teacher conference in which the kindergarten or first- or second-grade teacher tells you your child has a short attention span, needs instant gratification, can't focus, or doesn't apply himself.

What worries Sloan, whose area of research is how to protect children from computer misuse, is that there's an evolutionary process involved here. Research still isn't definitive about this yet, but the speculation is that certain cognitive connections are being bypassed. Because children under 7 or 8 have not yet reached the age of abstract reasoning, the early exposure may be changing the way they absorb material, potentially stunting intellectual development. Young children learn best with concrete, real materials. Does your 3-year-old make you crazy because he wants a printout of every computer drawing he generates? That's because the computer offers nothing concrete and real for him; the printer does. There's something else too: When a young child is on the computer, he's being provided with someone else's visual images at a crucial time in his development when he should be working on his own image-making capacities. The same thing is true with too much TV time, of course, but studies show parents monitor TV more than they do computer time; we've come to ascribe almost magical educational qualities to the computer.

On the social side of the developmental ledger, the news is also bleak. In interviews for my 1994 column, researchers said parents need not worry that computers interfere with a preschooler's ability to interact and socialize with peers. Their reasoning was that young children don't like to play on the computer alone. Here's what I wrote: "If they don't have a sibling or age-mate to be with them at the computer, they'll drag you over to it. Indeed, playing with age-mates on the computer can help with some social skills such as turn taking." Today, after finding more and more kindergartners who are nonverbal and don't know how to play with peers, researchers are understandably less comfortable with that advice. I found no researcher yet who is willing to say that it takes twenty minutes or twenty hours of computer time to reach a critical mass. What they do say is that time spent in front of the computer is time away from peer play. Since it is through hands-on play that young children learn and make sense of their world, time away from that potentially compromises social development and imagination.

So does all this mean your 4-year-old's fingertips should never grace a keyboard? That the 18-month-old who climbs on daddy's lap and says "Me too" should be gently but firmly told to climb back down?

The advice I like best comes from Vicki O'Day, a technology researcher at the Xerox Palo Alto Research Center who engages in cutting-edge research. She would not turn the 18-month-old out of your lap. When it comes to children of any age, she says the computer should always be used for a purpose. For instance:

- If your 3-year-old has a penchant for pandas, let him watch while you download pictures of pandas for him.

- If your 4-year-old loves to tell stories, offer to have her dictate one to you while you put it on the computer, then print it out for her to illustrate.

- If your 5-year-old has thank-you notes to write, let her do them via e-mail.

If the computer is an appliance, it's no different than the telephone; you don't pick it up and dial numbers at random for entertainment. It's easier if you start with this attitude when your children are 18 months old. If they're 4 and 6 and have been using the computer for years, it's hard, but not impossible, to backtrack. There are two ways to do that. One is to provide enough interesting alternatives in your home so that the computer is no more attractive than anything else. The other is to talk to your children about family values and to say that you've made a mistake about allowing certain games. The older your child is, the harder it is to do, but even an unhappy 9-year-old at some level can admire the courage behind your conviction and secretly be glad you are standing behind your values, even if belatedly so.

Steve Bennett of Cambridge, Massachusetts, who reviews software and is author of *The Plugged-In Parent*, calls himself a cultural realist. He does not minimize the dangers of computers for children, but as the parent of an 8- and 11-year-old, he says it's impractical and unrealistic to think you can keep kids and computers apart. Just as there are hardware and software, there needs to be "parentware," a term Bennett coins to elevate the importance of parental involvement. "You can't plunk your kid in front of the computer and expect something good to come out of it, even with the best software," he says. Every time a child under 7 sits at the computer, there should be a parent at her side, talking and interacting around it. In his home, the computer is one resource among many and it's not used as a baby-sitter or as entertainment. He enforces limits on screen time: His kids can have two half-hour sessions a day; interestingly, they rarely use it that often, going many days at a time without ever touching it. He also has restrictions on software: no "drill and skill," no shoot-em-ups, no Internet surfing.

Another researcher, Howard Budin, who is director of the Center for Technology and School Change at Teachers College at Columbia and who also reveiws children's software, says the best guideline for buying software is to look for programs that are open-ended and allow a child to do more than they could do with traditional media; software that supports a child's writing or drawing generally gets his approval. Like most other researchers, he doesn't like the Living Books series; they don't substitute for book reading, he says, and they don't teach children to read, just to learn what they have to do to get to the animation. At home, he subscribes to the "use it for a purpose" theory. His sixth-grade son spends his computer time on spreadsheets, graphics programs, and 3-D renderings. Asked to recommend one program for kids other than *Kid Pix*, he hesitates only for a second: *The Logical Journey of the Zoombinis*, he says, is a problem-solving software that operates on different levels and is appropriate for children of all ages.

By second grade, it's reasonable for children to be on the computer alone—however, always with a purpose, not for entertainment. Set limits around its use; forty-five minutes a day is reasonable, but only after homework, piano practice, or other responsibilities.

Internet interactions

Sometimes when your child is between 8 and 10, another big question surfaces: Does she belong in cyberspace? Personal safety is first and foremost on our minds, and for good reason. A child could unwittingly provide enough information for someone to find her *off*-line; it has happened. For this reason, every professional I've interviewed says that children under 10 should not be allowed to go on-line unless an adult is with them. For children 10 or older who want to go on-line, here are some basic rules to get your child to agree to:

- Never give your full name, phone number, or address without your parents' permission;

- Never agree to meet someone in person without your parents' permission;

- Never send your photo out on-line or post a photo on a homepage without talking to your parents;

- Never agree to engage in a private conversation;

- If a conversation makes you uncomfortable, turn off the computer and tell an adult. (As seemingly simple as this rule is, it seems to elude kids. They tend to think it would be rude.)

Safety is not the only issue to be concerned about, however. As fellow *Globe* columnist Ellen Goodman writes, "In many ways, parents today see the communications revolution as a coup d'état. The power to guide children, to shape and screen the cultural messages, was taken from our hands by the television in our living room and now by the information superhighway running through home, school, and library." Her point is that we aren't as powerless as we think. Just because the information is out there and available doesn't mean we can't control its access or affect its influence.

It's easy to see both the good and bad of the Internet. When Harry's daughter was 13, her favorite TV show was *My So-Called Life*. On-line, she found chat groups about it. That was good. "Rather than passively consume the show, she had an opportunity to think and talk about what she found meaningful and to download photos of the stars," says her father. "In that way, the Internet enhanced Amy's experience."

The problem was how much time she was spending doing it. As a computer professional, this father was more able than some parents to take the long view. He wants both his daughters to be able to navigate the Internet. "It will be a big part of their future even if we don't yet know in what way," he says. On the other hand, he notes, "I wouldn't want her on more than an hour a day." He set a limit for Amy of thirty minutes on school days and an hour a day on the weekends.

Knowing if on-line activity is good or bad for your child depends greatly on the individual. Media researcher Renee Hobbs says there are two crucial questions for parents: Which activity is not being done because he's on the computer? Is she developing a new skill from being on-line or honing existing ones? A chat room may build personal confidence in a shy child who finds a forum for expressing himself. But if an already social 12-year-old is just doing more socializing on the net instead of practicing violin, that's a negative. A Web site with lots of reading may be worth the time away from sports for a preteen who isn't much of a reader, but not for an overweight youngster who already buries himself in books and gets little physical activity.

Here's another important question Hobbs says we should be able to answer: Where does your child go when he's on-line? Most of us don't have the foggiest idea.

Just as parents are wise to see what's on the TV a child is glued to, so should we pay attention to what's on the computer screen, particularly if you have a child in the middle school years with a potential interest in sexual topics. There are lots of sites you don't want a 10- or 12-year-old going to because they are geared to sex and drugs. Pornography is not as available as parents have been led to think, according to many computer experts. Pornography is mostly available on bulletin boards and you need the phone number of a particular modem to get to it. On the other hand, a 12-year-old boy in the market for sexual content will find it. Parents with children of a certain age would be wise to purchase blocking technology. They would also be wise to make sure that any computer with a modem is in a public space in the house, not in your child's bedroom. When it's in the kitchen or family room, you can frequently and casually walk past and see what's she's up to without it even looking like you are paying attention. When it's in her room and you want to know what's going on, you're being intrusive.

Another powerful protective strategy is to provide our children with appropriate literacy skills for the Internet. Many of the most popular sites among preteens are nothing more than commercials, frequently for alcoholic beverages. Hobbs says the sites often are so beautifully assembled that the typical 12-year-old doesn't even know it's an ad. Mud sites are also very popular. These are interactive fantasy environments with multiple players who generally assume game identities. Many of them are addictive, not just in the sense that kids don't want to turn them off, but also because a child can't drop the persona when he goes off-line.

Internet use is also causing problems in school. Bill Schechter, a history teacher at Lincoln-Sudbury Regional High School in Massachusetts, says he knows the Internet has the capacity to be a tremendous tool for research, but so far he hasn't seen how. "I'm getting to the point where I'm not going to accept Internet research," he says, "The technology for cheating far outdistances a teacher's ability to recognize it. All I'm seeing is lazy Internet use, where kids use it as an excuse not to open a book, not to check sources, not to go to the library."

Software researcher Howard Budin says one of the problems is the vastness of the Internet; it overwhelms middle-school-age children. Last year, his son's fifth-grade research project required two Internet sources. "When he did a search for 'panda,' he turned up 54,000 entries! How could he deal with that?" he asks. Luckily, his son isn't allowed on the Internet without his dad right there, so Budin was immediately able to weed out thousands of entries that belonged to schools with pandas for mascots. But it took even an experienced navigator like Budin half an hour to get to the appropriate sites.

What children need to know from the first introduction to the net is that it is a source of information, not entertainment. Here are some ways to increase your child's on-line safety:

- Get him in the habit of asking questions: Who created this site I'm in and why? How credible is this source and/or information? Is someone benefiting from my using/believing it? The idea is to get children away from the automatic assumption that because they find information on-line it is therefore accurate. Applying critical thinking skills to on-line data is also important as schools go on-line. Parents should feel free to inquire if similar questions are being addressed in the classroom.

- If your child really wants a computer in his room, the compromise is to give him the computer but not the modem.

- In the classroom, make sure teachers are not putting kids on-line just for the sake of enabling kids to have access. You should expect to see them customizing use to make it interactive in an educational way. Researchers are increasingly urging schools to steer away from computer labs and to put computers in the classrooms instead. That way they're more likely to be integrated into the curriculum and to be seen as one more tool, along with the dictionary and pencil sharpener.

- Establish with your child an evolving list of favorite sites. Agree that you will be adding and subtracting to this frequently. This works best with a child going on-line for the first time, because you can set some standards and establish a "favorite places" menu. If he's already been on-line, ask him to give you a tour of his favorite sites. Ask why he likes each one but don't be judgmental; there are lots of really stupid environments that aren't dangerous, just dumb. In the course of any of this, if you find a site you don't want him to be in, shutting him down doesn't mean he won't go there again, it just means he'll know better than to share it with you. Which is why it's better to have him agree up front to an *evolving* list of favorite sites and why you need to communicate your values around these issues: "I don't like this site because . . ."

Facing the music

> "Back off, back off bitch,
> down in the gutter, lyin' in the ditch,
> you better back off, back off bitch.
> Face of an angel with the love of a witch.
> Back off, back off bitch, back off, back off bitch."
>   From "Back Off Bitch"
>   by Axl Rose, Guns N' Roses

Ever wonder what your middle-school-aged child is listening to on his headset? As bad as these lyrics are by Axl Rose of the group Guns N' Roses, they're mild compared to some of what our kids listen to. Lyrics are rife with four-letter words, messages of women as objects and men as tools, with the glamorization of violence and with sexist, racist, and homophobic themes. Music videos are even worse because the offensive lyrics have visuals to match. In fact, even if the lyrics are acceptable, don't assume the accompanying video will be. Often the image has nothing to do with the lyrics and is sexually explicit or violent even though the message is not.

With all this in mind, Laura decided one day to listen to her 11-year-old son's favorite Guns N' Roses tape. "All I had to do was listen once to know they were not the values I want for him," she says. "They were very sexist, appallingly racist."

Heated arguments ensued. She told Sam he couldn't listen to the music. Sam said he was the only kid whose mother felt that way. "Those mothers aren't paying attention," she retorted. "I am. I care." That registered, but what registered even more was when she quoted the lyrics themselves—unquotable here—to her son.

"Mom!" he said. "Don't say things like that!"

"But I'm just saying what they say on those songs! You mean it's okay to listen to that on a lyric, but it's not okay to say it?" she asked.

"What are you talking about? Those words aren't on that tape!"

Laura couldn't believe her ears. They listened to the tape together and to another, and then another. Sam was as surprised as Laura was incredulous.

"I just like the music," he said. "I guess I don't even hear the words."

> *Check your child's music for the voluntary labeling by record companies that indicates it contains explicit lyrics. This would obviously be music worth your while to listen to and talk about.*

Is Sam typical of other kids his age, or is he an exception? Driving carpool, I heard my son's friend, seated next to me in the front, singing softly with the radio. My ears perked up at "making love." Suddenly he asked the kids in the back, "Don't you think it's weird that the Spice Girls would tell her boyfriend that she wants to share him with her friends?"

This 9-year-old, at least, was paying attention to lyrics.

Even if preteens aren't buying the music for the lyrics and aren't buying what the lyrics say, we need to be paying attention. Parental laissez-faire on a subject like this is equivalent to saying "I approve." Indeed, by saying nothing you are saying a lot: You're saying that it is possible to have two sets of values, values for home and values for outside the family; that as long as what happens at home is kind and polite and decorous, you don't care what values he adheres to elsewhere.

That your child likes the music at all indicates he's trying to separate from you. Whether it starts at 8 or 12, it's a sign of healthy, normal development. As my sister says, think back to the music of your own preteen years. Elvis? The Doors? The Stones? Pink Floyd? Your parents didn't like it, did they? Didn't that make you like it more?

In almost every generation, music is one of the first battle lines that get drawn between parents and children; music is easily available and it speaks to the issues a child this age is dealing with. The typical preteen is coping with a number of fears and anxieties, but most especially a fear of isolation or of not being accepted by peers, and anxiety over changes in his or her body. One reason horror films are popular among 11- to 14-year-olds is that the monster's struggle with his body parallels how preteens feel about their bodies. Music serves a similar purpose. The middle-school-age child is breaking away from us—it's what he's supposed to do—and moving toward the peer group that is forming its own culture with heroes and icons, ideas and ideologies. Music typically becomes a means of articulating that culture and voices a child's deeply felt hopes, angst, desires, and fears. Lyrics tend to be reflective, which is one of the reasons kids can relate to them. Clearly not all kids are as oblivious to lyrics as Sam.

It's unrealistic to think we can convince them not to listen to their music, but it's perfectly reasonable to try to get them to evaluate what they listen to so they don't accept the lyrics as statements of fact. If we want our kids to be able to hear us, however, we need to come at them with an I-understand-you-like-this-music attitude rather than with value judgments ("This isn't music, it's just noise!") or outrage ("We raised you on good music!"). Such responses, even if true, will only make your child defensive and angry and reinforce her feelings of not being understood.

It's at this point that many parents turn to censorship. Researchers say it doesn't work and advise against it. In fact, they say it's the worst thing we can do: It gives a child reason to be angry with you, justification (in his mind) to sneak behind your back. Certainly if we think our role as parent is to be an educator, censorship cuts off all possibility of that. There's a philosophical problem with censorship, too. It's a value statement that says to a child "I am teaching that it is okay to control access to information," a value that may be hypocritical for most of us.

The strategy most professionals prefer is to get a dialogue going. One psychologist I know has worked out a deal with his 11-year-old son. Whenever Andy buys or trades a new CD or tape, he gives it to his father to listen to at night, after Andy is asleep. The next day, they compare notes: What did they each think of the guitar work, or the sax solo? What about the lyrics and the overall message? The dad, Tom, works hard to keep the conversation nonjudgmental. If Andy seems to him to be confused or have a wrong impression about a lyric, he might say: "I think there's another way to think about this." When Andy likes a song that Tom doesn't, Tom will ask, "What is it about this that makes you like it?" When the lyrics are particularly offensive to Tom, he might say, "What do you think about what this says about blacks/gays/women?" Tom is often surprised by Andy's answers, but he keeps his responses neutral in tone. The dialogue has become comfortable enough for Andy that he even revealed to his dad that there are some groups he only pretends to like because his friends like them. Rather than harangue

Andy for not being true to himself, Tom understands how important peer acceptance is at this age and says simply, "That's okay for now but keep this in mind: That is not the real you."

Tom loves music of all kinds and doesn't find this a chore. Others of us might find this strategy time-consuming and overly permissive. But something important is going on: Andy keeps coming back for more. Tom is building a trusting relationship and that can't be bad. It's not as if Tom is being a wimp about things, either. Although he keeps the conversations nonthreatening and nonjudgmental, he is very clear about his own values. "I want to be very sure Andy isn't walking away from any of this thinking it's okay to think or talk about women the way Axl Rose does," he says. "Andy tells me he likes it because it's 'naughty,' but he needs to know it's more than that. It's plain wrong."

Tom is convinced Andy hears his messages and he's optimistic he is internalizing them, too, although the jury is still out on that. He had a glimmer of his impact when he and his wife were particularly offended by the cover of a CD that depicted a scantily clad woman in chains. They had a heated discussion with Andy in which they said, "We have a real problem with this. This isn't the way we think about women. What kind of message does this send to your sister?" Andy still listened to the tape but months later, Tom and his wife had their reward. On one of their regular jaunts through a music store with Andy and his friend, they overheard him talk the friend out of buying that group's newest CD.

"I don't want to spend my money on this group," he said. "I think they're anti-women and I wouldn't want my sister seeing that CD cover. Your sister shouldn't see it either. It sends a bad message."

Notice that Andy said, "I don't want to spend *my* money. . . ." This is another important piece of strategy. Andy's parents do not buy music for him. If you're just starting off on this process or you want to be clear about where you stand, you might tell your child: "My conscience doesn't let me give you the money to buy CD's from a group with values so opposite to mine. But I can't stop you from spending your own money on it."

As tedious as this entire process may be, Tom and his wife are helping their child to be more aware of what he listens to, to evaluate and screen out messages. Equally important, they are keeping communication open and buying themselves insurance for the future, when there will be other critical issues in which they want to have input.

Superhero worship

For many parents of boys and for parents of some girls, personal values can force you to take a harder stand when it comes to superhero worship. Consider the dilemma of the mother of a 10-year-old boy who began collecting X-Men trading cards and comic books. The typical card is sexist, frequently obscene and pornographic, depicting women as sex objects, bound and chained, spandexed and coiffed. This mother was about to tell her son that she wouldn't allow him to spend her money on them and that he couldn't spend his own money on them, either, but at the last minute she decided to sleep on the decision before she laid down the law. The next day she discovered that all his friends were trading the cards, including his best friend, whose parents' values always coincided with hers. She decided to back off, voicing her disapproval but stopping short of censorship. Even that generated lots of unhappiness. A week later, she was vindicated. Her son's afterschool program sent home notices detailing which X-Men cards could be traded during the program.

According to the afterschool program director, this mother wasn't the only one thrilled at the policy. "Parents have come to see themselves as powerless in the face of superheroes, whether it's Dennis Rodman or Madonna," said the director.

Unfortunately, it's easy to succumb to this sense of parental powerlessness. If your son's best friend is collecting or is into something, anything, that you don't like, and especially if his parents are people whose opinion you respect, it's not unreasonable to think that perhaps there's something they know that you don't. Perhaps it's not as bad as you think. Perhaps you are overreacting and over-protecting.

What is the superhero fascination anyway? Mostly it's a sense of identity. Through the ages, young boys have always looked to warriors and heroes to gain a sense of what it means to be a man. When you are young and powerless, the world seems overwhelming and threatening. Heroes give young children a way to enter the adult world without feeling lost in it. But there's a difference between having a hero and a superhero. One is a real live person, someone you look up to and admire, someone who is human with a human story full of triumphs and failures, someone whose life offers valuable lessons. Superheroes, on the other hand, are not real. And once again, even though previous generations have had their share, the problem with today's typical superhero—from Spiderman to X-Men—is that even when they champion admirable causes, as many of them do, they use violence to achieve their goals. Even the *Batman* movies, which are very clever and have some great humor, even Superman, who is an altruistic character, leave children with an overall impression that violence is positive, not negative. And because these superheroes are available not just on TV but on videos and computer games, on bedsheets and T-shirts and lunchboxes, there is constant reinforcement for children of this negative, violent message. As Mary Pipher laments, the effect is cumulative. It's not as if a child is exposed to only one violent superhero. There are many of them in a child's life, each one worse than the one before.

The earlier a child is exposed to violent superheroes, the more problematic it can be. Research shows that 2-, 3-, and 4-year-olds who watch superhero violence (usually because it's the viewing choice of older siblings) are the ones most likely in later years to use violence and aggression themselves. Part of the problem is that superhero action totally dehumanizes the enemy, typically portraying the hero as all good and the enemy as all bad. Because preschoolers are developmentally unable to distinguish between degrees of right and wrong, they can get carried away with this dichotomy. If they watch enough, it begins to get into their head: "I am Good, therefore the other person is Bad. Because I am good, my behavior is justified and anything I do to the bad person is okay."

As parents of young children, the best thing we can do is limit exposure to superheroes. Even so, however, we need to be realistic: It's not only through firsthand knowledge that kids get exposed. As a preschooler, my son was never drawn to Teenage Ninja Mutant Turtles, never watched the TV show or the movie or collected the figures. But all his classmates did. As a result, he knew how to do all the kicks, he knew story lines, he got involved in the play, and, yes, he even had Ninja-sponsored bad dreams. In the face of this kind of exposure, we parents can only serve as a counterbalance by continually and clearly presenting our values and hoping for the best: "In our family, we don't think people should hurt each other, ever."

The older they get, the harder this is, but we are never powerless. First, get some data. If your child is caught up in a new kind of trading card or comic book, show some curiosity about it. When the characters have names such as Death Metal and Apocalypse and the stories that go with them involve vows to "drink [only] the blood of criminals" it's time to ask questions—"Tell me what these cards are about? What is it you like about them?" Express your views: "These make me really uncomfortable." "Would you like to see your sister wearing outfits like this? Would you like to see her treated like this?" At the very least, refuse to provide money to buy the items in question.

And now a few words for the good guys. While superhero worship is often problematical, hero worship is not. In fact, it's something parents ought to encourage. Real-life heroes create a certain sense of optimism for children, a feeling that they can grow up and become something successful and have a meaningful place in the world. Sociologist Gary Fine, who studies children's culture, says, "Kids identify with the hero and bask in the reflected glory of that person. That makes them feel happy." Fine is the author of *With the Boys: Little League Baseball and Preadolescent Culture*. By definition, a hero is someone a child looks up to and admires. All children need this but some need it more than others, especially children in troubled homes, children of divorce or abuse. Peak time for hero worship tends to be sixth grade, but research shows even very young children have heroes.

The first hero is usually a parent or relative. Nicole says her grandfather is her hero. "I like the way he handles things when he gets in trouble," she says. Matt, a fourth-grader, says Carl Yastrzemski is his hero. "He wasn't just a great athlete. He helps the Jimmy Fund and that helps kids who are sick." Chris wrote a homework assignment on his hero: "My heroes are people who care for people besides themselves and people who show courage. Magic Johnson showed courage when he heard that he was HIV positive. He wanted to help others and to speak out." The savvy parent and teacher will tap into these interests by encouraging children to soak up all they can about a person, reading and writing reports about them.

Girls have heroes as frequently as boys do, but their choice is more often someone they know rather than a celebrity, probably because fewer females are media figures.

If you think your child has glommed on to a hero who is not a good influence, don't say that flat-out. That will only make a child feel he needs to defend the person, which could make him identify with him even more. Instead, try to enlarge the child's world of experience and use the hero as a source of conversation about what the appeal is and what your values are. If you worry about your child emulating behaviors you don't like, brainstorm with her about other ways to handle the issue the hero is involved with. Some parents who disapprove of a child's choice of hero may feel competitive or threatened by him. If the hero fails in some way or turns from a positive influence to a negative one by getting caught for drug use, for instance, it can actually cause a child to be depressed. At some level, he may have relied on this person. He had an imagined connection to him. This may partially explain why so many children were so confused at the height of the scandals swirling around President Clinton.

With a little help—"Gee, this is really upsetting"—children usually rebound by rationalizing the hero's failure, dispensing with him and finding someone else. If the figure disgraces himself in some dramatic way à la Mike Tyson but remains heroic in the child's eyes, parents need to step in and remind him of the values his hero worship is blinding him to: "Tyson is still a phenomenal athlete and you can admire him for that reason, but he's no longer a hero because of the terrible way he treats women." Whether the hero is being dumped because his batting average dropped or because he's been jailed for rape, this is a loss for a child, a blow. Be sympathetic, help him mourn and then move on.

CHAPTER SIX

Living in a Changing, Complicated, and Sometimes Scary World

. . . .

When I was a grade school student, we had weekly drills in which we practiced crouching under our desks in case of a Soviet attack. During one of those drills in fourth grade, I asked my teacher, Mrs. Hamilton, a freckle-faced, wisecracking redhead whom I adored, what it was about our desks that made them so strong. She was uncharacteristically flustered. "They just are," she finally said. At home that night, I asked my father the same question. "What did your teacher say?" he asked. "Well, then, if that's what she said, then that's that." Now I had it on authority from two adults I trusted that these desks had some kind of magical qualities beyond their appearance, beyond the understanding of a child like me. As a 9-year-old in 1956, I was perfectly satisfied.

I don't know many 9-year-olds for whom that would work today. It's not just that we are raising our children to think for themselves and question authority; a child today would have access to enough information on his own to know that that answer is bogus.

Every generation of parents has to deal with issues their own parents didn't have to face, issues for which they have no role model. In that at least, we can take comfort. In previous generations, however, parents were almost always able to protect their children from information they considered inappropriate. It's not that the issues of homosexuality, sex, drugs, suicide, murder, or kidnapping are unique to our generation; what's different for us as parents is the uninhibited access to information that our children have to them, whether or not we, or they, are ready. For better or for worse, thanks to instant, constant, and multiple modes of communication, not to mention changed social mores, there's literally nothing our children aren't exposed to. As parents today, we are caught in a thicket. Our instincts are to protect them from information, much as our parents protected us. But today, what our children don't hear about from us at home, they hear about on the playground, in the bus, and from friends' older siblings.

Professionals tell us again and again that it is better for children of any age to hear an age-appropriate version of the truth from us than to get inappropriate and inaccurate versions of the truth elsewhere. Inevitably, the spin they put on it from their own imagination is more frightening than the truth doled out in sound bites they can handle. Figuring out what, exactly, the age-appropriate version of the truth is for any given child at any given moment is a daunting task, to say the least. Like the frazzled parent who answers the 3-year-old's "Where did I come from?" with a complicated explanation of conception only to discover the child wants to know if she was born in Philadelphia or Boston, sometimes the hardest part of knowing what to say is knowing what your child wants to know.

When the news raises anxiety

A 9-year-old who hears about a knife fight on a school bus in the next town shows good sense when he asks his bus driver if she'll save him a seat in the first row until he feels safe again. A 10-year-old who hears about the hole in the ozone layer and says he wouldn't want to travel to Antarctica has a healthy grip on a scary subject. But if the 12-year-old won't ride the bus at all, or the 10-year-old won't go on a Cape Cod vacation because the hole might move, anxiety has run amok.

There's anxiety and there's *anxiety*.

Our job as parents is to keep garden-variety anxiety from moving along the continuum to the italicized version. Unfortunately, life makes it hard for us. While researchers and clinicians have long agreed that some children are more anxious than others because of genetic predisposition, they are now considering another possibility: that increased exposure to frightening things in our world is causing more children to be more anxious, including those who are not wired to be that way naturally.

As a rule, children are adaptive and resilient. But if they get too much information at too young an age and it strains their cognitive abilities, it can begin to interfere with how they function. If in addition to that they have repeated personal or media exposure to whatever causes their anxiety, the problem gets compounded. Generally, the fallout is that they can't concentrate at school, want to stay close to home, can't fall asleep at night, or have repeated headaches or stomachaches. There are several studies that show just how all of this is creeping up on our children, including compelling research indicating that contemporary issues (fear of drive-by shootings, gangs, drugs, kidnapping, and nuclear war, in that order) are edging out what have long been considered the developmental fears of grade school children—big animals, ghosts, the dark, and being alone. A study by Harvard sociologist Ron Kessler shows that the number of 12- and 13-year-olds who were afraid to leave their neighborhood has doubled in the past decade, from about 2 percent to about 5 percent. Research by West Virginia University psychologist Tracy Morris concludes that rural children are developing anxieties that are unrealistic for where they live. Her favorite example is of a 9-year-old who didn't want to move with his family from a Midwestern town of 10,000 to one of 20,000. "He thought they wouldn't be safe because of what he'd heard on the national news about gang violence in some distant city," Morris says.

If a child is predisposed to be anxious, you'll see hints of it in the preschool years: cautiousness, unwillingness to venture into new situations, unhappiness at loud noises or strange smells. Once in elementary school, this is the child who may pick up a new worry a day: Is this the kind of pencil I'm supposed to have? Will Tim sit next to me? What if I don't know the answer? For the child who doesn't have this lowered threshold, anxiety is more likely triggered by specific events. A shooting that kills a merchant in town, even though it's not someone she knows, can so overwhelm a child that she can think of nothing else. She worries every time someone in her family goes to a store, and she may not want to leave you to go to school for fear you'll get shot while you're shopping. The trigger can also be ordinary events that combine to make her feel out of control.

> *Bedtime or the middle of the night is the wrong time to have a conversation about whatever is worrying your child; you'll only fuel the anxiety. A better strategy is a reassuring hug, a promise to talk in the morning, a trip to the kitchen for something to drink, and casual, unrelated conversation.*

To reestablish control, he may want things done in a certain way: clothes laid out precisely, breakfast served in a proscribed sequence, a goodbye kiss proffered only on the right cheek. For some children, these are no more than exaggerated superstitions that aren't a big deal. For others, if it doesn't happen in this way, their day is ruined. In extreme cases, this can lead to severe disorders. (If you're worried that apparent ritualistic behavior is getting out of control, talk to your pediatrician.)

The best antidote for anxiety, yours and your child's, is to talk about the issue and the feelings, something many of us purposely avoid. Parents who are anxious themselves may think their kids will catch their worries, or that by talking about something big and scary, especially if in involves children—the Oklahoma City bombing, the Jonesboro, Arkansas, murders—they will put ideas in their child's head. That thinking usually backfires. Without information and without our interpretation, children tend to read the wrong message into things, including even our actions. This is a concept you're going to read about often in this chapter, and nothing illustrates it better than this anecdote from a Wisconsin psychologist. One of his clients was the family of a first-grader. His parents reported that in the course of four months, their son had gone from being outgoing and happy to withdrawn and uncommunicative, and they couldn't figure out why. What the psychologist eventually was able to piece together was that the mother was afraid to drive in bad weather. She would send her son to school telling him that she would pick him up, but almost every winter day, she would call school to leave a message for him to go home with his friend's mother. Because she never explained to him why she did that, in the absence of information he concluded she didn't care enough to come herself. His friend's mom always came, after all, so she must love her son more than his mom loved him. A simple, age-appropriate explanation of the mother's anxiety—"It makes me nervous to drive in bad weather"—not only would have eliminated the possibility of her son's misinterpretation but also would have modeled for him that it's okay to talk about fears. The younger your child is when you start to do that, the better. Kids who grow up thinking fear is for sissies are more vulnerable for major anxieties later on.

The Tobin Elementary School in Boston is in a neighborhood where crime is high. One morning at recess, some fourth-graders saw it firsthand. As they were playing on the playground, shooting erupted across the street. The area filled with police, ambulances, and onlookers. It was only a matter of minutes before word reached them that a man had been killed. Holly Nathan-Colon was the student service coordinator at the school, responsible for interpreting violence to children in a way that would help them cope and also mitigate against their tendency to normalize it. As word reached them of the murder, she and her staff went into overdrive, meeting with small groups of students.

> *Never force or shame a child into facing a fear. Embarrassing or belittling him—"You're a wimp"—tends to become a self-fulfilling prophecy.*

"You can't pretend it didn't happen or minimize it," she explained. "You have to validate the fear. 'Yes, that really did happen. It's okay to be afraid.' After that, you can talk about ways in which they can be safe."

Situations at home are hopefully far less traumatic, but we can prepare our children in advance for the day something fearful comes along by giving them a secure and reassuring base to work from. That means being proactive. Point out now and then the ways in which you keep your family safe: You lock your doors when you leave the house, you leave porch lights on when you go out at night, you have rules about talking to people you don't know, about not getting into cars with people you don't know. Model behavior that has safety in mind and point it out when you do. If you are walking on the sidewalk with your 7-year-old and there's a group of unruly, intimidating teenagers in front of you and you cross the street to avoid them, saying nothing is as bad as saying "Look at these kids! Boy, they're scary-looking." The idea isn't to make a child frightened but to make him feel empowered. Say instead, "Those kids are so loud they make me uncomfortable. Let's cross here." As you're leaving the house to go on errands, mutter loudly enough for your daughter to hear, almost as if you're thinking out loud: "I want to be sure to lock the door. That's one of the ways I keep my family safe." If your child asks you, "Why do you put the porch light on when we aren't home?" answer honestly: "I do it for two reasons. One is so we won't trip when we come up the stairs in the dark, and the other is to keep our house safe. Robbers usually only go to a house that's dark."

Just as we need to take seriously the preschooler who says there are monsters in the basement (Ask: "Where is he? What does he look like? What should we do to make him our friend?"), we don't want to dismiss the fears of an older child whose hypothetical thinking causes her fears to expand and include local and world events. By not dismissing the fear, whether it's ghosts in the closet or holes in the ozone layer, you tell your child she can trust you to help her. Whether it's encouraging her to look under the bed with you for the ghosts or going to the library to read more about pollution solutions, you're helping her take responsibility for confronting her fear.

Sociologist Kessler says worry about local and national events is most prevalent among 12- to 14-year-olds. Nip it in the bud by being immediately responsive and specific; put things into perspective without making them worse: "Okay, realistically what are the chances that in the next five years, pollution would get so bad that the world's food supply would be threatened?" Because they are so good at hypothetical thinking, kids this age are great at coming up with all sorts of hypothetical "what if's:" What if the ozone layer got so big it covered North America? What if there was no space left for trash? What if Iraq really did unleash biological warfare? An antidote for the endless stream of "what if's" is a sense of control. Help your child develop an action plan: "What can we do in our family to not contribute to pollution?" At the same time, keep your child doing everything he is supposed to do. If you let the anxiety restrict or affect his life, you're fueling it. Often you can negotiate gradual progress. The 12-year-old may be too frightened even to ask the driver to save him a seat on the school bus, but he may buy into an action plan that calls for you to drop him at the stop closest to school for three days, then one farther away for three days, and so on, until he works his way back to his regular stop. If you share his worry about bus safety, it's okay to tell him so as long as you also talk about how you are coping: "I'm worried about the buses, too, so I've called the school to talk about increasing security on the bus. There's going to be a meeting for parents on Tuesday."

Whenever there is a national or local story that involves children and garners big headlines and discussion in the community, assume your children will tune in to it, even when other bigger stories don't make their radar screen. If there's a suicide, murder, or kidnapping that involves children or parents, your children need help interpreting what they hear. Even a 3- or 4-year-old who attends preschool or day care is likely to hear something about it. The Oklahoma City bombing comes to mind; so, too, does the Wayland, Massachusetts, story of Sarah Pryor. Sarah was 9 years old when she disappeared in 1986. Twelve years later, scientists identified bone fragments that belonged to her, and her parents finally were able to have a burial. The funeral got huge media attention in the Boston area. Every story repeated the original tragedy, and even though the kidnapping and murder were twelve years old, children reacted as though it had just happened. Many parents reported their children were afraid to walk home from the bus stop or from a friend's house.

A child who knows, even peripherally, the victim of any crime is obviously going to be affected more than a child who doesn't, but even children who don't know the victim may need intervention and monitoring. Since the concern is that a child will harbor a fear that grows out of control, the first rule of thumb is to find out what your child already knows. Begin by asking, "Have you heard about—?" If he has, he might say nothing more than "Yeah." Follow up with: "What do you think about that?" or "Do you have any questions about it?" Since you don't want to push it, and since many children won't respond, you could then say, "If you have any questions about it, feel free to ask me." If he hasn't heard about it and you know it's only a matter of time until he does, you can say something basic: "Well, there was a story in the news that people might be talking about. I thought I'd give you the facts so you'll have it straight." Then give a simple, straightforward explanation: "There was a bombing in Oklahoma, which is far from here, and a lot of people were killed, including some children. It's pretty awful."

Thankfully, the murder of a child is not something we hear about often, but when such a story makes the news, particularly if it is in your community but even if it is not, it is not safe to assume that your school-age child won't hear about it or that he will hear about it but not be troubled. Most likely, he will hear about it and be too scared or confused to talk about it. The fear that he will have, even if he doesn't voice it, even if your home is happy, healthy, and nonviolent, is this: What about me? Could this happen to me? Don't wait until your child shows you in some way that he's frightened; by then, he's already suffering. Bring the topic up: "Something very sad happened, I'm sure you'll hear people talking about it." Share the barest of details—a 6-year-old boy died, his father killed him. Answer any questions honestly but age-appropriately, which means staying as close to the truth as possible but not answering what isn't being asked. Most children take information in without registering a reaction, but if a young child is frightened by what he hears, it will most likely come out through a change in behavior. A kindergartner who was never clingy suddenly will be. He may be newly afraid of the dark, won't go into a room alone, or will manifest some other new fear. An older child may also have new fears or develop violent or gory themes in play or school work. Bed-wetting or sleep problems may crop up. Of course, these behavioral changes could be due to any number of things, but if they come in the aftermath of hearing about this news event, it's pretty safe to conclude they're connected. Sometimes the connection is obvious. In the wake of a story where a father is accused of murdering or kidnapping a child, if your child suddenly doesn't want Daddy to play with him or put him to bed, it's a no-brainer what's behind the change. If you're really unsure if there's a connection, ask him to draw a picture of what's on his mind. Remember, too, that some children are more vulnerable to these stories than others: A child whose life is chaotic, who has seen or experienced violence or has reason to think a parent may harm him, is most likely to personalize another child's murder. A child whose parents are divorced, especially if they are angry, is most likely to personalize another child's kidnapping. This child is the one teachers and parents need to monitor most, but he is not alone in his vulnerability. Any young child can become fearful as the result of these news stories; it goes with the developmental territory.

If you determine a specific crime or event is on his mind, a good question to ask is "Can you imagine this happening to you?" In the wake of a Boston area murder of a 6-year-old boy by his father, several school-age children I know in happy, healthy two-parent families asked their parents why a father would kill a child. It's often hard to come up with an answer, but you might try something like this: "Honestly, I don't know, I can't imagine it myself. But I will try to get the details of this story and I'll let you know if I do." You don't necessarily need to volunteer information after that, but you need to have information ready in case he brings it up again. A good response to a young child who persists might be "Why do *you* think a daddy might do this?" Since young children tend to put unrelated facts together, he might say it happened because of a behavior you yelled at him for, or he may associate the murder with the place he was in at the time he heard about it and think that place isn't safe anymore. Rather than try to disabuse a child of the fantasy he has created, provide extra doses of love and reassurance about your ability to protect him. Listen to your 4-year-old's version of why a father might do that and then say, "You know, Daddy and I love you and we will take care of you." That may be all she needs to hear.

With school-age children, changes in behavior may show up in school: A child may be quieter than usual, have trouble concentrating, or overreact. Because a child of this age can understand on a slightly more abstract level, she may want more detail. This is always a good opportunity to talk about the people in her world who are there to protect her in addition to you—policemen, firefighters, teachers—and about steps to take when there is danger. For most children, the trauma they experience from hearing about a child's murder is not lasting, unless the victim was someone they knew very well. In that case, you should consult a professional.

When children hear about suicide

Suicide is one of those topics children are aware of at younger ages than we think, certainly by 9 or 10. That does not mean we should talk about it to them when there is no context, but if they hear about a suicide, we should be prepared with honest, age-appropriate information. Because suicide is so prevalent among teenagers today, what you want your child to know from as early an age as possible is that you are available for her to talk to if she ever feels unhappy, lonely, or depressed; that suicide is neither glamorous nor normal; and that there is help for people who feel suicidal. In other words, consider talking to a child about suicide as a form of prevention, not just as a matter of helping her cope with upsetting information.

Of all the topics that are tricky to talk to children about, this may be one of the hardest because we are so uncomfortable with it ourselves. It's because of that discomfort that suicide tends to get shrouded in euphemisms, most commonly "He died by his own hand." Children tend to take statements like these literally. One preschooler, told that his teacher "took his own life," wanted to know "Where did he take it?" The best explanations for suicide, then, are ones that are truthful: "Your teacher ended his life. He killed himself." Psychologist Pamela Cantor of Needham, Massachusetts, past president of the National Committee on Youth Suicide Prevention, says honesty is so important on this subject because we want our children to trust us and feel they can come to us with their feelings. "If you hide or deny the truth about something like this, you jeopardize that trust," she says. They'll get the information sooner or later from someone else and then feel they can't trust you.

Before you dole out information about a suicide, however, find out what your child already knows, much as described earlier about a murder:

Dad: "Did you hear that Michael's brother died?"

Child: "Yeah. I heard he killed himself."

Dad: "I heard that, too. What do you think?"

A 7-year-old in this conversation might say, "What a dumb thing to do!" in which case you would agree and move on. But a 12-year-old might say, "Yeah, well, a lot of people kill themselves," in which case you need to say, "No, it's really very unusual," and give him more opportunity to talk. Your child's perception will depend, as always, on his age as well as on the relationship he had to the deceased. Expect a child under 12 to have an egocentric response: Did I do anything to cause it? Will it happen to me?

When the victim is someone they know, perhaps the older sibling of a peer, a child may be angry at the adults: "How could they let this happen?" They may also worry: "Will this happen to *my* older brother?" All these issues need to be addressed, but most important among them is the issue of blame and responsibility. You might say, "Almost anyone who knew Michael's brother feels guilty. I certainly do, even though I hadn't talked to him in a long time. Do you think there is something you did that made him kill himself?" Whatever the answer, this is your opening for some mental health education:

- **With preschoolers.** Be honest but careful with your language. It's okay to say, for instance, "Some people who get very sad or lonely don't realize that if they shared their sadness with someone else they would feel better." Or: "He couldn't see the good side of life and doctors say that thinking that everything is bad is a kind of sickness. He didn't realize there are doctors who can help a person who feels that way."

- **With a 6- to 8-year-old.** The explanation can be more detailed: "A person who kills herself has an illness in the brain. But since we can't see the brain, we don't always know when it isn't working right. Her thinking became unclear because of this sickness in the brain, and she didn't see any other way to solve her problems. There are doctors for this kind of illness, just like there's a doctor if you have a pain in your heart or your knee. It's too bad she didn't realize there are doctors who can help with these kinds of problems." If she asks you, "Am I going to kill myself?" a good response might be: "No. That person didn't understand that he could get help, but you know if you are feeling sad you could talk to us and we'd get you the help you need."

- **With an 8- to 12-year-old.** You can talk more abstractly: "When a person dies by killing himself, that person feels so much emotional pain and struggles against it so much until finally it is too exhausting to keep struggling. The person doesn't know he has choices. You need to know that no matter how bleak life looks, you can always come to me for help." With a child 12 or older, you might also extract this promise: "I want you to promise that if you ever thought you wanted to kill yourself, you would tell me or some other adult."

A child at any age is likely to ask "How did she do it?" It's a perfectly reasonable question (you're curious, aren't you?) but, once again, tricky to answer. You want to be truthful, but in a vague sort of way. You don't want to provide a recipe. A bad answer would be a dismissive one: "You don't need to think about that." A better approach is to ask, "What did you hear?" Your response should be honest—"Yes, he hanged himself"—without elaborating on how he accomplished that. For a child who probes further you might say, "I honestly don't know how a person goes about doing it," or "You know that you have to breathe to stay alive. Well, Michael's brother stopped himself from breathing, but I don't know exactly how he did it."

If your child seems preoccupied with this aspect of the suicide, no matter what his age, mention it to your pediatrician. Keep in mind, also, that dealing with the suicide of someone who was close to a child is extremely complicated, and professional help is suggested.

Alleviating fears about kidnapping

When a kidnapping makes the news, parents typically react in one of two ways: We say nothing in the hopes our child won't hear about it, or we say too much, causing a child to imagine she is in danger when she isn't. Obviously, neither response is helpful.

Even if you live far from where the kidnapping occurred, once it's in the public arena, either on the news a lot or in people's conversation, assume your child has heard about it. In 1994, there were twenty-seven alleged would-be child abductions in the Boston area. It was big news, in the headlines and TV news constantly, and it affected kids in big ways. At one of the schools where an alleged abduction attempt took place, an 8-year-old asked her parents to drive her to and from school every day, even though school was literally around the corner and she had always walked. A kindergartner at another school where an attempt was made told his mother one morning, "I'm worried strangers will hurt someone else, not me." The mother wisely suspected that wasn't his true worry.

Unfortunately, kidnapping is not as rare an occurrence as it once was, and news of any kidnapping has the potential to make school-age children anxious and increase their sense of vulnerability. Contrary to what our instincts tell us, not talking to a child fuels the fright because it feeds into a child's normal, developmental fear of people with evil intent, robbers, for instance. (At 10, my son still periodically asks, "What would you do if there was a robber in our house?" Usually there has been nothing I'm aware of to put the subject in his mind.) But talking to our children is not as simple these days as saying "Don't talk to a stranger." We need to be far more concrete and specific.

Maria, the mother of a kindergartner, got into a conversation one morning at the school bus stop with a 5-year-old girl who was also waiting for the bus with her mother. They were talking about ways to be helpful to other people. "What would you do if a man you didn't know asked you to help him find his lost puppy?" Maria asked.

"I'd help him," the girl replied, without hesitation.

"That's nice that you want to help people," Maria said. "But shouldn't you check first with an adult in charge before you help a stranger?"

"Oh, I know that," the child said. "My mom told me about strangers."

To this child, someone looking for a lost puppy was benign. He wasn't a stranger.

The conversation graphically illustrates that a young child's idea of a bad person typically doesn't include someone who is engaging or pleasant-looking; a bad person would have a gun, or be mean, badly dressed, or grotesque. Starting at age 3, children need to know that you can't always tell a bad person from the outside, that sometimes bad people are so tricky they *look good.* At the same time, it can worry a child if he thinks it is up to him to decide whether someone is bad or not. You can remove that burden by providing specific behaviors to be wary of: someone who needs help with directions; someone who has lost something, not just a puppy but his glasses or an earring; someone who says Mommy has been hurt. Present these scenarios as a rule: "If someone says/does this then you . . ." Place this person in a setting familiar to your child: What if you were in the supermarket and someone said, "Can you show me where the milk is?" "What if you were in front of our house and someone was looking for his son's bike?"

Give your child the opportunity to tell you her ideas for keeping herself safe too. You may be surprised at her answers. Boys 4 to 7 are quick to say "I know karate," or "No one could hurt me." This kind of all-powerful response is not necessarily meant to be taken literally. It is a child's way of presenting himself as more powerful than he really is because it makes him feel safe to have those thoughts. A good response is to translate for him: "You mean you would kick and

scream until someone came to help you? That's smart thinking."
Or: "You mean they couldn't hurt you because you would scream
your loudest and run your fastest? Your yell is so loud and you run so
fast, that would be good." If your child's response is a powerless
one—"There's nothing I could do"—the message to get across is
that he is not, in fact, helpless. The Massachusetts Children's Trust
Fund offers these rules to give a child to keep her safe and to feel
empowered. Try to present them matter-of-factly:

- Always check with an adult you know before changing plans or
  helping someone.

- Use the buddy system. Have someone with you at the mall,
  walking to school, riding your bike, or in any public place.

- If someone approaches you or says or does something that
  makes you feel uncomfortable, run away and tell an adult in
  charge. If they grab you, scream your loudest.

- Stay a grown-up step away from someone you don't know who
  tries to talk to you, or even from someone you do know who
  makes you feel uncomfortable.

The challenge, of course, is to provide information without
panicking him. That means you can't be panicky yourself. Knowing
the statistics on stranger abductions may calm your fears. According
to a national study on abductions done for the U.S. Department of
Justice, there are more than 350,000 child abductions a year by
someone who knows the child, usually a family member, and only
200 to 300 child abductions a year by strangers, when a child is
taken at least overnight by someone they have never seen before and
then held for ransom or murdered.

In addition to giving your children rules, help them learn to
identify adults in charge, people it is safe to go to for help: the
cashier in a store, a police officer in uniform, a teacher. It's also a

good idea to role-play with a child because children learn best by doing: "Pretend I'm someone you never saw before. What would you do if I said . . ." Ideally, this kind of discussion should take place periodically, in the same way you remind your child to look both ways when crossing the street. If you talk about this only in the wake of a crisis, it may make her more aware of people around her or may cause her to think someone is following her. If your child does report being followed, treat it seriously. Retrace her footsteps and call the authorities, even if you conclude that she imagined it. To her, it was real and she needs to know that she can count on you to take her seriously. If false alarms happen repeatedly, that can be a sign of a more serious anxiety and you should consult a professional.

Wrapped into these conversations should be a discussion about inappropriate touching. Begin by identifying the private parts of the body and naming the people who are allowed to touch you there, such as a doctor or nurse. Be sure to talk about the difference between okay touching and not-okay touching—"If someone touches any part of your body and it makes you uncomfortable, it's not okay"—and the difference between okay secrets and ones that are not okay: "If someone touches your private parts and wants you to keep it a secret, it's not okay." As long as these conversations are handled in a matter-of-fact and calm manner, they will not make your child fearful, which is the reason parents typically give for not having such talks. Indeed, study after study shows that children feel better about themselves and are less likely to be frightened if they have been given coping skills. It makes them feel less powerless.

Coping with environmental and other world catastrophes

About a week after the World Trade Center bombing in Manhattan, Tracy, 8, who lives in a Boston suburb, got up an hour earlier than usual, at six a.m., and joined her father for breakfast. Amid mouthfuls of cereal, she asked him, "Daddy, you work in a skyscraper, don't you?"

"Yep, thirty-fifth floor," he replied proudly. "Great views."

The next morning, she was there again. She wanted to sit in his lap. "Can you stay home from work today?" she asked.

On the third day, she cried and pleaded with him, "Daddy, pleasepleaseplease don't go to work today." By now, of course, both father and mother suspected something was troubling their daughter, and they began systematically to look at her life. Luckily, they put in a call to her teacher. It took only a brief conversation to learn that three days before her appearance at breakfast, there had been a current events discussion that included the World Trade Center bombing. Tracy had concluded that because her father worked in a skyscraper, he was in danger. As it turned out, other children in the class had come to the same conclusion about their parents who worked in downtown Boston buildings, and the teacher had received calls from them too. She regretted that she had not sent a note home alerting the parents to the discussion.

Young children have a way of personalizing everything, and catastrophes are no exception. Once again, for them it comes down to one basic issue: What about me? What about my safety? What adds to the terrifying nature of catastrophes today is that children are better able to visualize them from having watched disaster movies and from seeing scenes of real-life disasters on the TV news. A second-grader I know refused to eat anything for several days after he heard a discussion on the radio about radiation from a Russian power plant that had exploded and contaminated crops. Luckily, his mother had heard the same report. It had been a historical look at Chernobyl. The fact that this had happened years ago had escaped him. Sometimes what it takes to reassure a child is so simple that it doesn't occur to us. For instance, after the World Trade Center bombing, many children thought the building had been bombed many times. They didn't know that TV news programs were repeating the same footage over and over. Remind your child that they have instant replays on the news, just like they do on sports.

Parents shouldn't be surprised that what a child reacts most strongly to are natural or environmental disasters. From the earliest age, children relate to animals and nature in a kind of magical way. Seeing TV footage of oil-soaked birds and seals, whales trapped on beaches, elephant carcasses left to rot after being plundered for ivory—these disasters are very upsetting to children, and they often react with an intensity that astounds parents. Solid-waste disposal is an issue many school-age children glom on to in a very concrete way too. They see how much trash they produce in their own house and they worry: If everyone's house makes this much trash, what will happen? Will there be enough room for me to live in the world?

The antidote to unduly worrying children is to create an environment in which no subject is taboo. If a child cares enough to ask a question, she deserves an answer, not a dismissal. Telling her "You don't have to worry about that," or "That happened far away, it doesn't affect us," leaves room for imagination to flourish or for peers' inaccuracies to fill in the blanks. On the other hand, while you shouldn't shield children from the real world, you also shouldn't overburden them with responsibility or guilt. Help a child develop a sense of being part of the human community by achieving a delicate balance of raising consciousness and education, on the one hand, and, on the other, protecting them from what they are cognitively unable to process. What children need is information that is not only not too complicated but also has something positive they can hold on to and something concrete they can do to help them feel empowered, not depressed and helpless. About the trash problem, for instance, you could say, "Yes, it's true there is a problem. There isn't an endless amount of space for our trash. But there are things people can do. We can recycle. We can buy things in large packages, so we don't make extra garbage. We can reuse things, instead of throwing them away." Talk about options, come up with some plans and discuss them with other family members. Doing something always makes a child feel better. If a child pushes you on an issue— "But what if that did happen here?"—the best answer is "Scientists/

the President/politicians are working to make sure that it won't." Child psychiatrist David Fassler, who has written a number of books for children on health and environmental topics, offers this framework for an explanation to a child worried about something happening in the world—for instance, a civil war in which children are dying or starving—and suggests parents modify it to fit other situations:

"It's very scary to see this on the news, to see children who can't go to school or who are starving. It's a very sad, frightening situation to have this going on in the world. But even though this is on TV and it is real and it looks like we are right there, it's far away from here. You are safe in your house and your school. But it does make me want to figure out ways we can help, if it's possible, and it makes me want to figure out ways people can stop hurting each other. Do you have any ideas?"

Whenever you have this kind of discussion, check back with your child a few days later to see how she's put the information together. Don't be surprised if the facts have been twisted, not on purpose, of course. Tell her, "No, that's not quite what I mean," and restate your original message. Children whose misconceptions are never cleared up can have one misconception built on another. Some children are more vulnerable to this than others, especially those who are depressed or have experienced a trauma.

Helping our children feel safe should always be our bottom line with all of these issues. To do that, we need to be very direct in our reassurance. A good general answer for almost any topic would go something like this: "Yes, that's a difficult problem. Some things in the world are very troubling. But you are safe. We will always take care of you the best way we can." As trivial as that may sound to a parent, it's what children of any age need to hear. In addition, when it's clear that a child has some specific worry that is getting in the way of her ability to function normally, you need to be as reassuring as possible in as specific a way as possible. Once Tracy's parents figured out what she was so upset about, there was actually an easy solution. Management of the building had issued some new security guidelines in the wake of the WTC bombing, and Tracy's father was able to talk about that with her.

"You were right to be worried about how safe my skyscraper is," he began. "In fact, the people in charge of the building were worried, too, and they developed some new safety guidelines for the building. They added some security officers in the lobbies and they added metal detectors at the doorways, so if anyone tried to bring a bomb into the building, they would know it right away. I feel much safer working there now."

After that conversation, Tracy stopped showing up for breakfast at six a.m.

Talking about sex . . .

Two sisters, 4 and 8, are chattering in the tub together. Mom, in the next room, isn't paying much attention until she hears the word *sex*. She hears the younger say, ". . . he asked me to have sex with him . . ." The sisters giggle. Mom can barely breathe.

What is this all about, she wonders in a rush. *She's only 4 years old!* She is full of questions. Where does it lead, what does it do to them, what should she *do*? She reels from the possibilities. Are there kids in the preschool engaged in sexually explicit imitative behavior? Does this mean someone has been exposed to sexual abuse and, by extension, her daughter is in jeopardy? Is this the updated developmental equivalent of playing doctor? The mother quickly called Kathy Roberts, director of the preschool her daughter attended in Cambridge, Massachusetts. Roberts was surprised but not shocked.

"I've never before heard those specific words in a preschooler's mouth," she said, "but I have seen a steady escalation of sex talk among children at the school. Talk about looking sexy, being sexy. It's bloodcurdling for me."

Roberts is not alone. Kay Stritzel Rencken, a researcher and kindergarten teacher in Tucson who leads parents' and professional workshops on children's sexuality, says five years ago such talk among children would have prompted a referral to a social service agency. Today there's a tendency to assume it's just the price we pay for living in today's world.

Preschoolers don't know what they mean when they use or hear sexual words; surely the 4-year-old in the bathtub didn't know what her peer was talking about, and probably her 8-year-old sister didn't have a clue either. That's the good and bad news. "Whatever they hear, they want to make sense of," says early childhood educator Diane Levin. "They bring it into their play and their talk. There's nothing wrong with that process, that's normal." The problem is, no matter how hard they try to make sense of sexual information, they can't; cognitively, they just don't have the tools. It's like trying to read *Hamlet* when you haven't mastered *The Cat in the Hat*. It's exhausting. Even worse, it takes energy away from the issues they should be working on that are more developmentally appropriate, like learning how to share and take turns. And because of their lack of understanding, lack of experience, and lack of a context, the messages they do get are confusing and scary.

There's something else going on too. Researchers are seeing more play divided along gender lines. Because both boys and girls are pretty much dealing with the same developmental issues, a preschool teacher normally sees lots of gender-free play, girls playing with blocks and balls and boys enjoying dress-up and pretend play. But teachers around the country report less of that than usual. "It's hard to get girls to play with blocks and boys to go in the playhouse," says Rencken. Roberts sees more girls wearing nail polish and wanting to be "pretty." Levin fears this is symptomatic of a serious underlying problem. "What they need to figure out about being male and female is getting completely scrambled," she says.

At the heart of the issue is the high degree of sexuality that has become such an accepted part of our culture that we often don't see its influence until it hits us in the face. A mother describes waking up in a hotel room on vacation to find her daughter and son, 4 and 6, glued to a cable TV channel watching a couple engaged in oral sex.

A father watching football on TV blushes when a lingerie commercial for Victoria's Secret catches his preschooler's attention. A mother stammers when her kindergartner excitedly tells her there's a song on the radio about her Barbie doll and proceeds to sing some of it to her: " 'Barbie is a bitch.' What does that mean, Mommy?" she asks. As if this isn't bad enough, our children's toys are among the worst culprits. Levin, who researches the influence of toys and media on young children, says the end of the 1990s has seen a proliferation of toys for boys that are sexually grotesque and toys for girls that are sexually precocious. Spider Man action figures include a female character whose exaggerated breasts have antennae coming out of them; a female Spawn figure has carved skulls for breasts. She says the message this gives boys is that the female body is disgusting and sinister and that sex and violence go together. Cosmetic Castle, particularly popular among preschool-age girls, offers a wide selection of "real-life" makeup; Special Night Barbie shows how to dress up for a "night out." The message girls get is not ambiguous: What adults are doing is for you, too.

> *Constantly counteract media messages that show unrealistic body images by relating it directly to your child's experience: "Have you ever seen anybody with muscles like that?" "I don't know anybody who has a waist that tiny, do you?"*

Luckily, there are many things we can do as parents. Levin, Rencken, and others urge us to be more conscious of the impact toys and media have, including the Internet (see Chapter 5). Levin and her co-author, Nancy Carlsson-Paige of Lesley College, lecture nationwide on the detrimental effects some of these toys can have, and they urge parents not to buy the toys that feed into violent or precocious sexual behaviors and to tell toy store managers they don't like them, especially managers at toy superstores. Stay away from gender-specific toys, including color-coded ones, for preschoolers. Why does a girl need a pink bike anyway? TRUCE (Teachers for Resisting Unhealthy Children's Entertainment), an organization based in Cambridge, Massachusetts, publishes a good-toy and bad-toy list each year at Christmastime as a way to help parents make toy choices that feed into developmental stages in appropriate rather than harmful ways. Perhaps most important of all is that we not keep quiet on the subject. If we're outspoken enough as consumers, we might be able to change the tide, and if we're outspoken with our children, they will be better consumers themselves. Indeed, at the very least, we need to talk to our children; by not commenting on things like sexually grotesque action figures or cosmetics for 4-year-olds, the message they get is that these things are okay.

> *Children most likely to see sex as violent are boys with no positive male role models. If you're a single parent, look to your child's grandparents, relatives, or parents of friends for this modeling. Comment on it occasionally in a matter-of-fact way: "Grandpa and Grandma are so loving to each other. It's nice to see that."*

Helping our children cope also means we need to put aside any inhibitions we might have and talk to our children about sex and sexuality. No matter how embarrassing or disquieting it is for us, not talking about sex is a luxury we can ill afford. Look at these statistics from the national Centers for Disease Control: One million teenagers become pregnant nationwide each year, and more than three million each year contract a sexually transmitted disease, including AIDS. Talking about sex doesn't guarantee your child won't become a statistic, but it can go a long way. The more children know about sexuality, the more likely they are to act responsibly.

Talking about sex is not something that happens at a specific age or milestone—the day your daughter menstruates for the first time—and it's not a conversation that happens only once. Rather, it is a communication process that needs to begin far earlier than most of us realize: before a child talks.

In one family I know, the parents referred to their baby's toes as "piggy toes" from the moment he was born, as in "Aren't these the cutest little piggy toes you ever saw?" Years later, when he was in second grade, the boy came home from school one day furious at his mother. They were studying the body in school. "Why didn't you tell me they aren't really called piggy toes?" he demanded. "Everybody laughed at me!"

There wasn't long-lasting damage to the relationship here or to the trust between child and parent, but it illustrates the point professionals are anxious to get across to parents: Starting at birth, we should use the correct anatomical term for every part of the body, especially genitalia, because that sets a comfort level, a tone, and a foundation for future communication, not just for our child but also for us. Clue your child's grandparents, close relatives, and caregivers in on the words you do—and don't—want used for body parts. This may seem extreme, especially when we're talking about babies, but even with something as innocuous as piggy toes, sooner or later, there is an issue of parental credibility. Educators and authors Judith and Sol Gordon talk about the need for all of us to be an "askable parent." "That means your child will ask anything at a young age and come to you at an older age," says Judith. Their point is this: When our children are very young, if they think we aren't being straight with them, they'll stop asking us questions; by the time they're teenagers, they won't see us as a resource or care about our values.

There's another rule of thumb that makes good common sense

too. If a child is able to ask the question, we should be able to provide a straight answer that is as close as possible to his level of understanding. When questions about sex come up, don't be dismissive or judgmental. Not "That's not something you need to think about" but: "What does that mean to you?" A good answer for a preschooler who wants to know what sex is: "When grown-ups love each other, they express it by doing something called sex." A good general answer: "That's a grown-up behavior. It's not for children." You don't tell a 4-year-old about the trimesters of pregnancy but you also don't say that the stork brought him. If a 2-year-old asks, "What's that?" when she sees her cousin's penis, you might say, "It's called a penis. That's what boys have so they can go to the bathroom. Girls have a vagina." This question from a 2- or 3-year-old, by the way, is her way of making sure she has the right equipment, that a boy is supposed to have that thing between his legs and a girl isn't.

> *Always answer your child's question when she asks it, even in the middle of the grocery store. Never cut off her questions, give the wrong information or say "You're too young."*

A common question from a 3- or 4-year-old is "Why do you and Daddy sleep together and I have to sleep alone?" A good answer: "Because when a man and woman get married, they sleep in the same bed." To the 4-year-old who asks, "Where do babies come from," you might say: "The daddy has something called sperm and the mommy has something called an egg. When they join together, they make a baby grow. It grows in a special place inside the mommy, called the womb or uterus, until it's big and strong enough to be born." Language is important here, says Eric Johnson, a nationally known sex educator and author of many books on human sexuality. He says it's not a good idea to say the egg grows in the mommy's stomach, because it can fuel a child to imagine having one growing and to develop a stomachache as a result.

Simple answers are always best. If your child accepts the answer, that means he was comfortable with it and that's all you need to say. If he starts to giggle at your answer, that's a good tip-off that he's heard something from peers. Don't make anything out of the giggles, but you might ask, "Do you know anything about this already?" A child of any age who isn't satisfied with your answer will let you know, usually by asking more questions. When my son was 5, we were alone in the car on our way to a birthday party when he asked me how the egg and sperm "get together" (his words).

I patiently repeated what I had told him several times before: "The sperm comes out of the penis, and the egg is inside the mommy's vagina, so the daddy uses the penis to put sperm inside the vagina so the baby can start to grow."

"No, that's not it, Mom," he insisted. He was getting frustrated and so was I. There was something else he wanted to know, but I didn't know what it was and he didn't know how else to ask. Anxious not to give too much or inappropriate information, I just kept repeating the same thing in different ways. Finally he was exasperated.

"Mom. What I want to know is, how come the sperm doesn't fall out?"

The light bulb suddenly clicked on. I remembered the science book we had read a few days before. "You mean because of gravity?"

"Yes!" he said.

"Because the mom and dad are lying down," I said.

"Oh!" he said. And that was that.

By 8, sex becomes a topic among peers and your child may push for more information. Now it's appropriate to use the words *intercourse* or *making love*. Some time after 9 or 10, a child is going to start to figure out that sex isn't only for making babies, at which point you may want to say, in an appropriate context, that sex not only produces babies but also is pleasurable. When you do, however, you may want to couple it with the concept that sex requires responsibility. For instance, "Even though sometimes you want to have intercourse just for pleasure, you could end up making a baby anyway, so that's why sex is something that people should do only when they are old enough and mature enough to take that responsibility."

> *If your child walks in on you while you are having sex, remain calm, ask her to wait outside the closed door, put some clothes on, and go to her immediately. Explain you were doing something called making love, which is an activity parents do sometimes because they love each other.*

If your child hasn't asked any questions by age 5, initiate a conversation: "Have you ever wondered where babies come from? Would you like me to tell you?" No matter what your child's question, try to be as calm and matter-of-fact as possible in your response. It never hurts to end any discussion by asking, "Do you have any more questions?"

. . . drugs . . .

As he was about to give a talk on substance abuse among children, John J. Knight, director of the substance abuse program at Boston's Children's Hospital, suddenly got nervous. What he was about to say was controversial; he wanted a reality check. He turned to his colleague, S. Jean Emans, co-chief of the children's division of adolescent medicine.

"Jean," he said. "Do you think experimentation with alcohol and other drugs is a developmental norm?"

"Of course," she answered. "For everybody's kid but mine."

Nothing could have emboldened Knight more. One of his theses is that the not-my-kid syndrome is potentially as dangerous as a child's actual drug use. "If a parent's in denial, he or she isn't available to help a child. That's trouble," he says.

There's something else that presents trouble. Our children need our help sooner than we tend to offer it. Children enter what is known as the curiosity stage sometimes as young as 7 or 8, certainly by 9. Even though your child may not be ingesting anything or even thinking about ingesting anything, she is wondering: "Why do people like it? What does it feel/smell/taste like? Would I like it?" The typical 10- or 11-year-old still thinks concretely, and that's in our favor: "If I smoke, Mom will kill me"; "If I smoke, I might burn the house down." By 13, though, the thinking changes and begins to revolve around self-image: "If I smoke, will Amy like me more or less?" "If I don't smoke, will Tony still be my friend?" What's good about the curiosity stage is that kids are still young enough to be open to what we have to say. In order for them to hear our opinion, however, we have to be intuitive and sense questions are being asked even if they aren't verbalized.

When questions come up in a specific way—you're sipping a beer and your 9-year-old asks what it tastes like—Knight believes in settling the curiosity and offering a sip, although he wouldn't do that for a 13-year-old, who is at a different developmental stage and might be aware that you are violating the law by letting him drink even a taste. There is by no means professional unanimity on offering a taste to an 8- or 9-year-old. Many psychologists would allow tasting only in a religious context, for instance, wine at Passover or Communion. Anything else, they say, puts parents in the awkward position of seeming to have a double standard. Either way, it's important to stress that alcohol is an adult beverage. There's nothing wrong with saying it tastes good and that you like it, as long as you also say that you are careful not to drink any kind of alcohol very much or very often because alcohol isn't good for you. It is not too early, even with an 8- or 9-year-old to lay the groundwork for behaviors in the years to come: "We believe cigarettes, beer and other alcohol, as well as certain drugs like marijuana, are bad for your body and they are illegal. We know you don't want to try them now, and we don't want you to try them even later, but we know not all kids feel this way. You might feel some pressure from kids in school or you might change your mind and decide you want to try them. We want you to know you can always talk to us about this."

Also in this curiosity stage you can expect questions about what you did way back when. For many of us, this is a slippery slope. Better to be honest than to avoid the question, pretend it isn't a big deal, or lie and be caught in your lie years down the road. If you don't smoke/drink/use now, but once did, it's okay to admit it, along these lines: "I tried ——— when I was in high school/college. When I learned about how much it can damage the body, I realized it was a mistake and I stopped." If you had a substance abuse problem, admitting to it is far better than denial, especially if you can finish up by saying, "I realized I had a serious problem and I got the help I needed." If you drink socially now, tell your child, "Your mom and I drink socially/have wine a few times a week, but we're adults, our bodies are different, we know our limits, and besides, it's legal for adults."

It's important to lay this groundwork before your child hits middle school, because that's when your influence begins to wane. While what we do always sets a model—studies show parents who smoke or drink likely will have kids who do—by seventh grade, media and peer pressure are bigger influences. Lay this groundwork now, too, because curiosity can turn to experimentation in some children by the time they are 10, although 12 is more typical. What tends to fuel it is not only peer pressure but also puberty, which can begin as early as 9 for some girls, a fact many parents are woefully ignorant about. A child can wake up in the morning and have a body that looks very different to her/him than it did the day before, even though you might not notice a thing that's different. (Not that she'd point anything out to you or ask your opinion.) That's downright scary. What's happening to me? Who am I? Typically, a child looks to the culture to figure that out, to fill the gap between what he is and what he wants to be. This is often referred to as the Image Gap—he admires what he sees, but he isn't what he admires. Seeing this gap and being frightened by it is often what prompts a child to begin to dabble in drugs or alcohol. It's a way to be cool, to be like peers and/or to identify with a cultural image at a time when he feels very uncool.

Research shows that cigarettes are the drug of choice among middle-school-age kids. According to studies, preteens respond in droves to the advertising that's pitched their way, smoking Marlboros, Camels, and Newports more than any other cigarette. Cigarette lighters, especially those with tobacco company logos, are often status symbols. While owning one doesn't mean a child smokes, at the very least it means he has friends who value the cigarette culture. If he's not smoking yet, he may be soon. It's definitely time to make sure you are having ongoing conversations about smoking's dangers.

> *Tell your child: "I care about this because I care about your safety. Just like I want to know that you use your seat belt and your bike helmet, I want to know if you're putting something dangerous into your body."*

Other "gateway" drugs are inhalants, such as Wite-Out, gasoline, cleaning supplies, and beer. How does a 10- or 11-year-old get access? It depends on a lot of things, but kids can be resourceful, sneaking things out of the house or stealing. Older siblings commonly are abettors. Where does it happen? On the playground, at the park, in the basement of a friend's house. And it's just as likely to happen in the afternoon after school as it is on a Saturday night.

The first hint a parent may have that experimentation is going on is a funny odor on his clothes. You want it to be innocent and you convince yourself that it is. There's nothing wrong with thinking "I have a good kid, he'll do the right thing." The mistake we make is failing to recognize that temptation presents itself perhaps hundreds of times a year in various forms. Even though he may do the right thing ninety-nine times, even the best kid can be worn down. Circumstances change. Things happen. If you think your child is in the experimentation stage, a watchful eye is critical. Kids get addicted, even at 10 and 12. Kids also die as a result of poor judgment, even at 10 and 12. Luckily, there are many warning signs: falling grades, change of friends, change in dress style, bloodshot eyes, dilated pupils, clothing with unfamiliar smells on it, sudden preoccupation with money, sudden trouble at school.

One sign alone is enough to act on. A drop in grades could be perfectly innocent: The teacher's marking harder this term, or a team sport has taken time away from homework. But it may be something not so innocent. Who can afford not to know?

In confronting a child, we walk a fine line between being overly suspicious, which can ruin a relationship, and being overly permissive, which can ruin a life. Stick to the facts: "Mary, your grades went from B to D. That's worrisome in itself, but what has us really upset is that last night when you came home from the party, your eyes were red. We're wondering if you're trying some kind of drugs, or if you are with kids who are." Needless to say, don't expect this to be an easy conversation. If there's something to what you say, she's going to be shocked and maybe relieved you've figured this out. She might come clean, perhaps tearfully and with great promises. More likely, she'll be defensive and angry. Avoid accusations. If she offers you a blatant lie, listen to her story and repeat the facts as you have seen them, ending with something like "We seem to have different understandings of what's happened and I'm still worried." John Knight says that whatever you do, don't panic and don't run off to the emergency room unless, of course, there is reason. But it is perfectly reasonable to call the doctor and share your concerns. Tell your child if you're going to do that: "Something may be medically wrong and I want to take you to the doctor. I'm going to make an appointment tomorrow." No matter how miserably your child reacts, including shutting herself in her room and not talking to you, believe it or not, you have at least opened the door to communication. There can be no question in her mind that you care, and that counts for a lot. Whether you think there is experimentation going on or not, especially if she's lying to you, this is definitely a time to remain firm and consistent about limit-setting. Here are some good rules to consider:

- A party is off-limits if alcohol or drugs will be present or if there's no adult supervision;

- Get permission from your parent or another adult in charge before getting into a car with a teenage driver;

- No illegal substances or activities in the house. Caution: If a room search seems appropriate, do it only with your child's knowledge. If an 11-year-old reacts ballistically to that, that's reason alone to be worried.

Turn infractions into a trust issue: "You chose to smoke and to harm your body. Now I can't trust you. The consequence is that you can't ride your bike to the park with your friends, because I can't trust you to be responsible when you are with them."

Will setting limits like this turn into a power struggle? Absolutely. Will it be awful? Maybe. But at this age, it's worth it because you are setting guidelines for potentially even stormier years to come.

. . . *homosexuality* . . .

Dave has two sons, 6 and 9. "My brother is gay," he begins. "He loves my kids and they love him and he likes to spend time with them. I have no problem with that. What I do have trouble with is letting the boys go to his apartment. I don't think they need to be exposed to his friends. It's just not the role model I want for them. All of a sudden, my older boy is pushing me: 'Why can't we sleep at Uncle Peter's house? We sleep at Uncle Joe and Aunt Sue's. . . .'"

Like many parents, this father's ambivalent feelings about homosexuality make it difficult for him to understand his children's needs for honesty and information. Whether or not there is a homosexual or lesbian in your family, children begin in third grade to hear words such as *gay, lesbian, bisexual,* and *homosexual.* By not weighing in with his values, a parent leaves room for a child to form his opinions from random sources.

What this father doesn't see is that instead of helping or "protecting" his children, he's sending mixed signals that inadvertently say it's okay to discriminate against Uncle Peter and therefore against all gay people. Equally problematic, he's damaging his credibility with his sons, potentially losing the opportunity to communicate with them not just about this but about other things too. By not talking, the father also loses an invaluable opportunity to put his own spin on information.

When there is someone in your family who is gay or lesbian, acknowledge it as a fact of the family. Talk about it in the same way you would talk about what a great cook Aunt Ginny is or that Grandma is the only left-handed person in the family. With a preschooler, you might say: "Uncle Charles is gay. That means he loves another man." If a 4-year-old has a peer with a lesbian parent, you might say, "Some families have a mommy and a daddy and some families have only one mommy and no daddy, and some families, like Bryn's, have two mommies." Young children will accept this as matter-of-factly as you convey it, although some children, especially those who have a homosexual parent or know someone who does, may need extra reassurances because they feel different. Tell this child, "It's true our family is different, but every family is different in some ways. We're Jewish and Ricky is Buddhist, and John's family is Catholic. We also have two mommies instead of one mom and one dad. What matters most is that we love each other like any other parents in any other family, and we love you." (For more on differences within families, see the section later in this chapter entitled "If your family doesn't fit the stereotype.")

If your child doesn't have any contact with homosexuality, you should initiate a conversation about it by the time she's 8, for the simple reason that she will hear about it soon and it's better for her to get her information from you than from peers or popular culture. Find some context, either something in the news or a conversation about someone you know. Don't try to cram too much information in, but at least get the basics. Begin, as always, with a question: "Have you heard about homosexuality?" or "Do you know what the word *gay* means?" Then say something along these lines:

"Human beings experience different kinds of loving. Most men and women are heterosexual; that means they are attracted to and fall in love with someone of the opposite sex, like Mommy and Daddy. Some people are homosexual, which means they are attracted to and fall in love with a person of the same sex. If a man falls in love with another man, that's called being gay. If a woman falls in love with another woman, that's called being lesbian."

By age 8, children begin to ascribe meaning, including goodness and badness, to these differences, so you might want to add, "There are some people who think it's wrong to be in love with someone who is the same sex and you might hear people say bad things about gays or lesbians. Sometimes gays or lesbians are treated badly, called bad names, or denied rights. In our family, we believe in treating all people equally." An 8-year-old might also be wondering about how people fall in love. If he asks, you might say, "That's something we don't really know much about. I don't even know exactly why Daddy and I fell in love. People who fall in love usually have some of the same interests. They both like classical music or hockey or something. They usually also have something called chemistry, which means they feel this attraction to each other. But that's not something people experience until they are at least teenagers."

By 9, it's almost a given that a child will have heard derogatory comments firsthand. Don't wait to hear them come out of your child's mouth to say explicitly, "In our family, we treat people with respect. We don't call people names." This tells your child you treat all people equally, with dignity. A child of 9 or older might want to know how two people of the same sex have sex. A simple response might be "There are parts of a man's body and parts of a woman's body that feel good when they are touched," or "I'm not sure."

> Q: "Mom, what if I grow up to be a lesbian/homosexual?" A: "I would love you no matter what."

It's not uncommon for a school-age child to try out words and say things like "I think I'm a lesbian." A good response might be "What do you think that means, to be a lesbian?" Most likely, a young girl might say, "I hate boys!" Then you might respond, "A lot of girls your age only like girls and a lot of boys only like boys. It doesn't mean much about what you'll be like when you grow up." By 11 or 12, it's not unusual for a child who thinks he is homosexual to worry about it. Rarely will he voice the fear, however, so you should do it for him: "You know, a lot of kids your age think they are going to be gay or lesbian. If you think that, I just want you to know that those are normal thoughts. You could change your mind lots of times between now and when you become an adult or maybe not. Either way, no matter what, I would love you." Also behind the question may be a worry that a gay person isn't happy. Reassure your child that homosexual love relationships can be just as fulfilling as heterosexual ones.

All of this, of course, leads to the ultimate issue that every parent should confront: How would I react if my child was gay or lesbian? We'd all like to think that we'd respond with love. Which brings us back to the father with the gay brother. If Peter were his son instead, would he counsel someone else to keep their children from going to his house?

. . . and AIDS

AIDS scares a lot of children. To them, sex equals AIDS, AIDS equals death, therefore sex equals death. As a result, it's not unusual for them to conclude, as did one 9-year-old I interviewed, "When I grow up, I'll never have sex. I don't want to die."

This statement stunned the boy's parents, but it made perfect sense to Debra Haffner, president of the Sexuality Information and Education Council of the United States. She's heard lots of comments like that from children and while she's not surprised at the logic, she is worried about it. "We could be raising a generation of adults who will be sexually dysfunctional," she says.

Behavioral pediatrician David Schonfeld of Yale University says one of the biggest pitfalls for parents and teachers is that it's easy to be misled into thinking a child understands more than he does about AIDS. Even if a 10-year-old tells you that you can get AIDS only from sex, it's a mistake to drop the conversation there. "If you ask him what sex means, he might say holding hands, kissing, or hugging," says Schonfeld.

Children with such misconceptions could easily be terrified. Kissing, hugging, and holding hands are things *they* do, things their parents do. They could be living in fear of imminent death, if not for themselves, then for their parents. The children most at risk for this misunderstanding are those who are getting their information from peers without input from parents and/or without the support of any kind of curriculum in the schools.

Children who are in day care or preschool typically learn about AIDS without ever even hearing the word *sex*. They are taught that AIDS is a disease that can be transmitted by touching the blood of someone who has AIDS and are instructed matter-of-factly not to touch the blood of a bleeding child but to get the help of an adult. This is important protection for any child, in or out of day care. You can give it to her without frightening her and without raising a topic that is beyond her scope of comprehension by simply saying, "We don't touch someone else's blood." By 4 and 5, you can add, "There's a bad virus called AIDS that can make you very very sick and you can catch it if you touch the blood of a person who has AIDS. Since you can't always tell by looking whether someone is sick with AIDS, we have to be safe by not touching anyone else's blood. Even doctors and nurses wear special gloves when they have to bandage a wound that is bleeding."

School-age children may hear that AIDS can be transmitted through drugs and/or needles. Because they may not understand that this doesn't include the drugs you get from the pharmacy or the needle a doctor uses to give a shot, if a child resists shots or medicine or if you think they have had access to this tidbit, it would be wise to offer reassurance: "These are not the kinds of drugs/needles that can give you AIDS." School-age children tend to be more worried about AIDS than parents realize, because it gets a fair amount of media and TV attention. Children who don't know how it is spread may assume people get it the same way they get a cold. It helps to antici-pate this kind of thinking and look for an opportunity to say "AIDS is not the same as a cold. You can't get it from coughing or sneezing."

Fourth or fifth grade is the time to introduce the idea that AIDS can be transmitted through sexual body fluids and that there are ways to be safe from having that happen. It's not that a child needs to know this for himself, but it's a way to reduce her anxiety about you, especially if you are a single parent. Your child could worry that you will catch AIDS and die. If children learn about AIDS, its connection to sex, and safety precautions in the same breath, it reduces the likelihood that there will be fear attached to the concept.

Don't bring up AIDS without a context—that can be scary in itself. But if AIDS is in the news or you have some reason to talk about it, ask your child, "Did you ever worry that Mom and I might get AIDS? We don't have the virus, so we can't spread it to each other. And if we were worried that one of us had it, we know about the ways to protect ourselves." Children of single, dating parents could be so worried about this that it could fuel anger and upset over a relationship you are in. Let her know, "Just in case you're worrying, I know how to be safe from AIDS. I am taking care of myself."

If your child announces he never wants to have sex when he grows up, don't be dismissive. The worst thing you could say would be "Oh, don't be silly, you'll change your mind by then." Whether his concern stems from a fear about AIDS or from something else entirely, a good response would be something like this: "I understand that's how you feel about sex now. But sex can be a wonderful, intimate experience and many grown-ups enjoy it. They also know how to have sex safely, without worrying about getting AIDS. When the time comes, if you change your mind about having sex, we can help you learn how to have sex safely too." While it is important not to overwhelm a child with too much information or to lecture her, Haffner and others say it is not inappropriate to show a mature 8-year-old a condom and explain that a latex barrier can keep you safe. Personally, I can't imagine having done that with my son when he was that age, but there are plenty of other children just slightly older with whom I could imagine such a conversation.

There is one thing to keep in mind if your 9-year-old tells you he never wants to have sex. Most kids that age think sex is icky and disgusting. It's an age-appropriate response that has nothing to do with anything else except being 8 or 9 or 10 years old.

Clashing hormones

Not so long ago, the typical mother went through menopause years after her children went through puberty. Today, with more and more women becoming mothers late in life and with puberty beginning younger and younger, typically now about age 9, it's not unusual for the two events to occur under the same roof at the same time. The coincidence of timing can be like adding accelerant to the fire, but it is possible to keep the flames from consuming either one of you.

At 47, Laura no longer gets a regular period and she's having hot flashes and mood swings. Under the best of circumstances, this would be a time of turmoil and uncertainty as she grapples with femininity and aging. That her 11-year-old son, Steven, is sprouting facial hair, has a physique that is more manly than boyish, and is reconsidering his position that girls are awful is adding to her misery.

"We're going in opposite directions at the same time" is how she puts it. "It makes me profoundly sad, and even though I know my sadness is probably hormonally induced, this isn't easy." Well-known child and adolescent psychoanalyst Louise J. Kaplan offers this perspective: "For boys and girls alike, puberty is a time when their bodies feel out of control and so do they. That's hard enough on any parent at any age, but it's harder on the mother whose body also feels out of control, who also feels uncertain about the future."

Mothers may experience this differently, depending on whether their puberty-aged child is a boy or girl.

Mothers of boys. At a time in your life when you desperately need to feel needed, your son is going through a developmental stage where he is rejecting you big time. This can fuel a profound sense of loss. If he hasn't already shunned any overt show of affection, he will sometime in this 11- to 13-year-old range. If you're lucky, he'll only ban your kisses and hugs in public; at home, in private, he may still curl up next to you on the couch or look for a good-night kiss. Don't count on it, though. You may also find yourself the victim of verbal torment: "Your hair looks ugly today, Mom." "Why do you wear all that makeup? It looks awful."

He hasn't developed a mean streak. His behaviors are motivated by an overwhelming developmental fear of being overly dependent on you at the same time he needs to gain distance from unconscious incestuous feelings. Your attempts at hugs and physical closeness are anathema, your efforts at caregiving set off alarms: "If I surrender to tenderness, I'm not masculine enough." He'll flip-flop between finding fault with everything you do and asserting his masculinity in ridiculous ways. This can be both provocative and scary for mothers, but generally not as devastating as the loss of emotional closeness. Laura says, "We've always had a relationship where we can talk about anything. Now he's reticent to talk to me at all. It's an emotional kicker." To top it off, at the same time, the typical son bonds anew with Dad and the father becomes an ally against the mother. All of this is a function of your son's development and has little if anything to do with you. But since some women experience mood swings during menopause that make them unpredictable even to their spouse, a husband may think a son is justified in his antipathy toward Mom and may unwittingly contribute to his wife's feeling abandoned. As a result of the alliance, Mom typically becomes the disciplinarian, further putting herself at odds with her son. Thus the advice for fathers is to be careful to be a wife's ally as well as a child's, and to watch for alliances that become exaggerated or hurtful toward either.

Mothers of girls. Their sense of loss is complicated by feelings of competition and envy: "Here's my beautiful, nubile daughter on the verge of having everything, and here I am, at the end of my fertility, losing my looks, looking my age. Men don't even look at me anymore. She has everything I've lost!" The daughter, meanwhile, is struggling with what it means to become a woman. Confused by the changes in her body, wanting independence but frightened of it, she vacillates between wanting Mom's love, pushing it away, and then resenting Mom when it isn't forthcoming. To gain autonomy, the typical 10- to 14-year-old girl finds some other woman to adore and imitate, a teacher, camp counselor, mother of a best friend. Almost always, it's at your expense. There is a litany of things this person does better than you. The secrets she once shared with you are now reserved for the best friend, with doors literally slamming in your face. "Needless to say, this mother's self-esteem is getting battered by her daughter at a time when it's the last thing in the world she needs," says Kaplan.

> *Studies show mothers who have had a mastectomy or who are single or in unhappy relationships tend to have a harder time dealing with the coincidence of puberty and menopause and need to take pains to monitor their reactions to their child.*

How a mother copes depends on how she feels about menopause. If you buy into the cultural stereotype that this is a time of decline rather than of rejuvenation, you're more likely to view it negatively and therefore to be envious of a daughter and angry with a son and to overreact to either's budding sexuality. This mother has a hard time saying mentally, "I had my chance, now it's your turn," and she's likely to make some inadvertent mistakes that could further jeopardize her relationship with either child.

With her daughter, she might become too involved in her social life: She offers to chaperone the fifth-grade dance and ends up dancing with the boys. Robin Ohringer, a social worker in Cambridge who specializes in midlife women, says with great insight, "She doesn't want to share in her daughter's life, she wants to *be* her daughter." The effect this has on the daughter is to intensify the normal stage of rebellion, pushing away from Mom more than she needs or wants to.

Envy could propel a mom to overreact in the other direction, too, going off the scale over her daughter's sexuality. Guard against equating your daughter's budding sexuality with promiscuity; just because she doesn't want to wear a bra doesn't mean she's flaunting herself. This kind of reaction from a mother has the same effect of intensifying and exaggerating a daughter's need to push away. This is the daughter who is more likely to experiment with drugs and sex as a way to reject completely whatever it is she might otherwise need or want from her mother.

For a mother of a boy, it's not envy she needs to resist as much as the urge to keep him at her side. Some mothers set strict social limits on a son to keep him home more, or they infantilize him as a way to maintain control: "I'll do your laundry, you don't know how to separate colors." Others might devalue or tease a son: "You want to *shave*!" "Boy, is your voice squeaky!" At the other extreme is the mother who reacts angrily, abandoning or ignoring her son, just as she feels he's done to her.

The thing of it is, our children do still need us, just in different ways. Mothers who have the ability to look positively at their menopause will be best able to see that. Ohringer says, "Instead of resenting their kids' sexuality, they let it lead to reconnections with their own partner," and Kaplan says the mother who feels good about the changes in her own body will be better able to tolerate her child's sexuality, better able to let personal assaults roll off her back, and better able to keep from getting defensive or overly controlling. For instance, let your child know you are as available and interested as always, and that you can take her rejections in stride. You might tell her, "That's fine, if you want to shop for a bra with your friends. If you change your mind, I'm happy to go." Or, "I was thinking of going to your game tomorrow. Would that be okay or would you rather I don't?"

Apologize if you realize you are reacting differently to an event than you normally would—"I guess I'm overreacting, sorry"—but don't use your mood changes as an excuse for inappropriate parental behavior.

As Laura struggled with her own feelings, the biggest question she had was whether she should talk to her son about the changes in her body. "Normally, that would be something I'd talk to him about; in fact, I did tell him about my hot flashes last year. But now, given the emotional struggles he's having with his own body, I'm not so sure."

Certainly a preteen should hear the word *menopause* and know that your body is going through changes that sometimes make you uncomfortable, prevent you from sleeping well, or make you cranky. The degree of openness, however, depends on the child. You don't want to burden her or make her feel guilty or embarrassed about her own sexuality, and you don't want to cause her to worry about you. On the other hand, being secretive isn't a good idea either. Laura recalls sitting at the kitchen table one day when a hot flash came over her. She looked up to catch her son looking at her so strangely, she wondered if, in her out-of-body sensation, she might have said or done something weird.

"Are you okay?" he asked her.

"Well, I'm having a hot flash and I feel a little uncomfortable," she said.

Somehow, that made her feel better and, she thinks, him too.

When honesty counts:
1. If your family doesn't fit the stereotype

You don't have to be a sociologist to know that families today don't look like they did when we were growing up. In those days, having parents who were divorced was unusual; stepparents were practically unheard of; and if there was a kid in the class who was adopted, it was only rumored or whispered about. Today, it's impossible to live in America and not realize that families come in all sorts of configurations, from interfaith to multiracial, from two dads or two moms to no dad or no mom but a gram and gramps or a stepmom and stepdad. When the family we create is different from the family structure we grew up with, we can't turn to our parents as role models. What our parents took for granted—that the family was something fundamental, unchanging, and nurturing in and of itself—can be a struggle for us. How do we nurture our new concept of family and raise children who will be comfortable in it and empowered and validated by it?

When our children are very young, this isn't really an issue. To them, their family is just their family and they accept it for what it is without question or judgment. Psychologist Barbara F. Okun, a family therapist who specializes in alternative families, says that as long as parents provide a definition of what the family is—"In our family, we have two mothers"—and offer rituals and patterns that provide connections to and with each other, children will be happy and secure.

Parents and kids typically are fine with this until the day a preschooler comes home and asks, "Why don't other kids have a black daddy and a white mommy like I do?" This is likely to rattle you even though your child is doing what she is supposed to be doing developmentally: noticing differences. To her, these differences in family structure are matters of observation and she puts them in the same category as "Anna has straight hair and mine is curly," "John is a boy and I'm a girl." She isn't ascribing goodness or badness to them and neither should we. As long as we are able to respond to her observations honestly, simply, and matter-of-factly, a child will do fine. Louise Derman-Sparks, who is white, remembers when her son, who is black, was this age. As she picked him up at preschool one day, a classmate stopped them. "Is that really your mom?" he asked. Derman-Sparks, an early childhood educator who specializes in anti-bias education, was ready with an answer.

"I bet you're wondering if I'm Doug's mom because his skin is brown and mine is white," she said. The little boy nodded. "I am his mommy. What makes me his mommy is that I love him and take care of him." Children can also be coached to answer for themselves: "She's my mom even though her skin is white and mine isn't. I'm adopted." In biracial families, a good answer might be "My mother is white, my father is black; blend the two together and that's the color of my skin."

Okun says parents often get fooled into thinking that they need to give preschoolers more information because they keep asking questions. But children often come back at something many times because they absorb different pieces of information each time. On the other hand, some children this age who keep coming back to the issue may do it because they are picking up on a parent's discomfort. They're wondering "Is something wrong with me? Is this my fault?" Indeed, Okun says parents who don't talk honestly and openly about differences once they have begun to take on meaning to a child run the risk of causing him to feel ashamed: "There's something bad about our family."

By third grade, maybe sooner, a child may exhibit confusion about differences. This is partly a result of her own changing perspective, partly the result of peers' questions and biases. Hopefully, she will bring the issues home to you: "Mary says we aren't a real family because I'm adopted." A simple, honest approach is still the best strategy, although you can offer a little more information:

"There are some people in the world who don't like families like ours. Sometimes it bothers me, but mostly it doesn't because I know how wonderful and loving our family is." Because peers can be so mean by third and fourth grade, assume that there will be times when your child faces hostility. Don't let her be caught by surprise; anticipate things that might be said and prepare her for them. As much as you would like to shield your children from the meanness of the world, you do them better service not to isolate or insulate them.

The trick is to do this without heightening anxiety. While each family may have a set of beliefs about handling discrimination, Derman-Sparks says there are two rules:

- **Don't let a child deal with it alone.** "Children who feel unsupported have the hardest time and develop the most negative responses," she says, sometimes including hating and resenting their family.

- **Don't ignore even minor discrimination.** The longer you wait to intervene, the more likely it is that a child will blame himself for whatever happened and the worse he will feel. As soon as you are aware of a problem, contact the appropriate adult, whether it's the parent of a playmate, a coach, or a teacher. Let them know what happened, suggest how they might have handled it differently, and what, if anything, you want them to do now. If it turns out a teacher or coach is prejudiced, talk to the appropriate supervisor, the principal, for instance. If the parent of a playmate is, then you might want to distance your child from that family. Depending on the age of your child, you may even want to have a conversation with him about it: "You know how we've talked about people who have prejudices. Well, unfortunately, Joey's mother is one of those people. It makes me sad, but it also explains why you and I feel so uncomfortable around her." What, specifically, you say, will depend on your family values, but your child will benefit by open, honest, and thoughtful conversation around it.

Being part of a network of other families like yours is helpful for children at all ages. Young children need to see themselves reflected elsewhere in their world, while older children want to act and look and talk like their peers and want their families and parents to look like everyone else's too. This network of families is a place where that can happen. It also gives you a built-in support system that can help you tease out what's developmental for your child and what is due to sensitivity to your family's uniqueness.

Sooner or later, most children go through a period of development where they are unhappy with their family. For children in nontraditional families, this can be more poignant. What you get from your 9- to 13-year-old may range from an angry outburst— "I hate our family!"—to something more subtle: Perhaps he stops inviting friends to the house, or suggests casually that you don't need to attend his hockey games: "They really aren't a big deal, Dad, and I know it's hard for you to get there." Translate that to "It's embarrassing for my friends to see that I have two fathers and they're gay."

> *A child will be more willing to talk to you if you have shared your own stories of prejudice. When you're finished, ask him: "Has anything like this ever happened to you?"*

The best reaction is one that is neither defensive nor self-righteous. Avoid responses that force him to choose between his family and his friends or that invalidate his feelings: "You should be ashamed for being ashamed of us." A child shouldn't be made to feel he's a bad person or that he's betraying you for having normal feelings. While you don't want to push her to invite friends over, you can make it clear that you're open to finding a solution she can live with. Derman-Sparks says, "You don't want to give in to prejudice, homophobia, for instance, but you also don't want to be so rigid you drive your child away from you. He's just a kid. Don't ask him to do something out of principle that is beyond what he can cope with." Just because he doesn't want two fathers coming to his game doesn't mean he doesn't love you both, or that he's ashamed of you and wouldn't defend you. In fact, he probably would, more than you know. It's just that he's a kid at a stage of life when being different is tough to handle. Find a compromise: "You know we both love your games. How about if we take turns going to them?" This also is a good time to show a little empathy: "I know you wish we were like your friends' parents. I know it's hard being in a family that's different." If your preteen has never brought home stories of prejudice, don't assume it's because he hasn't run into it. More likely, you are sending messages that say "This topic is uncomfortable for me. Don't talk about it."

On the other hand, don't excuse behavior that is inexcusable, like bad-mouthing the family. Again, try empathy: "You must feel a lot of pressure to have said something like that. Something must have really gotten to you. Wanna talk about it?" Sometimes what's bothering a child about her family is not the big differences but the small ones: that you never get pizza for dinner or that you have lamb on Thanksgiving.

2. If a parent is absent

Eric, who is 6, has seen his father seven times in his life, and not once in the past year. When Eric asks why this is, his mother, Heidi, says, "Your father doesn't know how to be a father." One day recently he told her, "I'll be all grown up by the time I see him again."

If this breaks Heidi's heart, it also strengthens her resolve to be as open and honest with Eric about his absentee father as possible, given his age and stage of development. "What damages you in life is not the amount of tragedy you experience but how you heal from it," she says. "I want him to feel what he feels and be able to talk about it."

For all sorts of reasons, from single motherhood by choice to having a parent abandon the family, it's not uncommon for children today to grow up with only one parent. Absentee parenthood can take many forms, from no contact at all to irregular, unpredictable contact to semiregular visits. No matter what, this leaves a mark on a child. Perhaps the first dose of honesty is for the parent who is raising the child: Don't pretend this isn't a big deal. Even when the father is occasionally on the scene, what counts is not just physical presence but being present emotionally as well. Long Island psychologist Leah Klungness, who specializes in single-parenting issues, tells of an 8-year-old girl whose father visits her now and then with some regularity but never with any predictability. "Even though he sees me sometimes, my father doesn't really want to be with me," she told Klungness. "If he did, he'd turn off his beeper and cell phone."

It's children like these who have the hardest time. Klungness says that to see a parent a little but not enough to see his faults for yourself leaves the biggest developmental hole in a child's life, potentially even harder to heal from than a parent's death. One of the first thoughts this child has on the subject goes something like this: "My father is out there, but he chooses not to be with me. What's wrong with me?" It's a thought, she says, that can last well into adulthood. The advice professionals give to parents is not far from what Heidi instinctively realizes: Honesty in age-appropriate doses is, indeed, the best policy.

Typically, children whose fathers are not in their lives were abandoned before birth or shortly thereafter. Eric's father never married his mother and left when she was pregnant. No matter what caused your child to have only one parent, beginning when your single-parent family is created, even if your child is only an infant, tell the story of how your family formed. Andrea Engber, founder of the National Organization of Single Mothers, did that when her son Spenser was an infant. His father disappeared when she was pregnant, and by the time Spenser was 11, he had seen his father only three times. He says, "I have one father who made me, but he's not around, but I have one who loves me," referring to a longtime family friend. The advice his mother offers to other women in similar circumstances is not to be brutally honest but not to stray far from the truth.

The more infrequent, unpredictable, and unsatisfying the contact with an absentee parent, the more likely a child is to have fantasies about him that have nothing to do with reality. Kids put a lot of energy into imagining how different things would be "if my dad was here." That's not dysfunctional, it's human nature, says family therapist Claudia Jewett Jarratt, who specializes in children's loss and separation issues. If you know your child is doing this or even if you only suspect it, she suggests validating and empathizing with a child's hopes: "I know you wish things were different. I know you miss having a dad. I wish it were different, but it isn't." Stop short of instilling false hope: "Maybe he'll show up for your next birthday!" As tempting as it is to take away your child's hurt, it's better for a child to deal honestly with the disappointments he or she will undoubtedly face over time. But granting your child his wish in fantasy can be very healing: "It would be wonderful for you if your wish could come true and your father did show up for your birthday. What do you imagine he would say to you?"

Telling your child the truth begins with laying a foundation. When he's a toddler, talk about how families are different: "Sometimes both parents live together, sometimes children live with the dad and see the mom only once in a while. In our family . . ." If you can, point out other families where there are absent parents, even if the structure isn't exactly the same: "You know Jill at day care? She lives with her grandparents." Never tell a child the parent is dead if he isn't and don't give more information than he can handle. Don't tell a 3-year-old his father is a drug-dealing womanizer. You could say, however: "Your father takes something called street drugs. It's not medicine, not drugs a doctor gives you, but drugs that are bad for your body and confuse how you think. They make it hard for a person to be where he is supposed to be or do what he needs to do. That's why your father forgets to visit. When he makes a promise, he wants to keep it but then he can't." To a 4-year-old you could add: "This is a sickness and it's called an addiction." Other ways to help your child cope:

- **Have photos of the absentee parent available and/or on display in the child's room or in a specific place in the house.** That gives her permission to think about the parent and also tells her that just because someone isn't in her life doesn't mean they disappear from her heart.

- **Don't bad-mouth the absentee parent.** Sooner or later a child figures out that she is half that person, too. If you've said only bad things about the parent, she'll worry: "If my mother's a liar and a cheat, maybe I am too." Saying nothing about the person is equally bad, however, because it gives rise to inappropriate fantasies. If there's nothing good you can say about her, find something that is neutral: "Your mother loved strawberries, just like you."

- **Stay in contact with the absent parent's family.** The only caveat is if you think your child is unsafe with them, if they undermine you or glorify him.

- **Commemorate a parent's birthday as a way to acknowledge his existence and open a conversation:** "I was thinking about your dad. It's his birthday. It makes me sad for him that we don't have an address and can't even send a card." "What would you say if you could talk to him? What would you want him to say back to you?"

- **Don't pooh-pooh fantasies a child shares; she may never do it again.** Try instead to gently insert some reality: "You wish your dad were a person who brought you presents, don't you?"

There's a tendency for a child with an absentee parent to think it's her fault the parent isn't around—"He'd still be here if I were taller/shorter/smarter/more athletic." As the parent who is around, you need to give frequent reinforcement that you love her just the way she is: "Nobody wants you to be a different girl." By school age, you can be more explicit: "It's not that if you were smarter or more athletic, or a boy instead of a girl, that your father would be around more. This isn't about you. It's about what your father is able to do." A child who's having these thoughts may be very clingy and have difficulty separating. She's afraid you will leave, too, and she may need lots of reinforcement about your stability. If a preschooler has difficulty going to sleep at night, tell her, "I'll be here when you wake up and every other morning, too." Tell an older child: "Your father and I are separate people. I am not going to make the choice he made. I want to stay with you. Being your parent is my most important job."

In the elementary years, one of two patterns typically emerges: A child either tries to be perfect, hoping to bring the parent back, or he purposely gets himself in trouble, as if to say to the remaining parent "Let's see if you love me as much as you say. Let's see if you'll stick around no matter how bad I am." Misbehaving is also a way to be in control. He assumes friends, teachers, almost anyone in his life, will also reject him. If he gives them reason to, then when they do it's not for some arbitrary reason he can't understand.

If a parent has a history of not showing up, cushion disappointment by having an alternative plan: "He said he'd be here at two-thirty. How long do you think it's reasonable to wait? What's our plan if he doesn't come?" Use that opening to reinforce the idea that his no-show isn't the child's fault: "Your father has a problem keeping promises, not just to you but to everyone. It's one of the reasons we couldn't stay married." When broken promises pile up, Klungness suggests putting this spin on them: "When your father makes those promises, we need to put the words 'I wish' in front of them. He wishes he could take you sailing, but he isn't able to. He would like things to be different, too, but he has problems that get in his way." It's around this age that the typical child may begin to refer to an absentee parent by his name rather than "Dad." As she begins to grasp the emotional distance between them, a name that isn't endearing may feel more authentic.

3. If you had help conceiving

In the photographs, Michelle looks like any other pregnant woman. "That's me inside my mom's uterus," says 5-year-old Sammy, pointing to the picture. "Wanna know how I got inside her?"

It's not the kind of question adults expect from a 5-year-old, but then Sammy's story isn't typical either. "Well," he begins. "To make babies, you need a sperm from the dad and an ovum from the mom. Well. My mom's eggs didn't work so a very nice lady named Nancy gave my mom some of her eggs so they could make a baby with my daddy's sperm. Then they put me in my mom's uterus so I could grow." He flips the page of the photo album. "That's Nancy," he says, pointing to a picture of a pregnant Michelle arm in arm with another woman. "She's my egg mom."

This degree of openness may take many adults by surprise. As recently as the early 1990s, professionals, especially physicians, urged parents not to tell children that they are a product of collaborative reproduction, the term used to describe the voluntary help of a person who is involved in the creation of a child they will not parent. Sammy's parents' openness represents a sea change in how to handle the questions of whether, when, and what to tell these children. By the mid-1990s there was widespread agreement on openness and honesty. The turnabout is modeled on adoption research that established not only how important it is for children to know the truth about their origins, but also how much better they fare emotionally when they have access to the truth. The argument professionals make is that not telling your child jeopardizes your ability to be a good parent and your relationship with him.

Being truthful is for your mental health as well. Parents who don't tell their children report being troubled by a nagging worry: "Would my son feel different about me if he knew I wasn't his biological father? Would he resent me or reject me?" In subtle ways, this can affect how you parent, unwittingly causing you to be more or less permissive or more or less consistent. It can also confuse your child. Even very young children have an uncanny ability to pick up vibes from what we do as much as from what we say. Child psychologist Elaine Gordon, one of the nation's leading researchers on collaborative reproduction and its impact on families, says, "Children sense at an early age that something is different [about them]. Without information, they create misinformation." In other words, magical thinking takes hold, and we already know what that can do: Kids create a fantasy that can be detrimental.

For Gordon, an equally important reason not to keep this secret is because the older a child is when she finds out the truth, the more likely she'll feel betrayed. "You will almost always get her love back, but will she ever trust you again?" she asks. Gordon's motto to parents is succinct: "Tell early, tell gently, tell everything."

Tell even your baby. No, it's not that your baby will have any idea what you're talking about, it's that talking aloud about this— literally hearing these words come out of your mouth—will help you develop a comfort level with the topic. Hopefully, it will help you resolve any lingering tension or conflict so that by the time your child is old enough to take in some of what you're saying, you'll be rid of any emotional baggage. Not only that, but when your child is old enough to understand, she will have a comfort level too: She will already have heard words like *donor, insemination, sperm,* and *ovum.* They won't be scary or foreign-sounding.

When to have that conversation depends on your child. Sometime in the preschool years, he'll reach a point of development that pushes him to be curious about babies and where they come from. The first question is typically at age 3: "Was I in your tummy?" What your child is asking for is his birth story, not a biology lesson, so if he was in your tummy, no matter how he got there, all he needs is an honest answer, "Yes," along with the story of the day he was born: Where you were and what you were doing when he let you know he was ready to be born, the rush to the hospital, and the moment of birth: "We were so happy! Daddy squeezed my hand and we both cried."

If your child grew in someone else's uterus, this is the opening you've been waiting for: "You know what? You weren't in my tummy. Babies grow in a place inside a woman called a uterus, but my uterus can't grow a baby. Since Daddy and I wanted a baby really badly, we found a very caring lady who agreed to help us grow a baby. You grew in her uterus and when it was time for you to come out, Daddy and I went with her to the hospital to help you get born."

> *An analogy young children grasp easily: Sperm and ova are kinds of seeds that make a baby grow. Sometimes they don't work, just like some seeds in the garden don't grow.*

Let his attention span and interest level be your guide for how much to embellish: "Would you like to know what I was doing when I found out you were ready to be born?" With many children, this will be the end of the discussion. Others will ask for more detail, for instance, "What was the name of the lady?" If you have the information, give it.

The opening for the mother who carried her baby through sperm or ovum donation will come with two questions. One of them—"How are babies made?"—gives you an opportunity to explain that an egg from a woman's body and a sperm from a man's body come together to make a baby. The other—"How come some children look like their parents and I don't?"—gives you the chance to talk about how families are made in different ways. For instance: "In our family, something wasn't working in Dad's body and he couldn't make good sperm, so a doctor helped us find someone called a sperm donor to help us make a baby with my egg and the donor's sperm. Look what a good job we did! You!" Los Angeles marriage and family therapist Carole LieberWilkins, who counsels parents whose children are the result of donor egg, donor sperm, or adoption and who herself has a son through anonymous egg donation, remembers the first time her son asked about family differences. "He was 4 and he wanted to know why he didn't look like me," she says. "I told him, 'You don't look like me because you don't have that piece of me that makes us look alike. It's called a gene. Your genes come from the egg donor.'" Sometime in the first few school years, a child may begin to understand that genes help determine certain things about a person—how tall you'll be, the color of your eyes—and she may become concerned about not having Mom's or Dad's genes. Reassure her, "You'll still be a lot like us because we love each other and spend time sharing interests and doing things together, and that makes parents and children alike, too."

Conversations about origins are not one-shot deals. Be prepared to talk about this over and over again, including at times when you least expect it, like when you're driving carpool and your daughter asks, "Mommy, can you tell Jill the story of my sperm daddy?" (Hint 1: Keep it simple. Hint 2: When you get home, call Jill's mom and tell her what happened. Hint 3 is for Jill's mom: If you haven't already done so, use this opening to talk about the many different ways there are to make a family.)

In these early years, children accept the information you give them without having an emotional or social context to put it in. With the developmental shift that comes about at age 8, you may begin to see that something about the story makes him sad. It may be that he feels bad for the parent whose traits didn't get to be passed on, or sad for himself at not having those traits. He may also begin to think about the motives of the third person: Why is it that people want to donate? Why would a person want to have a baby and not mother it? Who is this person to me? If you have details, share them, but don't lie; you'll only have to mop up after yourself in the years to come.

LieberWilkins says her son's questions at first reflected curiosity, but when he was 7, she sensed a sadness she was sure was due to her inability to provide details. The next time he asked the donor's name, she asked him, "What would you like to name her?" He picked a name from his favorite TV show. When he wanted to know what she looked like and LieberWilkins didn't know, she asked him, "What do you think she might look like?" Only when he launched into a detailed description, did she realize the depth of his need for a connection and how important it is for parents to share whatever details they do have. Gordon says that parents' willingness to talk is a gift we give our children. "When they can access information on their timetable, that means they are developmentally ready and able to take in and assimilate it," she says. "When parents dole out information and then shut down, children may be getting facts but not be ready to process what they get, so it doesn't really do them any good."

If you took advantage of collaborative reproduction, have not yet told your child, and she's now 8 to 12 years old, don't wait any longer. Think of Gordon's "gentleness" approach, though. Don't just blurt out, "We have something to tell you. I'm not your real dad." Try instead: "We've been thinking about something we haven't told you because we thought you weren't old enough to understand and now we can see you're ready. . . ." Avoid using the word *real*, but if she says, "You mean you're not my real dad," a good response might be "Genetic material is one way a parent is real, but in every other way, especially how much I love you and care about you, I am your real father."

Be prepared for a range of reaction, including anger, confusion, and a sense of betrayal—"Why didn't you tell me, you lied to me all these years!"—as well as nonchalance. Some kids will simply say, in essence, "What's the big deal?" and mean it. If your child is angry or hurt, your best response is one that is open and loving: "We're sorry we didn't tell you sooner, maybe that was a mistake. But we're blessed you're here and now that we have told you, we'll answer any questions whenever you have them."

Whether your child is 3 or 8 the first time you have this conversation, what counts most is that you are having it. Second in importance is that you sprinkle any and all conversations liberally with comments about how much you wanted a baby, how grateful you are for the help you got, and how happy you are that she was born. The overriding idea is to leave your child with a message that is positive and unambiguous so she knows there is nothing bad or wrong about the way she was born.

Michelle expects that someday Sammy will meet his "egg mom," but only when he is older and only if he wants to. In the meantime, she and her husband and Sam go every year to a holiday party at the fertility center where Sammy got his start. There, he sees all kinds of different families who he knows also had help getting babies born. "My friend Elizabeth has two mommies, so they didn't have any sperms, not even sick ones," he says. "Her family *really* needed help to get started."

CHAPTER SEVEN

Birth, Death, and a Few Things in Between
. . . .

The birth of a sibling, the death of a parent, a child's own serious illness, moving—these are among the biggest stresses life has to offer; we can all identify them as dramatic and potentially traumatic events in the life of a child. Getting a grip on our children's unique developmental perspective may elude us, however, because we are so often active participants in the drama ourselves. I'm reminded of when my husband was hospitalized for many days for some serious surgery. Our son was 4 at the time. We had given him lots of advance preparation, he talked to Norm on the phone and visited him as soon as the many tubes were removed. I was careful as well not to disrupt his preschool schedule and to be home each night to put him to bed. I thought he was doing really well, until one of his preschool teachers gently suggested that he and I do something "fun" together. I thought it was a rather strange suggestion, given the situation, but the next day, when friends Lyle and Betsy urged us to come visit their new puppy, the teacher's words echoed in my head. My son's face lit up when I told him of the plan. The second we got to their house and romped on the floor together with the puppy climbing all over us, I could see what the teacher had meant. I had been very diligent about logistics for the week, but I had also, understandably, been very intense. My son had absorbed that intensity. He needed my permission to be silly and laugh. It lightened the load for both of us.

Children almost always will rise to the occasion, but they also need to be able to sink comfortably back down to their natural developmental level. We need to be able to tolerate their doing that and, more than that, to sometimes facilitate it.

Welcoming a sibling into the family . . .

One morning about a week after Meg and Jeff had brought baby Caroline home from the hospital, Meg was nursing in the kitchen. Avery, their firstborn who was not quite 2½, was watching intently. With every passing minute, she was getting increasingly frustrated. Finally she turned to her mother in a rage.

"Put that baby back in the refrigerator!" she screeched.

No matter the age or level of understanding, no matter how much preparation you've done or acceptance you seem to have fostered, sooner or later there will come a time when a firstborn isn't happy about the existence of a second-born. "Why would any sibling be happy about it?" asks registered nurse Judy Gundersen, coordinator of parent and childbirth education at Brigham and Women's Hospital in Boston, where she runs classes for soon-to-be siblings. "Whether he's been an only child so far, or one of several, his position in life is being usurped."

If there is a mistake parents typically make introducing a new baby into the family, it's thinking that if only they do a good job of it, they will avoid sibling rivalry. T. Berry Brazelton, America's beloved author, pediatrician, and researcher, tells parents, "You can *reduce* the sibling anger and resentment, but there's no getting around it altogether. That's a myth." He says sibling rivalry is normal and healthy, not to be prevented but to be managed.

Helping your child get ready means you have to be ready. As

soon as you know there's a baby coming, whether she's growing in your tummy or going to be adopted, parents and especially moms begin to make some emotional and psychological shifts. As excited as most parents are at the prospect of a new baby, they often are preoccupied with some negative or at least mixed feelings: Will I be spreading myself too thin? How will I carve out time for another child? Will I be able to meet the unique needs of each? Brazelton urges parents to acknowledge these doubts to each other. Otherwise your anxiety will affect your ability to parent your existing children.

> *If you're sick during your pregnancy and behaving differently as a result—for instance, spending lots of time in bed—don't relate it to the pregnancy. You're just sick.*

Even when a mother isn't anxious, the relationship with a child generally does change sometime during pregnancy. Many kids can sense Mom is different, but they don't know why. Some get clingy and whiny and hyperactive, others quiet and withdrawn. In the effort to reengage you, a toddler may tire you out, unwittingly making you more tired and unavailable. This can cause regression even before the baby is born.

Less than ten years ago, the consensus among professionals was to wait as long as possible to tell a toddler or preschooler that a baby was coming, at least until Mom's body was noticeably different. The thinking was that too much advance notice fueled anxiety. Because of a growing recognition of children's uncanny sensitivities to a mother, that thinking has changed. Now the growing consensus is to tell children at the same time that you tell other people. Anything else runs the risk they'll find out from someone else, by overhearing your conversations, or by picking up on vibes you're sending. It's a matter of trust that fuels this thinking: A big change is coming and a child of any age should hear about it from the person he trusts the most and who matters most in his life.

When you are telling your child, be simple and direct. Don't give more information than she can absorb: "A new baby is growing in a special place inside of me. When it gets born, it will be a part of our family." Avoid saying the baby is growing in your stomach; for some children, that can prompt sympathetic stomachaches or cause confusion about food and eating. If he wants to know where in your body, call it by its proper name: "In a special place called the womb (or uterus). It looks like it's my stomach, but it isn't really." Whatever you do, don't expect your child to be happy with the news. Gundersen tells a parent to imagine how you would feel if your partner came home one day and told you, "Honey, I really love you. You've been such a perfect partner and you make me so happy, I've decided to get another wife/husband. You won't mind, will you?"

When a baby is being adopted, the only thing that's different about the introduction is that the lead time may be longer. Tell a child as soon as you are officially waiting; don't risk that she'll overhear you talking about it on the phone or that someone else will tell her. Here's what you might say: "This may not happen for a long time, but we're starting to plan to have another child in our family. We're hoping to adopt a baby. When we know more, we'll tell you." Just because you raise the issue doesn't mean you have to keep talking about it, but let her know you're available to answer any questions she has.

Also prebirth:

- **Be realistic.** It's better to be honest about what babies are like than to bill them as playmates: "When babies are little, all they do is pee, poop, eat, sleep, and cry." Otherwise, your child will be not only disappointed but potentially angry at you for deceiving him. If anything, it's better to err on the side of underselling rather than overselling: "You know what? Babies are a little bit boring. They can't do anything themselves." As it gets closer to the birth, tell him, "In the beginning, babies take a lot of a mom's time because they can't do anything for themselves. That's hard for some little boys. If it's hard for you, I want you to tell me about it." This is worth repeating after the birth. Many times.

- **Tolerate negative feelings.** When your 3-year-old whines, "I don't want a new baby," resist the urge to say "Sure you do. It'll be fun!" That negates her feelings and doesn't get at what she really wants to know, which is "Will you still love me after the baby? Will you still take care of me?" Even though she isn't asking that in so many words, pretend she is. Tell her explicitly, "When the baby is here, I'll love you the same as now, and Mom and Dad will take care of you just like we do now."

- **Emphasize what's staying the same.** Most of us have a tendency to talk about all the things that will be different, because that's what we're focusing on. For young children, anything new and different is a threat. Instead of talking about her *new* room, her *new* bed, her *new* sister, focus on what will stay the same: "You'll still go to preschool. We'll still tuck you into bed every night. We'll still read a story." That's a source of comfort and security. Share this strategy with other caregivers and adults in your child's life, especially grandparents.

- **Make changes early in the pregnancy.** If you're moving your 3-year-old out of her room or an 18-month-old out of her crib, don't wait until just before the baby is coming. It'll give him one more reason to be angry at her. Make these moves months in advance and don't connect it to the baby. He's getting a big-boy bed because he's a big boy. Period.

- **Don't ask your child to help you name the baby, don't even solicit her opinion, unless you intend to use the**

name she chooses. Otherwise, she'll be hurt that you didn't. The same rule of thumb goes for other preparations. If you are redoing the nursery, don't ask her what color paint she likes unless you'll abide by her choice. One meaningful way to involve a child of any age is to ask her to draw a picture of welcome for the baby. Frame it and hang it near the crib.

It's not uncommon for a child to want to touch Mama's belly. Because these attempts can be clumsy, you need to let your child know right away that socking you in the tummy is not okay. Parent educator Linda Braun of Wheelock College and Families First, a parent information and counseling center in Cambridge, Massachusetts, tells parents to say that it hurts Mommy, not that it hurts the baby. That simple change in language can eliminate potential resentment. If poking at your stomach in a hostile way becomes frequent, assume it's anger and identify it for him: "I bet you're wishing there wasn't a baby inside there."

> *Help your child conceptualize the timing of the birth: "You know how far away Christmas is? Well, the baby won't be born until after that!"*

Braun assures that you're not putting ideas in his head with a statement like that. "The ideas are there," she says. "When you acknowledge them, it makes him feel safe because he now knows it's okay to have those thoughts. He realizes he doesn't have to feel guilty or repress the ideas or express the hostility in other ways. You accept him, mean thoughts and all." When hostile thoughts surface, pull out your child's baby album and tell the story of his birth and arrival. Do this with a child of any age and no matter what the circumstances of arrival: If the new baby is coming via adoption and your older child was adopted, too, talk about all the preparations you made before she arrived.

A subject that's come up in recent years is whether a sibling can be present at the birth. Although this is happening with increased frequency, most child development experts are not advocates. "Births can be scary and bloody," says developmental psychologist Phyllis Sonnenschein of Wheelock College. She discourages including siblings of any age. So does Brazelton. "I wouldn't say it's okay," he says. "If you want to do it, have an adult in the room with the child, completely at the child's disposal." In addition, all the medical professionals involved need to be comfortable with it.

If your firstborn comes to bring you and the baby home from the hospital, sit in the middle of the backseat with the baby on one side and her on the other. Give her a bunch of lollipops and ask her if she'd like to hand them out to her friends. Bill it not as an occasion to celebrate the birth but, rather, as one to celebrate her becoming a big sister.

Once the baby is home, a seesaw of emotion is very common. My favorite anecdote comes from a mom who, in three months, hadn't seen any hostility from her 4-year-old toward the baby. Driving in the car alone together one day, the 4-year-old suddenly cried out, "Mom, quick! Stop the car! I see a mailbox big enough to hold the baby!" This mother had all she could do to keep from laughing out loud. For most of us, the problem is keeping our anger in check. A good response acknowledges the jealousy a child is feeling and shows no anger at her for saying mean things, not even if she says, "I hate the baby!" Forget trying to talk her out of it by saying things like "You don't really mean that, honey." At the moment, it's exactly what she means, just as she also means it ten minutes later when she says, "I love my sister so much!" Letting her know you can tolerate all her feelings, including hostile ones, will help her feel safe. So tell her: "I understand how you feel, you're wishing there weren't a baby in our family right now. It's okay if you don't love the baby all the time." Similarly, if your child makes observations that are negative but true—"She's always crying!"—validate her perception: "You're right, she does cry a lot." Remind her this isn't forever: "You know, she won't always be like this."

For some children, jealousy, fear, and resentment may not surface until the baby is crawling or talking and literally infringing on her territory. Insecurity and indignation are such typical and normal responses that child psychiatrist Robert Nardone of Children's Hospital in Boston says if your child doesn't act out, you should wonder why. It's probably not because she's the most even-tempered, accepting child in the world but, rather, that she's keeping a lid on how she feels. You may be sending signals that lead her to think, "I don't dare let them know what's really going on inside me."

Almost all firstborns experience some regression. Whenever it happens, it means she's feeling threatened, frightened, and/or worried. Her thinking might go something like this: "I'm not getting the attention I want from Mommy. Maybe if I'm a baby, too, she'll pay more attention." When his sister was born, Bryan, 3, started talking baby talk, throwing tantrums, and appearing at his parents' bedside at four a.m. The first thing he would say was "Where's Meaghan?" It was just by luck, says his mother, that Meaghan was always in the bassinet and not in bed with her. The recommended strategy with regression is not to encourage or feed into it but also not to react angrily.

Psychologist Sonnenschein tells parents to be a little more permissive than usual and to build in lots more cuddle time. Try some gentle interpretation of the behavior and reinforcement for the big-girl things she does: "It seems like it would be nice to be a baby, but look at all the things you can do that the baby can't." Or: "You're such a big girl, you hardly ever want to sit on my lap anymore. What a good chance for a hug, now that you are sitting here." Whatever you do, says Sonnenschein, "get back to your regular limits for standards of behavior sooner rather than later." She says children are uncomfortable and confused if the limits you've always imposed suddenly disappear. Not only that, but when you remove limits, a child is forced to act out even more in order to find out where the limit *will* be set. If your child is pushing you harder and harder, that's probably a sign that you've disrupted her by being overly permissive.

Of all the regressive behavior you might see, the one that's trickiest to cope with is a child's desire to nurse. Unfortunately, there is not professional consensus on this. Sonnenshein, for instance, wouldn't offer the breast to any child who has been weaned, even just to try it. Child psychiatrist Clarice J. Kestenbaum agrees. She says, "It's simply is not appropriate. It encourages infantile behavior and might even hamper her other development." Brazelton, however, sees no reason not to allow a child to try it, as long as he is the one who initiates it, not you. "It's a way for him to test whether Mom is deserting him or not," he says. "It's letting him have access to Mother at a time when he is feeling shut out. Once he tries it, he won't want to do it again." Because this is a very personal decision, certainly there is no reason to offer the breast to an already weaned child if the idea makes you uncomfortable, but if you like the idea, factor in what the professionals say and go with your gut. If you don't want to do it, a proactive strategy is to distract your child while you nurse. Give him a snack at the same time the baby is nursing, or have a box with markers or toys inside that he can use only during feeding time.

There are some developmental differences that affect how children react to a baby:

Preschoolers. Three-, 4-, and 5-year-olds typically have the hardest time with a new baby. A girl, vying for a father's attention, perceives that he gave the baby to Mom and not to her and may be angry with him. A boy notices the powerful connection among Mom, Dad, and the baby and feels he has been betrayed. Some children may even think they have somehow failed: "I must have done something wrong, so they went out and got this baby." All of these feelings are normal, although they aren't always obvious. The younger the child, the less able she is to verbalize what she feels. Instead of displaying aggression or apprehension to you or the baby, she may project it on other things. "All of a sudden, she'll be fearful of thunder or the vacuum or a dog," psychiatrist Nardone says. Although these fears can also be part and parcel of the preschool years, if there's a new baby in the family, it's probably safe to assume there's a connection. The best antidote is to repeat that you still love him, that you'll always take care of him and play with him just like before. Words alone won't satisfy, though. Make special time for each parent to be alone with him, doing something of his choosing. Never leave your preschooler alone with the newborn, even if he seems to like the baby. Impulses come over children quickly. If he shows aggression toward her, tell him that he can talk or think about how much he doesn't like her, but he can't poke or pinch her. If you have to remove him from the baby, sit and talk with him. Otherwise, he'll feel abandoned and punished and resent her even more.

School-age. Their easier adjustment to the baby is partly because they have a life outside the family. But don't assume that a school-age child is having an easy adjustment just because it looks as if he is. By 8, a child is able to keep feelings of jealousy to himself. He may reason, "My parents will love me most if I'm really good." What mitigates against these feelings for a 6- to 9-year-old child is the degree to which his routines are disrupted. If Mom is still going to his hockey games and still helping with homework, he'll do better. It also will depend on how much responsibility you're throwing his way. Boys and girls alike enjoy caring for a baby, but if you overdo it, they'll get resentful.

Even though you may be dealing with various forms of sibling rivalry throughout your children's relationship, this period of adjustment may well be the most intense. Luckily it typically lasts only three or four months. Avery regressed for a while, climbing into her mother's lap whenever she saw her sister there. By the time Caroline was five months old, however, she was pretty much back to her old self and downright blasé. "I like my sister good," she says. "I *really* like food." In the weeks after Meaghan was born, Bryan only wanted Daddy to put him to bed. But one night he asked if Mom and Meaghan could say prayers with him. He wanted Meaghan to lie on his stomach with the blankets on them both. "I'm sleeping with my baby sister," he said proudly. It became a nightly routine for about four months, until Meaghan became too mobile to be content just lying there with Bryan. By that time, he thought she was too squirmy anyway, and he was happy to have Mom to himself. "This is cozy, isn't it?" he told her. "Just you and me."

. . . and a half sibling

When Matt was 9 and his half sister, Anna, was yet unborn, his father and stepmother made a serious tactical error. "They made me move out of my bedroom," says Matt, now 12. "I can understand why they did it. It's bigger and I'm only there once a week and she's there every day. But it ticked me off. One day it was my room and the next time I came, it wasn't my room anymore. They could have at least *asked*."

His father, Robert, and stepmother, Michelle, don't argue the point. "It was a bad mistake," Michelle says. "We should have talked about it with him."

Luckily, any resentment that was generated didn't last long. "I got over it because I had always wanted a brother or sister," says Matt. His stepmother says Matt and Anna, now 3, have an important relationship. "Anna is always sad when he leaves. And if I get angry with him, she'll say, 'Don't be angry with my Matt.' "

As for Matt, Michelle says, "I think he loves Anna deeply." Matt doesn't disagree with her. "She's cute, even if she is at the age where she's a pain," he says. It's a compliment not only to Anna but to all the adults in the family, including Matt's mother.

As difficult as the birth of a sibling can be, when the birth occurs in a stepfamily, there are layers of emotions and logistics that need to be worked through; all the sibling issues apply and then some. It's a double whammy. Here are some reasons why:

- A stepmother with a baby, especially her first, is likely to be less attentive to a stepchild. If the relationship between them was a good one, a stepchild can be even more than normally jealous; if the relationship was strained to begin with, this can add another degree of difficulty.

- A father with a new baby may be less accessible or have less time for a child he doesn't live with, perhaps even turning away from the child altogether. Whether the relationship with Dad is good or bad, a child can feel abandoned. She may even think she's done something wrong and that's why he isn't as attentive.

- A mother whose ex-spouse's new wife has a baby may feel hurt, sad, jealous, or angry. She may even be angry with her child, feeling he has betrayed her by being involved with this baby. Sensing his mother's anxiety, a child becomes anxious himself, perhaps assuming he has done something wrong but not knowing what.

- A mother who is having a baby and whose child from a previous marriage lives with her even part-time may at least temporarily feel more connected to her husband and the baby. This is more likely to be true if the relationship with her first child's father was very difficult and especially if memories of the child's birth and infancy are unpleasant, for instance, if his father was emotionally uninvolved or absent.

All of this plays out on top of a wide range of emotions within a half sibling: confusion, anger, guilt, joy, anxiety. In some families, parents are convinced the half sibling couldn't care less about the baby and even wishes the family ill because he is so negative or uninterested before the birth. More likely, a child is simply struggling to contain or sort out her feelings. There are all sorts of reasons she might be angry. If she doesn't like her stepmother, she may be even angrier with her after the baby is born because it is harder to hate someone whose baby you like, hard to hate her if you are connected through her baby. A child might be angry because she likes the baby in spite of herself or because she sees how much more her stepmother loves the baby than she loves her. When Elaine, a psychologist, was pregnant, her 7-year-old stepdaughter was able to tell her, "I'm afraid you'll love the baby more than you love me." Elaine remembers telling her she could understand why she might think that. "I told her, 'You and I have a special relationship that will never change. You're right that my feelings for the baby will be different than my feelings for you, but I will always love you too.' "

Most children aren't able to express themselves this forthrightly, so it's up to us to recognize that their resistance and negativity are more likely due to fear of change, not to an actual dislike of a baby. Research shows that half siblings overwhelmingly want the new family to succeed. Social worker Taube S. Kaufman, founder of the Combined Families Association of America, says a child who has been through divorce or the death of a parent knows that marriage isn't forever. "Because it's a terrible emotional burden to see a family fail, the typical child fantasizes that this baby will be the glue to keep the family together since it's the one person in the whole family that everyone is related to," she says.

The problem, of course, is that kids are much more sensitive to change of any kind than we are, so what upsets a child may not even register with us. Try some gentle probing: "It must be hard to see us not having as much time to spend with you," or "Isn't it amazing how much work and time a baby takes!" Whatever you do, avoid giving false reassurance. As with a young child awaiting the birth of a sibling, don't say, "Don't worry, nothing will change." Because most half siblings tend to be older, a dishonest or dismissive attitude will be recognized and resented. Be honest—"Some things will change"—and as specific as possible: "We'll be more tired because we'll be up a lot at night with the baby. So when you come over, you and I will still do something together every Saturday but for a while, it might not be very adventurous. Maybe this would be a good time for us to catch up on some videos."

Honesty between husband and wife is important too. Psychologist Patricia Peppernow of Cambridge, Massachusetts, says she's seen children get caught in the middle when the parent of the half sibling gets upset that his or her spouse loves the baby more than the stepchild. Because children of divorce are particularly sensitive to friction between adults, they pick up on the anger and assume they are to blame. In fact, it's unrealistic for the parent of the half sibling to think his or her new partner *wouldn't* love the baby more, and Peppernow urges parents to give each other permission to love each child differently.

The timing of the baby's birth is something else that can make a big difference. The more time a stepfamily has had to build up a history with each other, the more likely it is that a half sibling will view the baby as a positive addition. The younger the half sibling, the longer that wait should be, but anything less than two years as a family is tricky, even if a half sib is as old as 14, according to Kaufman.

How much time you spend together after the baby is born makes a difference too. Parents commonly assume that the best way to make this new family work is to spend all your time together. That usually backfires. Instead, each person in the family needs time alone with each other individual in all the various configurations possible: biological parent and child, stepparent and stepchild, husband and wife, baby and mother, baby and father, and baby and half sibling, but only if the half sibling is interested.

This turns out to be a critical point in most families. Matt is no exception. "I still spend a lot of time just with my dad," he says, "so I don't mind when I have to share him with Anna." In Matt's classmate's family, things have not gone as smoothly. "Tori thinks her father doesn't love her as much as he used to," says Matt. "Even when he promises to do something just with her, he ends up bringing the baby along. He always asks her if she minds, but she always says okay 'cause she doesn't want him to think she's selfish."

What also turns out to be a critical piece in a child's adjustment is the attitude of the biological parent who isn't the new mother or father. Matt's mother was welcoming to Anna from the start, taking Matt to visit in the hospital (she arranged for him to meet his father in the lobby) and sending a baby gift from them both. She has even invited Anna to visit Matt at their home. Tori's mother has not been nearly as generous. Tori's half sister was born on a weekend when Tori and her mother were scheduled to leave for a ski vacation in New Hampshire. Her mother insisted their departure could not be changed to accommodate a quick hospital visit to see the baby, even though Tori was dying to. As a result, Tori didn't see the baby until two weeks later, plenty of time for her to build up all sorts of fantasies about what was going on in her father's house. By the time of her first visit after the birth, she had developed a solid chip on her shoulder. Clearly, children need emotional permission from their biological parent who is not the parent of the baby to accept and/or love their half sibling. Without it, they feel torn and guilty. When this parent can offer support and be welcoming to the baby of an ex-spouse, it brings a child's world together. There's a big difference, for instance, between the ex-spouse who asks her child, "What's it like for you with the baby?" and one who says, "Your father never changed your diapers. Is he changing this baby's?" Or one who responds to a child's complaints about how much attention the baby is getting by saying "I'm not surprised, your dad never could focus on more than one thing at a time," instead of "It feels like you don't get enough time with your dad, huh?"

When the baby is born to the child's biological mother, the transition is usually easier, especially if the child lives primarily with her. Then the baby typically isn't considered a half brother or half sister but my brother or my sister. Then again, there are all sorts of individual differences. A half sibling who is 12 or 13 may think it's great having a baby in the family and love taking care of her, or he could think it's "stupid." Matt's stepmother has an older biological child, too, who was at first threatened by Anna, even though he is away at college. "He expressed the feeling more than once that he wasn't my only child anymore," says Michelle.

Making a move

From a child's perspective, there is no such thing as a good age to move, unless, of course, you are still an infant. At any other age, a move is traumatic, whether it's across town or cross-country. The change in routine, parents' preoccupation with it, loss of friends—these are all losses for a child that we tend to underestimate.

Tiffany was 8 when her family moved from the Midwest to a town south of Boston. The best part of moving, she says, was helping her parents, "especially being in charge of the goldfish in the backseat of the car. It didn't spill once. I also liked looking at the road signs, especially the ones that showed us our new street when we got there." She's not as forthcoming when she talks about the worst parts. "It was leaving my friends behind. Leaving my friends, my school, and my teacher made me sad. But I like my new school. It's very friendly," she says, three months after the move.

There are two major factors that enable a child to cope well: being part of the process and having parents with a positive attitude. The second is probably more important; this is one time when honesty is not always the best policy. Parents do need to acknowledge feelings truthfully—you can't pretend to be happy about the move if you aren't. But you may need to put on a happier face than you really feel in order not to burden your children. The problems most children have come not from being uprooted but from parents who are so preoccupied or unhappy that they are emotionally unavailable. If a child connects the change in parenting to the move, she'll try to take care of the parent in an effort to gain her back. That child will see the move as something to dread, says psychologist Sumru Erkut, and never come to terms with her own feelings. Parents, then, walk a fine line between being truthful and also positive: "It's true I'm sad to move, but I'm looking forward to new opportunities for our family." Don't say something like this: "I hope this will put us in better financial shape, but I'm not very optimistic."

No matter how well you present the case for the move, your children probably won't like the idea. Accept that as a given. In fact, the more pluses you put forward, the more negatives your school-age child will come up with. That doesn't mean you should stop presenting the good side of the move, only that you need to be prepared for lots of negativity. Don't try to stifle or minimize it. Kids who tend to make the quickest adjustments have parents who allowed them to vent. Okay, so, yes, this could make you crazy. Children can be *so* negative.

Here's how to keep their anger and your frustration under control:

- **Tolerate the anger rather than respond to it.** Keep saying sympathetic, empathetic statements that acknowledge feelings: "It's hard to move." "I know you'll miss your friends." "I know you don't like this." Avoid saying "You'll love it there," even if you think that's true. Not only aren't you acknowledging her feelings, but what if she doesn't love it, which of course she won't, at least not in the beginning.

- **Maintain limits for inappropriate behavior.** The prospect of a move makes the world seem unpredictable enough to a child; relaxing your parenting standards makes it even scarier. Apply the same limits that you always have even when you know inappropriate behavior stems from anger and frustration about the move.

- **Maintain routines right up to the day of the move.** The more normal you are able to keep their lives, the more secure children will feel. Tiffany's mother, Alma, a veteran of five moves since her daughter's birth, says routine is key to her success. "Whatever else I have to do, including move-related tasks, I squeeze in in between keeping the kids' routines on course," she says.

It's commonly held that teenagers have the most difficulty moving, but researchers say it's actually harder on kindergartners, first-graders, and preteens. They're developmentally more vulnerable. The younger ones don't have the coping mechanisms or social skills of even a second- or third-grader, while preteens are in the midst of physical and emotional changes that make them insecure under the best of circumstances. By the same token, although June, July, and August have traditionally been the months when most families move, current research indicates midyear moves can be easier on children. "It's harder for kids to make connections in the summer," says psychologist Erkut. "Hardly anyone is around and there's no mechanism for meeting the kids who are there." If you are planning a summer move, canvass the neighborhood in advance to find a child who will be around, or contact the school for names of classmates your child can meet during the summer. The advantage of a midyear move is that kids get plucked from one school environment into another. While the school layout and procedures may be different from what they left, school as an environment is something they know about. They know how to cope. If you move in the summer, don't send your child to overnight camp and move while he's gone. Being present for the move and seeing it actually happen grounds a child in the reality of it. Having your child simply show up after the fact may be easier for you and may seem like it would be easier for him, but it isn't.

The fact of a move should not be sprung on him while he's away, either. The time to tell children you're moving is as soon as it causes change within the family—Daddy is relocating sooner than the rest of you, or your house is going on the market—or when it's likely they might hear about it from someone outside the family. Otherwise, if you can be sure they won't hear about it first from someone else, give school-age children about a month's notice, preteens slightly more, and preschoolers slightly less. Too much time for even older children gives them time to worry and brood.

Many parents make the mistake of thinking that the sooner the new house is "normal"—that is, unpacked—the happier the children

Before the move:

- *If possible, visit the new community and the new house. Let him pick out the room he wants and have input into how it will be painted by offering choices: Which of these colors would you like for your room?*

- *It's important your school-age child feel that the part of her life she is leaving isn't disappearing forever. Encourage her to collect names and addresses in a book and to make a scrapbook about her life here. Plan for phone calls after you arrive and for visits back, if possible. Prestamp and address postcards for friends to send. Suggest inviting friends to a going-away party.*

- *Give him some sense of control. Let him pack his toys or decide which possessions will travel with him. Provide something to look forward to—"We'll have room for a dog now!"—but give him decisions to make about the new house only if you will abide by them.*

- *Give him a camera or video camera to take pictures of school, friends, and the house you are leaving.*

After the move:

- *Unless there are compelling reasons not to, keep him in the same grade.*

- *Create a ritual to mark the first night in your new residence: a picnic on the floor, pizza by candlelight.*

- *Arrange a tour of the school before your kids attend classes. Request someone from the class to serve as a buddy on the first day.*

- *Inquire at the school about cultural or stylistic changes that might affect your child. Differences in dress, in slang, or in music or sport or TV preferences can be a real impediment.*

- *Most children want their room exactly as it was before. Don't fight it.*

- *If the move requires a downscaling in lifestyle or living situation, find something to be positive about.*

will be. Researchers dispute that. "Spending your time unpacking means you aren't available to your kids," says Erkut. Alma, Tiffany's mother, says, "The first time we moved, Tiffany was 3. I did nothing but unpack for a solid week, plopping her in front of the TV. It was awful." This last move, the only rooms she unpacked immediately were the kids'. "Within the first twenty-four hours, their rooms looked perfectly normal. I didn't even bother with the kitchen, except for the few utensils we had in the car," she says. On Sunday, their first full day in town, instead of working on the house, Alma and her husband took the kids to explore the neighborhood.

A child of any age, even a toddler, can feel the loss of peer attachments. Although it's easier for parents to facilitate the making of new friendships for young children, there are some easy ways to help a 10-year-old too. While you can't do the inviting yourself, you can help provide access. Offer to provide rides to events for friends, encourage him to invite a friend to a movie or a sports event. If your child resists this kind of effort, try to find out what you can do that would be less threatening. Boys often have a harder time making the adjustment than girls, especially boys 9 or older, although sports can be a good entry. For girls, exclusionary behavior is likely to be a little more subtle; they may be the object of behind-the-back whispers and gossip about hairstyle, clothing, and mannerisms.

Unfortunately, you can't rely on your child to tell you she's being victimized. For one thing, she may not even realize it. If she does, she's likely to be afraid you'll do something that will embarrass her or make things worse. Unless you can see signs that your child is not having difficulty with peer acceptance (the phone is ringing, invitations are coming in), assume she *is* having a problem and ask her directly if she's feeling left out. Make it clear, however, that you see your role as helping her problem-solve, not that you will take over. Be supportive. Let her know what's happening to her is common but unkind. Be prepared to spend more time than usual with your children in this adjustment period. It can take up to a month before new friendships get made and five months before there's a friendship network similar to what they had before. After six months, if a child is still anxious and complaining, or if he's exhibiting any atypical behaviors, consult the teacher and school officials. Professional intervention may be helpful.

Overall, most children do well with a move and many even gain lifelong coping skills. As a veteran mover, Tiffany imparts this bit of practical wisdom for other children about to move: "Your friends will be with you in your heart. They'll also be back in your old neighborhood." No doubt her sense of humor helped make her transition easier, too.

How children perceive their own illness or injury

Your 5-year-old falls off his bike. He's crying, complaining that his knee hurts, and insisting on a Band-Aid. You examine his knee and find no sign of an injury. What would you say:

- "There's nothing wrong. You're a big boy, get back on your bike and go play."

- "Gee, that must have hurt, but it isn't even scraped. There's no need to waste a Band-Aid."

- "That must have hurt but it isn't even scraped. I don't think you need a Band-Aid, but if you think you do, let's get one."

When a child is sick or injured, a parent's first responsibility is to ensure his physical health and safety. But mental health counts for something, too, and our affect is as important as our first aid. What we say and how we say it send powerful messages that influence how children feel about sickness and how they respond to it, not just today but for the rest of their lives. Parents who think the first response above is the best may reason that it helps build character and instills self-confidence. Not so, says Gerald Koocher, chief of psychology at Children's Hospital in Boston. Dismissing the pain tells your child "Even though you hurt, you're not entitled to feel the way you feel." A continual diet of this message teaches a child that he can't trust his own feelings. "That can be very costly emotionally," says Koocher. He speculates that this child is likely to grow into an adult who thinks he has to hide his real feelings, not just about health but about other issues as well.

> *A father should be as involved in the care of a sick child as a mother, so a child sees both parents in a nurturing role and sees different styles of nurturing.*

The second response validates a child's feelings and expresses your concern but doesn't give the child any control, which is what he needs to avoid feeling out of control. It's the third response that professionals recommend. It acknowledges the child's feelings, shows some concern but not too much, and grants control. It's not self-indulgent, insists behavioral pediatrician Ellen Perrin of the University of Massachusetts at Worcester. "Every person has to participate in the management of his health. I'm big on kids being involved from an early age," she says. "If the child hadn't said 'I want a Band-Aid,' I would have asked him, 'What do you think will help?' "

It's easier to help with everyday aches and ailments when we have some idea of what's going on in our children's minds. Consider the typical preschooler who cuts his finger. His worry is that all the blood in his body will come out through this cut. If he breaks his arm, he believes *he* is broken. It's not unusual for a 3-year-old to notice a three- or four-day-old scab somewhere on her body and insist she needs a bandage. It's not that it hurts anew; rather, it's that she's afraid her insides will leak out through the scab. Even if you tell him that the cut will stop bleeding by itself or that it's just his arm that is broken, the typical preschooler won't really believe you. That's because a preschooler conceptualizes her body as a whole entity, not as a whole that has individual parts. Grant her her wish and apply the Band-Aid. You aren't babying her, you're responding to a developmental need. As you give her the Band-Aid, keep in mind that children this age worry about anything concrete they can see happening to their body. Tell her, "That mark means you are getting better, it's called a scab. Some kids wonder if they can leak out of a scab. It looks like maybe that could happen, but it can't." In other words, comfort your child by validating her worry and expressing confidence that nothing bad will happen.

Children 4 to 7 and sometimes even older mix magical thinking with egocentricity and typically think it's their fault they got sick. Confronted with yet another ear infection, a 5-year-old may blame himself for getting it: "I didn't wear my hat yesterday at preschool." Perrin, who is a pioneer in the field of understanding how children perceive illness, says not to let a remark like that go by. Tell him, "It's always a good idea to wear a hat in cold weather, but that isn't why you got sick. You got sick because when people are sick they have something called germs inside them. If the germs come out in the air and someone else breathes some of the air that has the germs, they might get sick, too. You can't see germs though, so there's no way to know if they are in the air or not. Sometimes, it just happens." Throughout most of the school-age years, children automatically assume all germs make you sick. Perrin says it's not until they are 11 or 12 that they understand finer distinctions, for instance, that their body has a reaction to a germ. It's not until 13 or older that they understand that the body is a system with everything interrelated.

If a child gets hurt because he did something wrong, he will feel guilty and worry that you won't take care of him. Take care of the injury before you address the wrongdoing. Tell him, "I know you're afraid I'm going to yell at you because you aren't supposed to ride your bike on the street. I'm not going to worry about that now. First I'm going to take care of your leg and see if you need stitches. Later on, we'll talk about what you did wrong."

Perrin says parents and pediatricians often err by assuming children understand more than they do or by ignoring them altogether. The typical parent, for instance, assumes his child isn't hurting unless he says he is. But some children don't complain even when they are in pain. They may not realize relief is possible or they may be afraid they need a shot. I'm reminded of my son who, even as a toddler, would complain only mildly about ear pain. When we'd get him to the pediatrician, the doctor or nurse practitioner would invariably be astonished that he wasn't howling in discomfort. Thresholds for pain vary from child to child, just as they do for adults. When you think it's likely your child is in pain and he's not complaining, instead of marveling at how tough he is, ask him: "Do you hurt anyplace?" That gives him permission to talk about it and shows empathy on your part. It also doesn't go overboard.

Children are not instinctively afraid of injury or sickness. Being frightened is something they learn, so a child's response to injury or illness is often based on his own previous experience—a shot that hurt—or on a parent's reaction. Do you hover and pet and cluck over him with an eagle eye when he's sick? Too much attention will make him overly worried about himself. Do you rush onto the soccer field when he's tripped during a game instead of letting the coach tend to him? Attention like that could make him think he's hurt worse than he is and make him question his ability to shake it off. On the other hand, if you underreact, a child feels at risk and uncared-for.

Go for the middle-of-the-road response that is both respectful and concerned without overdoing. Treat her as normally as possible, in a normal tone of voice. Hide your panic and concern. "Your child swallows some bleach," says Koocher. "You think, 'Oh God, he's going to die.' You can think that all you want, but saying that will hurt, not help, him. You've got to stay calm so he doesn't become panicky. You've got to say, 'I'm going to help you, here's what we'll do.' " Seeing that you are in charge comforts a child. You can help even a preschooler gauge his pain by drawing a horizontal line for him and showing that one end of the line is no pain, the other end is so much pain you can't stand it, and in the middle it hurts a lot but you can handle it. Then you can ask him, "Show me on the line how much pain you have." As he gets older, you can put numbers to the continuum. (This strategy also works for quantifying all sorts of emotions.)

> *When your child witnesses the serious injury or illness of a peer, raise the questions he's likely thinking. Magical thinking pushes even school-age children to come to irrational conclusions: "Jimmy had a seizure, I could too." "Cancer is catching."*

Studies show that the more information children have, the better they will cope with whatever is wrong with them, as long as the information is age appropriate. Neil Schechter, a developmental pediatrician whose research is on how children communicate pain and how parents react to it, says that when doctors take this into consideration, "There's a five-fold decrease in pain behavior like flinching, pushing the doctor away, crying, yelling." In the past, parents were asked to leave when children received stitches or shots or had blood drawn, because parents were seen as a distraction. Now pediatricians recognize that parents' presence can have a calming, normative effect on children, assuming the parents are under control. Asking your child how he feels and what he thinks is going on enables you to know how to meet his medical and emotional needs. It will also help you communicate at his level of understanding. A 3-year-old needs to be told more than that it's important to drink juice when she's sick. She needs to know that it's not just a rule someone made up, but that there's a reason for it: "Your body needs a lot of juices. Liquids help your body get better." This is comforting. It says to him "Mom is telling me to do this because it will help me get better." As children get older, you can add information. To a 10-year-old you can say, "When you have a fever, your body loses a lot of water, mostly because you perspire a lot. To get better, you need to replace the liquid you lost."

As they are beginning to recover from an illness, children often are at their most irritable and regressive. They don't understand why they aren't better already and they worry, "Maybe I'm never going to feel better again!" Sending them back to school or activities too soon can feed into that fear; not having their normal energy level back, they see other kids doing what they used to feel able to do and think they won't feel that way again. Cross off the days on a calendar to show them when they should feel stronger and back to normal.

Children's complaints should always be taken seriously, even if you think your child is a hypochondriac, even if he's only 2 years old. Yes, you run the risk of creating a child who cries wolf, but researchers say if you dismiss or ignore a child's complaints, you run a far greater risk of losing her trust. Parents and other caregivers need to validate themselves in a child's eyes. Every child needs to know you will take him seriously, that you are a concerned caregiver who is worthy of his trust and to whom he can bring his complaints. The reason you probably won't create a hypochondriac is because taking him seriously doesn't mean medication is always necessary or that a doctor needs to be called or that he's going to stay home from school. It just means you are a good listener. When you're unsure how seriously to take a complaint, a child's behavior is the best gauge. If he's alert and playing, he's probably basically okay. If a child persists with a complaint and you can't find anything wrong, keep a log to help your pediatrician. Note how long the complaint lasts, the time of day when it occurs, and whether there is a precipitating event or other symptoms. Whenever in doubt, check with your pediatrician.

Monitoring our own behavior is not as easy as monitoring our child's. The parent who is repelled by the sight of blood cannot necessarily change that, but she should work hard at containing her fear so it doesn't spill over to her child. The first time your child gets stung by a bee, it's fair to wonder if he'll have an allergic reaction and to get prompt attention. But it's alarmist to express a worst-case scenario—"Oh, my God, what if you're allergic?"—or to instill a fear of bees in a child every time one comes near. When you're unsure what to say or do in the wake of a child's injury, put yourself in his shoes. If you just fell off your bike and skinned both knees and your hand, would you rather have someone tell you "Don't worry, you'll feel better soon," or "Boy, I bet that stings!"

When a parent is sick

True or false:

- The old axiom "What little ears don't hear won't hurt them" is a good one to heed when a parent is sick.

- A 7- to 10-year-old's fear, usually unvoiced, is that a sick parent is going to disappear or die.

- When a parent is sick, a toddler worries more about what will happen to him than he does about what will happen to the parent.

- It is not unusual for a young child to think her parent got sick because the parent was bad.

Whether you are behind the bathroom door throwing up from a stomach virus or recuperating from gallbladder surgery, how well your child copes depends on honest communication at a level he can understand, a concept that often eludes us in the midst of our misery even when we know it intellectually. The answers to these statements—False, True, True, True—reflect the fact that when children don't have the information they need to make sense of what's happening, they make up stories. As we already know, their fantasies can be worse than the truth. Even a preschooler can see for himself when you aren't functioning normally. Telling him "Mommy's okay" presents him with a discrepancy that he needs to resolve somehow.

A young child, especially a toddler, worries not so much about your health but about your loss of availability to him: "You're not playing with me and I don't like it when I don't get as much of you as I want." A 2- to 4-year-old, after all, just wants you to be his mommy. For him, even when all you have is the flu, you're not his mother the way he knows you to be. He may think he's done something wrong and that's why you don't want to play with him. That can make him feel guilty or confused, especially when he hasn't done anything wrong. He may be angry with you: "I hate you [because you won't be my mommy like you always are]!" His worst fear is that you've stopped loving him and he may resort to all sorts of negative behavior to get your attention, a sign that you love him again. A child 6 to 9 may worry you are dying if your illness is just slightly out of the ordinary, for instance, if it keeps you in bed when you've never done that before, or keeps you from making dinner, or driving carpool. Children of all ages can have such egocentric responses that you are stunned at their seeming lack of concern.

Harrison was 9 when his father was in a car accident. As he was getting dressed for day camp one summer morning, a call came from the emergency room. He was standing near his mother when the phone rang, saw her sink to a chair as she listened, heard the worry and fear in her voice and listened to her questions: "Is he all right? Tell me what happened." Luckily, his father wasn't badly hurt and his mother, who was increasingly conscious of her son at her side, was able to change her tone of voice even before she put down the phone. "Daddy was in a car accident," she told Harrison. "Luckily, he only has some scrapes and bruises."

Before she was able to say more, Harrison had his first question: "Can I still go to camp?" His apparent selfishness took her breath away. She kept her mouth shut and let the conversation drift to other things as she took him to camp. But even as she worried about her husband and rushed to get to his side, she had this nagging thought about Harrison: "How can a child be that uncaring, that selfish?" As much to calm herself as to get information, after she dropped Harrison at camp she picked up her cell phone to call her friend who happened also to be a child psychiatrist. "That was just a defense mechanism," the friend reassured her. "It was a way for him to mask his real feelings. That Daddy was in a car accident and could have been badly hurt was such a scary thought that he needed to defend against it until he could brace himself and deal with it in bits and pieces in his own way. Knowing that his routine wasn't going to be disrupted enabled him to function."

Sure enough, when she picked Harrison up from camp at the end of the day, the first thing he said was "How's Daddy? I can't wait to see him!" Days later she was even more relieved when Harrison offered up what his thinking process had been. At a dinner table conversation, her husband talked about the combination of fear and relief he had when he realized he was okay. "That's how I felt, too," said Harrison. "The first thing I did was ask Mom if I could go to camp because I was really worried you were hurt bad, but I knew if she said I could go to camp, it meant you weren't hurt bad."

When you are sick or hurt, keep explanations to young children brief: "I know you want to play with me now and I'd like to play with you. But I'm feeling sick and I need to rest until I feel better." If you are going to have a procedure or be hospitalized, preschoolers need to know where you are going, how long you will be there, and as much other information as you can give about their routine while you are gone: "Grandma will pick you up from preschool, and she'll cook dinner and tuck you into bed." The details you provide about what is wrong with you should be limited, however. A 3-year-old won't understand surgery, gall-bladder, or operation, but she will understand that you have a booboo inside your body, that it makes you feel sick, and that the doctor will help you get better. It reassures a young child to know you're doing this by choice, that you have control over when and whether you do it, and that you have asked the doctors and nurses to help make you better. Phyllis Silverman, a psychiatric researcher who studies children's reactions to illness, change, and death, says preschoolers have a tendency to think you are sick because you were bad. Let them know that illness sometimes just happens, and that even though we can't control when it comes along, we usually know how to make it better.

> *Should a child under 5 visit you in the hospital? Yes, as long as she knows in advance what the hospital will look, sound, and smell like, and as long as you (or a roommate) aren't hooked up to a lot of equipment. If you're sitting in a chair instead of in bed, it's even more reassuring.*

With children 7 and older, you can be fairly specific and even talk about the medicine they use to make you sleep. It's a misconception to think you will frighten them by talking about this; most kids know about it from TV and school health education, and not being honest with a school-age child sets him up to be angry, hurt, and traumatized, to feel rejected and left out. As a result, no matter how routine the illness or surgery, he'll act inappropriately because he won't know what to expect or what is expected of him. These kinds of reactions can be exacerbated, too, because children see us as omnipotent. When we're sick, it's scary and threatening, and if a parent is ill for an extended period of months, it's not unusual for a child to become depressed, to act out, or to regress. When siblings' ages vary widely, the information each one gets should be different.

Tell the older one, "I'm explaining it to you in more detail because you're older. It's hard for your sister to understand this and we don't want to scare her." Be specific about which details she lacks, so he won't repeat them to her.

Both parents and other family members involved in a child's care need to be on the same page with all of this and all of the adults involved in your child's life—teachers, day-care providers, baby-sitters, parents of playmates—need to know what's happening. If you do a great job of explaining about your hospital stay to your 5-year-old and then Grandma answers her questions differently, the lack of consistency can undo all the good you did. Make sure all surrogate caregivers know exactly what your children have been told and how you want questions to be answered. Children always feel better when there is something concrete they can do. Let them know you would like notes and pictures.

Because hospital stays tend to be so short these days, it's the recovery period that is usually harder for a child to understand. Once you walk through the front door, a young child wants everything to be back to normal immediately and takes your presence as the signal for it to be so. When it doesn't happen that way, he may be angry. Pretending that you feel better than you do or trying to do something you're not up to will only make you feel worse and leave your child unhappy and confused, most likely thinking he's done something wrong. Explain that you are still healing inside, even though you look okay on the outside, that the situation is temporary (give time frames in small increments). Allow him to help you, even if it's just to bring you water. Many parents report that recovery periods helped them forge a new aspect to a relationship, especially fathers who previously only did physical things with their sons. This can be a good time to discover quiet-time activities you can do together, like puzzles or cards or having your child read to you.

A *child's hospitalization*

A child's own hospitalization is a different story, of course. Depending on the reason for the hospitalization and the hospital itself, there is likely to be lots of advance preparation, so much, in fact, that you may be amazed, especially if your own hospitalization as a child was a dismal, frightening event.

It was for Annie. The only advance notice she had came the morning her parents took her to the hospital. As they packed her bag they told her, "You're going to a hospital. You'll get a lot of ice cream there." They didn't stay overnight with her. "I remember waking up in a huge, huge bed in a large room," says Annie, now a mother herself. "I didn't know where I was. I was alone, confused and frightened. I got out of bed and walked down this giant hallway. It was scary. I still think about it."

> *It can comfort a child and help her gain control if you hug or hold her during a procedure like drawing blood, but if she needs to be physically restrained, a parent should never be the one to do it.*

It's not that her parents were bad or uncaring people. That was just the way things were done forty years ago. No more. As one of the preadmission nurses at Children's Hospital in Boston puts it, "There's more respect for kids today." Annie is grateful. When her 8-year-old son, David, had his tonsils out, she and her husband, Al, were coached by a nurse at Children's. When David asked if it would hurt, they were told to be truthful. "Yes, it might," they said.

"But one of us will be with you all the time and you'll have medicine to make the hurt go away." On the hospital's advice, they gave him a week's notice. The night before his admission, they made a mini party. Since he couldn't eat in the morning, they had pancakes for dinner and rented a movie.

"We were all nervous," says Annie. "It was hard for any of us to go to sleep, although in front of him we stayed calm. The only time he was tearful was once we were at the hospital, as they started to prep him, and then when we got to the place outside the operating room where I said goodbye. They even allowed my husband to go into the OR with him, but I knew I wouldn't be good at that."

The single most important coping tool you can give your child, no matter what her age, is the knowledge that you will stay with her, whether she's there overnight or not. Indeed, if your child needs to be in the hospital overnight, the first thing you want to know is the hospital's policy on sleeping in. If it doesn't allow parents to stay, find another hospital.

> *Some children are afraid they will never come home again. Assuage that fear by baking a cake together before hospitalization and freezing it. Tell her, "This will be for a family party after you come home. We'll eat it together, to celebrate."*

The next best way to help your child cope is to keep your own anxiety in check. The more anxious you are, the more your child will be. Deal with your anxiety by getting all your questions answered, not just the medical questions but the psychological ones—what do we tell him, what does he need to know—and the procedural ones about the hospital. This includes not only the policy on rooming in, but also such things as sequence of events—when will you be separated from your child presurgery? (after anesthesia induction is preferable)—and how often and in what way pain medication is administered. For all these issues, the person to turn to is the child life specialist, on staff at most hospitals. This is a new field of professionals who deal exclusively with the psychological and social impact of hospitalization on a child. Richard H. Thompson, a child life specialist and author of several child life textbooks, says that all children except newborns need some advance preparation. "That's what decreases anxiety and allows them to prepare themselves," he says. When and what you tell depends on your child. A good rule of thumb is one day's notice for each year of life; thus, you'd give a 7-year-old a week's notice, a 2-year-old, two days. Older children need more warning, but be guided by temperament, not age. A child who tends to be anxious needs less, not more, warning.

Children typically fall into one of two groups when it comes to coping with the stress of pain, according to Lonnie Zeltzer, head of the pediatric pain program at UCLA School of Medicine. Some are information seekers. "The more they know, the better they cope," she says. Even as preschoolers, these children ask a lot of questions and want to know why. For them, age-appropriate answers to their repeated questions is a coping mechanism, a kind of preparation. Other children are information avoiders. The more they know, the more anxious they get. "As you talk to them, they change the subject, avoid eye contact, leave the room," says Zeltzer. With that in mind, here are some suggestions as to what, exactly, you should tell your child about a hospitalization:

- **Infants.** Yes, even an infant deserves some communication. Since information won't mean anything to him, you could say almost anything, as long as you say something. Even though this may seem silly to you, it's a matter of trust. Keep it simple: "We're going to the hospital today."

- **Toddlers.** Again, simple is best: "We're going to the hospital so the doctor can fix your tummy."

- **Preschoolers.** This is the stage when imagination can take over, so add one more thought to what you would say to a toddler: "People go to the hospital to have something fixed in their body, not because they did something wrong. Mom and Dad will stay with you all the time." (Adjust that according to your situation.)

- **School-age.** Older children want and can handle more information. Combine facts with sensory information: "The hospital is in Boston. We'll drive there Tuesday morning. Dr. A. will be taking care of you. The lights are very bright in hospitals and sometimes there's a smell, kind of like a new Band-Aid." The older the child, the more detail you can add.

No matter how young or nervous your child might be, the most important thing to remember is not to lie. If there's a discrepancy between what he expects and what he experiences, that in itself can produce stress. It can also erode his trust in you and make future medical issues more difficult. So what do you do when you get tough questions, especially the heart-melter, "Mom, will it hurt?" Rather than give a definitive yes or no, Zeltzer suggests an answer that offers a range of possible sensations: "It might prick a little, or sting, or feel tingly." If your child presses you, answer with a "yes-but": "A blood test hurts for a very short period of time, like getting a shot. Other times if something hurts, there will be medicine to make it stop."

Even school-age children who have some anatomical knowledge are still full of misconceptions: If you open the body, do things fall out? How do you put them back inside? Answering questions like these takes some finesse. You don't want to avoid giving information, but you need to be careful with your language: Sometimes there's *pressure*, but not *pain;* medicine doesn't *put* you to sleep, it *helps* you sleep. These semantics are important for children 6 to 9 because control is such a big deal for them. The reason they need so much reassurance about anesthesia, for instance, is that they're afraid they will say or do something to embarrass themselves.

Perhaps the most important message to convey to a child of any age is one that says "I know you can cope and we'll be there to help you." Once in the hospital, make a point of praising your child, even if she's only marginally coping. Quips Zeltzer, "She screams all through a blood test? Praise her for how tightly she held your hand." Whatever you do, don't try to reason or threaten or promise a child who's very anxious. What he needs most is for you to be soothing and understanding, not angry and admonishing.

After a hospitalization, children may be more clingy or more fearful than usual, or give up a skill they had gained. This usually lasts a week or two. During this time, it's helpful to be supportive but not indulgent. The sooner you fall back into normal routines and normal limit-setting, the faster your child will readjust. Unlike when Annie was young, it is rare today for a child to be traumatized by a routine hospitalization. Her son certainly wasn't. After his recovery, he said, "It was good for me to go to the hospital because now I can tell my friends how okay it will be if they have to go there."

Aging, infirm, or dying grandparents

Maureen was often overwhelmed with sadness when she went to the nursing home to visit her father, who was suffering from Alzheimer's disease. When she and her husband would take their children, Johnny, 3, and Anna, 7, she felt even sadder. "We never knew what to expect when we got there. One week he was shouting, having a conversation with someone who wasn't there. Anna couldn't figure it out," she says. "My mother would say the children shouldn't go anymore, that they were being harmed by seeing their grandfather in such tough shape. But I thought it was a good thing for them to see us doing this as a family, to know we still cared for Pa."

Maureen's instincts were right. It is decidedly a good thing for children to be involved in the care of an aging grandparent with a chronic infirmity. This is not easy for anyone, but it is something more and more of us need to think about: An estimated 70 percent of aging parents in the United States receive some kind of care from their adult children who are also parents. As Maureen instinctively realized, it's important for children to see that we continue to love and care for our parents even when they are sick, even when they change physically and mentally, even when they can't love us back. These are the kind of messages that help a child to grow and mature and to understand the cycle of life. That's not to say there was anything wrong with Maureen's mother's instinct either; her desire to protect her grandchildren was equally intuitive. But Maureen learned that withholding information about Grandpa or access to him is not the way to do it.

Children will feel left out of the family. Like they don't count. Lacking a complete picture or accurate information, they'll make up their own story to fill in the gaps. A preschooler may think that what Grandma has is contagious; you're keeping her home from the visit so she won't catch it. Next time, when you want her to go with you, she may refuse, causing you to think she's uncaring and her to wonder why you aren't taking good care of her anymore. Psychologists who specialize in intergenerational family therapy say that magical thinking can lead a child of any age to think it's her fault a grandparent is sick. A child who is continually excluded from discussions also is at risk for long-lasting and potentially damaging effects: She may be learning that feelings, good or bad, are not to be talked about, and develop an automatic response to push feelings away. She could also be at risk to grow up unable to trust her own judgment about feelings.

In fact, there is a lot of information we can give children, as long as we do it in language they can understand. Look at all there is to tell a toddler or preschooler:

- It's no one's fault that Grandma is sick;

- Grandma can't help the way she is or what she says or does;

- She still loves us even though she can't tell us;

- Doctors are trying to make her better;

- Scientists are trying to find a cure for this disease;

- Grandma's sickness has a name. Tell even the youngest child what the disease is called; it's relieving for them to have a name to put to it.

With Alzheimer's and with some cases of advanced age, a grandparent's behavior can be confusing or scary to a child of any age. Point out behaviors she might see—"Grandpa mumbles a lot these days"—and look for questions she's asking nonverbally. A child who hangs back or doesn't offer a hug or kiss is not being mean. She doesn't know how to behave, and she's likely wondering, "Does Grandpa want to be kissed or not? If he doesn't recognize me, why should I say hello?" When the opportunity seems right, do some thinking out loud: "Sometimes I'm so confused when I see Grandpa. He seems so distracted, I don't know if I should kiss him or not, and sometimes he even makes me feel a little frightened. But then if I squeeze his hand or pat his back he seems to know I'm there. I think he likes knowing we're there even if he doesn't talk to us." Your child may not respond, but you will have helped him nonetheless.

There's another equally critical piece of information to convey, that what is happening to Grandma is not necessarily what happens to all old people. Renana Brooks, a psychologist who specializes in intergenerational therapy, tells parents to be sure that the infirm grandparent is not a child's only exposure to aging. "They need to see positive images of aging as well and they need reminders that not all people who get old lose their memory or need walkers or can't feed themselves," she says.

One element in all of this that parents often fail to come to grips with is that our children not only have to cope with a changed grandparent, they also have to cope with the change in you. The more frantic, angry, frustrated, sad, or depressed we are, the harder it is on our kids. Because they take their cues from us, if we don't know how to cope, neither do they. This puts added pressure on us, but intergenerational researchers like Brooks say it is not as difficult as it might seem. "It's better to show your sadness or your stress than to pretend everything is normal, as long as you don't overwhelm them," she says. It's okay to say something like "I remember when I used to be able to talk to Grandma about everything. It makes me sad that she doesn't understand what I'm saying now." What you can't share is the depth of that sadness. The overall message you want to give is that as sad as this is and as tough as it is, you can cope. Not a bad message to talk yourself into either.

Some children may express anger or resentment. Our automatic response to an outburst of "I hate Grandpa!" is "You don't really mean that." But at the moment, she *does* mean it. Rather than be dismissive of her feelings or reprimand her for having feelings she's perfectly entitled to have, respond with a question: "What is it about Grandpa that's making you so angry?" Most children will name something obvious: "I hate the way he looks/talks/smells, that he can't remember who I am, that he can't walk/play/read," etc. Offer an empathetic response: "It is hard to see Grandpa like this. For me too." Then go on to offer more information. Their anger is often fueled by a lack of understanding about the illness, a feeling of helplessness and/or an inability to know how to express their feelings. If the grandparent is living in your home, often it is not the person they are hating, but the situation: Having to give up her bedroom, maneuvering among weird-looking equipment, accommodating nurses' coming and going, adjusting to a higher level of activity than normal. She may be angry at you because you aren't as available for her. On the other hand, sometimes it *is* the person: Grandpa may have walked in on her when she was in the bathroom or embarrassed her in front of her friends.

Keeping your children's lives as normal as possible with as much of their regular routines uninterrupted will make them feel more secure in the midst of events that are so unsettling. This may not be easy. Don't push your child when you see signs that she's at her limit—staying in her room, not wanting to visit, waking up with nightmares—but help her to deal with the guilt she might feel as a result of backing off: "Can you draw a picture/write a poem, etc., for Grandpa so he'll know you're thinking of him?" Don't pressure a child to visit or make him feel guilty if he doesn't want to see him: "I can tell seeing Grandpa today would make you sad. Why don't we plan your visit a different day?"

If a grandparent is dying, what also helps enormously is enabling children to express their thoughts and emotions without feeling guilty. That helps relieve their sadness and the burden of their thoughts. "Children explicitly need your permission to have these feelings," says Brooks. Just as adults often need to grieve over the emotional loss before the death, children sometimes need to do that too. Brooks says children do this best through a ritual: Talk about Grandma, look at old pictures, cook her favorite recipe. In other words, preserve the positives of the person. This gets at the heart of what most parents worry about most. Maureen, for instance, says a source of great sadness for her has been that her daughter, who is old enough to remember Pa before he got sick, will only remember him as he was in his last year with Alzheimer's. "I wonder if that memory will have more power than all that came before it," she says. Maybe not. If we model a way to deal with our emotions and offer reminders of what the person once was, we will have given a child the tools she needs to piece together appropriate memories. Brooks is particularly insightful on this point. "Your job as a parent is not to make the world perfect to them or to defend it as always right," she says. "Your job is to provide some model and some process so your kids can deal with the imperfections life offers."

Remember, too, that children show their distress in ways we don't always recognize. A child who becomes withdrawn and doesn't want to play with friends, or who doesn't want to go to school or play sports, may feel guilty for being happy when he knows Grandpa is very sick or dying. If he seems angry with you, it may be that he thinks you don't really love Grandpa because you have moments when you laugh and are happy. This is when explanations are important, even if the questions aren't asked explicitly. Tell him, "There can still be moments of laughter and fun even though a person is dying. Even though he can't show it, Grandpa still enjoys our company and it makes him feel good inside to see us happy. He wants us to go about our regular lives. He knows that doesn't mean we love him any less."

> *Encourage your child to interact with the grandparent in whatever limited way is possible, bringing a glass of water, drawing a picture, singing a song.*

Instead of withdrawing, some children may giggle, tease, or poke fun at the grandparent whose illness-induced inappropriate behavior embarrasses him. Don't reprimand or punish him for it unless it was disrespectful or humiliating to the grandparent. At a later time, try to explain: "Grandpa's mind sometimes takes him back in time. He might have been remembering what it was like when he was 6 years old, and for a few minutes, he actually thought he was 6 years old again." Even though it can try your patience, repeat explanations often, especially to a child under 7, without an angry I-told-you-this-before edge to your voice: "Grandma can't help it, the sickness makes her not remember anymore." Young children get confused easily, they forget, and they can't extrapolate from one situation to another.

If you haven't so far been open with your child, it's never too late to start. Tell her, "Mom and I realized that we have been keeping all the information about Grandma to ourselves. We were doing that because we didn't want to worry you, but now we realize that not giving you information probably worried you more and wasn't really fair to you. You must be wondering what's going on and we want to tell you." Then plunge right in, in a way she can understand, with appropriate details. By 7, most children are wondering about death in some way, even if they aren't asking questions about it. With a sick and/or dying grandparent, the issue is even more likely to be on their minds. Don't bring the topic up out of the blue, but look for openings. A conversation in which you are providing information in general might be a good place: "The doctor says Grandma won't die for a long time and that she isn't in pain. He's always looking for new medicines for her." Or "The doctor says Grandma will die soon, maybe before the summer, but we don't know exactly when. When it gets closer, we'll talk about it more."

A sibling's chronic illness

"Sometimes I wish she weren't my sister," is how 12-year-old Tim began a conversation about his sister, Ria, who is 9. It's a typical enough comment, one that could be spoken by almost any sibling in America. But Tim's comment has particular poignancy because Ria has a severe case of juvenile rheumatoid arthritis.

When a child has a chronic illness, whether it's JRA or asthma or leukemia, the most immediate impact, of course, is on that child and the parents. But illness or disability also affects siblings. They can come to feel neglected and uncared-for, leaving them ripe for jealous, guilty, angry, or hostile feelings they don't understand and certainly don't know what to do with.

It's not a given that siblings will have adjustment problems, but it is a given that they have parents who are sometimes unavailable to them and that their stress level is sometimes very high. While parents may be unable to change those facts, we can be open and honest with our children; the more siblings feel they are part of the family, included in the process, the better they will cope. Massachusetts General Hospital pediatrician James Perrin, who researches how families adapt to having a child with a chronic illness, says that withholding information from siblings on the grounds that they are too young to understand only backfires. Feeling left out, they act out. For instance, siblings tend to act out when there is medical equipment in the home or when a medical professional comes to the house regularly, but once you explain in simple language what the machines or people do, a child is much more likely to take the paraphernalia in stride.

> *It's okay to cry in front of your children as long as you don't do it often. In fact, it can even be a model for them of how to handle their feelings: "I feel so sad this is happening to your sister. Sometimes it makes me cry."*

From the onset of an illness, children of all ages need concrete information at a level they can understand, including the real name of the disease. To Ria's younger sister Sri, who is 3½, their parents say often, "Your sister has a disease called juvenile rheumatoid arthritis. Her fingers and her knees don't always work. They hurt sometimes and she needs extra help to move. The medicines make them not hurt so much." As a child gets older, depending on her level of curiosity, more details can be shared as long as it is always at a level she can understand. To a 7-year-old: "Juvenile rheumatoid arthritis is a disease that causes joints not to work well. It's hard to predict when they will be painful or why it happens, but all these medicines are helping her."

As we've discussed elsewhere in the book, children need to know they did not cause this to happen. Because it is so typical and normal for a child to be angry with a sibling and to wish her ill, magical thinking causes him to blame himself for whatever is wrong. The thought is so common that parents should assume it's going through a child's mind. Tell your child specifically, explicitly, and repeatedly: "This is not your fault. You didn't make this happen." Even a child as old as 10 or 11 may harbor such thoughts. With an older child, though, your approach needs to be less direct: "I read somewhere that even kids your age might think that they're to blame for a sister's or brother's illness. In case you were wondering, you absolutely didn't cause your brother to get sick." A 10-year-old will rarely admit to you that this was worrying him. More likely, he'll tell you, "Gee, Dad, I'm not that stupid!" But it's information he's probably secretly glad to have.

There's another misconception children as young as 2 and as old as 13 need help with. They tend to equate love with the amount of time a parent spends with a child. Thus, another typical thought might go like this: "You spend so much time with Amy, you must love her more." Address this head-on, too, whether your child verbalizes the thought or not: "I spend a lot of time with Amy because her diabetes requires a lot of attention. That may make it seem like I love her more, but I don't. I love you each differently, because you are different people, but I love you each the same amount." It's also not uncommon for school-age children to be angry at the sick sibling for consuming so much of your time and even to wish, as Tim sometimes does, that she didn't exist. These thoughts can lead to feelings of intense jealousy, which can lead to guilt and then affect a child's sense of self-esteem: At some level, he knows the thoughts are uncharitable, mean, and wrong, but he can't help himself from having them and then thinks he's an awful person because he does.

As parents, we need to convey over and over again that these emotions are normal, okay to have, and okay to talk about. Label and identify them for your child. To a 3-year-old with a hospitalized sibling, you might say: "I know you must worry about your sister because she is so sick and I bet you also must wish I were home more often. It's okay to have that feeling, and it's okay to tell me about it." It's also appropriate to express your frustration at not having more time to spend with him: "Once the new medicine starts to work for your sister, I'll have more time for you. What can we plan to do together?"

Not surprisingly, the onset of an illness can be the most difficult time in a family as you struggle to adjust to a diagnosis and treatment plan. For siblings, the inaccessibility or preoccupation of a parent translates as a loss and so does the disruption of regular routines. The more information you can give them about why things are different, the easier it will be for them and the more you can expect them to be helpful and willing to make a contribution. To a preschooler, for instance: "We can't go to playgroup anymore because your sister needs to go to therapy and this is the only time the therapist can see her. I'll find some other group for us to do together, but in the meantime, can you help me take her to therapy? Can you be in charge of doors at the doctor's building while I push the wheelchair?" With older children whose schedules are disrupted, there are frequently substitutions that can work, friends who are willing to provide transportation when you can't carpool to ballet, aunts or uncles or family friends who will attend soccer games.

During a crisis, flexibility helps. Sometimes that means relaxing the limits for your healthy child—letting him stay up late so you can have some time together—but it shouldn't mean excusing inappropriate behavior. This may be trickier than it sounds; in the midst of a crises, you may be loath to come down on your healthy child, reasoning that life is so hard and complicated for him right now. But what you perceive as a kindness by giving your kid some breaks may come across to him as a lack of caring, especially when you don't set a limit around something that you always did: "Mom doesn't care enough about me anymore to be upset about what I did." This can cause a school-age child to push the limits even farther, just as a 2-year-old pushes the boundaries to see when you will impose a limit. Intervene when you catch your child acting inappropriately and don't be surprised if some of it is directed toward the sick sibling. Be clear and unequivocal: "Shutting the door in someone's face is plain rude behavior." Impose the same kind of limit you would under more normal circumstances and then, in a calmer moment, talk about the feelings you suspect are behind the behavior: "I think you did that because you think your brother gets more attention than you do." If crises crop up frequently because of the nature of your sick child's illness, create contingency plans that get talked about in advance so that your healthy children don't feel as though what happens to them is is an afterthought.

> *The child who cares for the sick sibling, who shows no jealousy or resentment and is always helpful, could be bottling up feelings. Give her openings to talk about them.*

In addition to meanness, there are two other troubling behaviors that typically crop up when there's a sick child in the family. Healthy siblings may:

- **Be embarrassed by the sister or brother who is ill.** The very first time this happens, you need to respond quickly and to the point: "Things have changed in our family and I admit it takes getting used to, but this is still our family and we stand together." Make a point to continue to invite your healthy children's friends to the house, as well as the friends of your sick child, if appropriate. Be matter-of-fact when they're there:

"All this equipment is for Tom's sister. She has trouble breathing and the machine makes it easier for her."

- **Insist the sick child is faking it.** This is very common among siblings and can really push a parent's button: "How dare you say such a thing!" Before you jump on him, however, examine the situation. You aren't with the kids every minute. Perhaps there are times when your sick child tries to use the illness or handicap in a manipulative way; that's as normal and healthy as it is for the healthy child to imagine that she's faking. If you see that there is some faking going on, tell your healthy child, "I can see you're right, but that doesn't give you the right to shut the door on her." If it's not true, your child may need more cognitive information: "I know it looks like her fingers should work. Some days they do, some days they don't. We can't tell by looking which days they are hurting."

Tim, who often complains his sister is faking it, says he knows deep down inside that she isn't. "Sometimes when I get angry it's because I wish she could do the normal things kids can do. I'm sad she can't have regular fun." Nonetheless, he says, "Sometimes, I just can't help having my bad feelings." He's absolutely right.

How children cope with death and grief

When a family member dies, parents face an especially daunting task. They must deal with their children's sadness at the same time they are grieving themselves. What's more, children show us their grief in such unexpected ways that we may be startled:

- A preschooler, told of the death of a beloved grandparent, brushes aside the information and says she wants to play.

- A 6-year-old whose father has died in a biking accident tells his mother, "Daddy wasn't very smart, was he?"

- An 8-year-old comes back from her mother's funeral and asks, "Now that Mom's dead, will I still be able to take ballet?"

- An 11-year-old is overheard telling a friend "it's no big deal" that his sister has died.

Fortunately, these responses are not as hardhearted as they sound. Children's grief doesn't look like ours. But just because a child doesn't look like she's sad doesn't mean she isn't. Just because her grief comes in spurts, sad one minute, happy the next, doesn't mean the grief is disingenuous. It isn't. This is just the way children are. Their reactions are firmly rooted in developmental stages:

- **Preschoolers.** The 3- to 5-year-old thinks death is reversible. Coming down on her, losing patience, punishing her, or trying to convince her otherwise will only frustrate you both. Instead, state the facts simply, honestly, and often: "Grandpa has died. That means he isn't coming back. When someone dies, it's forever."

- **Six- and 7-year-olds.** By 6, the typical child understands that death is irreversible, but because he feels so competent and confident of his own abilities, he thinks you can outrun death or outsmart it. He frames death in that context: "Daddy wasn't riding fast enough. That wasn't very smart. That's why he died." A child this age needs a supportive response that tells her we all die eventually, even very smart people, and that sometimes we die for reasons we just can't explain.

- **Eight- to 11-year-olds.** The selfish-sounding 8-year-old is, indeed, egocentric, but she can't help herself, so don't come down hard on her. Instead, meet her developmental need to know how things will change in her life: "I know Mom's income paid for your ballet and I know how much you love it, so when I figure out our finances, I'm going to try to find a way so you can still go. For now, you can still go and as soon as I figure things out, I'll let you know about next year."

- **Eleven- to 13-year-olds.** Perhaps most maddening is the flippancy of a preteen. His response is shaped by two issues. One is a need not to be different from peers; because none of his friends have siblings who have died, he's reluctant to show his feelings. A second issue for the 11- to 13-year-old is that he has only recently learned to control and modulate his emotions. Giving in to his sadness makes him feel unsafe; the flip response is a defense mechanism. With this age child, a parent needs to share his or her own feelings in a nonjudgmental way: "I'm feeling sad and your response doesn't help me. If you need to joke, don't do it around me."

Just because you don't see your older child cry doesn't mean she isn't crying in private. In fact, if your child isn't crying in front of you, ask yourself this: Are you crying in front of her? Many parents make a point not to cry in front of their children, a strategy researchers say is a mistake. In studies where grieving children were asked why they didn't cry in front of parents, they typically gave two answers. The first is that they don't want to add to our grief. They think that by showing us how sad they feel, it will make us sadder. The second is that many parents walk around with a stiff upper lip in the mistaken belief that that protects their children. The opposite is true. Because we are role models for our children, if we hide our sadness, they think that's the way they are supposed to behave too. Not only that, but we may inadvertently cause them to be angry or upset with us. When they don't see our grief, they may think we are unfeeling or that we didn't really love the person who died. It's important to be honest, then, not only in the information we give but also in expressing how we feel.

Answer questions truthfully even when the topic isn't one you are eager to discuss. It's not enough to say, "Daddy died at the tennis court." Kids need details just like adults do, always, of course, at an age appropriate level. Something like this might be okay for a school-age child: "Daddy was playing tennis and he got a pain in his arm. So he sat down on the court. The pain got worse and he fainted and his partner called the EMTs. . . ." For a preschooler, you eliminate the middle two thoughts.

Death itself should also be explained truthfully. Children take euphemisms literally. Counseling psychologist Maria Trozzi, director of the Good Grief Program of Boston University Medical Center, works with families and consults to schools on death and dying. She tells the story of a 5-year-old whose infant sister died at Christmas. His parents told him, "The angels took her." Five weeks later, they brought him to see Trozzi because he hadn't slept for more than an hour or two a night since then.

"Do you want to talk about your sister?" she asked him.

"No," he said. "I want to talk about the angels. Two things about them. There are lots of them and they are on the loose at Christmas. The second thing is they don't have headlights. You can't see them coming so you have to stay awake."

Because of religious faith, his parents genuinely believed their baby was in heaven with the angels. That would have been a fine thing to tell their son had they added just one more sentence to accommodate his concrete stage of thinking: "The baby's body is in her grave in the ground, but we believe her spirit is in heaven with the angels." Other times, parents use euphemisms as a way to protect a child, somehow thinking that it is kinder and gentler to stay away from the words *death* and *dead.* But that can backfire, too, even with an older child. Trozzi has known children whose parents made heaven sound so attractive that they tried to kill themselves so they, too, could go there. Answer honestly such questions as "Now that he's in the ground, will the worms get him?" (Answer: "No, he's inside that box we call a casket, remember? It keeps insects from going inside.") Putting him down for asking such a question or avoiding answering it is what will lead to fantasies that can become unmanageable for him—for instance, visualizing worms and insects eating his grandfather's face.

> *Take some of the mystery out of death by visiting a cemetery with your child who is 7 or older. Explain how a body is put in a casket and what the headstone is for.*

Also under the guise of protection, parents tend to keep children away from funerals and burials. Children need closure as much as adults, according to Rabbi Earl Grollman of Belmont, Massachusetts, an international lecturer and pioneer in the field of bereavement. "The burial is the best audiovisual aid in the world," he says. "A child knows definitively where a person's body is." Professionals generally agree that children 3 and older can go to a funeral and to the cemetery, with three caveats: Your child knows in advance what to expect; there is someone he loves other than you who will be with him at all times (the assumption is that you are too grief-stricken to give him the attention he needs); he isn't being forced to go. A child under 9 who does not want to go should not be forced or shamed into it. A child older than that shouldn't be forced either, but strongly encouraged, especially when it's a close relative. "Otherwise," says Grollman, "later on he'll feel that he didn't say good-bye."

In the weeks and months after a death, Grollman urges parents to be alert for angry and guilty feelings. He says, "Children as young as 4 can be angry at the person who died: 'Didn't he love me enough to stay alive?' Or they think they caused the death: 'I was bad, that's why he died.' Older children wonder, 'Why didn't the doctors save him?' 'Why did God let this happen?' " Rarely will a child frame his anger in questions, however. More likely, it will come out in inappropriate or regressive behavior or in physical symptoms. Tell your child, "All of us have angry thoughts sometimes. That doesn't make us bad, or mean we didn't love Grandpa." Or: "You did not cause your sister to die. Everybody fights with their sisters. That's just part of being human."

How we cope affects how our children do. While this can be difficult when any relative you loved deeply dies, it tends to be most problematical when the death is of another child. That's when remaining children are most likely to be left to fend for themselves emotionally. There's an all too human tendency for parents to think that a toddler or preschooler is too young to take in much, that the siblings weren't all that close anyway, or that a school-age child will be fine because he has his friends and routines. Unfortunately, what we see is not what we get. Just because a child is functioning and appears to be okay doesn't mean she is.

When a sibling has died, a child of any age is likely to think it's her fault, thanks to magical thinking. Hours before his brother was hit by a car, 4-year-old Ethan had argued with Adam over whose turn it was to ride the scooter. In a fit of anger, he shouted, "I hate you. I hope you die!" Lo and behold, his wish came true! He's convinced he is responsible. Even a school-age child's thinking can be somewhat magical: "I should have been able to stop the car."

Because a young child also has a very worrisome, if not egocentric, fear—"This could happen to me! To Mom, to Dad!"—she needs explicit and repeated reassurance. Tell her:

- What happened to your sister was not your fault;

- It won't happen to you or to anyone else in the family;

- We are doing all we can to keep you safe.

When a sibling dies, a child of any age may also feel guilty— "Why was I spared?"—and the guilt can translate to any number of emotions. In a family where an infant died of Sudden Infant Death

Syndrome, a preschooler turned incredibly clingy, making every separation into an ordeal. There was no way to get into the mind of such a young child, but eventually, with the help of a professional, the parents were able to piece together that, like most 3- or 4-year-olds, this preschooler had wished the baby would disappear. When she did, the 3-year-old was frightened by the power she perceived she had. She worried: "What did I do? What's going to happen to me? What if my parents know what I did?" Concluding her parents would be angry with her, she decided on the one thing that would make them happy: "I'll never leave them." Thus, the difficulty at separation. Once they were able to tell her it was her job to go to preschool and their job to go to work and it was okay for them to be apart for some time every day, the difficulties slowly diminished.

Similar guilt feelings can be aroused in a child who has witnessed at first- or secondhand a sibling's abuse, according to child psychiatrist Stuart T. Hauser, president of Judge Baker's Children Center. Imagine an older sister who hears her sibling's cries for help in the middle of the night, night after night, but instead of going to her rescue or telling an adult, she hides under the covers, grateful it's her sister and not her whom their stepfather visits. It doesn't take long for that relief to turn to guilt. Without the opportunity to talk about it, it becomes a burden, buried deeper and deeper, probably eventually affecting how she thinks of herself: "I'm a bad person. I could have helped my sister and I didn't."

> *The more clingy a preschooler is, the more likely it is that she is clueless about what has happened to her sibling and worried it will happen to her, too.*

How a child reacts to the abuse or death of a sibling will be influenced by the relationship the two had. In a family with many children, obviously not everyone will suffer the same. The child who was closest in age and therefore played together the most; the one who baby-sat the victim and served as protector and mentor; the one who looked up to the victim as a role model—these siblings are most vulnerable. Often the child who lost a sibling who served as a mentor or protégé will be quick to get into a new intimate relationship with a peer (girl- or boyfriend or best friend) or an adult (coach, baby-sitter, teacher). He's looking to replace some of the closeness he lost.

Research shows the children who feel the most underattended-to after a sibling's death are those whose parents may find relief by throwing themselves into a court case or a cause célèbre. Louise was the 10-year-old sister of a high school senior who died in a car crash just before graduation. Their mother threw herself into Mothers Against Drunk Driving (MADD). Years later, Louise describes her sister's death as the end of her childhood. "I was forced to grow up. I became a latchkey kid because my mom was never home after school anymore. She was always off talking to this group or something. I didn't just lose my big sister, I lost my mother, too." In another family, a child in similar circumstances remembers thinking his worst fears were confirmed. "I always thought my mother loved Julie [the sister who died] best. After Julie died, Mom was hardly ever around. I figured if she loved us, too, she would have stayed home to be there for us."

Another danger is the tendency by parents either to idealize a dead or victimized child or to overprotect a survivor. When the dead child is talked about only in superlatives—how wonderful, how talented, how this, how that—it devalues even a preschooler. How can any child feel he or she compares? On the other hand, the parent who idealizes the surviving child tends to hover and smother, not leaving her with baby-sitters, not allowing her to go to sleep-overs, sometimes too fearful to let her out of her sight. In its extreme, this interferes with social development because it doesn't allow for age-appropriate risk-taking. Keep an eye on your parenting in the wake of a child's death or ask someone else to keep tabs on it for you. The

question to ask yourself is this: Is your parenting dramatically different from what it was before? Research shows that parents make
more of an effort to help a child who had a good relationship with
the victim or to help the child who is obviously falling apart. The
one who appears to be doing fine, or who wasn't close to the sibling
in age or relationship, is apt to be left to her own devices. Unfortunately, research shows that the silent sufferer is the one most at risk.

No matter what a child's age at the time of a tragedy, parents
need to be prepared for new questions at each new developmental
stage and to initiate conversations about the death and the dead
sibling every once in a while, just to make the subject talkable. A
child may seem uninterested, even ignore you when you do that, but
don't stop talking. He is taking it in even if it doesn't look like he is.

If a parent dies

Josh was 6½ when his father, Don, died of a heart attack at the age
of 44. He didn't cry much at the funeral or even in the days and
months that followed. "I didn't exactly know what was going on
when my father died," explains Josh, who was 11 at the time of this
interview. "Actually," he adds, his brown eyes black with intensity,
"I cried more when I was 9 and 8. That was when I got the picture
that he was *dead*. That he wouldn't come back. That I wouldn't have
a dad anymore."

Most children go through a parent's funeral, even the first
weeks after the death, in a state of uncertainty and confusion, rarely
understanding fully what has happened no matter how age appropriate and accurate the information is that we give them. But when the
crush of family and friends recedes and the covered-dish dinners
stop coming, Mom or Dad's absence becomes much more tangible.

Now what?

As the weeks turn into months, the task for the surviving parent
is daunting. Even now, you are setting a tone for communication
and a model for coping that will last a lifetime. If you become de-

pressed, research shows there is a far greater chance your child will too. If you are stoic, it's likely you'll have children who never really express or understand their grief. Obviously, the middle ground is the way to go.

> *Research shows that children who do best after a death are those who are able to forge a new relationship with the person who died. Facilitate this by talking naturally about the person, having photos around, and by asking questions: "What do you think Daddy would say about that?"*

Almost all parents instinctively want to protect a child against any more pain. Fathers more than mothers have a tendency to want to get on with it, to solve logistical problems and move on. Believe it or not, this is not helpful. Preschoolers don't know what to do with their fears, especially the fear that they are to blame for the death. Without the chance to talk about it, they'll make up stories that they come to believe. Older children who don't get the chance to work through their grief can carry fears and misconceptions into adulthood and not want to have children because they don't want their kids to go through what they went through. Josh says that his dad got a stomachache just before he died, so for a long time after he died, Josh thought that he was dying whenever he got a stomachache. His mother, Nancy, says Josh and his sister were both terrified of going to sleep for weeks after their father's death. "I don't think it was so much that they thought they would die in their sleep," she says. "I think it was more because Donald died at bedtime and they associated his death with going to bed." Josh also says, "I worried a lot about my mom in the beginning. A real lot. Every second. When I was playing sports, I might be concentrating on the game, but I was still thinking about her. That she might die or get sick." That his mother was pregnant with Danielle heightened his concern about her. He knew someone else whose mother got very sick during a pregnancy. Now that he only had one parent, the thought that she might get sick and die was terrible to consider.

Glimpses of the permanence of a parent's death typically come to children in isolated moments. Nancy remembers one morning a few weeks after Donald died when Josh dropped a carton of orange juice. As she cleaned it up, he stood watching her and then, without any preamble, just said, "Daddy will never know what this baby is, will he?" Stephanie, Josh's younger sister, was 4 when Donald died, and she became Nancy's shadow. "She wouldn't take a bath in the bathroom he had died in. I had to get in the tub with her. I remember thinking to myself, 'If I have to do this all the time, I'll never make it.' She wouldn't separate from me, wouldn't change her clothes."

> *Always tell teachers the date of the anniversary of a parent's death, even years later. Children may be unable to concentrate around that time, no matter what their age.*

Children tend to feel more alone than adults do because they usually don't know anyone else whose parent has died. Josh, for instance, felt isolated from his peers until third grade, when a new boy in school had an absentee father. Josh remembers thinking, "I thought we could talk to each other. I thought I could be better friends with him than with anybody else because we could share not having a dad around." Indeed, the two boys became friends. "When my dad died," says Josh, "I kept feelings inside. It made me feel worse and worse. I would tell kids who go through this to be open with the parent they have. Talking helps a lot even though you think it doesn't. Talk to the person you feel most comfortable with. It doesn't have to be your parent."

Josh is right. Talking is what helps children grieve, but often they aren't able to talk to their remaining parent. They worry that if they talk to you, it will make you sadder, and that's scary for them. When a parent's death is sudden or traumatic, it can take a child up to two years to show grief, according to bereavement specialist Trozzi. "They need to feel the environment is safe," she says, which mostly means they need to see that you aren't going to fall apart. How you grieve becomes the model for your children. Crying in front of them is okay as long as they can see that you will not abandon them emotionally, that you can feel the pain, express it, and then pull yourself together and go on: "I'm feeling sad right now. Something just reminded me of Mom. I'll be okay in a few minutes."

Children typically need us to put the topic on the table: "I was thinking about Mom today and missing her. How about you?" Don't push your child if he doesn't respond, but don't stop providing the opportunities. With preschoolers who may not be able to verbalize, drawing can help. "Stephanie drew pictures like crazy," says Nancy. Even with our efforts, some children can't talk to us as freely as they need to, and professionals frequently recommend children's bereavement support groups.

> *Increased sibling fighting is common after a parent's death. It's a way for them to release tension.*

Children revisit a parent's death at each new stage of development, sometimes almost as if it's happening for the first time. This can be frightening to surviving parents, who may worry that something is wrong, or take it personally and blame themselves. In fact, it may have nothing to do with you. It's just part of the way children grieve. If a child's mother died when she was 3, at 6 she may want to know "What were the things Mom did for me? How did she take care of me?" At 8, she wonders, "What was she like? Am I like her?" and at 15, "Would I have liked her?"

No matter that these questions catch you off-guard or that you've answered them a dozen times in a dozen ways. Go through it again, and again, and again. As many times as your child brings it up, that's how many times you need to respond with patience and understanding. At each stage of development, she's hearing the answers differently because she is taking in the information in a new way. As she reworks and rethinks the death, she may be experiencing guilt and anger. For instance, a child may:

- **Hate the parent who died.** A preschooler as well as some young school-age children might feel, "I hate Mommy because she left," or "Didn't he love me enough to stay alive?" and then feel guilty for having such a thought. Because the anger is scary and the guilt freezes them up, they literally can't talk about it. A parent needs to provide gentle probes: "Some kids feel angry that a mom died and left them. I wonder if you ever do?" Whether she says yes or no or nothing at all, your response should be nonjudgmental, supportive, and simple: "It's okay to feel that way, if you ever do. All of us have angry thoughts sometimes after a person dies. I do. It doesn't make us bad people or mean we didn't love Mom."

- **Hate the parent who is alive.** A preschooler may actually say, "I hate you because you let Mommy die," but an older child is more likely to express this feeling by picking a fight with you and shouting, "Mommy would never be so mean to me!" What's happening is that your child is holding you responsible for not keeping his other parent alive. He's also blaming you for letting him, the child, hurt so much. On the one hand, these are healthy responses; it's good he's able to get out some feelings. On the other hand, they are scary feelings for him and for you. With a direct attack, "Why did you let Mommy die?" a direct response is needed: "It might seem like that happened. The doctors tried their hardest to make Mommy better." But what's also needed is for the two of you to miss Mommy together. Avoid a defensive or angry response: "Stop comparing me to Mom all the time. I'm here, she's not," or "You're not really angry with me, you're angry that Mom left." Instead, try this: "You're angry with me and maybe that's because there's something I'm doing that you don't like. That's okay. We can figure this out. I'm also wondering if you're missing Mom. We haven't talked about her in a while. . . ." Also reassure your child: "I'm not going away. I will be here for you."

- **Hate themselves.** Because young children typically blame themselves when a parent dies—"I was bad, that's why he died"—they can come to feel bad about themselves. One way this can play itself out is for the child to make life incredibly difficult for the surviving parent. He's testing you to see just how bad he really is. Because a parent may have less patience than usual, there's a tendency to be unable to tolerate the acting out and to respond angrily, to tell him he's bad or punish him. That reinforces his fears: "I *am* a terrible person." Better to try to take this acting out in stride and cope with it as you would any other inappropriate behavior. Then his reasoning is more likely to be "Maybe I'm not so bad after all." A child needs you to say explicitly, "Kids sometimes think they caused their parent to die. I wonder if you're thinking something you did caused Mommy to die. You didn't make her die, you know. . . ." You might even say, "Everybody has fights. Daddy and I had a fight before he died but that doesn't mean that's why he died." Don't be discouraged if he never responds to this line of reasoning. It's reassuring to him nonetheless.

A school-age child may also feel guilty, be angry with himself, or be worried he's a bad person because he can't remember the parent. Josh went through that: "I would worry because I would think I was forgetting my dad. 'Oh no, how did he talk? Was he nice or mean?' Not remembering made me feel bad, real bad," says Josh, who adds that this particular worry intensified when his mother remarried. Liking his new dad made Josh feel disloyal. Whenever he felt bad or thought he was forgetting his dad, he would get out pictures of his father. "Pictures help a lot," Josh says. "It makes you feel better to remember the good times. You'll never forget the person. I want to tell other kids that."

About one-third of children aged 6 to 12 become depressed after a parent's death, generally within the first eight weeks. Seek professional help if you're worried that's happening.

Trozzi and Silverman encourage parents to help children commemorate a parent in all different kinds of ways. It's empowering for them to put pictures up around their room, write stories, or watch videos. Talking about the parent provides healing. While this can happen informally—"That reminds me of the time Dad . . ."—it also occasionally needs to be more pointed. Trozzi suggests saying to your child, "I need to talk about Mom. How about if we have some Mommy time together?" The conversation can be about things you did and enjoyed together but also should be interspersed with comments such as "Mommy laughed just the way you do." Have these sessions only if you can maintain reasonable control of yourself. If you're melodramatic or uncontrollably weepy, it will be enough to make any child decide she doesn't want to do this again.

Remembering enables children to hold an inner representation of the parent, and that bodes well for healing. Some children talk to the dead parent or write letters to her or describe feeling as though the parent is watching them, much the way we sometimes imagine or talk to our conscience. As long as this provides comfort and doesn't interfere with his ability to function—he doesn't have to go "talk" to Mom before he decides what to eat for dinner—there's nothing wrong with it.

When asked what advice he would like to give to other children whose parent dies, Josh offers this wisdom: "Some kids think you will be upset forever. I want to tell kids, you will feel better. You won't stay in pain forever, but you'll still miss the parent."

Source Acknowledgments and Notes
• • • • • • • • • • • • • • • • • •

Chapter 1: Negotiating Independence

Imaginary friends
Interviews with psychologist Robert Brooks; researcher Peggy Stubbs; psychologist Malcolm Watson.

Dressing for success
Marilise Flusser, *Party Shoes to School and Baseball Caps to Bed: The Parents' Guide to Kids, Clothes and Independence* (Simon & Schuster).

Marshall Duke and Stephen Nowicki, *Helping the Child Who Doesn't Fit In* (Peachtree Publishers).

Arnold Gesell, Frances L. Ilg, and Louise Bates Ames (editor). *Infant and Child in the Culture of Today* (HarperCollins). Interviews with Flusser, Duke, and Ames; and also with early childhood educator Carol Seefeldt.

The sleep-over
Interviews with clinical psychologist Robert Pianta; clinical psychologist Carl Mumpower; psychologist Janette B. Benson; human developmentalist Barbara O'Donnel.

The minefields of friendship
Stanley Greenspan, *Playground Politics* and *The Challenging Child* (both Addison-Wesley).

Research also based on interviews with Greenspan and with Pamela Seigle, director of the Reach Out to Schools Project at Wellesley College;

psychologist Thomas J. Berndt; Marsha Rogers Canick, school psychologist with the Wellesley, Mass., school system; and Lois Lange, clinical social worker at the Maimonides School in Brookline, Mass.

Getting your kids to pitch in

Don Fontenelle, *How to Live with Your Children* (Fisher Books).

Evonne Weinhaus and Karen Friedman, *Stop Struggling with Your Child* (HarperCollins).

Judith Smith, *Child Management: A Program for Parents and Teachers* (Research Press).

Interviews with Fontenelle, Weinhaus, and psychologist Jacqueline Goodnow; and with child psychologist Carolyn Webster-Stratton.

Earning and handling money

Neale S. Godfrey, *A Penny Saved: Teaching Your Children the Values and Life Skills They Will Need to Live in the Real World* (Simon & Schuster). Godfrey is also the founder of the Children's Financial Network, which publishes a curriculum for kindergarten through third grade on how to handle money.

Research also included interviews with Godfrey; sociologist Jerome Rabow; sociologist Peter Adler; economist Debra Sherwin; family therapist Donald Gordon; and financial psychologist James W. Gottfurcht.

The first crush

Research included interviews with clinical psychologist Dee Shepherd-Look; early childhood educator Ric Hovda; elementary school teacher Mary Lou Dowd of Hingham, Mass., schools; early childhood educator Carollee Howes; psychologist Robert Pianta; psychologist Eda LeShan; psychologist Elaine Hatfield.

The dating game for 10-year-olds?

David Elkind, *The Hurried Child* (Addison-Wesley).

Research also included interviews with pediatrician Michael Weitzman; clinical and developmental psychologist Gil Noam; retired elementary school teacher Richard Salinger of Angier School, Newton, Mass.; and human developmentalist Anne Petersen.

A space of their own

Research included interviews with environmental psychologist Leanne Rivlin; early childhood educator Sylvia Feinberg; social psychologist Steven Schiavo; psychologist Jerome Tognoli; family life psychologist Frances Degen Horowitz.

Home alone

Bobbie Rowland, Bryan E. Robinson, and Mick Coleman, *Home-Alone Kids* (Lexington Books).

Research also included interviews with Rowland and with researcher Michelle Seligson; developmental psychologist James Garbarino; human developmentalist Brenda Bryant.

Chapter 2: Milestones of a Different Kind

When toddlers bite

Diane Lusk, *Nothing But the Best* (William Morrow).

Research included interviews with Lusk; and with clinical and developmental psychologist John M. Chavez; and psychologist Claire L. Poulson.

"Shut up! I hate you!"

Ellen Galinsky, *The Preschool Years* (Ballantine).

Joe Strayhorn, *The Competent Child*, (Guilford Press).

Research also included interviews with Galinsky and Strayhorn; and with child developmentalist Alice Sterling Honig and former preschool head teacher Susan Ackerman.

When good children use bad words

Research included interviews with child psychologist Rhoda Fisher; child psychiatrist William F. Fry; speech communication specialist Charles Gruner; child psychiatrist and pediatrician Gordon Harper; pediatrician Hank Harris.

"Timmy is a tattletale!"

Betty MacDonald, *Mrs. Piggle-Wiggle's Magic* (Lippincott/Raven).

Research included interviews with educational psychologist Larry Nucci; human developmentalist Judith Smetana; educator Pamela Seigle; psychologist Myrna Beth Shure; pediatrician Dorris E. Tinker.

Taking stealing seriously

Research included interviews with child psychologist and pediatrician Gordon Harper; psychologist Leah Klungness; researcher Susan McElroy; psychologist Ron Prinz.

Secrets

Notes: Recommended reading for children 5 to 7: *Uncle Willie's Tickles* by Marcie Aboff (Magination Press).

Research included interviews with early childhood educator Carolyn

Edwards; psychologist Betty Smith Franklin; family therapist Irene Goldenberg; clinical psychologist Robert Pianta.

Truthfulness doesn't come easily
   Research included interviews with psychologist Stephen Ceci; psychologist Paul Ekman; philosopher Owen Flanagan; psychologist Douglas Peters.

Young runaways
   Notes: Recommended reading for kids 4 to 7: *Running Away from Home*, by Nigel Gray (Crown). Statistics provided by the National Network for Youth, Washington, D.C., and the National Clearinghouse on Families & Youth, Silver Spring, Md., and from the Covenant House, a nationwide hospice for runaway teens, which has a tollfree hotline for runaway teens: 1–800–999–9999.
   Interviews were with family psychologist James H. Bray; child psychologist and Paulist priest Fr. Mark-David Janus; social worker Wendy Naidich; child psychiatrist Daniel Rosenn.

Playing with fire
   Notes: University of Rochester social psychologist Robert Cole has developed a fire prevention curriculum, Fireproof Children Education Kit ($39.95) for grades k through 6 and a multimedia package for preschoolers, "Play Safe, Be Safe" ($12). For information, write Fireproof Children at 1 Grove St., Suite 210, Pittsford, NY 14534.
   Research included interviews with Cole; child psychiatrist Stuart Goldman; psychologist David Kolko; Elaine Mesiti of the Boston Fire Department.

Chapter 3: School Days

Getting—and keeping—your child talking
   Linda Budd, *Living with the Active Alert Child* (Parenting Press).
   Judi Craig, *What Happened at School Today?* (Morrow).
   Jane M. Healy, *How to Have Intelligent and Creative Conversations with Your Kids* (Doubleday); also *Endangered Minds: Why Our Children Don't Think and What We Can Do About It* (Simon & Schuster).
   Elizabeth Fishel, *Family Mirrors: What Our Children Reveal About Ourselves* (Houghton Mifflin).
   Research also included interviews with Budd, Craig, Fishel, and Healy.

Teacher trouble

Stanley Greenspan and Nancy Thorndike, *Essential Partnership* (Viking Penguin); also *Playground Politics* (Addison-Wesley).

Research also included interviews with Greenspan; educator Janine Bempechat; educator Ja net Crouse; educator John Cheffers.

"Don't make me go to school!"

Robert Schachter, *When Your Child Is Afraid* (Fireside Publishing).

Research also included interviews with Schachter; psychologist Leah Klungness; elementary school nurse Ann Lowry, of Lenox, Mass.; school psychologist Wayne C. Piersel; behavioral psychologist W. Ray Rhine.

Starting a new year

"Turning Points," a study of adolescent development, published by the Carneigie Council on Adolescent Development, Ruby Takaniski, co-author. Also, surveys conducted by the National Council of Middle Schools.

Interviews with middle school educators Jean Dorcus and Fran Borelli of the Boston public schools; middle school consultant Jim Burns; early childhood educator Jerlean Daniel; early childhood educator Hope Dauwalter; educational psychologist Jacquelynne Eccles; early childhood educator Shirley Gallerani; human development specialist Marjorie Kostelnik; family therapist Judy Osborne; research developmental psychologist Ruby Takaniski; early childhood specialist Barbara Willer.

Kindergarten and first grade

Notes: for kindergartners: *When You Go to Kindergarten* by James Howe and Betsy Imershein (Morrow Junior Books).

David Elkind, *Miseducation: Preschoolers at Risk* (Knopf).

Howard Gardner, *The Unschooled Mind* (Basic Books).

Jane M. Healy, *Your Child's Growing Mind* (Doubleday).

Research also included interviews with Elkind, Gardner, and Healy; and with early childhood educator Sylvia Feinburg; psychologist Carol George; elementary school teacher Anne Martin, of Brookline, Mass.; developmental psychologist Barbara Rogoff; early childhood educator Jeri Robinson; early childhood specialist Barbara Willer.

School-age children and sleep

Richard Ferber, *Solve Your Child's Sleep Problems* (Simon & Schuster).

Stella Chess and Alexander Thomas, *Know Your Child* (Basic Books).

Research included interviews with Chess and with Ferber; child psychiatrist Donald Gair; psychiatric nurse Sue Korber.

Battling the bully

For information on "Bully Proof," a curriculum for fourth and fifth grades, or "Quit It!" a curriculum for kindergarten through third grade, contact the Publications Office at Wellesley College, (781) 283–2510. Cost is $24.95, postage included.

Books for parents and children to read together: *How to Handle Bullies, Teasers and Other Meanies, A Book that Takes the Nuisance Out of Name Calling and Other Nonsense* by Kate Cohen-Posey (Rainbow Books). *Bullies Are a Pain in the Brain*, by Trevor Romain (Free Spirit Publishing).

W. George Scarlett, *Trouble in the Classroom* (Jossey-Bass).

Myrna Shure, *Raising a Thinking Child* (Pocket Books).

Research included interviews with Scarlett and Shure, as well as with psychologist Robert Cairns; psychologist Robert Coie; research scientist Nan Stein; guidance counselor Judy McCarthy and social worker Carmen Wilson, both of the Up Island Region schools, Martha's Vineyard, Mass.; and psychologist Marian Winterbottom.

Overcoming test anxiety

Research included interviews with educational psychologist Harry O'Neil; educator Peter Airasian; Maryellen Donahue of the Boston public schools; research scientist Walt Haney; educator Lady June Hubbard; educational consultant Patricia Lawerence; principal Mary Nash of the Mary Lyons School, Brighton, Mass.; educational researcher Stephanie Sartain. Special thanks to Stephanie Sartain for sharing her doctoral research.

Extracurricular activities: too many too soon, too bad

Research included interviews with educator Mark Churchill; child psychologist Jeffrey Derevensky; early childhood educator David Elkind; human developmentalist Charles Flatter; child psychologist Richard Weinberg.

Chapter 4: Summertime

When school ends

Tiffany Field et al., eds., *Stress and Coping in Infancy and Childhood* (Lawrence Erlbaum Publishers).

Books to read with children leaving preschool: *My Teacher Said Goodbye Today*, by Judy Osborne (send $9.95 to Judy Osborne, Box 971, Brookline,

Ma., 02146); also *When You Go to Kindergarten,* by James Howe and Betsy Imershein (Morrow).

Research included an interview with Field, as well as interviews with school principal Bob Farrell and elementary teacher Marilyn Niehoff, both of the Bell Public School, Marblehead, Mass.; early childhood educator Shirley Gallerani; early childhood educator Irma Napoleon; educational psychologist Jerome Schultz;

"I'm bored!"

Interviews with early childhood educator Joan Bergstrom; pediatric psychologist Melanie L. McGrath; early childhood educator Jeri Robinson; parent educator Jim Van Horn.

Family vacation as oxymoron

Research included interviews with family therapist Linda Budd; clinical psychologist Mathilda B. Canter; psychologist Hy Day; child psychologist Carolyn Newberger.

Summer's pitfall: parenting in public

Marguerite Kelly, *"Marguerite Kelly's Family Almanac . . . A Helpful Guide to Navigating through the Everyday Issues of Modern Life"* (Simon & Schuster).

Patricia Henderson Shimm and Kate Baller, *Parenting Your Toddler* (Addison-Wesley).

Research included interviews with Kelly and Shimm as well as with family therapist Linda Budd; parent educator Fran Litman.

Conquering water fears

Mariane Garber, *Monsters Under the Bed and Other Childhood Fears* (Villard Books).

Research included an interview with Garber, as well as with child psychiatrist Betsy Bush; psychologist Richard Gallagher; psychiatrist Manuel D. Zane; Sue Green, waterfront director at Grossman Camp in Westwood, Ma.; Bob Shinn, director of Camp Quinobequin in Needham, Mass.

Is your child ready for overnight camp? Are you?

Research included interviews with child psychologist Thomas J. Berndt; Jeffrey Solomon, executive director of the National Camp Association; developmental psychologist Ruby Takaniski; child psychologist Richard A. Weinberg.

A homesick camper

Research included interviews with pediatrician Bruce Bogard; Barbara

Davis of the American Camping Association, New England Section; child psychologist Gerald Koocher.

Meanwhile, back at home: siblings left behind and *The returning camper*

Research included interviews with social worker Robert Ditter; family psychologist Peter Goldenthal; camp director Dan Isdaner; psychologist and camp consultant Bruce Muchnick.

Chapter 5: Our Children and the Media

The violent screen

David Elkind, *Understanding Today's Children* (Scott Foresman).

Diane Levin, *Teaching Young Children in Violent Times: Building a Peaceable Classroom* (Educators for Social Responsibility, Cambridge, Mass.) and *Remote Control Childhood? Combating the Hazards of Media Culture* (National Association for the Education of Young Children).

Jerome Singer, Dorothy Singer, and Diana Zuckerman, *The Parent's Guide: Use TV to Your Child's Advantage* (Acropolis Books).

Interviews with Elkind, Levin, and Jerome Singer; also with children's television advocate Peggy Charren; psychologist Leonard Eron; child psychologist Ava L. Siegler; child psychologist James Garbarino; educator Beverly Robertson Jackson; child psychiatrist John E. Meeks; Holly Nathan-Colon of the Tobin Public School, Boston; Pamela Seigle, researcher scientist; research scientist Ron Slaby; child psychiatrist and pediatrician Albert J. Solnit.

Even Disney can be the enemy

Note: To contact Mothers Offended by the Media (MOM), contact Jacqui Sears, Box 402, Southampton, MA 01073.

David Walsh, *The Selling Out of America's Children* (Fairview Press).

Interviews with Walsh; early childhood educator Diane Levin; communication researcher Joanne Cantor.

When television remakes romance

Note: Television programs that give positive messages about relationships include *Barney,* for 2- and 3-year-olds; *Blue's Clues, Sesame Street, The Puzzle Place,* and *Mister Rogers' Neighborhood,* for preschoolers; and for school-age kids, *Clarissa Explains It All* and *Punky Brewster.*

Interviews with communication researcher Julia Dobrow; communication researcher Renée Hobbs; communication researcher Bill Husson; child and adolescent psychiatrist Miriam Mazor.

Megabyte babies? Maybe not

Notes: Parents may want to subscribe to the *Children's Software Quar-*

terly, a newsletter that reviews software. Write to Children's Software Press, 720 Kuhlman Rd., Houston, TX 77024. Also ask about booklets on Internet use.

Steve Bennett, *The Plugged In Parent* (Times Books).

Jane M. Healy, *Failure to Connect, How Computers Affect Our Children's Minds, for Better or Worse* (Simon & Schuster).

Interviews with Bennett and Healy as well as educator and technology researcher Howard Budin; technology researcher Vicki O'Day; professor and technology researcher Douglas Sloan; educational policy analyst Ed Miller of Cambridge, Mass.; history teacher Bill Schechter of Lincoln-Sudbury Regional High School, Lincoln, Mass.

Internet interactions

Brad Schepp and Debra Schepp, *Kidnet: the Kid's Guide to Surfing Through Cyberspace* (Harper Books).

Interviews with educational consultant and software researcher Sari Boren; communication researcher Renee Hobbs; researcher Brad Schepp; educator David Whittier; as well as Howard Budin, Douglas Sloan and Vicki O'Day (see references immediately above).

Facing the music

Tim Scheurer, *Born in the USA: The Myth of America in Popular Music from Colonial Times to the Present* (University Press of Mississippi).

Interviews with Scheurer; also with sociologist Clinton Sanders; popular culture researcher Michael T. Marsden; popular culture specialist Donald F. Roberts, Jr.

Superhero worship

Gary Fine, *With the Boys: Little League Baseball and Preadolescent Culture* (University of Chicago Press).

Interviews with Fine; psychologist Bill Berkowitz; psychologist Roger Burton; sociologist Thomas Cushman; educator Irene Denty, director of the Lexington, Mass., Lextended Day Program; sports sociologist Janet Harris; educational psychologist Mary Anne Lyons; popular culture researcher Michael Marsden; early childhood educator Corly Petersen; sociologist Clinton Sanders; child psychiatrist Mohammad Shafii; psychoanalyst Stanley Teitelbaum.

Chapter 6: Living in a Changing, Complicated, and Sometimes Scary World

When the news raises anxiety

Notes: Books to read with your children: for 5-to 8-year-olds, *The*

Safety Book for Active Kids, and for 7- to 10-year-olds, *What Would You Do? A Kid's Guide to Tricky and Sticky Situations*, both by Linda Schwartz (The Learning Works). For 9- to 14-year-olds, *Now I Know Better: Kids Tell Kids About Safety*, a collection of essays by kids about accidents and injuries and precautions they wish they had taken, published by the Children's Hospital at Yale/New Haven and Millbrook Press.

Interviews with Ann Case of the student services department of the Wellesley (Mass.) public schools; forensic psychologist Ronald Ebert; child psychologist Nina Fish-Murray; educator and psychiatric social worker Virginia Kahn; pediatrician Eli Newberger.

When children hear about suicide

Notes: Books for school-age children coping with the death of a family member by suicide: *Tunnel Vision*, by Fran Arrick (Bradbury Press); *I Wish I Were in a Lonely Meadow*, published by the Dougy Foundation, Portland, Ore.; for the suicide death of a parent, *Grover*, by Vera and Bill Cleaver (New American Library). For parents: *The Seasons of Grief: Helping Children Grow Through Loss*, by Donna Gaffney (New American Library); *Child Survivors of Suicide: A Guidebook for Those Who Care About Them*, published by the American Suicide Foundation. To contact the foundation, write ASF, 1045 Park Ave., New York, NY 10028.

Interviews with psychiatric nurse Karen Dunne-Maxim; child psychiatrist Cynthia Pfeffer; child psychiatrist David Shaffer; counseling psychologist Maria Trozzi.

Alleviating fears about kidnapping

Notes: There are many good curricula on sexual assault prevention, especially "Kids and Company: Together for Safety," a sexual assault prevention curriculum for grades k through 6, published by the National Center for Missing and Exploited Children. Contact: 1–800–843–5678. Another good one is "Talking About Touching," a curriculum for preschoolers and kindergartens about sexual assault prevention, personal safety, and fire safety, published by the Committee for Children, Seattle, Wash., a nonprofit organization that develops educational material and training and client support for prevention of child abuse and youth violence. Contact: 1–800–634–4449. The committee also has a curriculum for grades 1 through 3, and 4 through 6.

Interviews with clinical social worker Susan Bartley; clinical psychologist Leslie Biron Campis; sociologist David Finkelhor; Jerry Hotaling, codirector of the National Study for the Justice Department on stranger abductions and family abductions.

Coping with environmental and other world catastrophes

Notes: Recommended for school-age children: *Let's Talk Trash, The Kid's Book About Recycling,* by Kelly McQueen and David Fassler (Waterfront Books).

Lynn Dumas, *Talking with Your Child About a Troubled World* (Fawcett Columbine).

Interviews with Dumas and Fassler; also with child psychiatrist Donald Cohen; child psychiatrist Jim Leckman.

Talking about sex . . .

Notes: To read with your child: *Love and Sex and Growing Up* (Skylark) by Eric Johnson, for children grades 3 through 6. For parents, *Raising a Child Conservatively in a Sexually Permissive World,* by Judith and Sol Gordon (Fireside).

Interviews with Judith Gordon and Johnson; pediatrician Susan Pauker; early childhood educator Diane Levin; sex educator Kay Stritzel Rencken; preschool teacher Kathy Roberts of the Dandelion School, Cambridge, Mass.; early childhood educator Fred Rothbaum.

. . . drugs . . .

Interviews with pediatrician and addiction medicine specialist Paul Fuller; developmental behavioral pediatrician John R. Knight; pediatrician Richard Heyman of the American Academy of Pediatrics Committee on Substance Abuse.

. . . homosexuality . . .

Interviews with sex educator Debra Haffner; sex educator and family therapist Gina Ogden; pediatrician Gary Remafedi; psychologist and sex educator Robert Selverstone; social worker Havi Stander;

. . . and AIDS

Notes: Reading for school-age children: *What's a Virus, Anyway?: The Kid's Book About AIDS,* by David Fassler and Kelly McQueen (Waterfront Books); for kindergartners through fifth-graders: *Does AIDS Hurt?* by Marcia Quackenbush, ETR Associates (Scotts Valley, Calif.).

Interviews with Quackenbush; sex educator Debra Haffner; pediatrician Martin W. Sklaire; health educator and consultant Lennie Roseman; behavioral pediatrician David Schonfeld.

Clashing hormones

Louise J. Kaplan, *Adolescence: The Farewell to Childhood* (Simon & Schuster).

Evelyn S. Bassoff, *Between Mothers and Sons: The Making of Vital and*

Loving Men (Dutton); *Mothers & Daughters, Loving and Letting Go* (Dutton).

Barbara Mackoff, *Growing a Girl: Seven Strategies for Raising a Strong, Spirited Daughter* (Dell).

Shari Thurer, *The Myths of Motherhood, How Culture Reinvents the Good Mother* (Penguin).

Interviews with Bassoff, Kaplan, and Thurer; psychologist Paul Wink; social worker Robin Ohringer.

When honesty counts: 1. If your family doesn't fit the stereotype

Notes: for information on the *Anti-bias Curriculum: Tools for Empowering Young Children* written by Louise Derman-Sparks and published by the National Association for the Education of Young Children, contact NAEYC at 1–(800)–424–2460. Two good books for preschoolers: *The Crayon Box That Talked*, by Shane DeRolf (Random House); *Daddy's Roommate*, by Michael Willhoite (Alyson Wonderland).

Barbara F. Okun, *Understanding Diverse Families* (Guilford Press).

Interviews with Okun; psychologist James H. Bray; preschool teachers Ginny Cohen and Bonnie Mark; early childhood educator Louise Derman-Sparks; social worker Peggy Kaufman; clinical social worker Francie Mandel-Folly.

2. If a parent is absent

Andrea Engber and Leah Klungness, *The Complete Single Mother: Reassuring Answers to Your Most Challenging Concerns* (Adams).

Claudia Jewett Jarratt, *Helping Children Cope with Separation and Loss*, rev. ed. (Harvard Common Press).

Jane Mattes, *Single Mothers by Choice: A Guidebook for Single Women Who Are Considering or Have Chosen Motherhood* (Times Books).

Also helpful: "SingleMOTHER," a newsletter published by the National Organization of Single Mothers, PO Box 68, Midland, N.C. 28107. For information, call 704–888–KIDS.

Interviews with psychologist Klungness; Engber; Jarratt; Mattes.

3. If you had help conceiving

Notes: To read with your children: for 3- to 7-year-olds, *Mommy, Did I Grow in Your Tummy?* by Elaine Gordon, available for $9.95 from E. M. Greenberg Press, 1460 7th St., Suite 300, Santa Monica, Calif. 90401. For 8- to 10-year-olds, *Let Me Explain: A Story About Donor Insemination*, by Jane Schnitter (Perspectives Press).

For adult reading: *Flight of the Stork*, by Anne C. Bernstein (Perspectives Press). *Talking to Children About Their Conception: It's Easier than You*

Think, by Carole Lieber Wilkins (avialable for $10 by writing to her at 1460 Westwood Blvd., suite 204, Los Angeles, Ca. 90024).

Ellen Sarasohn Glazer, *Choosing Assisted Reproduction* (Perspective Press).

Heidi Moss, Robert Moss, and Carol Frost Vercollone, *Helping the Stork: The Choices and Challenges of Donor Insemination* (Macmillan).

Interviews with Bernstein; Glazer; Gordon; Lieber Wilkins; Moss; Vercollone.

Chapter 7: Birth, Death, and a Few Things in Between

Welcoming a sibling into the family . . .

Note: There are many wonderful books to read with your young children about the birth of a sibling. Here are a few suggestions: *The New Baby*, by Fred Rogers (Putman); *One Frog Too Many*, by Mayer and Mayer (Dial Press); *Peter's Chair*, by Ezra Jack Keats (Harper & Row); *The Lapsnatcher*, by Bruce Coville (BridgeWater Books); *Baby Wants the Moon*, by Salvatore Murdocca (Lothrop Lee & Shepard). For school-age children, *Happy Birth Day*, by Robie H. Harris (Candlewick Press). Also recommended: *That New Baby: An Open Family Book for Parents and Children Together*, by Sara B. Stein (Walker & Co.).

Interviews with parent educator Linda Braun; child developmentalist Bettye Caldwell; child psychiatrist Clarice J. Kestenbaum; developmental and behavioral child psychiatrist Robert Nardone.

. . . and a half sibling

Taube Kaufman, *The Combined Family: A Guide to Creating Successful Step-relationships* (Insight Books).

Patricia Papernow, *Becoming a Step-Family* (Analytic Press).

Marilyn Coleman and Larry Ganong, *Relationships in Remarried Families* (Sage Publications).

Interviews with Kaufman; Papernow; Coleman.

Making a move

Note: *The Preschool Years* (Ballantine) by Ellen Galinsky is one of the best books on children 3- to 6-years and devotes a section to moving.

Interviews with Galinsky, and with psychologist and researcher Sumru Erkut; child psychologist and researcher Frederic Medway; and psychologist and researcher Eric Vernberg.

How children perceive their own illness or injury

Note: Two books that incorporate children's physical health needs with developmental and growth issues: *Taking Care of Your Child*, 3d edition, by Robert H. Pantell, MD, James Fries, MD, and Donald Vickery, MD (Addison-Wesley); and *Your Child's Health* rev. ed., by Barton D. Schmitt, MD (Bantam).

Interviews with parent educator Gloria Jurkowitz; child psychologist Gerald Koocher; behavioral pediatrician and researcher Ellen C. Perrin; developmental pediatrician and researcher Neil Schechter.

When a parent is sick

Interviews with early childhood development specialist Susan Ginsberg; psychologist Judith Gordon; child psychiatrist Joseph Jankowski; clinical psychologist Bruce Masek.

A child's hospitalization

Note: Books to read with your children under 5: *A Hospital Story*, by Sara Bonnett Stein (Walker & Co.). For school-age children: *Hospital Journal*, by Ann Banks (Penguin).

Interviews with registered nurse Janet Hamilton; clinical health psychologist Barbara Melamed; developmental pediatrician and researcher Neil Schechter; child life specialist Richard H. Thompson; pediatrician and researcher Lonnie Zeltzer.

Aging, infirm, or dying grandparents

Notes: Recommended for children 7 to 11, *The Sunsets of Miss Olivia Wiggins*, by Lester J. Laminack (Peachtree Publishing).

Interviews with intergenerational clinical psychologist Renana Brooks; intergenerational family therapist Alan Entin; intergenerational family therapist Elaine Rodino; geriatric psychiatrist Gary Small.

A sibling's chronic illness

Note: The Sibling Support Project is a national network for siblings of chronically ill children based at Children's Hospital and Medical Center in Seattle. Its services are free and it can hook you up to sibling support groups wherever you live. Contact them at PO Box 5371 CL-09, Seattle, WA 98105. The Web site http://www.chmc.org/departmt/sibsupp offers direct links to chat sites for siblings, Sibkids, for younger brothers and sisters, and Sibnet for siblings 10 or older.

Interviews with pediatrician Betsy Bush; child psychiatrist and researcher David DeMaso; behavioral pediatrician and researcher Ellen Perrin; pediatrician and researcher James Perrin.

How children cope with death and grief

Note: To read with your child: *Talking About Death: A Dialogue Between*

Parent and Child, by Rabbi Earl Grollman (Beacon Press); *Straight Talk About Death for Teenagers* (Beacon Press), also by Grollman. For parents: *Helping Bereaved Children*, by Nancy Boyd Webb (Guilford Press).

Interviews with Rabbi Grollman; developmental psychologist and psychiatrist Stuart T. Hauser; social anthropologist Sheila Kitzinger; pediatrician Robert Reece; child psychologist Joseph A. Shrand; counseling psychologist Maria Trozzi; clinical social worker Webb; bereavement counselor Malka Young.

If a parent dies

Interviews with clincal psychologist and family bereavement researcher Simon Shimshon Rubin; social worker and researcher Phyllis R. Silverman; counseling psychologist Maria Trozzi; child and adolescent psychiatrist and bereavement researcher Elizabeth Weller.

Index